The Hartmann Era

The Hartmann Era

Edited by

Martin S. Bergmann

OTHER

Other Press
New York

Production Editor: Robert D. Hack

This book was set in 11 pt. Apollo by Alpha Graphics of Pittsfield, NH.

10 9 8 7 6 5 4 3 2 1

Library of Congress Cataloging-in-Publication Data

The Hartmann era / editor, Martin S. Bergmann.
    p. cm.
"Conference proceedings, October 18–19, 1997, New York, N.Y."
Includes bibliographical references and index.
ISBN 1-892746-22-0 (alk. paper)
    1. Psychoanalysis—History—Congresses.   2. Freud, Sigmund, 1856–1939—Congresses.
3. Hartmann, Heinz—Congresses.   I. Bergmann, Martin S., 1913–
BF173.B4675 2000
150.19'52'09—dc21   99-089140

Sponsored by the Psychoanalytic Research & Development Fund, Inc.

Conference Proceedings
New York, NY

Representatives of the Fund:
  Mortimer Ostow, M.D., *President*
  Sidney S. Furst, M.D., *Professional Director*
  Henry Nunberg, M.D., *Vice President and Treasurer*

Initial Presenter, Chairman of the Conference,
and Editor of the Proceedings:
  Professor Martin S. Bergmann

Invited Participants:
  Jacob A. Arlow, M.D.
  Harold Blum, M.D.
  Dr. André Green
  William I. Grossman, M.D.
  Otto Kernberg, M.D.
  Anton Kris, M.D.
  Peter Neubauer, M.D.
  Albert Solnit, M.D.
  Clifford Yorke, Dr.S.C.B.

Contents

Introduction

On behalf of the Psychoanalytic Research and Development Fund, I would like to welcome you. We are both pleased and proud to have assembled this distinguished group for the purpose of evaluating a major period in the history of psychoanalysis.

The Psychoanalytic Research and Development Fund was organized in 1956 under the leadership of Herman Nunberg for the purpose of conducting research in the clinical and theoretical aspects of psychoanalysis. To my knowledge, we are the only free-standing organization devoted solely to this purpose.

To date, the fund has carried out close to twenty research studies. Several involved the preparation of papers on a given topic, followed by a weekend meeting of the authors during which the papers were discussed and evaluated. The papers (often revised), as well as an edited record of the conference discussion, were then published in volume form. These included conferences on psychic trauma, the future of psychoanalysis, and the interface between psychoanalysis and psychotherapy.

More commonly, we assembled a group of ten to twelve psychoanalysts, who then met monthly for a period of three years or more to investigate a specific topic. The method of approach involved the detailed examination of psychoanalytic case material presented by the participants. In order to maintain focus and continuity, the proceedings of each meeting were transcribed. Each case was studied for at least several months and up to one year. On conclusion, a summary of the case material, along with the results and conclusions of the study, were prepared for publication, usually in volume form.

Subjects explored using this approach included the following:

Psychoanalytic study of perversions
Psychodynamic approach to drug therapy
Psychoanalytic study of aggression
Reconstruction in psychoanalysis
Psychoanalytic study of antisemitism
The "long" analysis
The older patient in analysis
The long-term effects of sexual abuse in childhood
Gender identity disorder
Affect regulation: practice and theory.

In addition to studies of adults, we have conducted a series of investigations of significant topics in child psychoanalysis. The approach was similar to that employed in the adult studies, and included the following:

An observational study of infants
Early child development
Psychoanalytic study of siblings
The many meanings of play in child analysis
The coordination of the analytic and the developmental goals in child analysis.

The results of these studies were published in volume form, or in papers that appeared in professional journals.

Some time ago, Martin Bergmann suggested a study of the history of psychoanalytic ideas and theories. We considered this topic too broad to be encompassed in a single study. Not one to give up a good thing, Martin then suggested that we study one specific period—namely, the one dominated by interest in ego psychology. This suggestion was enthusiastically accepted as both important and doable.

Sidney Furst

I

THE HARTMANN ERA AND ITS CONTRIBUTION TO PSYCHOANALYTIC TECHNIQUE

MARTIN S. BERGMANN

After World War II and into the 1980s, there were many psychoanalysts who were convinced that the era of psychoanalysis (known in the United States as ego psychology), with its emphasis on the role of the ego, the ego's capacity to neutralize both aggression and libido, and its connection to developmental psychology, had significantly advanced American psychoanalysis and given it a privileged position among psychoanalytic societies. Even though Hartmann and his coworkers saw themselves as the legitimate heirs to Freud's legacy, in my view the Hartmann era did more than expand classical psychoanalysis: it modified it substantially.

There was a time in the United States when Hartmann was regarded as the undisputed leader of American psychoanalysis. The praise that Schafer (1970) bestowed upon Hartmann can be taken as an example.

> Heinz Hartmann's contributions to psychoanalytic theory (1939, 1960, 1964) rise up before the student of psychoanalysis as a mountain range whose distant peaks with their immense vistas and rarefied atmosphere it is scarcely possible to reach. And yet the student must not only attempt the arduous climb, he must try to get above that range so that he can include Hartmann's work within his own vision of psychoanalysis. [p. 425]

Schafer was one of the first to recognize that Hartmann did more than just extend Freud's work.

> Hartmann was engaged in revisions in psychoanalytic thought and modes of thinking about psychoanalysis that are, in some respects at least, revolutionary, their modest and emendatory tone to the contrary notwithstanding. . . . One of the fundamental revisions in Freudian thinking undertaken by Hartmann is the dissolution of its dualistic framework, its crudely dialectical bias, it orienting itself so far as possible by means of great polarities. [p. 426]

This praise notwithstanding, Schafer's paper was one of the first by the younger generation of psychoanalysts to be somewhat critical of Hartmann's theory.

It was the 1939 monograph that received the highest praise. Thus Rangell (1986): "In 1939 the year Freud died Hartmann published his famous monograph which defined the direction of psychoanalysis for the next three decades. The baton had been passed between the two men" (pp. 1–2).

Eissler's (1971) praise was just as enthusiastic:

> The future historian of psychoanalysis will probably regard Freud's scientific career as having been prematurely terminated by death, . . . Yet, if fate had granted a few more years he might well have put the keystone to his work by writing three essays on the theory of the ego and its function, thereby creating the counterpart to his first book on clinical theory, which he wrote in 1905. . . . The observational data that are requisite for the assumption of an ego function are not yet determined—which is one of the reasons one may speak of the present state of "wild" ego psychology. [pp. 522–523]

Eissler's statement amounts to a conviction that had Freud lived longer he would have followed in Hartmann's footsteps, at the same time improving upon Hartmann by delimiting the number of ego functions.

Young (1989) wrote that Hartmann's 1939 monograph was one of the most influential psychoanalytic publications since Freud. Peltz (1989), writing in the same symposium, stated: "His greatly expanded view of the ego and its functions put that agency of the mind on a par with the id (and the superego) without diminishing psychoanalysis as a depth psychology" (p. 559). Hartmann was given credit for a new emphasis on organization in theory and practice. In this view, psychoanalysis after World War II was in danger of stagnation, of living off Freud's heritage without adding anything new. It was Hartmann who, by the new emphasis on the ego, opened up new horizons and unleashed creative forces within psychoanalysis.

Criticism of Hartmann by his peers already appeared in 1961 in a paper by Glover. There were also those who believed that Hartmann and his followers had turned away from the unconscious, the most valuable part of psychoanalysis, as they preached conformity and adjustment. It was argued that they misread and misunderstood Freud and buttressed their misunderstanding by the English standard edition to Freud's work, a translation that does not mirror Freud's thinking faithfully. Finally, they defined analyzability so narrowly that only a few could pass through the eye of that needle. George Klein (1976) said:

> Ego psychology as it is currently formulated is without dynamic foundations, a graft on the clinical concepts of psychoanalysis. . . . Ego theory looks more like a potpourri identical with many of the concerns of academic psychology and without any distinctively psychoanalytic meaning. [pp. 7–8]

Even more sharply, Hartmann was accused by Edelson (1986) of neglecting the empiricism of the psychoanalytical situation as a source of data in favor of abstract theorizing, thus setting psychoanalysis back for a whole generation.

Anna Freud (1966), in her essay in honor of Hartmann's 70th birthday, recalled the opposition that his 1939 book evoked. There were those who objected that he turned away from psychopathology in order to obtain for psychoanalysis the status of general psychology, theoretical thinking taking precedence over clinical concerns. But, above all, it was feared that his ego psychology would endanger the psychoanalytic concern with instinctual drives and the unconscious. Although Anna Freud spoke of these concerns as belonging to the past, there were others who thought that the danger was all too real.

I have shown elsewhere (Bergmann 1997) that psychoanalysis is both a discipline and a movement. As a discipline it is open to new ideas. As a movement it has its orthodoxy. Hartmann and his followers departed from Freud in many significant ways. At the same time, it was important for Hartmann to anchor his findings in Freud. This anchoring was found in *The Ego and the Id* (1923a), Chapter III, where Freud said:

> We have reckoned as though there existed in the mind—whether in the ego or in the id—a displaceable energy, which, neutral in itself, can be added to a qualitatively differentiated erotic or destructive impulse, and augment its total cathexis. Without assuming the existence of a displaceable energy of this kind we can make no headway. The only question is where it comes from, what it belongs to, and what it signifies.
>
> It seems a plausible view that this displaceable and neutral energy, which is no doubt active both in the ego and in the id, proceeds from the narcissistic store of libido—that is desexualized Eros. [1923a, p. 44]

It is of historical interest that so casual a remark by Freud, that he neither repeated nor followed up, became the historical nucleus for Hartmann's psychology.

Hartmann's name has become almost synonymous with psychoanalytic ego psychology. It is therefore important to point out that ego psychology antedated the Hartmann era by a number of decades. The leading ego psychologist was Otto Fenichel. It is of historical interest to know Fenichel's appraisal of Hartmann. I quote from Fenichel's classic of 1945.

> Hartmann, in a very interesting paper, tried to show that adaptation has been studied by psychoanalysts too much from the point of view of mental conflicts. He points out that there is also a "sphere without conflict," originating, it is true, in antithesis between organism and environment. Because of the importance of these antitheses, the term sphere without conflict seems misleading, as tending toward an undynamic point of view. The ego's maturation is a result of the continuous interplay of the organism's needs and the environmental influences. [Fenichel 1945, p. 52]

With those few sentences Hartmann is dismissed—so much for prophecy. Fenichel, whose book appeared in 1945, had no foreknowledge of the significant role that Hartmann would play in the next chapter in psychoanalytic history.

In the last years of his life Freud became convinced that the normal ego is an ideal fiction (Freud 1937, p. 235). The ego of the analysand is, to various degrees, damaged and therefore cannot assist wholeheartedly in the work of analysis. The deformation in the capacity of the ego to test reality makes the analysand treat past dangers as if they were present dangers. In such a case, recovery itself is seen as a danger. This line of reasoning led Freud to a pessimism about the possibility of psychoanalytic cure. Hartmann's ego psychology can be seen as a reaction against Freud's pessimism about the role of the ego in the process of cure.

The program of the Hartmann movement was stated in the preface of Hartmann's festschrift (Loewenstein et al. 1966), which bears the title *Psychoanalysis—A General Psychology*: "To refind, systemize, and increase our knowledge, thus advancing psychoanalysis as a general psychology" (p. ix).

Hartmann himself has stated: "The consistent study of the ego and its functions promises to bring analysis closer to the aim Freud has set for it long ago—to become a general psychology in the broadest sense of the word" (1964, p. x).

> In an implicit way from its beginnings, and quite explicitly in the last two or three decades, psychoanalysis has set out to lay the groundwork for a general psychology, including normal as well as pathological behavior. [1947, p. 37]

> By developing ego psychology, analysis has more and more come to include in its scope phenomena that previously had been studied by other methods. . . . It is the specific nature of this method, and the insight into the unconscious processes, that frequently let the common object of observation appear in a different light; and above all, analytic knowledge allows one to assign the observed facts their proper place in the structure of personality. [p. 38]

As to whether Hartmann was right in his claim that this was also Freud's intention depends on how we read a famous passage written by Freud (1926b):

> I have assumed, that is to say, that psychoanalysis is not a specialized branch of medicine. I cannot see how it is possible to dispute this. Psychoanalysis is a part of psychology; not of medical psychology in the old sense, not of psychology of morbid processes, but simply psychology. It is certainly not the whole of psychology, but its substructure and perhaps even its entire foundation. [p. 252]

There have been a number of studies evaluating the contributions of Heinz Hartmann to psychoanalysis: Rangell (1965), Loewenstein

(1966, 1970), Schafer (1970), Blanck and Blanck (1974). In 1986, *Psychoanalytic Inquiry* devoted an issue to a reappraisal of Heinz Hartmann's contribution to psychoanalysis (Bornstein et al. 1986). In 1989, the *Psychoanalytic Quarterly* devoted an issue to Hartmann (Friedman et al. 1989). To my knowledge, this essay is the first to deal with the Hartmann era. Terms like "the Hartmann group" or "the Hartmann era" raise a number of new problems, but I will discuss them at the end of this essay.

In her forward to Blanck and Blanck (1979), Margaret Mahler said:

> From Freud's structural theory, through Anna Freud's elaboration of the defensive functions of the ego, Hartmann's elaboration of theory in his collaborative work with Kris and Loewenstein, Jacobson's description of the process of differentiation of self and object representations, and Spitz's and my work on direct observations of children—became a body of knowledge known as "ego psychology." This ever expanding body of knowledge that ego psychology represents what has become a most important fundamental theory upon which many clinical and theoretical works have been based in recent years. [p. 9]

The sense of unity of the Hartmann period as well as its optimism and self-confidence are clearly expressed in these remarks.

Hartmann differed from other founders of schools such as Melanie Klein and Kohut in that he had no avowed disciples. The list of those psychoanalysts whom I call Hartmannites is a list of coworkers rather than disciples. These include Ernst Kris, Rudolf Loewenstein, Edith Jacobson, Margaret Mahler, Annie Reich, Kurt Eissler, Max Schur, and David Rapaport, to name only those who were most influential. This group consisted almost exclusively of psychoanalyst refugees who settled in New York. It is indeed surprising that so small a number of analysts affected the course of American psychoanalysis to the extent that they did. I hasten to add that during the same period there were many active and creative psychoanalysts who cannot be counted among the Hartmannites. These include Hermann Nunberg, Franz Alexander, Robert Waelder, Helene Deutsch, Phyllis Greenacre, Laurence Kubie, Mark Kanzer, and a number of others. Some of these, such as Greenacre and Stone, were friendly to the ideas of the Hartmann group, but Hartmann's influence was not central to their thinking. Such a line of de-marcation is subjective, and in many instances I relied on my own per-sonal recollections.

The fact is that the Hartmann school remained confined to the United States. With the exception of Anna Freud and Willi Hoffer, who may be regarded as honorary members of this group, no thinker in Europe or South America drew inspiration from Hartmann.

It will become clear as I go on that the Hartmann era was charac-terized by a psychoanalytic optimism not found in Freud's writings. The question arises: From what source did the group draw this opti-mism? Nearly all the participants were refugees from Hitler's Europe. None were what we called (Bergmann and Jucovy 1982) survivors of the Holocaust, since they reached American soil before the promulga-tion of Hitler's final solution. Only Edith Jacobson had been in jail, but even she was a political prisoner. As a group psychoanalysts had a better understanding of the events to come, and left Germany and Austria when members of other professions lingered. Psychoanalysts also had better connections abroad. Ernest Jones and others helped them to emi-grate. Most of them prospered in the United States beyond what they achieved in Europe. All these factors may have contributed to their op-timism, but above all, I suspect, that it was the victory over Hitler's evil empire that released this optimism.

The relationship between Erikson and the Hartmann group is of interest. Like Hartmann, Erikson developed an ego psychology of his own. Like Hartmann, he also stressed adaptation. Erikson emphasized that every phase in the life cycle is characterized by a task that must be solved. Rapaport (1959) believed that Erikson and Hartmann's con-tributions are complementary (p. 16). Rapaport's efforts at integration met with little success. Erikson was better known and more influen-tial beyond the confines of organized psychoanalysis, while Hartmann dominated American psychoanalysis.

The cohesiveness to the Hartmann group was enhanced by their opposition to Melanie Klein's ideas. A close alliance grew up between the Hartmannites in New York and Anna Freud and her followers in London. In 1945 the annual *Psychoanalytic Study of the Child* began to appear. Its managing editors were Anna Freud, Hartmann, and Kris. The lead paper was written by Hartmann and Kris and was entitled "The

Genetic Approach to Psychoanalysis." The opening sentence of that paper is worth quoting:

> The word "psychoanalysis" is commonly used to designate three things: a therapeutic technique, which we here call "psychoanalytic therapy," an observational method to which we here refer as "the psychoanalytic interview," and a body of hypotheses for which we here reserve the term "psychoanalysis." [p. 11]

On the whole, this definition follows Freud's 1923 Encyclopedia articles, where Freud said:

> Psychoanalysis is the name (1) of a procedure for the investigation of mental processes which are almost inaccessible in any other way, (2) of a method (based upon that investigation) for the treatment of neurotic disorders and (3) of a collection of psychological information obtained along those lines, which is gradually being accumulated into a new scientific discipline. [1923b, p. 235]

If we follow the nuances, a marked difference reveals itself. Psychoanalysis is now called "the psychoanalytic interview." Along the same lines, being in analysis was replaced by being under "psychoanalytic observation." To enhance the scientific status of psychoanalysis, where Freud spoke of "psychological information," Hartmann and Kris spoke of hypotheses. Freud's enthusiastic embrace of sexual seduction as a cause of neurosis was now termed the "seduction hypothesis." The great revolution that Freud brought about when he changed from the topographic to the structural point of view in 1923 will now be labeled the "structural hypothesis." The cautious language did not mean that the Hartmann group was less certain of its findings than Freud was; it was designed to appeal to scientists beyond the confines of psychoanalysis.

Since Hartmann was *primus inter pares*, the first among equals, the question arises why the era should be named after him. First, Hartmann's book of 1939, *The Ego and the Problem of Adaptation*, formed the kernel of the ideas that later were developed by the whole group. Second, Hartmann combined the capacity to develop ideas not found in Freud with the capacity to build bridges going back to Freud. Under his leadership the group could see itself as Freud's true heirs, even though they differed in many essentials from Freud. Since psychoanalysis is not only a discipline but also a movement, the need for the innovator to maintain a sense of continuity is important.

Hartmann and his associates would not have subscribed to this view, for Hartmann saw psychoanalysis as developing along a straight line. Hartmann divided psychoanalytic history into three periods. During the first, attention was directed towards the drives and their development (psychosexual phases). This was primarily an analysis of the id. From 1926 on the emphasis shifted to the ego from the point of view of its defenses against the id. The third period was reached in his own book, *Ego Psychology and the Problem of Adaptation* (1939). In this third era it is the ego and its autonomous development that is the center of psychoanalytic interest.

I. THE CONTRIBUTION OF THE HARTMANN GROUP

What makes the Hartmannites into a cohesive group are not only concepts and ideas they shared but also a set of passionately held beliefs. I would enumerate these as follows:

1) The truly great discoveries of psychoanalysis, such as the Oedipus complex, transference, and free association, are behind us, but, like a conqueror who rushes forward leaving unexplored territory behind him, Freud did not stop to systematize his findings. Trained clarifiers are needed to coordinate various propositions. Psychoanalysis is in dire need of systematization. As Kris (1947) put it:

> Sooner or later the ever more precise empirical test becomes an essential element in the development of any system of scientific propositions. In the development of psychoanalysis this moment seems to have arrived. [p. 14]

2) Cherished beliefs of Freud that no longer meet the test of science have to be weeded out. The two prime examples are Freud's acceptance of the Lamarckian view that acquired characteristics are inherited and Freud's belief in the death instinct (1920). In their paper entitled "Notes on the Theory of Aggression" (1949), Hartmann, Kris, and Loewenstein bypassed Freud's death instinct theory, maintaining that this hypothesis cannot now, or in the foreseeable future, be checked against empirical evidence. Freud thought that aggression can be mitigated by fusion with the libido. Hartmann, Kris, and Loewenstein thought that it could be accomplished through *deaggressivization*, a term

they coined as parallel to desexualization. The term *neutralization* was applied to both drives.

Waelder (1960), commenting on the change introduced by Hartmann, Kris, and Loewenstein, said:

> This hypothesis is, of course, contingent upon the assumption that destructiveness is the manifestation of an instinctual drive. And since every mitigation of destructiveness implies a degree of conservation of the object, it would have to be shown either that this conservation contains no element of love, or if it does, that love is only a consequence, not a cause of the process. [p. 153]

In his Freud lecture of 1965, Waelder suggested that to apply the term *neutralization* where there was no previous history of overt sexual interest is unjustified. For example, when a 1-year-old enjoys a tune there is no evidence of neutralization (p. 13).

The possibility that the aggressive drive, like the libido, could undergo neutralization brought the Hartmann group into conflict with Freud's belief in the death instinct. Melanie Klein and her school, on the other hand, took Freud's death instinct seriously. The emphasis Klein put on the paranoid position suggests that mastering the death instinct was for the young child a most important task. The ego psychologists from Fenichel (1974) on, including Hartmann, Kris, and Loewenstein (1949), were reluctant to accept the death instinct into their metapsychology. Even Anna Freud was dubious.

> Psychoanalytic study of aggression has its starting point at Freud's *Beyond the Pleasure Principle* (1920). This publication had the double result of, on the one hand, moving the hitherto neglected topic of aggression into the limelight but, on the other hand, of burdening and hampering its clinical investigation by drawing it into the center of a theoretical dispute. [1972, p. 170]

Freud's death instinct operated beyond the pleasure principle, but even this hypothesis became questionable. I recall a remark attributed to Stalin: "Revenge must be eaten cold." Whatever one may think about this remark, Stalin's aggression operates under the pleasure principle.

Lichtenstein (1961) contrasted Freud's view on man in *Beyond the Pleasure Principle* (1920) with Freud's view of the two principles of mental functioning. In 1911, Freud followed Darwin with the following modification: since man can no longer rely on instincts the way animals do, the pleasure principle in man safeguards adaptation. Having no instinct to rely upon, man learns to make choices on the basis of the reality principle, which is itself an outgrowth of the pleasure principle. By 1920 Freud is no longer a Darwinian, with the introduction of the concept of the repetition compulsion, which operates beyond the pleasure principle; the libido is in continuous struggle against its immortal adversary, the death instinct. The new theory fundamentally changed the model of the way the human mind functions. Hartmann's task, as Lichtenstein understands it, was to undo the damage that was done to psychoanalysis by the introduction of the death instinct. It was the ego system that, according to Hartmann, took over the adaptive regulation. By transforming the conflict between libido and the death instinct into the dual instinct theory of aggression versus libido, Hartmann, Kris, and Loewenstein (1946) staved off a conceptual crisis in psychoanalysis. Grinker (1957) expressed similar ideas.

The controversy between Freud and the Hartmann group is one of the examples of controversies in psychoanalysis that the discipline itself is incapable of resolving. Whether one agrees with Freud that Eros is needed to mitigate aggression, or with Hartmann that aggression can be neutralized, becomes a matter of personal preference. Such a preference may be due to the prevalence of one school or another, or, more likely, connect to some unconscious pessimism or optimism over which the analyst has no control (Grossman 1995). In deference to Freud, Hartmann and his followers suggested a moratorium until biology confirms or disconfirms Freud's beliefs. The Lamarckian view was already discredited by geneticists. Freud's death instinct hypothesis was much more difficult to prove or disprove.

3) The area of promise for new psychoanalytic ideas will come primarily from infant and child observations, secondarily from data obtained from child analysis. Hartmann (1950) hoped that the future reconstructive data furnished by psychoanalysis would be compared and checked against longitudinal observations from childhood on. Eventually, Kris carried out this project at the Yale Study Center. Hartmann was keenly aware of the fact that the psychoanalytic method alone cannot provide the necessary data about the undifferentiated phase during which the demarcation lines between the ego and the id, and between the self and the object, are not yet drawn. Furthermore, psychoanalysis could not provide data on the preverbal stage (p. 102).

Hartmann does not mention the controversial discussions between Anna Freud and Melanie Klein in this context, but that controversy which took place between 1941 and 1945 centered almost entirely on this early period that is not open to direct psychoanalytic observations.

The new emphasis on developmental psychology yielded a number of important new concepts, the most important being the development of the infant from *need satisfaction* to *object constancy* and the gradual separation between self and object representation. Most of the work of Spitz, Mahler, and Jacobson was derived from these two concepts. These ideas also aroused considerable opposition (Kohut 1977, pp. 84–90). Data from infant observations were said to have no relevance to what psychoanalysts encounter in the psychoanalytic situation. André Green (1975a) put it thus: "psychoanalysis has yielded a large part to the fascinating ascendancy of child analysis" (p. 282).

4) Central to Hartmann's theory was the view that the ego was the organ of adaptation. Since Darwin, adaptation was a prerequisite for survival. Natural selection operated blindly through the survival of the fittest. Man alone had developed the ego as the organ through which adaptation takes place. In the 1939 monograph Hartmann stated, strictly speaking, that the normal newborn human and his average expectable environment are adapted to each other from the very first moment (p. 51). To be successful, the ego functions must have some autonomy from the drives. By the prominent place that Hartmann gave to adaptation, the environment was reintroduced as a potent force into psychoanalytic theory. During the Breuer–Freud (1895) period of emphasis on trauma, the environment was decisive in the formation of hysteria, but after the publication of *The Interpretation of Dreams* (1900) and *Three Contributions to the Theory of Sexuality* (1905) the emphasis shifted to the psychic reality of each person, with the fixation points of the libido as the main cause of mental illness. Hartmann's emphasis on adaptation redressed the balance in favor of the environment. Human development takes place in an "average expectable environment." Unexpected and below average environments affect children particularly, but also adults, bringing about either shock or stress trauma.

Hartmann did not intend to equate adjustment with mere conformity, but, as his influence became felt during the Eisenhower era, many critics of Hartmann interpreted his psychology as subservient to the American status quo. Analysts on the continent looked on Hartmann's work with dismay, fearing that these new formulations would undo Freud's understanding of the inevitable tension between individual and culture.

In a chapter entitled "Psychoanalysis and Science: American Ego Psychology," Nathan Hale (1995) described Rapaport as second only to Hartmann himself.

> A new attempt to systemize Freud's general theory of the mind into tightly woven linked propositions was undertaken by a "stiff, prickly, immigrant Jew," David Rapaport, who had suffered since childhood from a rheumatic heart condition. A refugee psychologist from Budapest, he possessed a strong Kantian philosophical bent, extravagant erudition, and a driven capacity for work. He was a passionate polemicist, discussing "abstract metapsychology with the thunder of a Hebrew prophet," and had little of the cool, magisterial detachment of the aristocratic Hartmann. [p. 237]

Rapaport is given credit for the recognition that dissidents of psychoanalysis Adler, Rank, and Horney played a role in the creation of ego psychology.

Rapaport (1967) made the new point of view explicit. The new thesis is: the environment does not foist adaptation on the id; adaptedness of the organism to the average expectable environment is primarily a given (p. 600). In a similar vein Rapaport wrote that secondary process is not simply imposed by reality but is built upon previously given foundations of adaptedness (p. 603).

Below the surface, not officially acknowledged, we find in Rapaport a highly critical attitude towards Freud. Because the ego has the capacity for relative autonomy from the drives, as well as from the environment, this double autonomy gives man his capacity for adjustment. This capacity was hailed by Rapaport, often at the expense of earlier psychoanalytic findings.

> Behavior is determined not only by unconscious motivation but also certain reality conditions. For example, a cigar can be just a cigar and not primarily a penis symbol. . . . It is a difficult job to create concepts which take account of both intrapsychological motivations and reality adaptation. . . . What is the aim of psychological treatment? . . . We all would agree that liberation from crippling defenses is the aim of our work. In the meantime, however, there is also something we keep in the back of our minds and some of us may even keep it in the

foreground: The patient needs to find his place in society and lead a useful, productive life. [1954, p. 587]

In 1957 Rapaport added:

It took quite a while to realize that this discovery does not compel us to embrace a solipsistic theory in which a chimney is primarily a phallic symbol and only secondarily the means of letting smoke out of a house. It was some time before we began to take account of the chimney as a smoke stack because these realistic meanings were not the focus of our early interest. [pp. 723–724]

The cigar quote comes from Freud, the one time when he was not a Freudian and denied the unconscious reason for his dependency on smoking cigars. We note the social conformity, when Rapaport speaks of the patient's need to find his place in society. Today it is not easy for us to sympathize with Rapaport. Was there ever a time that psychoanalysts forgot that chimneys serve a real function? The realistic meanings of chimneys are of interest to architects and fireplace owners. In psychoanalysis they have only a symbolic meaning. Was it really necessary to rediscover that the chimney is not always a symbol for the phallus? To my ear, hostility towards Freud is discernible here.

To the traditional assumptions of Freudian metapsychology, the dynamic, economic, and structural points of view, Rapaport and Gill (1959) added the adaptive point of view.

Rapaport (1960, p. 62) emphasized another difference between Freud and Hartmann. Freud's stress on drives and constitutional factors described society as restricting human nature, while psychoanalytic therapy aims to liberate human nature from social bondage. Hartmann (1939) introduced the concept of *social compliance* patterned after Freud's *somatic compliance*. In Hartmann's view social institutions mold, foster, and help the development of the individual, aiding the capacity for adaptation. What to Freud was a coercive force was to Hartmann a benevolent molding institution.

5) Rapaport (1951, 1957) expressed the moral fervor that lies behind the idea of ego autonomy. The healthy ego is slave neither to the drives nor to the environment. Such an ego solves problems, makes choices, and permits pleasure. Sandler (1987) noted, however, that Rapaport did not stress the autonomy from the superego sufficiently. This is a far cry from Freud's pessimism about the ego's subservience

to superego, id, and the reality principle in the ego and the id and the emphasis on the inevitable hostility we all bear towards civilization that Freud wrote about in *Civilization and Its Discontents* (1930a). Both Hartmann and Rapaport assumed that the autonomous ego finds the best solutions for adaptation, but Rangell (1986) disagreed (p. 17). Autonomy can be anti-adaptive. Rangell also saw creativity associated with "the greatest amount of autonomy" (p. 17). Freud and most other analysts writing on creative individuals stressed that creativity emerges from conflict and is an attempt to resolve intrapsychic tensions.

The attainment of this double autonomy became a new ego ideal and contributed to the enthusiasm of the Hartmann group. While Freud only wished to lighten the burden of neurosis so that the former neurotics can stand up to the ordinary miseries of life, the idea of double autonomy went beyond what Freud had envisioned. There is something majestic in Rapaport's description of the autonomous ego and its powers. It reminds one of Nietzsche's superman, except that the autonomous man is not amoral. Gitelson (1962) pointed out that the adult is autonomous and therefore a relatively closed system, while the anaclitic baby is an open system that makes him more dependent on the environment.

6) To the psychoanalyst's vocabulary Hartmann added *change in function*. It is not enough to know how a certain character trait or a certain sublimation originated, for in subsequent development one or more changes in functions can take place. What once was in conflict may secondarily become autonomous; what once was a defense against an instinctual drive may become independent and continue to flourish as an autonomous ego function. When Hartmann spoke of a conflictual situation becoming conflict-free he called the change *secondary autonomy*. Secondary autonomies can become so powerful that they are irreversible. Not to take them into account may open psychoanalysis to the accusation of fostering a genetic fallacy. The term *change in function* facilitated the separation between how something originated from what it later became. When psychoanalysis uncovers the instinctual origins of sublimatory activities, the change in function can become a liberating insight. Under the pressure of the superego many analysands condemned sublimatory activities once their origin had been unmasked; a change in function was a term analysts could use to counteract such self-accusations.

The term *change in function* had important implications for psychoanalytic technique. As the function changes, in its new form it belongs to the autonomous part of the ego. It is therefore neither necessary nor desirable to analyze those parts of the personality that have undergone this change. As a result, ego psychoanalysts became much more careful in what they analyzed and what they left unanalyzed.

A recent paper by Pine (1996) may serve as illustration. A 7-year-old boy begins treatment because he is still soiling. During treatment he makes various attempts at mastery. These include covering the office with paper pellets shot from a gun; at another time he soaks toilet paper into wet pads and throws them from a window on passers-by; at a later stage in development he brings to the office a bag of pennies. The bag tears, spilling the pennies. Each one of these events represents a progression from soiling, and at every junction the therapist asks himself whether the connection between such activities should be made conscious or left unanalyzed. Every one of those steps represents a *change of function*. The analyst's behavior is largely determined by the amount of anxiety that these activities engender. By contrast, analysts less aware of ego development would be inclined to analyze every one of these manifestations.

7) The new conceptual language enabled Hartmann (1953) to see schizophrenia in a new light. Freud (1924) understood neurosis as a conflict between id and ego, and psychosis as a conflict between ego and reality. In the *Outline of Psychoanalysis* (Freud 1940) he suggested that the break with reality can result either from changes that take place in the real world or be due to an increase in strength of the instincts. To these Hartmann (1953, p. 184) added that the ego's own capacity to act as a moderator between the id drives and reality is impaired. Strictly speaking this was not a new finding because Freud (1937) mentioned the possibility that ego itself may undergo deformation, but this was related to the problem of a successful analysis, not to schizophrenia.

Hartmann accepted Freud's idea that the loss of reality in schizophrenia is the result of the detachment of the libido from objects and withdrawal into the self, but added that the self can also be flooded with non-neutralized libido and aggression. Deneutralization, in turn, makes it more difficult to differentiate between libido and aggression (1953, p. 193). Deneutralized aggression is absorbed by the superego, which now torments the ego.

8) In 1962, that is, after Kris's death, Hartmann and Loewenstein published the last of the joint papers on superego formation. The super-

ego was conceptualized as a unique and epochal event, which coincides with the passing of the Oedipus complex. Superego functions deal specifically with moral issues. One of the main functions of the superego is to render the person less dependent on outer forces. Persons who have a fully developed superego owe allegiance to no external force. The superego has little effect on the self-representations but becomes the main agency for repression of the incestuous–libidinal wishes, as well as the aggressive ones. Moral pride and high moral self-esteem are the feeling states that accompany the consolidation of the superego. The ego ideal was not conceptualized as an independent structure, but as a function of the superego.

9) The ego itself, Hartmann postulated, should become the object of psychoanalytic scrutiny. Unlike the repressed id, which pushes upward into consciousness and is held back by the countercathexes of the ego, the ego itself offers no help to the analyst in exploring its own defenses. They reveal primarily as a resistance. Anna Freud put it (1965b): "So far as the ego functions are concerned, the analysand is served in almost equal measure by observations inside and outside of the analytic setting" (p. 22). Ego functions should be examined with the same dispassionate interest as were the psychosexual fixation points during the first period of psychoanalysis.

Almost all the ego functions, like memory, can be observed better by other methods than by the psychoanalytic interview. There are some ego functions that play an important role in the success or failure of any analysis, for example, the ego's capacity for integration. The integrative function of the ego, however, all too often becomes liberated only in the course of analysis itself.

10) High on the list of methods "outside the analytic setting" were the clinical tests developed by Rapaport in his book *Diagnostic Psychological Testing* (1945–1946). Before Rapaport, psychological testing in general, the Rorschach and the TAT particularly, was used to gain access to unconscious content. Rapaport employed a battery of tests as a way of obtaining a picture of ego functioning. In discussing the Rorschach test, Rapaport said:

> From the Ego-psychological point of view, the form responses refer to processes of formal reasoning which should pursue their course without anxiety and affects intruding into and disrupting them. Form responses apparently represent the calm—or as Hartmann put it, the

conflict-free—sphere of the Ego. Therefore, they stand for the autonomy of the perceptual and thought processes from encroachments by unconscious factors. [vol. II, p. 189]

Our general rationale of form responses . . . has emphasized that these responses refer to the cultural demand that will be directed by formal relationships of reality, that we become aware of these relationships through "delay of impulse," and that we keep a large segment of our thought processes "conflict-free" and undisturbed by the pressure of affects, anxieties, phantasies. [vol. II, p. 206]

Although only few clinical psychologists grasped the connection between Hartmann's ego psychology and the battery of psychological tests, it was an attempt to study ego functions in a systematic way. Psychological testing became the road for clinical psychologists to become psychoanalysts.

In the chapter on assessment of pathology, probably under Rapaport's influence, Anna Freud (1965b) provided a special section to ego and superego development. She asked the diagnostician making a metapsychological profile:

(a) To examine the intactness or defects of ego apparatus serving perception, memory, motility, etc.;
(b) To examine and study in detail the intactness or otherwise of ego functions (memory, reality testing, synthesis, control of motility, speech, secondary thought processes). To look out for primary deficiencies. To note unevennesses in the levels reached and to include results of intelligence tests. [p. 142]

In 1946 Hartmann, Kris, and Loewenstein noted that the three foremost functions of the ego—thinking, perception, and action—are frequently put in the service of the superego or of the id.

Thinking may be used for gratification of instinctual, as well as self-critical tendencies. In pathological cases, e. g., in compulsive thinking, it can become a substitute for masturbation. In psychoses, e. g., in paranoid delusions, it is overwhelmed by id and superego functions. [1946, pp. 30–31]

In 1950 Rapaport published his massive anthology *Organization and Pathology of Thought*. The confidence of the Hartmann era is reflected in such statements as: "Psychoanalysis appears to contain the outline of a broad theory of thinking." The book aimed to bring together the contributions of psychology, psychiatry, and psychoanalysis to the nature of thought. The richest source for the psychoanalytic theory of thinking is Freud's (1900) *Interpretation of Dreams*. Rapaport was famous as a teacher of Chapter 7 of that book. The basic model of thinking consists of drive tension, which in the absence of the drive object (the mother or caretaker) mounts and results first in the hallucination of the wish. During this period memory traces of previous gratifications are activated. When the hallucination fails to bring gratification, it is gradually followed by ideas; these are less strongly cathected than the hallucinations, but they too act both as indicators of the tension as well as safety valves for drive tension. Anna Freud expressed a similar thought when she pointed out that anxiety contributes to human intelligence. Memories become organized in relation to drive derivatives. These constitute the primary processes. A conceptual organization, which constitutes secondary processes, is gradually superimposed. Ultimately they prevail, because, unlike hallucinations, they can bring about real gratification. Thus, thinking becomes goal-directed. Crucial to Rapaport's thinking was the idea that the involuntary delay of gratification is eventually converted into the ability to delay and achieve internal control.

In that book Rapaport (1950) interpreted symbols as a primitive form of thinking.

> Plato used symbolic myths whenever he was not yet sufficiently in command of the idea to give it a discursive-logical form. In the rest of his writings, however, he was a master of inference and logical proof. Thus, his myths in relation to his other creative products may be justifiably labeled as regressive. [p. 217]

Freud recognized the importance of symbolism in dreams under the influence of Stekel in the third edition of *The Interpretation of Dreams* published in 1911 (Freud 1900). In 1916 Jones published his classic paper on symbolism, in which he concluded that only what has been repressed need be symbolized and only what had been repressed is capable of symbolization. In 1923 the philosopher Ernst Cassirer published his three-volume book, *The Philosophy of Symbolic Forms*. Cassirer's ideas in turn reached the English-speaking world through the work of Susanne Langer (1942). Under Cassirer's influence the capacity to create and use symbols became the very essence of what makes us human.

These views entered psychoanalysis through Melanie Klein's pivotal paper on symbolism (1930), followed by the work of Hanna Segal (1957). This line of thought was further developed in the works of Winnicott and André Green. Hartmann acknowledged the work of Klein on symbolism, but it played no role in his thinking. Even Kris (1952), who wrote about art, did not discuss the role of symbol formation. One gets the impression that the interest in symbol formation was avoided by the Hartmann group because of their fear that it would play into the hands of the Kleinians.

11) Much of the energy of the Hartmann period was devoted to the development of a complex metapsychological vocabulary. Hartmann found it important to differentiate the cathexis of an ego function, the cathexis of the aim towards which the function is directed, and the cathexis of the object through whom the aim is to be achieved (Hartmann 1955, p. 220). Hartmann found it useful to distinguish three kinds of developmental processes: those that occur without any influence by the external world; those that are triggered by average expectable events in the outside world such as the birth of a sibling; and those that are dependent on atypical or traumatic experiences, such as the death of a parent. The Hartmann group also introduced a differentiation between maturation and development: *maturation* refers to physical and psychic growth that is genetically determined and therefore largely independent of the environment; *development* is directly dependent on the child's interaction with the environment.

Jacobson (1964) introduced the differentiation between self-representation and the "wished for self image." The "wished for self image" should not be confused with the "grandiose self" and "idealized self representations" (Milrod 1982, p. 97). The "grandiose self" and the "idealized self representations" must be curbed before the "wished for self image" can be formed. The "wished for self image" must also, according to Milrod, be further differentiated from the ego ideal. It is evident that students of psychoanalysis during this period had considerable difficulty in understanding and using productively such subtle differentiations. Further differentiations introduced were: between primary and secondary autonomy; self and object representation; and the genetic origin of a symptom or character trait, as distinguished from its current function. The mastery of this language resulted in a certain feeling of elitism. Those who did not master it were considered confused. Anyone who used terms such as *internalized objects* or *introjects* was suspected of Kleinian leanings. The correct term to use was *object representations* (Jacobson 1964).

To give an example, after making the distinction between the wishful self image and the ego ideal, Milrod (1982) said: "The psychoanalytic literature is filled with examples of their confusion" (p. 98). The English usage is also cited as contributing to this confusion. What is noteworthy is that these metapsychological differentiations were just being conceptualized, and yet those who did not understand them were accused of confusion.

Eventually it became necessary to develop a special dictionary to accommodate the language of psychoanalytic ego psychology. This was done by Moore and Fine (1990), in *Psychoanalytic Terms and Concepts,* while the French equivalent, *The Language of Psychoanalysis* (Laplanche and Pontalis 1973), spoke a different tongue.

12) With the aid of these new data and as a result of better systematization, psychoanalysis, it was hoped, would become transformed into a general psychology with significant implications for all social sciences. Kris (1953) put it elegantly:

> Psychoanalysis provides the focal point for a new science of man of which the outlines are here and there visible. Psychoanalytic therapy and psychoanalytic psychiatry in general provide the most essential set of data in the building of this new science. [p. 475]

Hartmann (1959) maintained: "The etiology of neurosis was studied before the etiology of health, though psychoanalysis always aimed at a comprehensive general psychology" (p. 342). There is no evidence in Freud's writings for this assertion.

Freud also believed that psychoanalysis has a contribution to make to culture beyond the clinical and the therapeutic, but he saw psychoanalysis as contributing depth to the social sciences, based on the new understanding of the unconscious and the resultant intrapsychic conflict. Freud in 1926 said:

> For we do not consider it at all desirable for psycho-analysis to be swallowed up by medicine and to find its last resting place in a text-book of psychiatry under the heading 'Methods of Treatment', alongside of procedures such as hypnotic suggestion, autosuggestion, and persuasion. . . . As a 'depth-psychology', a theory of the mental

unconscious, it can become indispensable to all the sciences which are concerned with the evolution of human civilization and its major institutions such as art, religion and the social order. . . . The use of analysis for the treatment of the neuroses is only one of its applications; the future will perhaps show that it is not the most important one. In any case it would be wrong to sacrifice all the other applications to this single one, just because it touches on the circle of medical interests. [1926b, p. 248]

In Freud's view, it was the discovery of the unconscious, and not ego, that made psychoanalysis so important for the social sciences.

Hartmann and his group visualized a psychoanalysis so modified that it would appeal to other sciences, resulting in an interdisciplinary approach where psychoanalysis would influence other disciplines and continuously profit by observations made in other fields. They wished to undo the scientific isolation from which Freud could not extricate his movement.

13) Hartmann's concept of neutralization of both the sexual and aggressive drives and his concept of the autonomous ego and its conflict-free sphere are the main bridges that lead from psychoanalysis as a theory of neurosis to psychoanalysis as a general psychology. Drive neutralization was conceptualized as essential for the building up of object relations, reaching object constancy, where the object matters independently of the state of need. Rapaport (1951) considered neutralization to be the main difference between primary and secondary processes. The secondary processes that take reality into account and accept Aristotelian logic operate with neutralized energy, whereas primary processes under the sway of instinctual wishes operate with deneutralized energy.

The function of psychoanalysis was correspondingly redefined as the restoration of autonomy of ego functions that have been lost or diminished by conflict, or by instinctualization and repression (Beres 1971, p. 23).

In an influential paper written in 1955, Schur linked resomatization with the prevalence of primary processes and failure of neutralization. To the extent that this happens the ego cannot control anxiety because self and object representations are not separated. Patients who suffer from psoriasis punish the object by attacking the self. The hostility is meant for the mother, but the skin has to bear the brunt of such hostility.

14) Freud's concept of primary narcissism was redefined in terms of an early undifferentiated phase. Object libido does not result from transformation of narcissistic libido, but both emerge from an undifferentiated matrix. In general the concept of differentiation, which plays a peripheral role in Freud's thinking, became central to this group and particularly important in the understanding of borderline psychotic phenomena. The crucial concept became the separation between self representation and object representation; when these remain fused or confused psychic structure cannot develop fully (Jacobson 1964).

15) A differentiation between ego and self was made by Hartmann: he realized that the ego in Freud's paper on narcissism (1914), which can be cathected with libido at the expense of object libido, was not the same ego that Freud conceptualized as a term during the structural phase, when he differentiated between ego, superego, and id. Hartmann suggested that the cathexis of the ego with libido be called the *cathexis of the self*. This opened the way to the study of the self as an independent psychic entity. Jacobson (1964) described the development of the self in greater detail. In infancy the self image is fluctuating and unstable, inflated by omnipotence and narcissistic wishes and deflated under superego pressure and harsh reality. Under favorable conditions images of the self become increasingly realistic.

> . . . with advancing psychosexual and ego development, with the maturation of physical and mental abilities, of emotional and ideational processes and of reality testing, and with increasing capacity for perception and self perception, for judgment and introspection, the images become unified, organized, and integrated into more or less realistic concepts of the object world and of the self. [p. 22]

The new interest in the self brought with it a new interest in the sense of identity. The cathexis of the self can become sexualized and when this happens it results in sexual overestimation of the self (Hartmann 1953). Masturbation becomes the preferred form of sexual gratification.

16) Freud worked with two often contradictory metaphors. The *archaeological* model implies that all that was repressed is still alive in the unconscious and pressing upward to consciousness through various derivatives. This metaphor dominates *Civilization and Its Discontents* (1930a), where Freud says explicitly that nothing that has come into existence will ever pass away. It also dominates Freud's paper "On

Construction in Psychoanalysis" (1937). In the other metaphor, the *transformational* model, Freud suggested that even powerful wishes undergo transformation to such an extent that the original wishes can no longer be recaptured. This model dominated Freud's (1924) paper on "The Dissolution of the Oedipus Complex," as well as his theories on female sexuality and masochism. The Hartmann era stressed the transformational model, which was less concerned with the dominant points of fixation and more aware of human development beyond childhood. Hartmann (1952) felt that Freud's assumption that repressed impulses remain unchanged in the id was in need of revision. This was accomplished by another member of the Hartmann group, Max Schur (1966). In his book Schur paid homage to the Hartmann group. It contains an unexpected conclusion:

> I assume that certain autonomous apparatuses serve the development not only of the ego but of the id as well. . . . The concept "wish" and its development are to be understood in such terms. [pp. 199–200]

On the subject of the genetic relationship between ego and id, psychoanalytic theory developed three models. First was the model of Freud, in which the ego develops out of the id and becomes that part of the id that is in contact with reality (Freud 1923a). Second was Melanie Klein's model (1932), where the ego functions from the very beginning of life, its main function being the defense against annihilation anxiety. This early ego operates primarily by use of projection and introjection. In 1946 Klein added that one of the most important functions of the ego is integration. The third model, that of Hartmann, postulated that both ego and id develop out of the undifferentiated matrix.

I do not believe that psychoanalysts become agitated over pure problems of metapsychology. We, therefore, must ask what these models imply. In my view, Freud's model was designed to highlight the fact that man accepts the reality principle slowly, reluctantly, and incompletely. As the ego grows, so does the capacity of the person to accept reality. Hence the famous "where id was, there shall ego be." The Kleinian model implies that the margin of libido over aggression is slim at best, and a special psychic structure, the ego, is needed to defend man against his self-destructive tendencies. The purpose of the Hartmann model was to bring psychoanalysis out of its isolation and connect it with currents in biology and sociology. It is the most optimistic of the three, and implies the greatest trust in the human capacity to grow and develop. In this view conflict is not ubiquitous, and, even where the ego is involved in conflict with the id, secondary autonomy can develop so that what was once in conflict can become conflict-free once more.

17) In a paper written in 1950 entitled, "Notes on the Development of Some Current Problems in Child Psychology," Kris (1950b) introduced into psychoanalysis the significance of systematic longitudinal direct observation of children, how they develop, and how they solve or fail to solve phase-specific problems. Kris hoped that these direct observations will complement and supplement data observed in the psychoanalytic interview of adults associating to their childhood. The Yale University Child Study Center became the place where these longitudinal studies were conducted. These made it possible to test psychoanalysis, not only as a post-dictive discipline but also its capacity to predict future developments. Some predictions were made even before the infant was born, by interviewing the pregnant mother about her attitude toward the future child and by learning about her character structure. Similarly, attempts were made to evaluate the role of thumbsucking as a predictor of future development (Kris 1957, p. 182).

Anna Freud noted: As a result of such comparisons he (Kris) went so far as to state that the traumatic significance of an event is not laid down from the time of its occurrence but that the further course of life seems to determine which experience may gain significance as a traumatic one.

In the Wolf Man Freud (1918) had already assumed a latency period for trauma, but Kris went further to imply that the future, and not the event itself, can decide what will become traumatic.

At the height of this work a whole family, parents and children, were in analysis simultaneously. The therapists met to compare the analyses of the various family members. It was a challenging task to observe how the same event affects each member of the family differently. The difficulties in comparing this mass of data were very great, and the results of these costly and time-consuming investigations have not been published in full. Whether or not the results warranted the expenditure in time and money of this enormous work remains to be judged by a future investigator.

18) In the 1939 monograph, Hartmann made a significant contribution to psychoanalytic technique:

> Interpretations not only help to regain the buried material but must also establish the correct casual relations. . . . We cannot assume the ways in which children connect their experiences and which later become conscious in the course of psychoanalysis, could not satisfy the requirement of a mature ego. . . . The mere reproduction of memories in psychoanalysis can, therefore, only partially correct . . . the incorrect connections of elements. [p. 63]

The analyzed person is different from the nonanalyzed one, not only because he has a richer access to his past, but because his life history has undergone a reorganization of cause and effect, bringing the biography closer to the reality principle. Kris's later papers developed the implication of this significant insight. In his later work Hartmann never cited clinical cases, and it has often been said that he wrote as if he were not familiar with psychoanalytic therapy. Nevertheless, Hartmann's ideas influenced psychoanalytic technique decisively, but primarily through the work of others. The Hartmann group believed that psychoanalytic technique lagged behind psychoanalytic theory. They wished to update the technique so that it could reflect the new understanding of the role of the ego. They were concerned with two issues: the more precise timing of interpretations, and the derivation of psychoanalytic technique from the structure of the ego.

In December 1948 a panel entitled "Technical Implication of Ego Psychology" was held at the midwinter meeting of the American Psychoanalytic Association. Both Hartmann and Kris read papers at that symposium (Hartmann 1951; Kris 1951). Loewenstein also published a paper on technique (Loewenstein 1951). The paper by Hartmann was essentially programmatic in nature. He believed that in 1948 psychoanalysts knew more theoretically than they could use technically. A great deal of accumulated psychoanalytic wisdom was transmitted from teacher to pupil along anecdotal lines. To understand neurosis, health had to be understood. The intrasystematic conflicts within the ego had to be studied to match the psychoanalytic understanding of intersystemic conflicts between ego, id, and super-ego.

Kris cited the example of a child who had been to the dentist and in his analytic hour proceeded to damage objects belonging to the analyst and to break the sharp points of pencils. Kris suggested that three lines of interpretations are possible. First, one can draw the attention of the child to the retaliatory castration in his play; that would lead directly to the discussion of the castration complex. This is the approach of id analysis. Second, one can show that he has turned the passive experience in the dentist's office into an active one. Third, one can interpret that he has identified himself with the aggressive dentist. Their emphasis on different approaches was new and emerged in part out of the disagreements with Kleinian technique. Kris favored the third as the broadest and most conducive to self observations. Ultimately all three interpretations are necessary, but the sequence in which the interpretations are given makes the difference.

Kris then presented a case of an academician who could not advance because he was incapable of publishing. The patient had previously been analyzed by an id analyst (Schmiedeberg 1934), who had uncovered that during his adolescence he had occasionally stolen sweets and books. The stealing was later transformed into a tendency to plagiarize. At a still later time, he developed a prohibition against the plagiarism that resulted in his inability to publish his findings. Kris did not aim at a rapid access to the id. He explored the surface, and by doing so he discovered an intermediary defensive structure. The patient had developed a tendency to ascribe to others his own ideas, a kind of reverse plagiarism, and developed his working inhibition as a reaction to it. The previous analyst had emphasized the conflict between id and superego; Kris the subtle defensive structure of the ego. In keeping with the Hartmann era, without awareness of this intermediary structure the patient could not be cured of his working inhibition. This clinical example should also be read as a polemic against the Kleinians. Whether inexact interpretations can nevertheless be curative is still an open question (Glover 1931).

In Freud's work and in the Kleinian technique, the timing of interpretation does not play a major role. When Freud understood the individual variation on the Oedipus complex that every patient presented, he disclosed it to the patient. He relied on the resistance that this interpretation engenders to introduce the second phase of the analysis, that of working through. The analysand resists the interpretation, the analyst persists, and eventually the analysand becomes convinced and accepts the interpretation, ushering in the termination phase. In this technique the structure of the ego did not have to be taken into account.

By contrast, Loewenstein's paper (1951) stressed the slow sequence of interpretations. Any interpretation to be effective should include elements that are known to the patient together with unexpected connections. It should deal simultaneously with causes that are currently alive, as well as with events in the past that influence the analysand.

In the beginning of analysis a patient describes a number of events that strike the analyst as having certain similarities. The analyst's first task is then to show the patient that all these events have elements in common. The next step is to point out that the patient behaved in a similar way in all these situations. The third is to demonstrate that this behavior was manifested in certain circumstances such as competitive situations. A further step in a later stage of the analysis would be to show that in these situations rivalry does exist unconsciously but is replaced by an avoidance of competition. In a still later step it will be shown that the behavior originated in certain critical events of his life, such as the oedipal period. The interpretation extends in installments though the analysis, and only in late stages of treatment does an interpretation become complete. In 1954 Loewenstein stressed that success in psychoanalysis depends on autonomous functions such as the intactness of memory and reality testing. It cannot proceed without the capacity for self-observation. The analyst represents to the analysand another autonomous ego more capable of resisting distortions, provided that the analyst himself is free from countertransference. In Loewenstein's formulation conflicts between the drives and the defenses are submitted to the scrutiny of the autonomous functions of the ego and, as a result, better solutions to the conflict are found. Rubenfine (1967) reported that Lowenstein explained that controlled regression in the analytic situation takes place because fantasies are put into words during the process of free association, whereas the fantasizing person is usually satisfied merely by images. Furthermore, the interpretation of the analyst also brings these products under the control of the ego (p. 201). Loewenstein's approach had the unexpected effect of slowing analyses to a snail's pace.

One of the most influential papers on technique of the Hartmann era was the so-called parameter paper by Eissler (1953), "The Effect of the Structure of the Ego on Psychoanalytic Technique." Eissler postulated that, to the extent to which we understand the structure of the ego, we can devise varieties of techniques ideally suited to each individual patient. Hysterics can reasonably adhere to the basic rule and recovery can be attained by interpretation only. Phobic patients resemble hysterical ones, but at a crucial point the interpretation has to be supplemented by suggestion or even command that the patient confront his phobic fear. Parameters can be applied only under three conditions: when interpretation alone cannot bring recovery; the parameter must never transgress the minimum necessary; the parameter can be used only if it leads eventually to its own elimination by further interpretations. Unanalyzable parameters could cause irreparable damage to the analysis, and might make successful termination impossible.

Freud (1918) had used two parameters with the Wolf Man. He promised the patient complete recovery from his intestinal pains, a promise that implied omnipotence. The other parameter became necessary when the analysis stagnated. Freud felt forced to set a termination date for the analysis. Freud's parameters were neither minimal nor self-eliminating. In working with schizophrenics and delinquents the concept of parameter does not apply, since the whole technique has been modified.

Eissler (1958) added the concept of *pseudo-parameters*. These are used when direct interpretation arouses unmanageable resistance. Examples of pseudo-parameters are jokes told by the analysts. With the aid of a joke Eissler suggested an interpretation may be "smuggled in" without arousing as much resistance, because the pleasure gained from the joke acts as a bribe taking the resisting ego by surprise.

In time, the concept of the parameter acquired within psychoanalysis a status reminiscent of mortal sin. It was never entirely clear how one is to know in advance whether a parameter will prove analyzable or not. In a footnote that proved to be particularly influential, Eissler warned that even such a harmless act as giving a cigarette to the analysand (those were the days when both patient and analyst smoked) could endanger the further course of the treatment. The elimination of the effects of the parameter was modeled on the belief that the transference relationship itself can be resolved at the end of the analysis.

A year after the publication of the parameter paper, Stone (1954) criticized the demand that the parameter must terminate before the end of the analysis as too severe. I (Bergmann 1988) argued that the demand that transference be resolved at the end of the analysis runs counter to our understanding of the formation of object relations, from which the psychoanalytic situation is not immune. An object relationship view would assume that, even in an analysis devoid of parameters, an object relationship develops that survives termination.

In keeping with the spirit of the Hartmann era, Eissler assumed that defense mechanisms are initially fed by unneutralized energy. In the course of development this energy can become delibidinized and deaggressivized and thus become useful in building psychic structure. The schizophrenic ego cannot achieve this degree of neutralization. One of the important parts of any psychoanalysis is to demonstrate to the analysand what functions of the ego have become impaired at what time and in what way.

On the positive side, Eissler introduced a sense of order into the question of what behavior other than interpretation is permissible and desirable. What was in the realm of anecdotes, where older analysts would tell the students of particularly successful deviations from standard technique, was now subject to rational considerations. In this sense his paper had a liberating effect. On the other hand, his severe warning of possible consequences had a frightening effect, particularly since he never spelled out why deviations from strict interpretation can have such dire consequences. It is of historical interest that in 1950 Hanna Segal successfully analyzed a schizophrenic patient with parameters. She visited him in the hospital and at home.

Schafer (1994) criticized Eissler:

> Eissler's parameter was progressively and perversely made into a coercive, if not punitive, concept. . . . Eissler's paper seems unacceptably finalistic, restrictive and uncritically committed both to assumptions about continua in development and pathological states and to an operational approach to diagnosis. [p. 721]

To my ear Schafer's criticism is harsh, particularly if we take into account the historical period in which Eissler's paper appeared.

Orgel (1995), also writing under the rubric of a classic revisited, stressed the "political" aspects of Eissler's paper. It was directed against the ideas of the "Widening Scope of Psychoanalysis" advocated by Leo Stone (1954). It was also directed against Alexander's emphasis on corrective emotional experience (Alexander and French 1946). Orgel believed that every meaningful parameter permanently changes the transference.

He was particularly critical of Eissler's withholding the information about why the parameter was introduced until a later date. He felt that the freedom to use parameters gave the analyst magical powers.

19) The Hartmann period had a marked influence on the way psychoanalytic case histories were written. To my knowledge, the first case history written under Hartmann's influence was by Margaret Brenman's (1952) "On Teasing and Being Teased and the Problem of Moral Masochism." It appeared in 1952 in the same volume of *The Psychoanalytic Study of the Child* in which the historical symposium on "The Mutual Influences between the Ego and the Id" appeared. In Brenman's opinion, recent modifications in psychoanalysis had made it possible to look upon moral masochism as an example of a complex configuration resulting from the interplay of primitive unconscious drives with defensive processes and adaptive implementations. It is the third emphasis that make us aware that we are in the Hartmann era. This impression becomes even stronger when we read:

> Human development is not simply a direct instinctual expression, nor merely a defense mechanism, but a highly organized hierarchically stratified set of functions designed simultaneously to express aggression, however circuitously, and to obtain gratification of infantile needs in fact or fantasy however long delayed. [p. 281]

Annie Reich's paper of 1958 entitled "A Character Formation Representing the Integration of Unusual Conflict Solutions into the Ego Structures" broke new ground. Already the title foreshadows the fact that character will be treated in a new way. The case is that of a psychologist, presumably a candidate, married, a father, well liked, and functioning productively. The relevant paragraph reads:

> His history, as will be shown, reveals an abundance of traumatic situations, difficult conflicts, and a preponderance of repressed pregenital and sadomasochistic strivings. Conditions for the formation of good object relations and healthy identifications were far from favorable. Nevertheless, the all-over result of this complicated development was an amazingly positive, one might say ego-syntonic, one. Important sublimations were formed; libidinal strivings found acceptable forms of expression; lasting object relationships were established. [p. 251]

Reich is interested not only in pathology but also in finding how successful solutions emerge out of psychic adversity.

As a third case history, Victor Rosen's (1955) "A Reconstruction of a Traumatic Childhood Event in a Case of Derealization" is a case of a man who showed bizarre behavior during treatment. He became amenable to therapy only after Rosen made the reconstruction that during his third year of life the patient witnessed a suicide attempt by his mother. The patient reacted to the reconstruction not as a discovery but as a permission to remember. The father had tried to make the child believe that he fantasized the event. In this case, the Hartmann era is represented by one important sentence: "Significant figures in the child environment denied the reality of the event and prevented the usual process of repression from taking place" (p. 217).

20) The new emphasis on neutralization raised the question how it relates to the earlier concept of sublimation. Hartmann (1955) noted that Freud's *sublimation* usually referred to deflection of the sexual drive from instinctual aims to culturally approved activities. It was seen as an alternative to repression offering some discharge. Hartmann subordinated sublimation to neutralization. Kris (1955) suggested that *neutralization* be used when we are dealing with energy transformation and sublimation for the displacement of the goal. Kris admitted that the two are interdependent. He cited some examples: in dancers we might expect strong exhibitionistic wishes; in actors a capacity to change identifications rapidly. The success of the activity depends on the degree of autonomy. In my view, this formulation is difficult to prove, since we have no way of ascertaining detachment from conflict except by the success of an activity. Another observation by Kris is clinically easier to verify: "In every process of creation a gradual emergence from conflict plays a part" (p. 153). Any analyst working with creative analysands can verify that this is so. Kris observed children at easel painting, and noted that some were closer to drive discharge while others could be seen as attempting neutralization and sublimation.

21) Hartmann's ego psychology also affected applied psychoanalysis. In his 1960 presidential address to the American Psychoanalytic Association entitled "Ego Psychology and the Study of Mythology," Arlow said:

> Psychoanalysis has a greater contribution to make to the study of mythology than demonstrating, in myths, wishes often encountered in the unconscious thinking of patients. The myth is a particu-

lar kind of communal experience. It is a special form of shared fantasy, and it serves to bring the individual into relationship with members of his cultural group on the basis of certain common needs. Accordingly, the myth can be studied from the point of view of its function in psychic integration—how it plays a role in warding off feelings of guilt and anxiety, how it constitutes a form of adaptation to reality and to the group in which the individual lives, and how it influences the crystallization of the individual identity and the formation of the superego. . . . Society can exist only because the impossible burden of instinctual renunciation which communal living demands can be abrogated nightly in dreams. Personal dreams and daydreams are made to be forgotten. Shared daydreams and myths are instruments of socialization. The myth, like the poem, can be, must be, remembered and repeated. [1961, pp. 375, 378–379]

Since Abraham's "Dreams and Myths" (1909), classical psychoanalysis equated the two, dreams being private myths and myths collective dreams. Arlow's approach emphasized the difference by introducing the role of culture and education and, by implication, social adjustment.

Classical psychoanalysis emphasized the connection between early infancy and the work of the painter or the writer. The model was Freud's "Leonardo Da Vinci" (1910), restated in connection with Goethe when Freud received the Goethe prize (1930b). Psychoanalytic biographies of the Hartmann era veered away from this model. Greenacre's (1955) *Swift and Carroll* emphasized early ego development. Niederland's (1965) biography of the archeologist Schliemann emphasized the problem of identity: "All through his life Schliemann was never sure whether he was the dead brother inside or the living one outside the grave" (p. 375). Beyond the Hartmann group important psychoanalytic biographies, like those of Edith and Richard Sterba's study *Beethoven and His Nephew* (1954), contained no reconstruction of childhood memory and no analysis of Beethoven's music. The most popular of the biographies of this era—those by Erikson, *Young Man Luther* (1958) and *Gandhi's Truth* (1969)—did not originate in the Hartmann sphere of influence. Erickson stressed phases of psychosocial development spanning the whole life cycle. He emphasized particularly the identity crises that often take place in adolescence. While these biographies are different from each other in methodology and depth, they all depart from the classical model (Bergmann 1966).

In the field of biography, Eissler's massive two-volume *Goethe: A Psychoanalytic Study* (1963), extending over 1500 pages, broke new ground. To Eissler, Goethe was the very model of genius; where ordinary mortals succumb to psychic pathology, the genius creates a healthy and organizing disease. Goethe had an incestuous fixation on his sister Cornelia. Her marriage brought him close to suicide, but these dangerous impulses were sublimated into writing the story of *Werther's Sufferings*. Eissler believes that the fixation on his sister saved Goethe from psychosis and overt homosexuality. In Eissler's view the seven years in which Goethe loved Charlotte von Stein without sexual consummation were curative for him. The relationship between the two was never sexually consummated. Older than Goethe and mother of seven children, Charlotte von Stein acted as a "proto-analyst." Eissler sees her role as analogous to the role Fliess played in Freud's life. In some respects the book can be read as a dialogue with Hartmann on the limits of neutralization. Eissler's book is based on the conviction that for Goethe the unconscious "served functions not ordinarily achieved by the unconscious which made possible a magnificent achievement without ever feeling harassed or pressed for time" (p. xxxiii).

> Hartmann sees the proof of neutralization principally in the stability of ego functions, their resistivity against regression and sexualization, which he calls degrees of secondary autonomy of the ego. Yet I think one can regard the stability of ego function as firmly established only when they also operate adequately so long as they are charged with great quantities of instinctual energy. [p. 1412]

> I am trying here to demonstrate a factor that plays its great role in a certain type of healthy person and can be called "drive dependability." . . . Such "drive dependability" as one finds in Goethe, combined with eminent ego structure, was responsible for a life story of such magnificence that even the highest degree of neutralization could never achieve. [p. 1414]

> The ego has the capacity to turn the cathexis of the forbidden imagery to the ego-acceptable imagery of the created work . . . preserves its instinctual quality despite the profoundest changes of aims. . . . I used the term "sublimation" as a change of instinctual aim and not as a transformation of energy. [p. 1415]

Hartmann's neutralization threatened to replace Freud's sublimation. Eissler, like Kris (1955), attempted to create a bridge between the two concepts.

II. SKETCHES OF INDIVIDUAL CONTRIBUTORS TO THE HARTMANN ERA

In a previous section I attempted to describe the main contributions of the Hartmann era. In this section I will deal with specific contributions of some of the members of this group that I consider particularly significant.

Rene Spitz

Rene Spitz (1887–1974) was one of Freud's own analysands. The work that made him famous in psychoanalysis appeared in the first volume of the *Psychoanalytic Study of the Child* (1945), entitled "Hospitalism." Spitz reported a fact that was well known to students of institutional care of infants, but not to psychoanalysts: that between 70 and 90 percent of all infants put into foundling homes die in their first year of life. The rate of death was particularly noticeable when the infant was separated from his mother from 6 to 12 months. These deaths took place even when the physical care of the infants was good. Deprived of maternal care, these children developed an extreme susceptibility to infections.

In the same journal a year later (1946) Spitz (together with K. Wolf) published a paper entitled "Anaclictic Depression." The term was analogous to Freud's *anaclictic love*. They studied the stages infants go through after separation from the mother. The infants first became weepy, then began to withdraw, averted their faces, and ceased to take part in the life around them. They lost weight, developed insomnia, and failed to thrive.

Spitz and Wolf (1946a) compared their findings with Freud's (1917) "Mourning and Melancholia."

> We suggest that when the mother substitute is a good one, depression does not develop. Where the mother substitute turns out to be

an aggressive, unloving personality, the parallel to adult melancholia is enacted in real life. Just as in melancholia the ego is oppressed
by a sadistic superego, here the body ego of the infant is oppressed
by a sadistic love object substitute. [p. 335]

It is more difficult to replace a satisfactory love object than an unsat-
isfying one. Accordingly depression is much more frequent and much
more severe in the cases of a good mother–child relationship. [p. 336]

We encountered biting phenomenon in some of the depressed children, but not in all. . . . The biting activities *never* were in evidence
during the depression; they appeared after the depression had lifted.
[p. 340]

These data have shown that the infant depends on the mother for
love to a degree not suspected by Freud, who assumed that the child is
born in a narcissistic state and only later develops object relations. Spitz
and the editors of the *Psychoanalytic Study of the Child* (1946a,b) were
not aware of the theoretical magnitude of this discovery. Instead they
used the data to refute Melanie Klein's claim to the universality of the
depressive position. The assumption of classical psychoanalysis that the
infant's first stage of life is narcissistic was not challenged.

In 1946 Spitz and Wolf (1946b) wrote a monograph entitled "On
the Smiling Response." They established that between 6 and 8 months
stranger anxiety appears in the infant. The infant who earlier went
happily from one adult to another now as the result of a newly acquired
diacritic discrimination becomes bashful or anxious when a stranger
appears. Normally the 8-month anxiety takes between 1 and 10 minutes for the infant to overcome. However, in the anaclictically depressed
child it can take over an hour before contact is established.

In 1957, Spitz published *No and Yes*, where he observed that around
15 months the baby begins to say no to everything and does so with
unconcealed glee. Under unfavorable conditions the no phase can fail
to appear or is greatly reduced. This negative behavior, so abhorrent
to many parents, is prerequisite for the development of an independent self. Eventually this insight had an effect on psychoanalytic technique. It was now realized that analysands may belatedly try to make
up for what they did not achieve as toddlers; they achieve it by saying
no to every interpretation given by the analyst. Analysts learned to

understand and tolerate the negativity of their analysands in a way they could not do before.

Arlow reviewed this book in 1958 and noted that:

In this present work Spitz has effected a most impressive synthesis of psychoanalysis with ethology, experimental psychology and embryology. So far, no comparable study of the maturation and development of a specific ego function has appeared. [p. 579]

The emphasis on relating psychoanalysis to ethology, experimental psychology, and embryology is entirely in keeping with the aims of the Hartmann period.

A later book entitled *The First Year of Life* appeared in 1965. There Spitz enumerated stages that universally take place at crucial junctions in development. These were the smiling response, the 8-month anxiety, and autoerotism. Spitz differentiated between two systems of sensations: the *coenesthetic* and *diacritic*. Coenesthetic sensations are mostly extensive and visceral, effected by the smooth musculature and the sympathetic and parasympathetic nervous organizations. Diacritic sensations are intensive, involving striated musculature and the central nervous system. In the neonate only coenesthetic organization prevails; the diacritic evolves slowly.

Spitz stressed that maturational processes in the baby foster the development of the structure of the child's ego:

It can never be sufficiently stressed that object relations take place in a constant interaction between two very unequal partners, the mother and the child. Each provokes the response in the other; that this interpersonal relationship creates a field of constantly shifting forces. [p. 204]

These observations mark the transition from ego psychology to object relations theory. Spitz further concluded that disturbances in the maternal personality will be reflected in the disorders of the child. He differentiated pathology created in the child by improper mother–child relationships and maternal insufficiency. Among the improper relationships he included oscillations between pampering and hostility, cyclical mood swings and compensated hostility. If insufficient mothering is not compensated for by adequate caretakers it will lead to psychogenic deficiency diseases. In my own work I have noticed that even if a substitute maternal object is supplied in the form of a nanny, there is always the danger that envy and hostility between the mother and the caretaker may destroy some of the beneficial effects of the maternal substitutes.

Another observation reported by Spitz that had a far-reaching effect on psychoanalysis was that the breast is not a visual percept, but a content percept (p. 69). The nursing baby does not look at the breast, but looks at mother's face. Similarly he looks at her face and not at her breast when she approaches him. Spitz's finding was enthusiastically embraced by Erikson.

> The motherly person, by letting her face, as it were, shine upon the newborn's searching eyes, and by letting herself be verified as a comprehensible image, thus may be called the first reality. And indeed some infants can nurse with open eyes, they are apt to stare continuously at the mother's face while at her breast. Thus vision becomes the leading perceptual modality for the organization of the sensory space, for reality testing, and for adaptation. [quoted in Brenman-Gibson 1976, p. 334]

This observation was at variance with the Kleinian point of view, where the split between the good and bad breast plays a major role in development during early infancy. That some men and women are fixated on the breast, to the exclusion of the whole person, is well known; they relate to others only as *part-objects*. In light of Spitz's findings, such a fixation need not be a regression to the first stage of normal development but rather a disappointment in the face of the mother, when the mother cannot, for reasons of her own depression, show the infant a responding face. In light of these findings the reclining position, when the analysand is deprived of looking at the analyst's face, appeared in a new perspective. Analysts had a better way of understanding why some people have difficulty accepting the couch. I have observed that frequently during the termination phase some analysands ask to sit up and establish eye contact with the analyst.

At the same period, Winnicott (1953) was conducting parallel studies centering on the role of the transitional object, but Winnicott was in the camp of Melanie Klein. None of his publications appeared in the *Psychoanalytic Study of the Child*, nor did Spitz mention Winnicott's work in his book. The gulf separating the work of the Hartmann ego psychologists and the work of the Kleinians in England had few bridges.

Spitz's work had a great influence on psychoanalytic technique. A paper published in 1956 under the unassuming title of "Countertransference" contained revolutionary ideas. There Spitz introduced the term *diatrophic* (from the Greek meaning "to support throughout"). The term was first applied to the infant as taking place after the anaclictic phase (the term *anaclictic*, meaning "to lean on," was coined by Freud in 1914 when he differentiated anaclictic from narcissistic object choice). During the diatrophic phase the child forms secondary identifications with his parents (the child feeds the teddy bear). Spitz recommended that as the analysand is entering an anaclictic transference the analyst should respond in a diatrophic manner.

Gitelson (1962), in his opening remarks to the International Symposium in the Edinburg Conference, stated that a patient's need for help arouses in the analyst the diatrophic attitude and the anaclictic–diatrophic equation is responsible for the rapport that is the harbinger of transference. "The analyst's task is equivalent to the steadiness of the effective mother" (p. 201). Thus, with little fanfare, a major change was introduced into psychoanalysis. Where the Oedipus complex was central, the analyst stood mainly for the father. Now an earlier phase took precedence, with the emphasis on preoedipal constellations; the analyst's role became increasingly that of the mother. Many analysts did not go along with this change and they were labeled derisively as "oedipalists."

Edith Jacobson

Edith Jacobson received her psychoanalytic training in the Berlin Psychoanalytic Institute in the later 1920s and began publishing psychoanalytic papers in the 1930s. She was interested in the evolution of the wish for a child in women and in boys. Together with Karen Horney, she was instrumental in changing the psychoanalytic view about the formation of the superego in women. In the United States she was highly regarded for her writings on depression and melancholia.

Jacobson's 1964 book on *The Self and the Object World*, itself an elaboration of an earlier article by the same name (Jacobson 1954), was one of the most important texts of the Hartmann era. Written in an abstract metapsychological language, it was the most comprehensive statement about normal development from birth to psychic consolidation.

The first chapter in that book is a dialogue with Freud, whose concepts of primary narcissism and primary masochism Jacobson attempted to modify. What makes this chapter difficult reading is her wish to be both an extender and a modifier of Freud's views. She suggested that Hartmann's undifferentiated matrix replace both Freud's primary narcissism and primary masochism. In Jacobson's view, in normal development pleasurable and unpleasurable experiences and object images emerge in the first 6 months. Libido and aggression are also not yet differentiated, and discharge of unpleasure takes place silently into physiological channels. With further maturation the early infantile wish for oneness with the love object yields to the desire to become like the object. The good and the bad images of the mother become consolidated into one person. Simultaneously, object images become object representations and are differentiated from self representations. Eventually, when developments are favorable, the real parents become differentiated from the idealized parents, and realistic self representations are differentiated from the earlier idealized images of the self. Finally, a coherent self emerges. "The images become unified, organized, and integrated into a more or less realistic concept of the object world and the self" (p. 22).

The aggressive drive becomes modified into ambition and envy. Eventually sexual identity is added to the earlier sense of identity. The superego emerges as a comprehensive reaction against oedipal and narcissistic strivings. If the superego establishes a dominant control over the cathexis of the self representation, superego fear becomes the leading affect signal.

That we are in the Hartmann era can be seen from the following:

> Normal identity formation appears to rest on the ability of the psychic organization to develop and achieve an optimal secondary autonomy of superego and ego in its handling of reality and of the drives, of intersystemic conflicts and of tensions within all systems. [p. 27]

In spite of the complexity of the language, Jacobson's book succeeded to show the complex interaction of the developmental forces that are necessary for normal development to take place. As a result, psychoanalysis became better aware of the great variety of factors that can impede normal development. It increased the interest of psychoanalysts in ascertaining the developmental point in a life history at which pathology first become evident.

In her Freud lecture Jacobson (1967) attempted to combine Hartmann's (1953) modification of Freud's understanding of schizophrenia with ideas expressed by Katan (1954). Katan was interested in the schizophrenics' *residual personality*, those ego functions that remain intact despite the illness. By focusing attention on ego functions Jacobson found:

> There are delusional psychotics who, despite their impaired reality testing in the areas of their psychopathology, may be able, for instance, temporarily to engage in highly intellectual work. Other patients may show such a severe deterioration of the ego functions that they are incapable of working even though they may not suffer from any overt psychotic symptoms, such as delusions or hallucinations. [p. 14]

Looking at psychotics from this new perspective, Jacobson was able to arrive at new conclusions about the relationship between psychotics and the reality world. In her view the psychotic needs the external world to help him or her to prevent the dissolution of both ego and superego structures, which, in turn, creates the psychotic breakdown. While they cling to reality, psychotics also try to mold reality to suit their special needs, and either reject or at least deny those aspects of reality that do not meet their needs. "Psychotics give up reality and replace it by a newly created fantasy reality only if reality fails to lend itself to their purposes and to help them in their conflict solution" (p. 20). Jacobson thus highlighted that the psychotic withdraws from reality only after he had tried to mold it to meet his needs. This interpretation of psychosis was acceptable to psychoanalysts of other schools and was incorporated into Kernberg's (1980) own frame of reference.

Margaret Mahler

Margaret Mahler had been a prominent child psychoanalyst in Vienna before the Hartmann era began. Her earlier studies were what I designated as the work of an extender. They dealt with the subject of tics in children (Mahler and Rangell 1943). It was her contact with the Hartmann era that made it possible for her to make original contributions that rank among the most important findings in the history of psychoanalysis. Mahler began to study mothers and toddlers in a normal setting, where she could observe the separation–individuation process of the young child from his mother, with its many variations. However, the conclusions that she reached, although based on observations, cannot be said to be derived from them, no more than Freud's case histories can be said to have given rise to psychoanalytic theory. Any other observer in Mahler's place would not have drawn her conclusions from her observations. Like Freud, she brought something unique to the data. Such an interaction between data in the outside world and the unique endowment of the analyst may very well be at the core of the psychoanalytic creative process. It seems that psychoanalytic discoveries are made at the crossroads between data of observation and the inner life of the investigator.

Mahler found that prerequisite for good adult functioning, including the capacity to love, is an adequate symbiotic phase where the infant has an intense relationship with one adult before the infant can begin to separate from this all-important love object, the mother or her substitute.

In my paper written for the Mahler festschrift (1971), I drew attention to the point that Plato anticipated this finding when he described lovers as two people who desire nothing more than to be melted into one. I showed that the human need to fall in love is based on this wish, as well as the need to refind the symbiotic partner; symbiotic longings are awakened in the state of falling in love. However, symbiotic refinding for the adult cannot literally be a repetition of the symbiotic experience. Symbiotic elements must blend with later capacities, otherwise the lovers will be inseparable when this need is met. Mahler believed that under favorable conditions the symbiotic phase comes to a natural nontraumatic end. This was different from the way classical psychoanalysts formulated the *weaning trauma*. Nor was it necessary, in Mahler's view, that the father act as a separator between mother and child, as the father appears in the work of Chasseguet-Smirgel (1985). When all goes well, the symbiotic partner helps the infant to "hatch" from the symbiosis. The optimism that characterized the Hartmann era also animated Mahler's work.

If the child is offered a congenial environment and the mother is capable of responding appropriately, first to the symbiotic needs of the child, and later to the need for separation and individuation, the main difficulties of the preoedipal phase will be mastered, and the child will be strong enough to weather the vicissitudes of the Oedipus complex.

Mahler's stages, which follow the separation–individuation process, are in turn divided into four subphases. From 10 to 16 months, the first separation–individuation subphase was called *differentiation* by Mahler. In this subphase the body image develops. The second stage was called the *practicing* subphase, when adequate mirroring is essential and autonomous ego functions begin. It is characterized by an elated mood. Difficulties encountered in this developmental phase reappear in adults in whom success and accomplishments do not evoke the ordinary expected elation. The third, called the *rapprochement* subphase, begins at about 18 months. It is the most vulnerable subphase. During this subphase the child wanders away from the mother, seeking his or her own interest in the outside world. But it is crucial that when the child wishes to return for "refueling" the mother be there for the child. A separation trauma is likely when the mother overestimates the independence of the toddler, or if she herself feels hurt by the separation and wishes, consciously or unconsciously, to retaliate by not being there when the toddler returns. While this separation is described in interpersonal terms, it has an intrapsychic corollary. During the separation–individuation phases, the self of the child as an independent entity is slowly emerging.

The fourth phase involves the consolidation of individuality and the beginning of emotional object constancy. Separation anxiety in Mahler's world is not inevitable; it depends to a significant extent on the availability of the mother. Once the individuation process takes place, the autonomous ego functions, so important to the Hartmannites, come into operation. If symbiosis is the precondition for the capacity to love, a successful negotiation of the separation–individuation subphases deepens the capacity to love. Object constancy is essential if lovers are to sustain their love during periods of separation.

In the process of separation–individuation, object constancy is attained during the third and fourth year. By object constancy Mahler means "that the maternal image has become intrapsychically available to the child in the same way as the actual mother has been for sustenance, comfort, and love" (1968, p. 222).

In her formulations Mahler (1971) belongs to the Hartmann group when she says that the rapprochement crisis is helped by the developmental spurt of the conflict-free sphere of the ego. However, the fact that her chosen field was direct observations of the symbiotic and separation–individuation phases that involve the mother opened her work to a two-person psychology. This endeavor brought her closer to object relations theory.

In her 1963 Brill Memorial lecture Mahler assigned a significant role to the deficiencies of integration and internalization, deficiencies that leave a residue that will later appear in "borderline" personalities. In her Freud Lecture (1971) she stressed the desperate clinging of such children during the rapprochement subphase. Aggression may be unleashed and sweep away the good object and the good self representation. The child then has to resort to splitting in order to defend the good object against the aggressive drive. Out of the split emerges the good mother of symbiosis for whom we long "from the cradle to the grave" and the image of the dangerous re-engulfing mother of separation. Many of the difficulties that adults experience in loving are due to the coexistence of the longed-for mother of symbiosis, and the fear of the re-engulfing mother of separation. Melanie Klein's good mother appears here as the mother of symbiosis and the bad mother as the re-engulfing mother. Klein's influence is evident, but to quote Klein favorably was one of the unspoken taboos of the Hartmann era.

In a paper published in 1966, followed by a series of books (1974, 1979, 1986) Gertrude and Rubin Blanck translated Mahler's findings on the importance of the separation–individuation phases into a technique of psychotherapy. They envisioned that the finding of ego psychology opened a new approach to the treatment of what they called "less structured personalities." These patients, the Blancks thought, require from the therapist, above all, the building up of the missing ego structure. To cite one example: when a borderline patient dreams that he killed the therapist the aggression should not be interpreted, but the dream should be used to stress the difference between thought and action, helping the patient to reduce guilt. Parameters are used in this therapy, but they should remain unanalyzed.

The Blancks organized their own school, but whether it is possible to help people build up ego structure by ignoring the unconscious, the id wishes, and passionate transference manifestation seems to me dubious.

How Mahler fitted into the Hartmann frame of reference can be seen in her contribution to the Hartmann festschrift (Loewenstein et al. 1966). Her paper was entitled "Notes on the Development of Basic Moods."

> Our reconstructive and observational data suggest that, in those small children who show "the basic depressive mood," not enough sound secondary narcissistic libido has remained available, beyond the period of mastery, to be vested in the "objects and objectives" of his expanding world, and particularly not enough to cathect his own self representations. Too great a portion of his unneutralized aggression (Hartmann, Kris and Loewenstein, 1949) is being taken up by the mechanisms of splitting and projection—a potentially pathological combination of defense, which serves to ward off the child's hostility (aggression) and his fear of annihilating the love object by his aggressive ambivalent fantasies while he struggles to restore this state of oneness with the love object. [p. 161]

> Sound secondary narcissistic cathexis of the self, and for maintenance of structural harmony between the ego and the ego ideal, does not seem to be as readily available to these children as to those who have not suffered acute loss of self esteem and depletion of trust in the love objects, during the second 18 months of life. [p. 167]

That melancholics suffer from low self-esteem and tend to regard others as better than themselves is well known. What is interesting in Mahler's formulation is that she does not stress the severity of the superego, preferring the formulation of deficiency in secondary narcissism. Mahler emphasized that the need to control aggression exhausts the meager supply of secondary narcissism that is available.

Mahler's findings challenged many of the basic tenets of classical psychoanalysis. Was the Oedipus complex still the nucleus of the neurosis, or do borderline patients, and even neurotics suffer from a faulty development that took place during the symbiotic phase or in one of the four separation–individuation subphases?

Mahler's Freud lecture (1971) stressed the relationship between borderline phenomena and difficulties in the separation–individuation process. What marks the borderline patient are failures in internalization, separation anxiety, and the failure to synthesize the good and the bad self and the good and the bad object images. There is a surplus of unneutralized aggression, and delusions of omnipotence alternate with feelings of utter dependency and self-denigration. Developmental failures, in turn, are conducive to creating defenses. If they persist into adulthood, defense mechanisms also persist and are not likely to be given up even when the developmental failures have been made conscious. The Hartmann era differentiated between developmental failure pathology and pathology from intrapsychic conflict, but failed to suggest what alterations in technique this realization would necessitate.

One of the important results of Mahler's work was the realization that mothering is a difficult task indeed. To meet the needs of the infant the mother must be able to foster and enjoy the closeness of the symbiotic relationship. But the very same mother, a few months later, is asked to support the need of her infant to become an individual in his or her own right. Mahler's findings influenced child rearing, but the implications of her findings for the analytic process remained less clear. Others, particularly Gertrude and Rubin Blanck (1974, 1979, 1986), created a psychoanalytic psychotherapy based primarily on Mahler's findings.

Kernberg (1980) found that Mahler's work corresponded to his own findings. "I fully agree with Mahler that a large majority of patients with borderline personality organization present intrapsychic structural organization and conflicts related to those of the rapprochement sub-phase" (p. 109). Schizoid personalities have difficulties based on the differentiation subphase. Psychotic identifications go further back to the symbiotic phase, in which the separation of the self from the nonself is abolished, the self and object representations are re-fused. Functioning on the symbiotic level, they experience idealized ecstatic merger states, as well as terrifying aggressive ones. Kernberg took the concepts of Mahler and Jacobson from the Hartmann frame of reference into object relations theory.

Anna Freud

Anna Freud's classic *The Ego and the Mechanisms of Defense* appeared in 1936. It antedates Hartmann's *Ego Psychology and the Problem of Adaptation* by three years. It was the most important book on ego psychology after Freud's *Inhibition Symptom and Anxiety* (1926a), which initiated ego psychology. The advent of ego psychology had an impact on psychoanalytic technique. The leading ego psychologist before World War II was Fenichel. (For further discussion of the early phase of ego psychology, see Bergmann and Hartman 1976.)

Paul Gray (1982) stressed the resistances that Anna Freud's 1936 book evoked among analysts, not excluding Freud, who referred to her work only once. Gray demonstrated convincingly (to my mind) that Freud originated the impetus for ego psychology but was not himself an ego psychologist.

Paying homage to Hartmann in the festschrift in his honor, Anna Freud (Loewenstein et al. 1966) wrote "Links Between Hartmann's Ego Psychology and the Child Analyst's Thinking."

> The child analyst's thinking, governed as it is by the developmental aspects of the human personality, does not thrive on the basis of drive psychology alone, but needs to range freely in the whole theoretical field of psychoanalysis, according equal significance to id, ego, and super-ego, to depth and surface, as Hartmann does. This creates the specific links between his work and the child analyst's thinking. [p. 17]

> So far as I am concerned, I have tried to take care of this by establishing the concept of *developmental lines,* contributed to both from the side of the id and of the ego development; these developmental lines lead from the child's state of immaturity to the gradual setting up of mature personality and are, in fact, the result of interaction between maturation adaptation, and structuralization. [p. 21]

In 1947 Anna Freud founded the Hampstead Child Therapy Clinic. It became a leading institution for the training of child psychoanalysts and child therapists. The children were seen five times a week for fifty-minute sessions, usually for a number of years. In the mid-1950s a major research project was undertaken under the leadership of Joseph Sandler, called the Hampstead Index. Had this project been undertaken a few years later, in the age of the computer, it would have been much easier. At the time, however, the therapists, at the end of the working day, were asked to classify the material they obtained on index cards. A team of researchers correlated their findings under various headings. It was hoped that this effort would lead to more precise use of analytic terms and thus bring psychoanalysis closer to a scientific method by integrating psychoanalytic theory with direct clinical observations. As this work proceeded, it became apparent that the great majority of concepts Freud and other analysts coined, when subjected to a rigid, quasi-experimental test, were ambiguous and had to be further refined. Difficulties were encountered with such basic concepts as the pleasure principle, superego, ego ideal, identification, internalization, self and object representations, and adaptation. As a result, a large number of papers were published by Sandler and his coworkers, most of them appearing in the *Psychoanalytic Study of the Child* and reprinted in Sandler (1987). Clarification of concepts was one of the most important goals of the Hartmann era, but whether the human psyche will ever lend itself to be treated with such precision is, in my opinion, doubtful.

Classical psychoanalysis had created a developmental psychology based essentially on psychosexual phases that the libido undergoes in the process of maturation. The organizer of this developmental table was Abraham (1924). These were correlated with stages of object love.

Stages of Libidinal Organization	Stages of Object Love	
VI. Final Genital Stage	Object-love	Post-ambivalent
V. Earlier Genital Stage (phallic)	Object-love with exclusion of genitals	Ambivalent
IV. Later anal-sadistic Stage	Partial love	Ambivalent
III. Earlier Anal-sadistic Stage	Partial love with incorporation	Ambivalent
II. Later Oral Stage	Narcissism (total incorporation of object)	Ambivalent
I. Earlier Oral Stage (sucking)	Auto-erotism (without object)	Pre-ambivalent

Abraham's table is still the backbone for Fenichel's classic of 1945. He reproduced the table with some modifications and added a third column, Points of Fixation. In Fenichel's hierarchy schizophrenia was seen as a fixation on the first oral stage. Manic-depressive psychosis was the fixation on the second oral phase. Paranoia was the fixation point on the early anal-sadistic phase, and compulsion neurosis of the late anal phase. Hysteria was the fixation of the phallic phase, and finally normality and the capacity of love were the attainment of the genital phase.

A final attempt to expand the table by including stages in reality testing and differences between boys and girls, as well as ego development, was made by Robert Fliess (1948), a psychoanalyst and son of Wilhelm Fliess, who was Freud's confidant during the discovery of psychoanalysis. By that time the table became so cumbersome that it had lost its usefulness.

One of the most important books of the Hartmann era was Anna Freud's *Normality and Pathology of Childhood* (1965). Written in her characteristically lucid style, it embodied some of the most revolutionary ideas of the Hartmann era. Abraham's table was basically static. By contrast, Anna Freud's concept of developmental lines allowed greater fluidity. In certain children, ego developments go further than their psychosexual development or their object relations. Each individual was now seen as a unique combination of various interacting lines of development.

> What we are looking for are the basic interactions between id and ego and their various developmental levels and also age-related sequences . . . [these] are comparable to the maturational sequence of libidinal stages for the gradual unfolding of the ego functions. [p. 63]

Going beyond the classical table of Abraham, Anna Freud sought to compare the maturational sequences of the libidinal stages with the development of ego functions, illustrating the interaction between ego and id. Some ego functions start early and their development may be subject to discontinuous maturation, while other ego functions, such as reality testing and adaptation, emerge later. These functions are dependent in turn on the maturation of the ego.

Ernst Kris

In the section on technique I have already referred to Ernst Kris, but I could not there do justice to the magnitude of his many contributions. His paper on preconscious mental processes (1950a) opens with two quotes from Freud (1940). These were particularly important to the Hartmann group: the advice to wait until what you wish to inter-pret what has become preconscious. "The inside of the ego, which compromises above all thought processes, has the quality of being pre-conscious" (p. 162). In his paper on the preconscious Kris explored the difference between recognition and recall, a subject dear to academic psychologists, as well as the relationship between fantasy and creativ-ity. Like Hartmann's papers this paper straddles the territory between psychoanalysis and academic psychology.

Together with Hartmann, Kris can be seen as the co-creator of the Hartmann era. Kris was an art historian before he became a psycho-analyst. At 28 Kris became a member of the Vienna Psychoanalytic Society and was appointed as the editor of *Imago*. Among the Hartmann group he was the analyst who was personally close to Freud through his marriage to Marianne Rie, whose family was close to the Freud fam-ily. In 1952 Kris published *Psychoanalytic Explorations of Art*. It was one of the most important books in applied psychoanalysis during the Hartmann era. The artist, as Kris saw him, had shifted his narcissism from himself to his work.

> If this shift outlasts the process of creation, the work gains a perma-nent place in the artist's life; in extreme cases he might find it diffi-cult to part from what he created. If the shift of interest lasts only while the work in being produced, the artist may look upon his ear-lier work with moderate curiosity or detachment; or the work may become dissatisfying, unbearable evidence of failure. Psychoanalytic observation suggests that such unfavorable judgments tend to be experienced as directed against the art work as part or substitute of the self. [pp. 60–61]

That we are in the realm of ego psychology is evident from such state-ments as:

> The process can also be described in terms of ego psychology. When the artist creates during inspiration he is subject to an ego regression but it is a partial and temporary ego regression, one controlled by the ego which retains the function of establishing contact with an audi-ence. The artist identifies himself with his public in order to invite their participation. [p. 167]

The normal artist creates not to transform the outer world, but to depict it for others he wishes to influence. The psychotic artist creates in order to transform the real world; he seeks no audience and his modes of expression remain unchanged once the psychotic process has reached a certain intensity. [p. 169]

Kris coined the phrase "regression under the control of the ego." The phrase became popular and created a literature of its own (Weissman 1967).

When the artist creates during inspiration he is subject to an ego regression but it is a partial and temporary regression, one controlled by the ego, which retains the function of establishing contact with an audience (Kris 1952).

I will deal with three pivotal papers that Kris wrote in 1956, a year before his death at the age of 57. Since Glover's influential book (1955) on technique, it was customary among psychoanalysts to measure the progress of a psychoanalysis by the emergence of new memories. As long as new memories were forthcoming, the analytic process was at work. Only if over a long period no new memories were forthcoming was there a reason to be concerned that the analysis had become stagnated. In two papers dealing with memories (1956a, 1956b) Kris brought forth a reevaluation of this basic assumption. He observed that the function of remembering itself can become hypercathected, when a rich past is preferred to the drab presence. Some patients have a tendency to treat their memories as treasured possessions, which they present to the analyst as a myth of their autobiography. Unless the therapist is alerted to it, such a personal myth is often strong enough to survive psychoanalysis intact. The personal myth falsified self-representations and replaced them with wishful self-representations. The term was akin, but not identical, to Winnicott's (1960) *false self*.

To recognize the existence of the myth of autobiography, its influence, and the damage it caused is a painful part of working through. The analyst who uncovered the personal myth ferrets out falsification of memories, lacunae in the continuity of biography, and other distortions. One of the damaging effects of the personal myth is that it compels patients toward actions that fulfill the demands of the myth. Many purposes are served by the myth, including idealization of parents, concretizing family romance fantasies, denying early traumatic events, and screening early depressive or anxiety states. In keeping with ego psychology, Kris stressed the defensive function of the personal myth.

Such myths also have a comforting function, acting as a substitute for a love object and masking the grave limitations of the real parents.

These thoughts led Kris to the all-important distinction between memories always preconsciously available, where censorship is directed towards their full meaning, and genuinely repressed memories. At the same time the line of demarcation between memories and screen memories is fluid. The present always exerts pressure on what can be recalled. The need for meaning plays havoc with actual childhood events, creating new combinations and recombinations.

To cite an example of my own: one of my analysands, who lost her father during her first year of life, created a belief that she alone was loyal to his memory and therefore had a special relationship with him. Instead of developing the usual oedipal wishes toward her stepfather, she remained attached to the fantasy of her dead father, who now belonged entirely to her. While mother and siblings accepted the stepfather as the father, my patient remained aloof from him. Her attachment to the dead father contributed to a state of permanent mourning for him, giving the personality of the patient a persistent depressive cast.

Kris succeeded to dethrone the central position of memories. Stress trauma, covering many years, usually appeared in memory as a single event. Conversely, traumatic events like seduction at an early age did not appear in sharp outline.

Kris's approach to remembering had an effect on psychoanalytic technique. Instead of focusing on an often hypothetical single traumatic event and reconstructing that event, attempts were now directed towards capturing the affective atmosphere of a whole period in the life of the child (Kennedy 1971). Experiences are stored as patterns, and it is with such patterns that the analyst works.

As to the recall of traumatic events, Kris cited a child named Dorothy in her third year of life (1956b). Her younger brother had been born when she was 2. The relationship between her parents had been and continued to be stormy; a beloved dog had chewed the tail of her cat; a few months later this dog had been run over. Her grandfather had died. Kris questioned the probability that future analysts would be able to recover these events discretely separated from each other.

The task of reconstructing these events at some future date will be beyond the capacity of any analyst. All occurrences are subject to the selective scrutiny of memory. Events are molded into patterns and psychoanalysis does not deal with events, but with the patterns into which these events have been arranged by the selective scrutiny of memory. Dorothy's ego would have the task of putting all these events into a coherent structure that would make sense to the child in her third year of life. Would she be able to assimilate the events or would they overtax the integrative function of her young ego, forcing her to develop a personal myth?

In the paper "The Vicissitudes of Insight in the Course of Psychoanalysis" (1956c), Kris applied to the analytic hour an idea that he had first developed in 1935 in his studies on art. He differentiated between two types of regression. In the first, the ego is overwhelmed by regression resulting in pathology. In the second, the regression takes place under the control of the ego. Artists in particular were thought to be capable of such creative regression. In this paper he applied this concept to the analytic hour itself. It is related to the two previous papers by demonstrating optimal conditions under which childhood memories or fantasies emerge. In the "good hour" the analysand is not straining to find new memories; they appear unbidden. The capacity to uncover new memories coincide with the capacity to grasp the significance of what had been uncovered. In the "good hour" memories appear in context, symbolizing significant events, or change related to the relative strength of ego, id, and superego.

While psychoanalysts had known for a long time that certain analytic hours were regarded by both patient and analyst as particularly productive, Kris's analysis of "the good analytic hour" (1956c) opened a new vista. After the publication of this paper, and probably because of his early death, implications of this paper remained unrecognized. He described first the morphology of the "good hour." Typically it does not start propitiously. It is usually disjointed. A recent experience is recounted and transference manifestations are usually negative. Such hours generally begin by recounting a recent experience. The analysand is restless. He or she then expresses negative feelings towards the analyst. But at a certain point in the hour a marked change occurs. Everything seems to fall into place. A dream is told with no resistance and is associated to. New memories become available. Often all that the analyst need to do is ask one or two questions and the analysand sums up the work alone.

Kris differentiated the "good hour" from the "deceptively good hour." In the "deceptively good hour" the patient wishes to obtain the analyst's love and so produces associations the analyst would appreciate. The "deceptively good hour" appears when the transference is fueled by either strong merger, or by competitive wishes. The analysand is making his own interpretations because he wishes either to be merged with the analyst or to be ahead of him. When free associations are not autonomous, a "good hour" cannot emerge. In keeping with the vocabulary of the Hartmann period, Kris stressed that neutralization of aggression took place early in the hour, brought about by the verbalization of the negative transference, and thereby freed the integrative functions of the ego. This "good hour" is fueled by energy that comes from the autonomous functions of the ego, which in turn makes insight possible.

In 1956 I was still a young analyst and Kris's "good hour" had a considerable influence on my technique and my subsequent teaching. I tried (Bergmann 1993a) to develop some of the implications of Kris's discovery. He rightly recognized that the "good hour" cannot consciously be brought about by either patient or analyst. He was also right in assuming that a long period of preparation must take place before analysands can have "good hours." I added that technical errors on the part of the analyst can interfere with the emergence of the "good hour." These include interventions early in the hour, raising questions or giving interpretations that deflect the flow of the association into channels that occupy the analyst or seem urgent to him, rather than following the flow of the hour itself. The special significance of the preconscious is evident within the analytic process of the good hour.

When the analysand is blocked and the analyst leaves him or her to struggle alone, the analysand, feeling deserted, gives up the search. When the analysis is blocked the analyst should direct his or her attention solely to the nature of the block, and help the analysand to resume the flow of the associations. The analyst should not interfere and try to interpret ahead of the analysand when the latter is working by himself or herself. Although Kris and Bion belonged to different psychoanalytic schools, Bion (1967) insisted that the analyst approach every hour "without memory and desire" and be ready to receive whatever the analysand communicates; in this respect the two had much in common.

In different ways Kris's three papers focused on the role of the integrative functions of the ego. At times the mere asking for a connection between different topics within one hour stimulates the integrative function of the analysand's ego. Or, to give another technical example, when the associations to a dream fail to make the transition from the manifest to the latent content intelligible, the analyst can invite the patient to simply enumerate the various themes present in the dream and in the associations. A mere invitation is often enough to stimulate the integrative functions. Alternately, the analyst may examine free associations to a dream to discover why they failed to reach toward an interpretation. He will then discover that free associations were not productive, because they took place under the domination of the superego, or because anxiety or depression prevented them from being productive. The emphasis on neutralization of aggression and on the liberation of the integrative functions of the ego mark this paper as belonging to the Hartmann era.

Kurt Eissler

As I am writing, Kurt Eissler is the only member of the original Hartmann group still alive. I have already referred to him in the section on technique and psychoanalytic biography, but these two contributions do not do justice to this very productive thinker. In sheer volume and the range of his writings, Eissler has no equal in the Hartmann group. In 1955 Eissler published his first book, *The Psychiatrist and the Dying Patient*. The book opens with a discussion of three thanatologies, those of Freud, Ehrenberg, and Heidegger. In Eissler's opinion the psychiatrist has to help in the process of dying, particularly those men and women who have lost their faith in religion. For the purposes of this essay, Chapter 10, "Death and Ego Formation," is of special interest. The reader will recall that the Hartmann group disavowed Freud's death instinct. Throughout his life Eissler was a fierce defender of Freud. In this book he faced the challenge of how to reconcile Hartmann's view on aggression with Freud's theory of the death instinct. That we are in the Hartmann era is indicated by statements such as:

> The constant operation of the environment upon the child's drives converts them gradually into an ego. [p. 81]

> The frustration of drives can furnish the energy with which to build an ego and only in the situation of frustration can an ego become conscious of itself. . . . Each act of frustration raises aggression in the infant's organism which is not yet regulated by an adaptable ego structure. . . . The arousal of libidinal energy and the aggression elicited by frustration—unite and probably neutralize each other. In this way a store of neutralized energy is built up which can be used for the formation of ego structure. [p. 83]

> Pleasure might have been the premium that lured life further and further away from its origins. . . . The ego succumbs as soon as all potential avenues of pleasure are blocked. [p. 85]

Eissler concludes: "Constructions necessary at present in order to visualize the early steps of ego formation do not seem to contradict Freud's theory of the death instinct" (p. 87). Eissler thus believes that he succeeded in bringing Hartmann and Freud into harmony with each other with regard to the death instinct.

Although neither Rapaport nor Kris were physicians, the Hartmann group was not interested in the question of lay analysis, so important to Freud. Eissler was an exception. In 1965 he published a massive book entitled *Medical Orthodoxy and the Future of Psychoanalysis*. Still at the height of the Hartmann period, Eissler expressed the fear that, in spite of the continuous growth of the American Psychoanalytic Association, a decline in the creativity in psychoanalysis was noticeable. He suggested that this decline was due to the restrictive alliance with medicine and the systematic exclusion of gifted lay analysts. In this view Eissler followed Freud's pamphlet on lay analysis (1926b).

Eissler's book was reviewed by Bion (1966) where he said:

> Eissler and I cannot see the same patient. Even if this were possible the patient would not be the "same" when seen by him and when seen by me. . . . If members of the movement can learn from Eissler the issues involved it becomes more likely that diversity of opinion will not menace group unity or group unity the integrity of the individual. [pp. 578–579]

The point of view of the two-person psychology could hardly have been expressed more forcefully.

In this book a different attitude toward ego autonomy is discernible. It seems that the confidence of the Hartmann message suffered a defeat. The autonomy of the ego is now seen as a pretense and illusion. Man's basic madness is emphasized. Ego psychology cannot encompass either man's creativity nor understand his degree of destructiveness (Eissler 1965). Creative writers, such as Shakespeare, Dostoevski, and Goethe, have penetrated the furthest into the thicket of man's mind; all have emphasized that we are born mad and live unhappily.

The same pessimism permeates Eissler's long essay (1975) "The Fall of Man." The essay goes back to Freud's *Beyond the Pleasure Principle* (1920) and *Civilization and its Discontents* (1930a), into a terrain usually avoided by the Hartmann group. "Man's history is an unending chain of suffering leading finally to the present, in which the whole of mankind seems threatened with annihilation" (p. 589). The inorganic world is stable, but the organic shows variance. Bacteria antedate homo sapiens and they will continue to propagate after man's extinction. Organic evolution was nothing but a senseless and painful detour.

Animals do not have to make decisions; they are born with the wisdom of preceding generations. In anthropogenesis animal instincts underwent degradation and became drives. The change from instinct to drive increased the flexibility of man, but, unlike animals, he must choose his own path. Man fell because he stepped out of nature. The change from oral instincts to oral drives resulted in a luxurious growth of aggression. Culture undid the parsimony of aggression that characterizes the animal world. In Eissler's view the degradation of man appears vividly in the gratification of the sexual drive. The normal intercourse is closer to animal behavior, while the pervert behaves in an exquisitely human way. The human psychic apparatus has an abundance of energy at its disposal, but this energy is not used necessarily in the service of the welfare of the species. While the aggression of animals is only in the service of their survival, the aggression of man goes much further. Eissler quotes the poet Rilke, who interpreted the biblical Cain and Abel myth to mean that murder came before death.

Another force contributing to the fall of man is cultural narcissism. It makes it possible for man to give up his life for an idea. Eissler quotes Horace's dictum *dulce et decorum est pro patria mori* (it is sweet and proper to die for one's fatherland). Because of cultural narcissism, history is full of national and religious wars and at the present time these are threatening our survival.

> One can hardly overrate the detrimental effect of cultural narcissism. It shows up in an overrating of one's language, national and Church membership, political system and whatnot. It is a major psychological factor contributing to wars. It is based on to the next generation and therefore involves a fixity and a tenacity that are incompatible with optimal cultural growth. [p. 627]

Animals have to suffer whatever pain is inflicted upon them. Man alone knows that he will die, but he has at his disposal the ability to put an end to his suffering by suicide. "The price man has to pay for being the only species that knows about death is all too great for the privilege of being the crowning product of the process of differentiation" (p. 633).

Particularly relevant to the discussion of the Hartmann era is Eissler's belief that every species is better adjusted than man, for adjustment means using one's potential to its maximum in the confrontation with reality. The proud credo of Rapaport in the double autonomy of man from his instincts and his environment is no longer evident. I have discussed this essay at some length, not only for its intrinsic interest, but also because, in the perspective of this work, it reads like a magnificent obituary to the Hartmann era.

III. THE PASSING OF THE HARTMANN ERA

Clio, the muse of history, has a reputation of being fickle. History can never be an exact science. We never know all the forces that make one era pass into another. We respect great historians because they offer new insights into the hitherto unexplained processes of change.

The transition from early id analysis to ego psychology did not take place in a sociological vacuum. As Kramer (1996) has recently pointed out, psychoanalytic ideas became popular in the 1920s due to a cadre of writers and intellectuals such as Walter Lippman, Eugene O'Neill, Edna St. Vincent Millay, Sherwood Anderson, and Van Wyck Brooks. They were rebels against Puritan morals and turned to psychoanalysis in the search for sexual freedom and personal transformation.

> The golden age of psychoanalysis, from 1945 to 1965, which many of us can still recall, raised Freud to the status of a cultural hero in America. Every analyst had a full caseload, and those with middle-

European accents had two-year waiting lists whether they were good or not. [p. 44]

Kramer's "golden age" coincides with the Hartmann era.

In modern psychoanalysis, adaptation is the criterion of health. Theoretically, the mentally healthiest individual is no longer the most sexually gratified one, but the one who is best adapted to the world in which he lives—the individual who, in theory, has reached an equilibrium between the gratification of his instinctual needs, his moral needs, and the demands of reality. [p. 46]

What Kramer labels as "modern psychoanalysis" represents, in the vocabulary of this essay, the Hartmann era. Kramer concludes that modern psychoanalytic thinking is more consonant with conservative values than with liberal ones.

In the realm of ideas, even after an era has passed, many of its formulations have been absorbed into the mainstream of thought. Busch (1993) enumerated some of the ways Hartmann's influence persists even when he is no longer consciously remembered. Automatically psychoanalysts keep in mind ego functions, threats to ego integrity, and restrictions of ego functions that interfere with free associations. We are much more aware than classical analysts were of deviations from the expectable environment and the typical interactions that analysands remember with their caretakers. Busch believes:

While ego analysis was championed in print, its translation into understandable, workable approaches in the clinical situation lagged behind. . . . Thus Hartmann's legacy is that while he opened a window to the subtleties in understanding ego functions, the shade remained drawn on the clinical ego. [pp. 165–166]

In this essay I tried to show that while there is truth in the statement if Hartmann is considered in isolation, if we include Loewenstein, Kris, and Eissler the Hartmann group developed a highly coherent theory of technique unique to this group.

A great deal depends on whether we believe that every period in psychoanalysis merely extends the work of the previous one, or whether we think that significant modifications have taken place. I have argued that we understand the history of psychoanalysis better if we differentiate between heretics, modifiers, and extenders and see Hartmann as a modifier rather than only as an extender of Freud (Bergmann 1993b;

see also Richards 1994). But my point of view cannot be said to be the prevailing one. Thus Kafka (1989):

> As Hartmann extended the scope of Freud's formulation of general psychology, so Brenner has extended Hartmann's legacy. Brenner's contributions have emphasized the ever present influence exerted by infantile drive derivatives. He has suggested that these drive derivatives, together with the defensive and superego forces are invariably represented in every psychic formation throughout life. [p. 580]

In my view, just as Hartmann and his co-workers modified rather than extended Freud, so Brenner (1982) modified Hartmann. To conceptualize psychoanalysis as substituting a better compromise formation of relative health for the previous compromise formation of neurosis, as Brenner did, is based on the belief that the core conflicts are not resolvable. It reemphasized the ubiquity of conflict and compromise rather than the conflict-free sphere of the ego. Wyman (1989) recorded similar conclusions when he wrote: "For Hartmann compromise of conflict would be only one of the tasks of the 'organizing functions of the ego'" (p. 624).

One looks in vain in Brenner's book for any of the terms so dear to the Hartmann era: conflict-free sphere, neutralization, secondary autonomy, or change in function. The same considerations apply to Arlow's work on basic fantasy (1969a, 1969b). The Hartmann era set out to clarify Freud, to remove contradictions and, we might say, to "sanitize" Freud. But Freud proved to be the stronger thinker, overcoming the effort to tame him. For Freud after the Breuer period, intrapsychic conflict was central. Hartmann and Rapaport sought to reduce the role of conflict in psychic life. The question remains whether this effort should be seen as a modification of Freud, or as a covert rebellion against him. We know from the controversy with Jung that Freud strongly disapproved of an effort to dilute his contribution and make him more acceptable to the nonpsychoanalytic world.

When I speak of the passing of the Hartmann era I do not mean that psychoanalytic ego psychology as a whole has lost its significance, but only that phase that is associated with Hartmann and his co-workers has passed. For example, when Brenner (1987) states that by working through we mean conducting a competent analysis with the tools of ego psychology, he refers to the earlier period of psychoanalysis, prior to the Hartmann era.

Wyman (1989) observed that Hartmann's ideas are no longer mentioned in the analytic literature. I conducted a small experiment of my own. I examined the 1993 volume of the *Journal of the American Psychoanalytic Association* because I believed that if Hartmann's work is still alive it is likely to be found there. The index shows that Hartmann was mentioned 31 times, Kris 18, and Jacobson 8. By contrast Melanie Klein had 46 references, Kernberg 45, and Winnicott 39. Hartmann's ideas were stated mainly in an historical context. For example, "Hartmann's work has proven to be both an important contribution and an unwelcome diversion" (Busch 1993, p. 161).

In retrospect it was Loewald's (1960) paper that signaled the onset of the passing of the Hartmann era. The full impact of that paper was not recognized until much later (Fogel et al. 1996). For Loewald the aim of psychoanalysis is the resumption of growth rather than the resolution of conflict. Regression during analysis leads to integration on a higher level. Psychoanalysis does not end with the resolution of the transference, but rather by the permanent internationalization of the analyst as a new and more mature object. The image of the analyst as a mirror, so important to Freud, gave way to an emphasis on a two-person psychology in which the process of interaction between analyst and analysand is crucial. The relationship of analyst to analysand recapitulates, for Loewald, important interactions between mother and child. From across the ocean, Loewald's ideas were supported by the object relations theorists like Winnicott and Balint, all challenging the premises of the Hartmann era.

The last encounter between the ego psychologists and the continental psychoanalysts who were opposing Hartmann's influence took place during the International Congress in London in 1975. In his pre-congress paper Green (1975b) argued that for twenty years a debate was going on between those analysts who wish to restrict the scope of psychoanalysis and those who wish to expand it. Prominent among those who wished to restrict were members of the Hartmann group, Anna Freud, Eissler, Loewenstein, and Sandler. Those who supported extension were the British object relations theorists Fairbairn and Balint, Kleinians Rosenfeld and Segal, but also Leo Stone and Otto Kernberg. The latter are not afraid of severe regressions taking place during analysis, nor do they fear the psychotic core that is to be expected behind the wall of rigid defenses. In Freud's formulation, the obverse of neuroses were the perversions. Green (1975b) argued that the psychoses have replaced perversions: "We are less interested in perverse fanta-sies than in psychotic defense mechanisms. Analysis of neurotics is deductive, the work with borderlines is inductive" (p. 5). Working with neurotics one can follow a model, while with borderlines a technique has to be invented for every new case. While the neurotic suffers from castration anxiety, the borderline patient suffers from the contradic-tion between separation anxiety and intrusion anxiety. He needs the object, that is, the psychoanalyst, to permit structural integration to take place. The nonengaged observing psychoanalyst is not available for such an integration.

Green did not refer to Loewald, but similarities between them are evident.

> The patient's material is not external to the analyst, as even through the reality of the transference experience the analyst becomes an inte-gral part of the patient's material. The analyst even influences the communication of the patient's material. . . . More and more fre-quently we see analysts questioning their own reactions to what their patients communicate, using these in their interpretations along with (or in preference to) the analysis of the content of what is communi-cated, because the patient's aim is directed to the effect of his com-munication, rather than to the transmission of his content. [Green 1975b, p. 3]

With most of her peers no longer alive, Anna Freud (1976) could only reiterate that in psychoanalysis the method of inquiry is identi-cal with that of cure; that by the interpretation of the repressed through transference and resistance analysis the adult ego can be helped to undo the pathological conflict solutions to which the weak ego of childhood submitted. Thus, neurotic structures will be replaced by more adap-tive ones. Anna Freud recognized that there are patients not born with average expectable physical and mental equipment, nor raised in an average expectable environment, and forced to develop deviant or borderline features. In such patients the most correct uncovering of the past does not bring about intrapsychic change. Working with such patients may help them to cope better with the destructive aftereffects of their pathology, but they remain inaccessible to psychoanalytic cure. Thus, Anna Freud offered little hope for the growing number of psy-choanalysts and psychotherapists who have to deal with such patients.

To adopt her counsel meant to become increasingly isolated from the main tasks of psychotherapy today. Because increasingly such patients demand our attention, the interest in the many fascinating questions raised in the Hartmann era seemed to many less urgent. Gedo's (1996) judgment is even harsher: "Hartmann's version of ego psychology has been rejected by the great majority of analysts because of its neglect of derivatives of the earliest phases of developments" (p. 168). The younger generation of graduates of the New York Psychoanalytic Institute (Shaw 1989) find Hartmann's monograph "hard to comprehend" (p. 593). "He is using psychoanalytic theory and concepts, but no longer in the psychoanalytic setting" (p. 600).

In addition to the general laws of change where every thesis gives rise to its own antithesis, it seems to me that the Hartmann era did not survive the deaths of its creators for the following reason: it did not live up to its promise to create a psychology beyond the realm of conflict. As a result, it had less to offer to the social sciences than it believed. Also, as the Eisenhower era came to a close and the turbulent sixties began, when the crisis of identity deepened and cultural narcissism increasingly became the norm, Kernberg, Kohut, Erikson, and Loewald were more in tune with the new generation than the Hartmannites. An antithesis appeared among Rapaport's disciples. Metapsychology was at the center of interest within the Hartmann group and it was against this emphasis on metapsychology that Rapaport's students rebelled. In a famous essay, "Two Theories Or One?" George Klein (1976) challenged the belief that metapsychology is a higher and more abstract theory than the clinical theory of psychoanalysis. To him and his circle, psychoanalytic metapsychology was a survivor of an antiquated nineteenth-century science long overcome in the sciences themselves, but not revised among psychoanalysts. The emphasis on supposedly physical forces is devoid of meaning and inappropriate in dealing with the complexity of human beings (Gill 1976, Gill and Holtzman 1976).

We do not have at our disposal a history of the development of psychoanalytic ideas. Most psychoanalysts are familiar with the development of Freud's own thinking from the Breuer period to the last formulation in the 1920s. Developments after Freud's death have not been traced with a similar care. The Hartmann era can be seen as a response of some of Freud's disciples to Freud's death, and the Kleinian school can be seen as the other. The two developed in opposition to each other and only recently have attempts been made to bridge the gap between the two.

When one era passes its contribution is not erased. It leaves behind a series of new problems not envisioned earlier. All too often psychoanalytic practitioners remain unaware of the connection between the historical period and the new problems that emerged as the aftermath of that era. As already stated, one of the strongest interests of the Hartmann era was its belief in the pivotal significance of direct child observations. Anna Freud, in an essay celebrating Hartmann's 70th birthday said:

> In his paper 'Psychoanalysis and Developmental Psychology' (1950), Heinz Hartmann gives expression to the revolutionary view that '. . . we come to the conclusion that psychoanalytic psychology is not limited to what can be gained through the use of the psychoanalytic method.' [1965a, p. 31]

What Anna Freud designated as "revolutionary," namely the role of infant observations and infant research, gave rise to a major debate. Analysts belonging to different schools have remained in opposition to the relevant of infancy studies. Kohut (1980) stated:

> The framework within which Spitz's and Mahler's theories belong and within which the statements find their meaning is the framework of sociology. In other words, however psychologically insightful and sophisticated these great contributions are, they deal in essence with social relationships and they must therefore formulate their findings in sociological-interactional, transactional terms. [p. 450]

> We do not focus our attention on the baby's anxiety vis-á-vis strangers (Spitz), his clutching of substitutes for the unresponsive and unavailable mother (Winnicott), or the affective and ideational swings that accompany his reluctant move from symbiotic existence to individuality (Mahler) as if these phenomena represent primary and circumscribed psychological configurations. From the vantage point of self psychology these phenomena are secondary, their meaning and significance becoming understandable when seen from the point of view of man's abiding need for self object throughout the whole span of life. [p. 479]

The Kohut debate with the role of Spitz, Mahler, and Winnicott gains interest if we realize that major philosophical concepts have entered into the psychoanalytic discourse. Whether man is developing from symbiosis to independence or out of a need for a permanent self object for the rest of his life are major philosophical issues. They show us how dependent psychoanalysis is on a *Weltanschauung,* Freud's protestations notwithstanding.

André Green and Kohut do not usually belong to the same camp, but their view of Mahler's work has much in common. "Margaret Mahler, during a private exchange with me, has confessed that she had to recognize that, as far as in the intrapsychic world was concerned, her research could not be of any use" (Green 1996, p. 12). Elsewhere Green, writing not only against Rapaport, but against the whole spirit of the Hartmann era wrote:

> In wanting to clarify the theory, they have suppressed contradictions which would have been better respected until psychoanalytic experience allowed a better formulation of what they concealed. A fruitful obscurity is worth more than a premature clarification. [Green 1977 in Green 1986, p. 192]

In line with this thinking Green (1996) advocates a greater degree of indeterminacy than either Freud or the Hartmann era would have favored.

Object relations theorists who wanted to demonstrate that the libido is object seeking rather than pleasure seeking welcomed infant studies as proof of their point of view. The debate on the nature of the libido is, in my opinion, another example where psychoanalysis is dependent on a point of view that does not emerge out of its own observations and depends therefore on philosophical, or if we prefer, unknown unconscious needs that determine the point of view of the psychoanalyst.

We owe the Hartmann era another controversy that so far has not been resolved, the debate between developmental arrest and intrapsychic conflict as they impinge upon the psychoanalytic process.

For Mahler the attainment of separation–individuation was the high point of the infant's development. By contrast, Stern's (1985) attachment theory emphasizes "period of core relatedness" and of the "pervasive feelings of connectedness and interpersonal well-being" (p. 241). "The concept of emergent relatedness assumes that the infant from the moment of birth is deeply social in the sense of being designed to engage in and find uniquely salient interactions with other humans" (p. 235). Fundamental philosophical differences are echoed in this debate. Mahler wrote in the spirit of European enlightenment, epitomized by the famous statement of Goethe that the greatest bliss of humanity is the attainment of individual personality (personlichkeit), while for Stern this is replaced by the bliss of intimacy.

My own work on love was stimulated by contact with Mahler's work (Bergmann 1971). Subsequently, when I formulated a psychoanalytic theory of love (Bergmann 1987), I saw falling in love in terms of regression to infancy. Sometimes this regression remains under the control of the ego. At other times the regression sweeps away ego control. The weaker the ego structure, the further the regression of love. This is one of the main reasons why so many people feel the fear of loving and also fear the necessary regression into the psychoanalytic situation.

As the post-World War II American hegemony over Europe came to an end, new European voices appeared that directly addressed those analysands considered too sick to be treated by the standard psychoanalytic method. In Darwinian terms the willingness of the Kleinians to treat borderline and psychotic patients made them better adjusted to the changes in culture. In France, Lacan, Chasseguet-Smirgel, Joyce McDougall, André Green, and others began to speak in a new key.

With the possible exception of Jacobson, the Hartmann group avoided entering into any serious discussion with Klenians or with Winnicott. Hartmann quoted Klein's work on symbol formation, and Kris (1955) co-opted Winnicott's finding of the same year on the positive role of illusion for the infant: "The capacity for appropriate illusion seems to constitute one of the earliest stages of neutralization" (p. 171).

In spite of the emphasis on adaptation, the Hartmann group showed surprisingly little interest in the outside world. Hitler, World War II, and the Holocaust left no discernible impression on their thinking. This is all the more surprising because they were Hitler's refugees. Denying what happened in Europe appears to have been a necessary defense for their adaptation to America.

The Hartmann group discovered much that is valuable and exciting, but because it did not harness these findings into a therapy with patients beyond neurosis it lost its appeal. Limiting the practice to physicians, whose earnings had to be on par with other physicians, demanding that the analysand come four to five times a week and be neurotic rather than borderline, the population available for psychoanalysis of necessity became restricted to a double aristocracy—an aristocracy of mental health as well as a financial one.

My claim that the Hartmann period has come to an end does not imply that it ceases to be influential. I have shown how much my own work is indebted to Kris. There are many ego psychologists, notably Paul Gray (1973, 1982, 1986) and Fred Busch (1995), who in their detailed emphasis on working with the ego follow Loewenstein's and Kris's footsteps, but the spirit of conquest that characterized the Hartmann era is no longer in evidence. As I conclude this study, I would like to admit to a subjective bias. Some aspects of the Hartmann era I have discussed more fully than others. I have given more space to those features that I consider relevant today. I also asked myself why I consider this historical survey to be worth the effort. Ours is an age of disclosure and I should, therefore, state some personal reasons for doing so. The Hartmann period was the period I grew up in as a psychoanalyst. Edith Jacobson was my analyst. It never occurred to me to question the fact that American psychoanalysis was far ahead of Europe. While I lived through the Hartmann period, I could not have understood it from within the way I presented it in this essay. The fact that we had personal contact with a number of psychoanalysts who had reservations about the Hartmann period, like Paul Federn, Robert Waelder, Theodore Reik, and Bertram Lewin, presented a continuous challenge. But the Hartmann group opened new vistas and was the most innovative force during that period. It is because they were so productive that they deserve to be commemorated.

With what excitement my wife and I attended the twice monthly meetings of the New York Psychoanalytic Society, as well as the meetings of the American and the International Psychoanalytic Societies. We devoured every new article and book. I can see them all occupying the first rows at the meeting of the New York Psychoanalytic Society—Heinz and Dora Hartmann, Ernst and Marianne Kris, Rudolph Loewenstein and Elizabeth Geleerd, Kurt and Ruth Eissler, Max and Helen Schur, Margaret Mahler, Edith Jacobson, and Annie Reich. To listen to their deliberations evoked the kind of awe one feels when one is privileged to witness the birth of a new era. Their day has passed.

Other issues are agitating a new psychoanalytic generation. I realize now that I wished to erect a monument to that era, not written by a true believer, but by one who recognizes their shortcomings as well as their creative spirit.

References

Abraham, K. (1909). Dreams and myths: a study in folk-psychology. In *Clinical Papers and Essays on Psycho-Analysis*, ed. K. Abraham et al. New York: Basic Books, 1955, pp. 153–209.

———— (1924). A short study of the development of the libido, viewed in the light of mental disorders. In *Selected Papers of Karl Abraham*, trans. D. Bryan and A. Stachey. London: Hogarth Press, 1948, pp. 418–501.

Alexander, F., and French, T. M. (1946). *Psychoanalytic Therapy, Principles and Application*. New York: Ronald Press.

Arlow, J. A. (1958). Review of *No and Yes—On the Genesis of Human Communication* by Rene A. Spitz. *Psychoanalytic Quarterly* 27:579–580.

———— (1961). Ego psychology and the study of mythology. *Journal of the American Psychoanalytic Association* 9:371–393.

———— (1969a). Fantasy, memory, and reality testing. *Psychoanalytic Quarterly* 38:28–51.

———— (1969b). Unconscious fantasy and disturbances of conscious experience. *Psychoanalytic Quarterly* 38:1–27.

Beres, D. (1971). Ego autonomy and ego pathology. *Psychoanalytic Study of the Child* 26:3–24. New Haven, CT: Yale University Press.

Bergmann, M. S. (1966). The impact of ego psychology in the study of myth. *American Imago* 23/3:257–264.

———— (1971). Psychoanalytic observations on the capacity to love. In *Separation–Individuation: Essays in Honor of Margaret Mahler*, ed. J. B. McDevitt and C. F. Settlage. New York: International Universities Press, pp. 15–40.

———— (1976). *The Evolution of Psychoanalytic Technique*, ed. with F. Hartman. New York: Columbia University Press.

———— (1987). *The Anatomy of Loving*. New York: Columbia University Press.

———— (1988). On the fate of the intrapsychic image of the psychoanalyst after termination of the analysis. *Psychoanalytic Study of the Child* 43/3:137–153. New Haven, CT: Yale University Press.

———— (1993a). Reality and psychic reality in Ernst Kris's last papers: an attempt to update his findings. *Psychoanalytic Inquiry* 13:372–383.

———— (1993b). Reflections on the history of psychoanalysis. *Journal of the American Psychoanalytic Association* 41:929–955.

———— (1995). The historical roots of psychoanalytic orthodoxy. Paper read at the 1995 Meeting of the International Psychoanalytic Association in San Francisco. Appeared as "Las raices historicos de la orthodoxia psychoanalytica." *Revista de Psychoanalysand Tomo* 52:645–660.

———— (1997). The historical roots of psychoanalytic orthodoxy. *International Journal of Psycho-Analysis* 78:69–86.

Bergmann, M. S., and Jucovy, M., eds. (1982). *Generations of the Holocaust.* New York: Basic Books.

Bion, W. (1966). Review of K. Eissler's *Medical Orthodoxy and the Future of Psychoanalysis. International Journal of Psycho-Analysis* 47:575–581.

———— (1967). Notes on memory and desire (including five discussants and author's response). *Psychoanalytic Forum* 2/3:271–280.

Blanck, G. (1966). Some technical implications of ego psychology. *International Journal of Psycho-Analysis* 47:6–13.

Blanck, G., and Blanck, R. (1974). *Ego Psychology Theory and Practice.* New York: Columbia University Press.

———— (1979). *Ego Psychology II.* New York: Columbia University Press.

———— (1986). *Beyond Ego Psychology: Developmental Object Relations Theory.* New York: Columbia University Press.

Bornstein, M., et al. (1986). A reappraisal of Heinz Hartmann's contributions. *Psychoanalytic Inquiry* 6/4:495–601.

Brenman, M. (1952). On teasing and being teased. *Psychoanalytic Study of the Child* 7:264–285. New York: International Universities Press.

Brenman-Gibson, M. (1976). Notes on the study of the creative process. *Psychological Issues* 9/4 (Monograph 36):326–357.

Brenner, C. (1982). *The Mind in Conflict.* New York: International Universities Press.

———— (1987). Working through, 1914–1984. *Psychoanalytic Quarterly* 56:88–108.

Breuer, J., and Freud, S. (1895). Studies on Hysteria. *Standard Edition* 2.

Busch, F. (1993). "In the Neighborhood": aspects of a good interpretation and a "developmental lag" in ego psychology. *Journal of the American Psychoanalytic Association* 41:151–177.

———— (1995). *The Ego at the Center of Clinical Technique.* Northvale, NJ: Jason Aronson.

Cassirer, E. (1964). *Philosophe der Symbolischen Formen.* Darmstadt: Wissenschaftliche Buchgesellschaft.

Chasseguet-Smirgel, J. (1985). *The Ego Ideal: A Psychoanalytic Essay on the Malady of the Ideal,* trans. Paul Barrows. New York: Norton.

Edelson, M. (1986). Heinz Hartmann's influence on psychoanalysis as a science. *Psychoanalytic Inquiry* 6/4:575–600.

Eissler, K. R. (1953). The effect of the structure of the ego on psychoanalytic technique. *Journal of the American Psychoanalytic Association* 1:104–143.

—— (1955). *The Psychiatrist and the Dying Patient.* New York: International Universities Press.

—— (1958). Remarks on some variations in psychoanalytic technique. *International Journal of Psycho-Analysis* 39:222–229.

—— (1963). *Goethe: A Psychoanalytic Study.* Detroit: Wayne State University Press.

—— (1965). *Medical Orthodoxy and the Future of Psychoanalysis.* New York: International Universities Press.

—— (1969). Irreverent remarks about the present and the future of psychoanalysis. *International Journal of Psycho-Analysis* 50:461–471.

—— (1971). *Discourse on Hamlet and HAMLET.* New York: International Universities Press.

—— (1975). The fall of man. *Psychoanalytic Study of the Child* 30:589–646. New Haven, CT: Yale University Press.

Erikson, E. (1958). *Young Man Luther: A Study in Psychoanalysis and History.* New York: Norton.

—— (1969). *Gandhi's Truth: On the Origins of Militant Nonviolence.* New York: Norton.

Fenichel, O. (1945). *The Psychoanalytic Theory of Neurosis.* New York: Norton.

—— (1974). A review of Freud's "Analysis, terminable and interminable." *International Review of Psycho-Analysis* 1:109–116.

Fogel, G. I., Tyson, P., Greenberg, J., McLauglin, J., and Peyser, E. R. (1996). A Classic Revisited: Loewald on the Therapeutic Action of Psychoanalysis. *Journal of the American Psychoanalytic Association* 44/3:863–924.

Fliess, R. (1948). An Ontogenetic Table. In *The Psychoanalytic Reader: An Anthology of Essential Papers with Critical Introductions,* ed. R. Fliess. New York: International Universities Press, pp. 285–290.

Freud, A. (1936). *The Ego and the Mechanisms of Defense.* New York: International Universities Press.

—— (1965a). Diagnostic skills and their growth. *International Journal of Psycho-Analysis* 46:31–38.

—— (1965b). *Normality and Pathology in Childhood: Assessments of Development.* New York: International Universities Press.

—— (1966). Links between Hartmann's egopsychology and the child analyst thinking. In *Psychoanalysis: A General Psychology, Essays in Honor* of *Heinz Hartmann,* ed. Loewenstein et al. New York: International Universities Press, pp. 16–27.

——— (1972). Comments on aggression. *International Journal of Psycho-Analysis* 53:163–171.

——— (1976). Changes in psychoanalytic practice and experience. *International Journal of Psycho-Analysis* 57:257–260.

Freud, S. (1900). The interpretation of dreams. *Standard Edition* 4 and 5.

——— (1905). Three contributions to the theory on sexuality. *Standard Edition* 7.

——— (1910). Leonardo da Vinci and a memory of his childhood. *Standard Edition* 11.

——— (1914). On narcissism: an introduction. *Standard Edition* 14.

——— (1917). Mourning and melancholia. *Standard Edition* 14.

——— (1918). From the history of an infantile neurosis. *Standard Edition* 17.

——— (1920). Beyond the pleasure principle. *Standard Edition* 18.

——— (1923a). The ego and the id. *Standard Edition* 19.

——— (1923b). Two encyclopaedia articles. *Standard Edition* 18.

——— (1924). The dissolution of the Oedipus complex. *Standard Edition* 19.

——— (1926a). Inhibition symptom and anxiety. *Standard Edition* 20.

——— (1926b). The question of lay analysis. *Standard Edition* 20.

——— (1930a). Civilization and its discontents. *Standard Edition* 21.

——— (1930b). The Goethe prize. *Standard Edition* 21.

——— (1937). On constructions in analysis. *Standard Edition* 23.

——— (1940). An outline of psycho-analysis. *Standard Edition* 23.

Friedman, L. (1989). Hartmann's "Ego Psychology and the Problem of Adaptation." *Psychoanalytic Quarterly* 53:526–550.

Gedo, J. (1996). *The Languages of Psychoanalysis.* Hillsdale, NJ: Analytic Press.

Gill, M. M. (1976). Metapsychology is not psychology. In *Psychology versus Metapsychology: Psychoanalytic Essays in Memory of George. S. Klein,* ed. M. M. Gill and P. Holtzman. *Psychoanalytic Issues,* 4/4:71–105.

Gill, M. M., and P. Holtzman, eds. (1976). Psychology versus metapsychology: psychoanalytic essays in memory of George S. Klein. *Psychoanalytic Issues* 4/4.

Gitelson, M. (1962). The first phase of psychoanalysis. *International Journal of Psycho-Analysis* 43:194–205.

Glover, E. (1931). The therapeutic effect of inexact interpretation: A contribution to the theory of suggestion. In *The Technique of Psycho-Analysis.* New York: International Universities Press, pp. 353–366.

————— (1955). *The Technique of Psycho-Analysis.* New York: International Universities Press.

————— (1961). Some recent trends in psychoanalytic theory. *Psychoanalytic Quarterly* 30:86–107.

Gray, P. (1973). Psychoanalytic technique and the ego's capacity for viewing intrapsychic activity. *Journal of the American Psychoanalytic Association* 21:474–494.

————— (1982). "Developmental lag" in the evolution of technique for psychoanalysis of neurotic conflict. *Journal of the American Psychoanalytic Association* 30:621–655. Also in 1995: *The Ego and Analysis of Defense.* Northvale, NJ: Jason Aronson, pp. 27–62.

————— (1986). On helping analysands observe intrapsychic activity. In *Psychoanalysis: The Science of Mental Conflict: Essays in Honor of Charles Brenner,* ed. A. S. Richards and M. S. Willick. Hillsdale, NJ: Analytic Press, pp. 245–262. Also in 1995: *The Ego and Analysis of Defense.* Northvale, NJ: Jason Aronson, pp. 63–86.

Green, A. (1975a). Potential space in psychoanalysis. In *On Private Madness.* Madison, CT: International Universities Press, pp. 277–296, 1986.

————— (1975b). The analyst, symbolization and absence in the analytic setting. *International Journal of Psycho-Analysis* 56:1–22.

————— (1977). Conceptions of affect. In *On Private Madness.* Madison, CT: International Universities Press, pp. 174–213, 1986.

————— (1996). What kind of research for psychoanalysis? *International Journal of Psycho-Analysis* 5:10–14.

Greenacre, P. (1955). *Swift and Carroll: A Psychoanalytic Study of Two Lives.* New York: International Universities Press.

Grinker, R. (1957). On identification. *International Journal of Psycho-Analysis* 38:379–390.

Grossman, W. (1995). Psychological vicissitudes of theory in clinical work. *International Journal of Psycho-Analysis* 76/5:885–899.

Hale, N. (1995). Psychoanalysis and science: American ego psychology. In *The Rise and Crisis of Psychoanalysis in the United States: Freud and the Americas, 1917–1985.* New York: Oxford University Press, pp. 231–244.

Hartmann, H. (1939). *Ego Psychology and the Problem of Adaptation,* translated by David Rapaport. New York: International Universities Press, 1958.

————— (1947). On rational and irrational action. In *Essays on Ego Psychology: Selected Problems in Psychoanalytic Theory.* New York: International Universities Press, pp. 37–68.

————— (1950). Comments on the psychoanalytic theory of the ego. *Psy-*

choanalytic Study of the Child 5:1–27. New York: International Universities Press.

———— (1951). Technical implications of ego psychology. In *Essays on Ego Psychology: Selected Problems in Psychoanalytic Theory*. New York: International Universities Press, pp. 142–154.

———— (1952). The mutual influences in the development of ego and id. *Psychoanalytic Study of the Child* 7:1–50. New York: International Universities Press.

———— (1953). Contribution to the metapsychology of schizophrenia. In *Essays on Ego Psychology: Selected Problems in Psychoanalytic Theory*. New York: International Universities Press, pp. 182–206.

———— (1955). Notes on the theory of sublimation. *Psychoanalytic Study of the Child* 10:9–29. New York: International Universities Press.

———— (1959). Psychoanalysis as a scientific theory. In *Essays on Ego Psychology*. New York: International Universities Press, pp. 318–350.

———— (1960). *Psychoanalysis and Moral Values*. New York: International Universities Press.

———— (1964). *Essays on Ego Psychology*. New York: International Universities Press.

Hartmann, H., and Kris, E. (1945). The genetic approach to psychoanalysis. *Psychoanalytic Study of the Child*. New York: International Universities Press 1:11–30. Also in *Psychoanalytic Issues*, 1964, 4/2:7–26.

Hartmann, H., Kris, E., and Loewenstein, R. (1946). Comments on the formation of psychic structure. *Psychoanalytic Issues*, 1964, 4/2:27–55.

———— (1949). Notes on the theory of aggression. *Psychoanalytic Issues* (1964) 4/2:56–85.

Hartmann, H., and Loewenstein, R. (1962). Notes on the superego. *Psychoanalytic Study of the Child* 17:42–81. New York: International Universities Press.

Jacobson, E. (1964). *The Self And The Object World*. New York: International Universities Press.

———— (1967). *Psychotic Conflict and Reality*. New York: International Universities Press.

Kafka, E. (1989). The contribution of Hartmann's adaptational theory to psychoanalysis, with special reference to regression and symptom formation. *Psychoanalytic Quarterly* 58:571–591.

Katan, M. (1954). The importance of the non-psychotic part of the personality in schizophrenia. *International Journal of Psycho-Analysis* 35:119–128.

Kennedy, H. (1971). Problems in reconstruction in child analysis. *Psychoanalytic Study of the Child* 26:372–385. New Haven, CT: Yale University Press.

Kernberg, O. (1980). *Internal World and External Reality: Object Relations Theory Applied*. New York: Jason Aronson.

Klein, G. S. (1976). Two theories or one? In *Psychoanalytic Theory: An Exploration of Essentials*. New York: International Universities Press, pp. 41–71.

Klein, M. (1930). The importance of symbol formation in the development of the ego. In *Contributions to Psycho-Analysis, 1921–1945, Vol. II*. London: Hogarth Press, pp. 236–253.

———— (1932). *The Psycho-Analysis of Children*. London: Hogarth Press. Also in 1948: *Contributions to Psycho-Analysis, 1921–1945, Vol. II*. London: Hogarth Press, pp. 17–374.

———— (1940). Mourning and its relation to manic-depressive states. In *Contributions to Psycho-Analysis, 1921–1945, Vol. I*. London: Hogarth Press, pp. 311–338.

Kohut, H. (1977). *The Restoration of the Self*. New York: International Universities Press.

———— (1980). Two letters and reflections on advances in self psychology. In *Advances in Self Psychology*, ed. A. Goldberg. New York: International Universities Press, pp. 449–554.

Kramer, Y. (1996). Freud and the culture wars. *Public Interest* 124:37–51.

Kris, E. (1947). The nature of psychoanalytic propositions and their validations. In *Selected Papers of Ernst Kris*. New Haven, CT: Yale University Press, 1975, pp. 3–23.

———— (1950a). On preconscious mental processes. In *Selected Papers of Ernst Kris*. New Haven, CT: Yale University Press, 1975, pp. 217–236.

———— (1950b). Notes on the development and on some current problems of psychoanalytic child psychology. In *Selected Papers of Ernst Kris*. New Haven, CT: Yale University Press, 1975, pp. 54–79.

———— (1951). Ego psychology and interpretation in psychoanalytic therapy. *Psychoanalytic Quarterly* 20:15–30.

———— (1952). *Psychoanalytic Explorations in Art*. New York: International Universities Press.

———— (1953). Psychoanalysis and the study of creative imagination. In *Selected Papers of Ernst Kris*. New Haven, CT: Yale University Press, 1975, pp. 473–493.

———— (1955). Neutralization and sublimation: observations on young children. In *Selected Papers of Ernst Kris*. New Haven, CT: Yale University Press, 1975, pp. 151–171.

———— (1956a). The personal myth: a problem in psychoanalytic technique. In *Selected Papers of Ernst Kris*. New Haven, CT: Yale University Press, 1975, pp. 271–300.

———— (1956b). The recovery of childhood memories in psychoanalysis. In *Selected Papers of Ernst Kris*. New Haven, CT: Yale University Press, 1975, pp. 301–342.

———— (1956c). On some vicissitudes of insight in the course of psychoanalysis. In *Selected Papers of Ernst Kris*. New Haven, CT: Yale University Press, 1975, pp. 252–271.

Kris, M. (1957). The use of prediction in a longitudinal study. *Psychoanalytic Study of the Child* 7:175–189. New York: International Universities Press.

Langer, S. (1942). *Philosophy in a New Key: A Study in the Symbolism of Reason, Rite and Art*. Cambridge, MA: Harvard University Press.

Laplanche, J., and Pontalis, J. (1973). *The Language of Psycho-Analysis*, trans. D. Nicholson-Smith. New York: Norton.

Lichtenstein, H. (1961). Identity and sexuality: a study of their interrelationship in man. *Journal of the American Psychoanalytic Association* 9:179–260.

Loewald, H. W. (1960). On the therapeutic action of psycho-analysis. *International Journal of Psycho-Analysis* 41:16–33.

Loewenstein, R. M. (1951). The problem of interpretation. *Psychoanalytic Quarterly* 19:501–539.

———— (1966). Heinz Hartmann's psychology of the ego. In *Psychoanalytic Pioneers*, ed. F. Alexander et al. New York: Basic Books, pp. 469–483.

———— (1970). Heinz Hartmann. *Psychoanalytic Study of the Child* 25:12–15. New York: International Universities Press.

Loewenstein, R., Newman, L., Schur, M., and Solnit, A., eds. (1966). *Psychoanalysis—A General Psychology: Essays in Honour of Heinz Hartmann*. New York: International Universities Press.

Mahler, M. (1963). Thoughts about development. In *The Selected Papers of Margaret S. Mahler, Vol. 2, Separation–Individuation*. New York: Jason Aronson, pp. 3–20.

———— (1966). Notes on the development of basic moods: the depressive affect. *In Psycho-analysis: A General Psychology, Essays in Honor of Heinz Hartmann*, ed. Loewenstein et al. New York: International Universities Press, pp. 152–168.

———— (1968). *On Human Symbiosis and the Vissitudes of Individuation, Vol. 1, Infantile Psychosis*. New York: International Universities Press.

———— (1971). A study of the separation-individuation process. *Psychoanalytic Study of the Child*. New Haven, CT: Yale University Press, 26:403–424.

Mahler, M., and Rangell, L. (1943). A psychoanalytic study of maladie des tics. *Psychiatric Quarterly* 17:579–603.

Milrod, D. (1982). The wished-for self image. *Psychoanalytic Study of the Child* 37:95–120. New Haven, CT: Yale University Press.

Moore, B., and Fine, B. (1990). *Psychoanalytic Terms and Concepts.* New Haven: Yale University Press.

Niederland, W. G. (1965). An analytic inquiry into the life and work of Heinrich Schliemann. In *Drives, Affects, Behavior,* vol. II, ed. M. Schur. New York: International Universities Press, p. 36.

Orgel, S. (1995). A classic revisited: K. R. Eissler's "The Effect of the Structure of the Ego on Psychoanalytic Technique." *Psychoanalytic Quarterly* 64/3:551–567.

Peltz, M. L. (1989). On the origins of contemporary structural theory: an appreciation of "Egopsychology and the Problem of Adaptation." *Psychoanalytic Quarterly* 58:551–570.

Pine, F. (1996). The "ego" in the session. Paper read at the Symposium: Freudian Psychoanalysis Today. New York University Post-Doctoral Program, New York. November 9–10, 1996.

Rangell, L. (1965). The scope of Heinz Hartmann. *International Journal of Psycho-Analysis* 46:5–30.

———— (1986). The executive functions of the ego: An extension of the concept of ego autonomy. *Psychoanalytic Study of the Child* 41:1–37. New Haven, CT: Yale University Press.

Rapaport, D., et al. (1945–1946). *Diagnostic Psychological Testing, I and II.* Chicago: Year Book Publishing.

———— (1950). *Organization and Pathology of Thought.* New York: Columbia University Press.

———— (1951). The autonomy of the ego. In *Collected Papers of David Rapaport,* ed. M. Gill. New York: Basic Books, pp. 357–367.

———— (1954). Clinical implication of ego psychology. In *Collected Papers of David Rapaport,* ed. M. Gill. New York: Basic Books, pp. 586–593.

———— (1957). The theory of ego autonomy. In *Collected Papers of David Rapaport,* ed. M. Gill. New York: Basic Books, pp. 722–744.

———— (1959). Introduction: A historical study of psychoanalytic ego psychology. *Psychoanalytic Issues* 1/1:1–17.

———— (1960). The structure of psychoanalytic theory: a systematizing attempt. *Psychological Issues* 2(2):1–158.

———— (1964). Present day ego psychology. In *Collected Papers of David Rapaport,* ed. M. Gill. New York: Basic Books, pp. 594–623.

Reich, A. (1958). A character formation representing the integration of unusual conflict solutions in the ego structures. In *Psychoanalytic Contributions.* New York: International Universities Press, 1973, pp. 250–270.

Richards, A. D. (1994). Extenders, modifiers, heretics. In *Spectrum of Psychoanalysis: Essays in Honor of Martin S. Bergmann*, ed. A. K. Richards and A. D. Richards. Madison, CT: International Universities Press, pp. 145–160.

Rosen, V. H. (1955). The reconstruction of a traumatic childhood event in a case of derealization. *Journal of the American Psychoanalytic Association* 3:211–221.

Rosenfeld, H. (1958). Contribution to the discussion on variations in classical technique. *International Journal of Psycho-Analysis* 39:238–239.

Rubenfine, D. (1967). Notes on a theory of reconstruction. *British Journal of Medical Psychoanalysis* 40:195–206.

Sandler, J., ed. (1987). *From Safety to Superego: Selected Papers of Joseph Sandler*. New York: Guilford.

Schafer, R. (1970). An overview of Heinz Hartmann's contribution to psychoanalysis. *International Journal of Psycho-Analysis* 51:425–446.

——— (1994). A classic revisited: Kurt Eissler's "The Effect of the Structure of the Ego on Psychoanalytic Technique." *International Journal of Psycho-Analysis* 74:721–728.

Schmiedeberg, M. (1934). Intellektuelle Hemmung und Ess-storung. *Z. Psychoanal. Päd.* 8:107–116.

Schur, M. (1955). Comments on the metapsychology of somatization. *Psychoanalytic Study of the Child* 10:119–164. New York: International Universities Press.

——— (1966). *The Id and the Regulatory Principles of Functioning*. New York: International Universities Press.

Segal, H. (1950). Some aspects of the analysis of a schizophrenic. *International Journal of Psycho-Analysis* 31:268–278.

——— (1957). Notes on symbol formation. *International Journal of Psycho-Analysis* 48:391–397.

Shaw, R. (1989). Hartmann on adaptation: an incomparable or incomprehensible legacy? *Psychoanalytic Quarterly* 58:592–611.

Spitz, R. A. (1945). Hospitalism. *Psychoanalytic Study of the Child* 1:53–74. New York: International Universities Press.

——— (1946). Hospitalism: a follow-up report. *Psychoanalytic Study of the Child* 2:113–117. New York: International Universities Press.

——— (1956). Countertransference: comments on its varying role in the analytic situation. *Journal of the American Psychoanalytic Association* 4:256–265.

——— (1957). *No and Yes: On the Genesis of Human Communication*. New York: International Universities Press.

——— (1965). *The First Year of Life: A Psychoanalytic Study of Normal and Deviant Development of Object Relations.* (In collaboration with W. Godfrey Cobliner.) New York: International Universities Press.

Spitz, R. A., and Wolf, K. M. (1946a). Anaclictic depression. *Psychoanalytic Study of the Child* 2:313–342. New York: International Universities Press.

———— (1946b). The smiling response: a contribution to the ontogenesis of social relations. *Genetic Psychological Monograph* 34.

Sterba, E., and Sterba, R. (1954). *Beethoven and His Nephew.* New York: Pantheon Books.

Stern, D. N. (1985). *The Interpersonal World of the Infant: A View from Psychoanalysis and Developmental Psychology.* New York: Basic Books.

Stone, L. (1954). The widening scope of indications for psychoanalysis. *Journal of the American Psychoanalytic Association* 2:567–620.

Waelder, R. (1960). *Basic Theory of Psychoanalysis.* New York: International Universities Press.

———— (1962). Psychoanalysis: scientific method and philosophy. *Journal of the American Psychoanalytic Association* 10:617–637.

———— (1965). *Psychoanalytic Avenues to Art.* New York: International Universities Press.

Weissman, P. (1967). Theoretical considerations of ego regressions and ego functions in creativity. *Psychoanalytic Quarterly* 36:37–50.

Whyte, L. (1960). *The Unconscious before Freud.* New York: Basic Books.

Winnicott, D. W. (1953). Transitional objects and transitional phenomena. *International Journal of Psycho-Analysis* 34:89–97.

———— (1960). Ego distortion in terms of true and false self. In *The Maturational Processes and the Facilitating Environment: Studies in the Theory of Emotional Development.* New York: International Universities Press, pp. 140–152.

———— (1967). The location of cultural experience. *International Journal of Psycho-Analysis* 48:368–372.

Wyman, H. (1989). Hartmann, health and homosexuality: some clinical aspects of "Ego Psychology and the Problem of Adaptation." *Psychoanalytic Quarterly* 58:612–639.

Young, M. (1989). Heinz Hartmann, M.D.: an introduction and appreciation. *Psychoanalytic Quarterly* 58:521–525.

II

PREPARED CONTRIBUTIONS
OF THE PARTICIPANTS PRIOR
TO THE CONFERENCE

2

The Hartmann Era

JACOB A. ARLOW

Of the participants in this conference, I believe only Peter Neubauer and I were actually part of the so-called Hartmann era. At the time we were either students or recent graduates of the New York Psychoanalytic Institute. Having received into its faculty some of the outstanding European psychoanalysts, the New York Institute's prestige was enormous. It was considered the outstanding psychoanalytic center in the United States. The presence of Hartmann, Kris, Loewenstein, Annie Reich, and Margaret Mahler, among others, in large measure enhanced its influence.

Those were indeed heady days for psychoanalysis in general. The standing of psychoanalysis within the medical profession and with the general public was at an all-time high. During the war, medical officers, using psychoanalytic principles, had achieved notable results with cases of battle fatigue. Through the news stories and the media the public came to appreciate the remarkable potential of psychoanalysis. Furthermore, during great wars and immediately afterwards, there appears to be a tendency for the boundaries of what is considered admissible sexual behavior to be broadened. Psychoanalysis appeared to many to offer a scientific rationale for sexual liberation. Since so much unhappiness was presumably the result of repressed sexual impulses, psychoanalysis was readily perceived as a liberating potential for personal happiness.

There were, furthermore, political reverberations of this promise from psychoanalysis. One British psychoanalyst suggested that, if every Cabinet member in the world was given a psychoanalysis as part of his official portfolio, statesmen would then make rational and realistic decisions and bring about a world of peace and order. Some left-wing liberals saw great promise for improving the world by combining Marx and Freud. This was a time when any intellectual worth his salt, at least in the New York area, was expected to be knowledgeable about psychoanalysis and perhaps to have undergone the experience himself.

The power of the dynamic unconscious fascinated the public and creative artists so that, on stage, screen, and in literature, various works of art enhanced psychoanalysis and intensified its appeal. Moss Hart's *Lady in the Dark* and Ingrid Bergmann's role in *Spellbound* contributed who knows how much to the aura surrounding our discipline. Perhaps even more significantly, within the medical profession and the wider world of academia, psychoanalysis was not only being accepted; it was being welcomed and even courted. There was a time when any candidate for the position of Chief of Psychiatry in a medical school was expected to have had psychoanalytic training. Psychoanalytic principles were applied not only to the clinical psychiatric entities. They were incorporated into general medical concepts as well. It is a short jump from the dynamics of hysteria to the concepts of psychosomatic medicine. This is the period that saw the founding of the American Psychosomatic Society, a movement dominated in its early years by psychoanalysts, many of whom worked side by side with medical researchers studying such conditions as asthma, peptic ulcer, hypertension, cardiac illness, and skin diseases. As a matter of fact, the Columbia psychoanalytic training program was first called the Program for Psychoanalytic and Psychosomatic Medicine. In academia, in the departments of literature, sociology, psychology, and anthropology, psychoanalytic concepts were being assimilated and applied to the respective disciplines. For many a fledgling analyst, psychoanalysis seemed to be the queen of the sciences, in keeping with the view that Freud expressed in 1913 on "The Claims of Psychoanalysis to Scientific Interest." Conditions were more than ripe for transcending the view of psychoanalysis as a psychology of conflict and illness and according it the status of a general psychology. This was the background in which the so-called Hartmann era developed.

Hartmann was the outstanding exemplar of this protean image of psychoanalysis. By virtue of his prestigious family, the unusual education he had received, his commanding presence, and the fact that he was more or less personally anointed by Freud, Hartmann came to be the unchallenged, designated spokesman for psychoanalysis. He saw it as his role to reconceptualize and transform psychoanalysis from the psychology of conflict to a general psychology. For this journey the logical point of departure seemed clearly to be the problem of adaptation. Some fascinating biographical questions arise, issues of which only a few simple facts are in my hands. As I understand it, Hartmann had been an analysand of Sandor Rado, although at a later date, at the personal invitation of Freud, Hartmann had what was called a "didactic analysis" from the master himself. I assume that Hartmann was closer to Freud than Rado, but of this I cannot be certain. At the invitation of the New York Psychoanalytic Institute, Rado had come to the United States some years earlier with the charge to supervise and lead the Institute's training program. At the time when Hartmann's leadership was ascendant at the New York Institute, Rado left for Columbia, where he organized the Psychoanalytic Clinic and its training program. In his lectures to the students at Columbia, many of which I attended, Rado was unsparingly critical of the New York Psychoanalytic Institute, which he repeatedly referred to as "82nd Street." Many of the classic psychoanalytic terms, like "cathexes" or "psychic structure," were interdited.

While I know very little about the history of the personal relations between these two figures, what struck me was that they both took the problem of adaptation as their point of departure for the elucidation of psychoanalysis. Rado, in fact, called his approach to psychoanalysis "adaptational psychodynamics," and this indeed was the title of the book in which he expounded his views of psychoanalysis (1969). His approach to the issue of adaptation differed widely from the views of Hartmann.

It would seem that Rado stressed the superficial, so-called ego aspects at a level that Waelder (1962) referred to as clinical theory. He was really using a different terminology from classical psychoanalysis and, by emphasizing what he referred to as the reparative maneuvers of the mind, his approach turned out to be quite different from Hartmann's.[1]

Contrary to Rado, Hartmann's approach was steeped in that most controversial part of psychoanalysis, the theory of drives. That theory, Freud had said, constitutes the mythology of psychoanalysis. Like the gods of classical antiquity, they are unseen forces whose reality we apprehend only through the results they effect in human behavior. Taking his cue from a comment by Freud about drive energy available to the ego that was from the very beginning neither libidinal nor aggressive, Hartmann developed and expanded concepts like primary and secondary autonomy of ego functions, neutralization of drive energy, fusion and defusion of the drives, and so on. Employing such concepts, he undertook to broaden the understanding of how psychoanalysis could be employed to clarify those aspects of psychology seemingly independent of psychic conflict and beyond the reach of the psychoanalytic situation. All of this seems to me to reflect the optimism and self-assurance of psychoanalysis at that time in history. Autonomous functioning, conflict-free areas, and neutralization indicate how Hartmann tried to resolve many difficulties in explaining behavior, both within and outside the clinical setting, by resorting to concepts that shifted the emphasis away from psychic conflict in favor of transformation of psychic energies. Specialists in other fields favorable to psychoanalysis, however, found little use for these energic conflicts, and challenges within the field to such ideas as completely neutral psychic activity were numerous. I too found it difficult to accept many of these concepts and with Brenner, on several occasions, raised several challenges on how these ideas could apply to such activities as perception and creativity. Explaining phenomena in terms of cathexis and decathexis, instinctualized and deinstinctualized energy, seemed to us to be tautological, inasmuch as the nature of the drives was determined by the clinical manifestations and the clinical

---

1. The reminiscences of both Hartmann and Rado have been recorded in the oral history program of Columbia University by Bluma Swerdloff. It is possible that the material contained in those interviews might illuminate significantly our understanding of the background and origins of the Hartmann era.

manifestations were then used as evidence for defining the nature of the drive.

One follower of Hartmann, for example, attempted to illustrate the usefulness of the concept of neutralization by attempting to make a distinction between hostility and aggression, as if there were no unconscious instinctual concomitants to adaptive aggressive behavior. Kris was well aware of these difficulties. In one of the sessions of the Kris Study Group, someone raised the question, "If one of the signs of progress in psychoanalytic therapy is the diminution of the aggressiveness of the superego, and its functioning transformed in terms of completely neutral, not instinctualized, control, what would the ideal superego, completely free of instinctual charge, be like?" Kris laughed and said that essentially the concept as outlined was correct but added, "but I doubt it would make a very effective or useful superego."

The main point I want to make is: Was there really a Hartmann era as it is generally understood? I think that the phenomenon was basically a local situation, primarily in New York, with some connections to New Haven and London. In New Haven, there was the Yale Study Group, whose main figures were Solnit and Ritvo, who had worked with Kris in the Child Development Center. While the influence of Hartmann seems to loom large in this period, we have to take into account the fact that the major psychoanalytic periodicals of the United States at that time were also under the influence of New York trained analysts, e.g., the *Psychoanalytic Quarterly*, the *Journal of the American Psychoanalytic Association*, and the *Psychoanalytic Study of the Child*. One should note, moreover, that in 1955, at a panel on sublimation at which the main speakers were Hartmann and Kris and the principal discussant was Loewenstein (a panel on which I served as the reporter), the colleagues who participated in the discussion were Bak, Rosen, Wangh, Mahler, Mary O'Neil Hawkins, Elizabeth Geleerd, Augusta Alperts, Bertha Borenstein, Robert Fliess—all of these were from New York. It should also be noted that not one voice was raised in contradiction or challenge to the views presented by Hartmann, Kris, and Loewenstein. Everybody agreed.

To fully appreciate the situation of psychoanalysis in the United States at the time, one must take note of the fact that while the literature of the time contained many references to Hartmann, the actual influence of Hartmann's ideas on individual analysts in their practice and in other work was rather limited. It was also a time when many new institutes were springing up, most of them originating around an important training analyst from Europe, sometimes a husband and wife team, to whom the members of the newfound institutes remained loyal. New York, being so large and having had a longer history, was the exception to this rule of institutional genesis. This may have been true perhaps also in Chicago. In Boston there were two dominant couples, the Deutsches and the Bibrings; Philadelphia was Waelder's domain; Cleveland belonged to the Katans; Detroit had the Sterbas. The graduates of the institutes just mentioned, as well as those of the San Francisco and Washington institutes, bore mainly the imprint of the local leading figures. One might say that the situation resembled very much the small Greek city-states in classical antiquity or perhaps the small town courts of the independent Chasidic rabbis in Eastern Europe.

For me the Hartmann era had a definite ending. It took place in March 1958 at the symposium at New York University under the aegis of Sidney Hook (1959). The symposium was devoted to the issue of "Psychoanalysis: Scientific Method and Philosophy." The meeting was arranged around a lead presentation on philosophy and psychoanalysis given by Hartmann. When Hook and other philosophers, not all of whom were opposed to psychoanalysis, posed their challenges, Hartmann remained silent. For some reason he could not muster the necessary arguments to defend his views. It took Robert Waelder, a few years later when he reviewed the book that was the record of that symposium, to delineate, in a magnificent, classical essay, the issues involved.

That may have been the beginning of the end, but the final word was really given by Anna Freud at a Hunter College lecture in her paper on "Difficulties of the Path of Psychoanalysis" (1969). As she very clearly and very precisely pointed out, the optimistic feeling of the previous era was eroding. A new generation had arisen, a generation that did not look inwards towards a self in conflict, but saw its ills and difficulties as a result stemming from the hostile influence, the untoward demands, and the rigid attitudes of society. If there really was a Hartmann era, Anna Freud's talk at Hunter College marked the definitive end of that period.

References

Arlow, J. A. (1949). Anal sensations and feelings of persecution. *Psychoanalytic Quarterly* 17:79–84.

———— (1955). Report of panel on sublimation. *Journal of the American Psychoanalytic Association* 3:515–527.

Fenichel, O. (1945). *Psychoanalytic Theory of the Neuroses.* New York: Norton.

Freud, A. (1969). Difficulties of the path of psychoanalysis: past, present viewpoints. In *Writings of Anna Freud*, vol. 7, p. 39.

Freud, S. (1913). The claims of psychoanalysis to scientific interest. *Standard Edition* 13:165–192.

Hook, Sidney (1959). *Psychoanalysis, Scientific Method and Philosophy.* New York: New York University Press.

Rado, S. (1969). *Adaptational Psychodynamics: Motivation and Control,* ed. J. Jameson and H. Klein. New York: Science House.

Staercke, A. (1920). The reversal of the libido sign and delusion of persecution. *International Journal of Psycho-Analysis* 1:231–234.

van Ophuijsen, J. H. W. (1920). On the origin of feelings of persecution. *International Journal of Psycho-Analysis* 1:235–239.

Waelder, R. (1962). Review of "Psychoanalysis, Scientific Method and Philosophy," ed. S. Hook. *Journal of the American Psychoanalytic Association* 10:617–637.

3

The Idealization of Theory and the Aim of Adaptation: The Passing of the Hartmann Enterprise and Era

HAROLD P. BLUM

Shortly after his arrival in the United States in 1941 and until his death in 1970, Heinz Hartmann was the preeminent personality and undisputed leader of American psychoanalysis.

Hartmann was President of the International Psychoanalytical Association from 1951–1957 and had worldwide respect and analytic influence. *Ego Psychology and the Problem of Adaptation* (1939), an expansion of his 1937 Vienna lecture, was widely read and acclaimed and, in its published English translation (1958), became the first monograph of the *Journal of the American Psychoanalytic Association*. In the analytic generation, from 1945–1965, hardly a paper was written, at least in the United States, without a Hartmann citation. His ideas then dominated analytic discourse. As Bergmann (this monograph) and Schafer (1995) have noted, Hartmann did more than conserve and systematize psychoanalytic theory. More than modest modification, Hartmann actually proposed extensions and revisions, radical in some respects. The complexity and depth of his contributions can only be evaluated multidimensionally and from different perspectives inside and outside psychoanalysis. During the Hartmann generation, controversy and criticism of his ideas tended to be minor or muted, with idealization rather than analytic evaluation of his "ego psychology."

Given the heretofore acknowledged greatness of the man, the scope of his work, the monumental general psychology which he attempted to create, it is rather astonishing how interest and utilization of his ideas and propositions have declined. The most influential analyst of the immediate post-World War II era has been nearly effaced from contemporary psychoanalytic thought and writings. This calls for the type of psychoanalytic investigation and review that Bergmann has undertaken. It is an extraordinarily rich and erudite study. However, the disenchantment and lack of interest in Hartmann is so striking and pervasive that I am not sure that many analysts will be interested in reading the papers of this Symposium.

In my own reconsideration of Hartmann's contributions, I shall particularly emphasize problems connected with his idealization of theory, with the ambiguous aim of adaptation, and with paradoxical denial of reality while emphasizing adaptation. Nazism, the war, and the Holocaust were disregarded, and traumatic adaptation was absorbed into rarified, reified theory. His attempts to make psychoanalysis a general psychology rather than primarily a psychology of unconscious conflict, in his time, were admirable yet also served as a wishful and defensive fantasy. He wished to have other disciplines, for example biology and sociology, not only allied but integrated into psychoanalysis. However, his idealized aims could not be realized, with ensuing disappointment and diverging theories.

Attempts to reconstruct the sources and motives as well as the consequences of Hartmann's propositions inevitably involve methodological problems and pitfalls. Such historical reconstruction is both easier at some distance from Hartmann and from his era and legacy and harder with the overlay and alterations of time. This reconstruction of an era in the historical development of psychoanalysis is inevitably subject to personal bias, conjecture, and misinterpretation (Blum 1994). The evolution of ideas and the development of theory are vastly overdetermined. Hartmann and his co-workers were attempting to deal with a number of problems in psychoanalytic theory. They wanted to learn much more about early development and mental functioning and to enlarge the psychoanalytic edifice well beyond the foundation left by Freud at his death and the inception of World War II in 1939. The term *ego psychology* is a misnomer since Hartmann's propositions were structural and multidimensional, encompassing far more than the ego. Despite the limitations of the Hartmann era, psychoanalysis was advanced and systematized in many areas. Though his own theoretical contributions tended to be isolated from clinical psychoanalysis, he and his co-workers, E. Kris and R. Loewenstein, refined the theory of technique, with clinical applications. Hartmann's objectivity and concept of a relatively conflict-free sphere are critical, if now controversial, issues related to interpretation and insight.

The issues I shall confront are, therefore, in no way meant to shift from idealization to devaluation of Hartmann or to indicate a lack of appreciation for meritorious achievement and disappointed effort. Like Einstein, his grand "unified field theory" was fated to fail, although it would also have important and stimulating ramifications. Heinz Hartmann had special interests in adaptation, the relationship of the individual to his surround or environment, the ego functions particularly subsumed under the reality principle, and the impact and internalization of social and cultural pressures and tradition. It is in this context that I shall initially explore the relationship of Hartmann's innovative formulations to their time and place in the society and culture in which they were proposed. However, the correlation of the life and work of a creative person does not change the value or validity of his contributions, independent of their creator.

Although Hartmann did not write about World War II and the Holocaust, I believe they had a significant impact, along with intra-analytic and intrapsychic forces, on the direction of his thinking. The Holocaust is one of the two defining events of this century, the related other being the atomic bomb and the threat of nuclear holocaust. From an analytic viewpoint, Hartmann's denial and silence cannot be without significance. He wrote about conflict-free function and the problem of adaptation while conflict raged in reality. In many respects, Hartmann's silent avoidance was a collective defense, shared by much of the analytic and intellectual community. A latency period of recovery has been observed prior to exploration of other massive historical trauma, though the Holocaust was unprecedented. Perhaps it is only with time and distance from the Nazi era and the war that we can review Hartmann's concepts in the light of history: adaptation, autonomous functions, neutralization, the sphere free from conflict, social compliance, deinstinctualization, and deaggressivization. These terms were introduced into psychoanalysis at a time when adaptation to Nazi tyranny and persecution was becoming impossible and when most Jews, analysts, and humanitarians either had fled or were hoping and preparing to take refuge from Germany and Austria. The Jewish analysts did not resign from the German Psychoanalytical Society. Their "resignation" was a euphemism for expulsion. Like so many other uprooted and humiliated refugees, they responded to a grave external danger situation by flight and migration.

The exodus led to the transplantation of European psychoanalysis largely to the United States, where two-thirds of the emigrés settled. This involved almost the entire Vienna Psychoanalytical Association, with more than one hundred analysts and candidates leaving and only three analysts, including August Aichorn, remaining in Austria during the war. Most of the refugee analysts did not speak fluent English, and a struggle for personal, economic, and professional survival meant multiple hardships and severe problems of adaptation. All were concerned about the safety and welfare of family and extended family.

At first there were the usual defenses of denial, isolation, and rationalization, alongside pessimistic/realistic expectations that things would only get worse. Denial competed with concurrent awareness of impending disaster. Freud stated in 1933, after the Nazis had burned his books, "In the middle ages they would have burnt me; nowadays they are content with burning my books" (Jones 1957, p. 182). He actually had been prophetic long before in March 1909 when he wrote to Jung, "One way or the other the Jew will be burned" (p. 211). He wrote in 1933 (to A. Zweig) of dark times and of feeling sorry for his children and grandchildren. In 1935, Freud wrote to Arnold Zweig, "Everything around is growing ever darker, more threatening, and the awareness of one's own helplessness evermore importunate" (p. 139) and "I see a cloud of disaster passing over the world" (p. 101). In 1937, when Hartmann was his analysand, Freud wrote of the worship of anti-Semitism in Austria and Germany, and noted, "the noose around our necks is being tightened all the time" (p. 154). Hartmann noted that he discussed a wide variety of issues with Freud, in addition to direct analytic work. It is not possible that the Nazi threat was not discussed, with thoughts of escape and migration.

Most of Europe's psychoanalysts and psychotherapists were Jews or partially Jewish and married to Jews. The pioneers of psychoanalysis were largely assimilated Jews. They considered themselves humanitarians and world citizens or mainstream professionals. Jewish identity was revived and thrust upon them by the virulent and contagious surrounding anti-Semitism.

Unlike the vast majority of his analytic colleagues, Heinz Hartmann had occupied a privileged position in Viennese society. He was only one-quarter Jewish, and his father had been the Austrian Ambassador to Germany after World War I. A great historian and professor of history at the University of Vienna, his father arranged for Hartmann to avoid declaring a religious affiliation and compulsory religious instruction.

His early schooling was at home. Hartmann became scientist, philosopher, physician, and musician. He met the leading politicians, physicians, and artists of his day in his parents' home. As a young adult he assisted his ambassador father, so Heinz Hartmann was certainly educated concerning contemporary political and social trends. He began reading Freud while a youth, and wrote "The Fundamentals of Psychoanalysis" (1927) while in training analysis with Sandor Rado. This first analysis with Sandor Rado has been relatively overlooked. Both Rado and Hartmann were to write on adaptation. It may not be insignificant that Rado left the New York Psychoanalytic Society to found Columbia and a school of adaptational psychoanalysis not long after Heinz Hartmann had achieved prominence in the New York Psychoanalytic Society and Institute.

Hartmann's retrospective denial of danger in 1937 and 1938 points to minimization of the very real menace to civilized society. If there was no danger, why did he emigrate? Hartmann's statement (Swerdloff 1963) that he feared conscription into the German army implies denial. Part Jewish and married to a Jew, he would probably have been conscripted to a concentration camp. When he left Austria in 1938 he traveled to France and then left France for Switzerland, presumably because of Swiss neutrality and sanctuary. Hartmann sought the safety of neutral Switzerland before journeying on to New York in 1941. He retained his European roots and chose to be buried with his wife in Switzerland.

Hartmann's work followed the Symposium on the Theory of Therapy at the IPA Congress in Marienbad in 1936, the publication of Anna

Freud's (1936) *Ego and the Mechanisms of Defense,* and the publication of Freud's (1937) *Analysis Terminable and Interminable.* It was certainly timely and appropriate from within psychoanalysis for further attention to ego development, ego functions, and structural change. However, one would have thought that there would be even more compelling reasons to deal with the ego's relation to reality and problems of traumatization, adaptive strain and defense, flight or fight, and so on. An analytic "business as usual" prevailed in the literature. At the time of greatest external peril, the concept of an average expectable environment was introduced into psychoanalytic discourse and writings. In its historical and social setting the average expectable environment was not only an innovative analytic concept but a wishful fantasy. The environment was neither average nor expectable nor available for safe or secure adaptation. For the Jews and for all those who opposed the Nazis or who were considered to be in opposition by the Nazis, there was no fitting ecological niche and no possible adaptation without flight or fight. The theoretical concept of an average expectable environment would also be criticized in the future as it became apparent that it courted science fiction. The environment was often subject to unexpected change and highly variable. Each parent–child dyad is different, and different during different phases of development. Intrapsychic and interpersonal conflict are universal and ubiquitous (Brenner 1982). External reality and unconscious fantasy were reciprocally influential (Arlow 1969). The environment was often subject to unexpected change and highly variable.

Ignoring the environment while attending to it, Hartmann contributed to enlarged understanding of the relationship between endowment and environment that eventuated in adaptation. He proposed that the human infant is preadapted, equipped to make changes in itself and then to change the environment. Adaptation could be progressive and regressive, and both progressive and regressive adaptation could be constructive. Avoiding the persecutory external environment, he elaborated a theory in which progressive adaptation coincides with normal development, while regressive adaptation could be maladaptive, adaptive, or both in different ways. Regressive flight into fantasy might, in the long run, support problem solving or the subsequent alteration of external reality. He spoke of a process of adaptation and of a process of internalization that potentiated and permitted the achievement of adaptation. "The inner world and its functions make possible an adaptation process which consists of two steps: withdrawal from the external world and return to it with improved mastery" (Hartmann 1939, p. 58).

Withdrawal from the external world into theory did not necessarily subserve improved mastery. Introducing the concept of ego interests, self-preservation was described as the chief such interest. Referring to social values and individual drives, religion and education exemplified *social compliance* (analogous to Freud's concept of somatic compliance) (Peltz 1989). These fascinating psychosocial excursions were not analyzed in relation to types of withdrawal; withdrawal from external reality to internal theory, and withdrawal from one external reality to a new, nontoxic environment where adaptation was possible. A complemental series of avoidance and awareness, intrapsychic defense and external adaptation, may be inferred from Hartmann's (1939) differentiation of three types of developmental processes: "Those which occur without any essential and specific influence of the external world; those which are coordinated with two types of experiences (. . . are triggered by average expectable environmental situations . . .); . . . those which depend upon atypical experiences" (pp. 103–104). Atypical experience and the need to construct or to find a more hospitable environment are rather abstract and tangential references to the essential problem that humanity confronted. He described the need to negotiate an adaptation of the internal and external milieus.

While innovatively and ingeniously expanding psychoanalytic theory, Hartmann (1939) introduced the problem of a psychoanalytic theory outside of conflict, an adaptation involving psychosocial fit and social compliance! For Jews, attempted social compliance with the Nazi regime was ultimately maladaptive and a prescription for disaster. In adaptation Hartmann also introduced a concept that was not clearly defined. The concepts were separated from analytic data and from psychosocial peril. They were experience-distant rather than experience-near, immediately relevant to the human or "inhuman" condition. Shaw (1989) described Hartmann's ideas as of "incomparable value as well as incomprehensible density" (p. 592). While Hartmann indicated that conflict could provoke problem solving and ego adaptation, he wondered how both the conflict-free and the conflict spheres interacted in the process of adaptation. He (Hartmann 1939) assumed, "The observation underlying the concept adaptation is that living organisms blatantly fit into their environment. Thus, adaptation is primarily a reciprocal relationship between the organism and its environment" (pp. 23–24). These formulations are not entirely internally consistent and depend not so much upon an achieved synthesis but rather a mix of psychoanalysis, biology, ecology, and sociology. Adaptation thus becomes part of adapting psychoanalysis to a general psychology and, particularly, to a social as well as developmental psychology. Data obtained from psychoanalysis and data obtained from other spheres are commingled, and it is difficult to judge which data and which organizational model are used for many of the formulations.

While stimulating the study of all aspects of development, particularly ego development, rather than libidinal phases, he seemed to base his concept of adaptation primarily on an analogy of an animal's adaptation to its environment. Since Hartmann indicated how much the ego, with functions of anticipation, language, and intelligence, was the unique organ of adaptation and self-preservation in humans, it was strangely inconsistent that he chose to emphasize that biological prototype of adaptation. The human ego was influenced by the environment and its adaptation, unlike animal instincts. If the application of these ideas to clinical psychoanalysis remained obscure, so did their application to social reality. Hartmann's (1939) monograph in German appeared at a time of frightful persecution and the outbreak of World War II. The formulations of the conflict-free sphere, of autonomous functions, an average expectable environment, and adaptation as an internal–external fitting together were the reversal and opposite of the reign of terror in the actual surround. The horrors of the war and the Holocaust, hitherto unimaginable atrocities, the traumatization of generations, and genocide were relatively eclipsed during the Hartmann era.

During the heyday of the Hartmann era and the popularity of psychoanalysis, there was little thought that "this too shall pass." In those heady days, there was an idealization of Hartmann and his eminent colleagues, of psychoanalytic theory and abstract metapsychology, and of psychoanalysis itself. Psychoanalysis would not only enrich and inform but would surely encompass psychology and the allied professions. Indeed, at the time, psychoanalysis had a greater impact upon American psychiatry than it had upon psychiatry in any other time or place in history. Psychoanalysts were often chairs of departments of psychiatry. Psychoanalytic teaching and principles permeated psychotherapy. An offshoot of psychoanalysis, psychoanalytic psychotherapy was often depicted as a lesser form of treatment for those whom, for one reason or another, psychoanalysis was unavailable or inappropriate. Little did the ego psychologists foresee that idealization would be followed by disillusionment and devaluation. Psychoanalysis declined in popularity and prestige coincident with the death of Hartmann in 1970. It was the end of a glorious and glorified era.

The superfluity of analytic patients would then be followed by a paucity of analytic cases. The present generation of analysts are largely practicing psychoanalytic psychotherapy. The decline of psychoanalysis was not due to the passing of Hartmann, although the influence of many pioneers has gradually dissipated with their death. The idealization of psychoanalytic theory and therapy and vast social, cultural, and economic changes, competing modes of treatment, and insular shortsightedness within psychoanalysis all contributed to the present devaluation of psychoanalysis. In more recent times, diatribes against psychoanalysis and Freud have been associated with lack of interest in psychoanalytic treatment. As the tide turned against clinical psychoanalysis, psychoanalytic thought in academia and the universities paradoxically began to thrive. Beyond medicine and psychology, psychoanalysis was increasingly applied to literature, history, philosophy, art, and anthropology. General interest in unconscious motive, conflict, character, development, and sublimation was, nevertheless, associated with diverging theories. Self psychology, object relations theory, intersubjective formulations, countertransference relativism, and deconstruction challenged classical views of neutrality and objective interpretation (Blum 1996). Theoretical pluralism and eclecticism were embraced.

Economic theory was particularly subject to major criticism and increasingly disregarded. Energic concepts were little used in *Ego Psychology and the Problem of Adaptation* (1939) but were prominent in Hartmann's later individual and co-authored writings and in the literature of the Hartmann era. Quantitative assumptions had been related to the conflict model but were no longer considered necessary, useful, or explanatory. The energic concepts are replete with anthropomorphism and the concretization of metaphor. The different descriptions of energy changes appeared to be based upon a thermodynamic or reified mechanistic model which "ran out of steam." Degrees of neutralization did not resolve the problems inherent in Freud's earlier metaphors involving energy reservoirs, for example, the transformation of primary narcissism into secondary narcissism, narcissistic love into object love. The damming up and discharge, transformations, fusions, and defusions of aggressive, sexual, and partially neutralized energy, the various shadings of bound and mobile energy, the pretentious terminology of cathexis, decathexis, and anticathexis have virtually disappeared from psychoanalytic discourse and are essentially an extinct language (Wyman 1989). This does not mean that issues of peremptory demands or of primary and secondary processes are no longer relevant. Quantitative intensities appear in clinical discussions but without abstract elaboration. Economics do not convey meaning, representation, or cause and effect, and they may be regarded as tautological. Further, the effort to depict forces, energies, and structures resulted from and contributed to the idealization of psychoanalysis as a science. It borrowed from the hard science terminology of physics and presented psychoanalysis as though it was easily classified with the natural sciences. Energic transformations really amounted to a form of pseudoscience, an arcane set of constructs that intoxicates the intellect and obscures rather than explains analytic data. The intricate and exotic energy transformations replaced issues of unconscious conflict and fantasy and their genetic reconstruction. Clarification and interpretation remain much closer to human experience than the description of hypothetical energies. The later deidealization of metapsychology was not a matter of decathexis but disillusionment with exalted pseudo-explanation. Psychoanalysis could retain scientific status without being a nineteenth-century natural science. Moreover, just as Freud (1895) had abandoned the project for scientific psychology, biopsychological propositions about mental energies could not be sustained.

Hartmann's (1939) important concepts of primary and secondary autonomy and the conflict-free sphere later were amalgamated with energy formulations. Autonomous functioning operates with neutral energy; the primary autonomous ego functions utilize a neutral energy to start, and the secondary autonomous functions are those that during development have become relatively independent of conflict and presumably operate with neutralized energies. Neutralization became equivalent to desexualization and deaggressivization. The developmental transformations involved in concepts of *change of means* and *change of function* were also overshadowed by energic transformations. The energy terminology actually handicapped Hartmann's powerful and influential analytic contributions. Hartmann especially emphasized both innate ego functioning and ego development in the context of object relations. He was attempting to reformulate developmental and structural psychoanalysis without being fixated to the narrow base of libido theory.

Freud's (1923) formulations of ego growth and ego strength were inconsistent and removed from a position of emphasizing the ego as "only a helper to the id; it is also a submissive slave" (p. 56). Freud (1926) later asserted the power of the ego and his changed view of an active ego and its functions. Hartmann's concept of secondary autonomy is analogous to Freud's developmental concept of signal anxiety. Overwhelming traumatic anxiety is transformed developmentally into a thought-like signal. The ego responds to a danger signal that is also a hybrid affective and cognitive communication. The development of signal anxiety signals a major change in function with implicit intrasystemic considerations. The ego is not overwhelmed but is able to anticipate, communicate, and effectively respond. Functions of anticipation, coordination, and defense are integrated into a new organization. Autonomous ego functions are impeded and encroached upon by the defensive functions of the ego, but they may also be organized with various degrees of harmony, subserving Hartmann's adaptation to reality. While employing energy theory, Hartmann was attempting to move psychoanalysis away from such global concepts as ego activity to consideration of specific ego functions. These functions changed during development and in relation to other functions and agencies. If the ego was deformed by its own defensive activity, if ego energies were depleted by excessive and pathological defense, Hartmann wanted more particular specifications of the different ego functions and their mutual influence. He was as interested in ego growth as in ego regression, more particularly in progressive as well as regressive alteration of functions. In the unconscious id, contradictory impulses could coexist without clash or conflict. Drawing attention to the conflict-free ego, Hartmann was also interested in intrasystemic conflict, as well as traditional intersystemic conflict.

Hartmann's (1950) interest in intrasystemic issues greatly contributed to psychoanalytic developmental and structural theory. Hartmann's consideration of the ego led from global ego concepts to functions and process. The introduction of self and object representations
had important theoretical consequences that altered contemporary
psychoanalytic thought. Theoretical inferences from child and adult
analysis, and from infant observation and research, were enormously
stimulated and exponentially advanced during the Hartmann era. In
fact, as Hartmann (1950) emphasized that "psychoanalytic psychology is not limited to what can be gained through the use of the psychoanalytic method" (p. 103), disharmony and conflict arose within the
ranks of psychoanalysis. An attempt to learn from other fields while
contributing to them led to a clash with those who firmly rejected
such "nonanalytic" endeavors and wished to rely only on the data of
the analytic situation. From this viewpoint, abstract metapsychology
and the utilization of arcane energies did more than idealize psychoanalysis as a natural science. Psychoanalysis was a complete science,
a superordinate science that could encompass other disciplines. It was
a unified, glorified field theory that could obtain all the answers
through the analytic method within the analytic situation. The translation and recasting of ordinary analytic discourse by energy propositions offered a veneer of greater scientific credibility. This abstract restatement of function, content, and conflict appealed to the
narcissism of analysts and their idealization of psychoanalysis. Esoteric energy had little, if anything, to do with clinical comprehension and interpretation. The analysis of defense was not facilitated
by the discourse of anticathexis or the proposition that defense
operates with partially neutralized aggressive energy. At the same
time, inconsistencies in Hartmann's formulations, such as conflating
drive and defense in terms of aggressive anticathexis, stimultane-
ously exposed prior oversimplified polarities. Change of means and
function, overdetermination, progression and regression to and from
secondary autonomy permitted psychoanalysts to consider new
orders of complexity. Earlier models were questioned and new
models could be considered without departing from psychoanalytic
principles.

External aggression and traumatic experience with diminished
ability for adaptation was avoided concerning the Holocaust and emi-

gration; it was then reengaged in Hartmann's elegant studies of aggression. Hartmann's interest was presumably stimulated by the aggression from without, and by formidable problems in the psychoanalytic theory of aggression. Having made the ego the basis of adaptation and discarded older concepts of ego and self-preservative instincts, Hartmann (1949) and co-workers turned attention to the aggressive drive. The nature of the aggressive drive, its sources, aims, and goals needed further clarification and coordination with ego and libido theory. Reaction to the prior denial of silence concerning Nazi aggression and hostility may have further contributed to Hartmann's compensatory elucidation of the aggressive drive. During the Hartmann era, aggression became coequal with libidinal impulses in studies of conflict, and Freud's (1937) suggestion concerning free aggression and the disposition to conflict was further supported. Hartmann's failure to formulate an aggressive drive completely congruent and symmetrical to the sexual drive does not diminish his great accomplishment regarding the importance and vicissitudes of aggression.

The value of Hartmann's theorizing is exemplified in his contributions concerning psychic structure and the regulatory functions of the ego and the superego. Hartmann (1939) described the importance of processes of internalization and the gradual human development of internal regulation in place of external controls or rigid stereotyped animal instincts. Hartmann's interest in internalization, organizing principles and layers of organization, intrasystemic as well as intersystemic conflict and disharmony, has been compared to government (Rangell 1965, Schafer 1976). Organization, centralized regulation, the coordination of structures and their functions, threats from within and without, choices of responses to danger, and such all suggest government as a model of the mind. Effective and stable government required capacities for functional adaptations to changing circumstances in different parts of the realm. In fact, several of Hartmann's specific interests correspond to those of Freud's three impossible professions: psychoanalysis, government, and education. Hartmann's father, an ambassador and historian, was the principal organizer at the university level for education for the working class (Eissler and Eissler 1964). Hartmann's paternal grandfather, an author and professor of German literature, was also a leading German politician. Government and its policies and processes appear to be one of the many determinants of Hartmann's model of the mind. In this model he was closer to contemporary systems theory than Freud's earlier model of the psyche seeking minimal stimulation. Hartmann's regulation, coordination, internalization, and identifications building up increasing complex and realistic self and object representations replaced antiquated constancy and nirvana principles. Hartmann tended to minimize his own innovative departures from Freud and highlight his clarifications and systemizations of Freud's formulations. His contributions concerning governmental organization and regulation, so much involved with the individual in society, were paradoxically counterposed and amalgamated with pseudoscientific psychoeconomics. He loved the play and interplay of ideas and the development of complex hypotheses and propositions. The nature of government and the governing of people could be partially eclipsed by impersonal energies and apparatuses. Could these models refer to a dehumanizing dictatorship as well as protective government? The danger of totalitarian terror and tyranny could be condensed and disguised within the tyranny of the drives and of the superego. Denial of an extremely pathological menacing milieu was reflected in the counterpart of an "average expectable environment." Hartmann's references to the classics omitted current events and living history. There was hardly a word from most of the expatriated analysts of the Hartmann era about the experience of being a refugee, emigration, and the strain of adaptation to a new country, culture, and language. It would take succeeding generations before the Holocaust and its continuing influence would be investigated and appreciated (Bergmann et al. 1982) inside and outside psychoanalysis. Hartmann would have been pleased with the search for objectivity, with relatively autonomous observation and relatively conflict-free evaluation of the era in which he figured so prominently. Partially based upon denial and idealization, his lofty goals could not be attained. Illusion was succeeded by disillusionment. Hartmann's denial in fantasy fortunately did not extend to denial in action. His emigration to the United States enormously contributed to the growth and vitality of American psychoanalysis. Hartmann remains an enduring influence upon psychoanalytic thought, internalized in the continuous evolution of psychoanalysis.

References

Arlow, J. (1969). Unconscious fantasy and disturbances of conscious experience. *Psychoanalytic Quarterly* 38:1–27.

Bergmann, M. (2000). *The Hartmann Era*. New York: Other Press.

Bergmann, M., Jucovy, M., and Kestenberg, J. (1982). *Generations of the Holocaust*. New York: Basic Books.

Blum, H. (1994). *Reconstruction in Psychoanalysis: Childhood Revisited and Re-created*. New York: International Universities Press.

——— (1996). An analytic inquiry into intersubjectivity: subjective objectivity. *Journal of Clinical Psychoanalysis* (in press).

Brenner, C. (1982). *The Mind in Conflict*. New York: International Universities Press.

Eissler, K. R., and Eissler, R. (1966). Heinz Hartmann: a biographical sketch. In *Psychoanalysis—a General Psychology*, ed. R. Loewenstein et al. New York: International Universities Press, pp. 3–15.

Freud, E., ed. (1970) *The Letters of Sigmund Freud and Arnold Zweig* (1927–1939). Translated by Elaine and William Robson-Scott. New York: New York University Press.

Freud, S. (1895). Project for a scientific psychology. *Standard Edition* 1.

——— (1923). The ego and the id. *Standard Edition* 19.

——— (1926). Inhibition, symptom, and anxiety. *Standard Edition* 20.

——— (1937). Analysis terminable and interminable. *Standard Edition* 23.

Hartmann, H. (1939). *Ego Psychology and the Problem of Adaptation*. New York: International Universities Press.

——— (1950). Comments on the psychoanalytic theory of the ego. *Psychoanalytic Study of the Child* 5:74–96. New York: International Universities Press.

Hartmann, H., Kris, E., and Loewenstein, R. (1949). Notes on the theory of aggression. *Psychoanalytic Study of the Child* 3/4:9–36. New York: International Universities Press.

Jones, E. (1957). *The Life and Work of Sigmund Freud*, vol. 3. New York: Basic Books.

Loewenstein, R. M. (1951). *Christians and Jews: A Psychoanalytic Study*. New York: International Universities Press.

McGuire, W., ed. (1974) *The Freud/Jung Letters, 1906–1914*. Princeton, NJ: Princeton University Press.

Peltz, M. (1989). On the origins of contemporary structural theory: an appreciation of *Ego Psychology and the Problem of Adaptation*. *Psychoanalytic Quarterly* 58:551–570.

Rangell, L. (1965). The scope of Heinz Hartmann. *International Journal of Psycho-Analysis* 46:5–30.

Schafer, R. (1968). *Aspects of Internalization*. New York: International Universities Press.

———— (1995). In the wake of Heinz Hartmann. *International Journal of Psycho-Analysis* 76:223–236.

Shaw, R. (1989). Hartmann on adaptation: an incomparable or incomprehensible legacy? *Psychoanalytic Quarterly* 58:592–611.

Swerdloff, B. (1963). Interview of Heinz Hartmann. Oral History Series, Columbia University.

Wyman, H. (1989). Hartmann, health, and homosexuality: some clinical aspects of "Ego Psychology and the Problem of Adaptation." *Psychoanalytic Quarterly* 58:612–639.

4

Illusion and Disillusionment in the Attempt to Present a More Reasonable Theory of the Mind

ANDRÉ GREEN

The time has come when every psychoanalyst should be aware of the importance of the history of psychoanalysis. *"Après-coup,"* thanks to Martin Bergmann, we realize that we have been through a Hartmann era. There has been a Hartmann phenomenon as very few theoreticians of psychoanalysis were credited for such a kind of almost cult of ideas if not of personality. But history, as Martin Bergmann recalls, is not easy to make. What we were lacking, up till now, was not only a history of the facts, events, and struggles that agitated our field but a history of ideas, which is of tremendous importance to us. Bergmann's essay will remain as a hallmark to evaluate a period of the psychoanalytical movement.

GEOGRAPHY: THE MAP OF HARTMANN'S CONQUESTS

History is frequently inseparable from geography. Martin Bergmann's essay, which encompasses so many aspects, mentions some indications about this but does not linger. How is it that, in comparison with the recognition and rapid success spreading all over the United States, Hartmann's work raised so small an interest beyond its native borders? Without even mentioning its total absence in Latin America, in Europe its influence was limited to the agreement of Anna Freud and her group. There was a mutual support between Anna Freud and Hartmann. Hartmann helped Anna Freud, who was in the minority in her own society, weakened not only by the Kleinians but also by the Independents.[1] Those who were not "Annafreudians" only paid lip service to Hartmann's work. But even in Anna Freud's group, Sandler admits that the development of Hartmann's conceptions followed a different path in England because of their exposition to the ideas of the other groups of the British Society. So we can argue that the wide success of Hartmann was linked to a sort of isolation, the Americans being convinced of their superiority. How far did political reasons contribute to this self protection? In the rest of Europe, Hartmann's work had little influence. In France, Lacan's hard criticism is not enough to explain the insusceptibility of the French analysts, as even those who were opponents to Lacan were not inclined at all to follow the American new wave. Above all the French denied the claim that Hartmann was Freud's heir. The French, whose group extended beyond Lacan's followers, also pretended to be in the line of the master of Vienna and they stood opposite to the Hartmannian Freud. The main areas of disagreement were about the differences in the concept of ego, their understanding of energy, the emphasis on the effects of drive and desire, the attention to what governed Freud's inspiration, the reference to pleasure for instance, and the emphasis on a radical discontinuity between conscious and unconscious. Let us remember in passing that Kohut's ideas also failed to be accepted. Melanie Klein's ideas were known and quoted but the Kleinian graft did not blossom on the other side of the channel. All this was not based on an attitude of orthodoxy but on the shared feeling that Freud was right. I am speaking here of the period during which Hartmann's ideas imposed themselves in the USA. Later on, the situation became more complex with the birth of Lacanism. Bion's ideas are more respected and Winnicott is the larger post-Freudian reference, except Lacan, of course.

---

1. By the way, it is not possible to say that Winnicott was in the camp of Melanie Klein. He used to oppose her on many grounds. Up till now the Kleinians are, in general, hostile to Winnicott.

THE ALLEGIANCE TO HARTMANN

To speak of a Hartmann era is more than justified, as Hartmann's work was so influential that many of the psychoanalysts of this period accepted his language and conceptions while defending original ideas that could be presented independently from this background. The most conspicuous case is that of Edith Jacobson, whose work was respected and admired largely beyond the United States. It is no surprise to see that it was easy for Otto Kernberg to reinsert her ideas in the new frame of object relations theory. One can say the same of other psychoanalysts mentioned by Bergmann: Spitz and Mahler, whose contributions can be considered worth discussing without necessarily adopting their ego-psychological patronage. On the other hand, some extreme Hartmannites such as Rapaport, whose hostility to Freud is noticed by Bergmann, express views that appear unacceptable to many because they imply an entirely different conception of the mind, in which the exclusively psychological interpretation modifies substantially the Freudian viewpoint. Here we are beyond disagreement because it is a new paradigm that is presented, breaking the basic assumptions of the theory it wants to change. Was Rapaport a modifier or an heretic according to Bergmann's classification? I would opt for the latter. When we come back to the practice of analysis, we agree that the works of Annie Reich, and even those of Loewenstein, can remain very valuable beyond their reference to many of Hartmann's concepts.

A most strange case is Eissler. Though labeled a Hartmannite, his deepest inspiration, as shown in the ideas of "The Fall of Man" in Bergmann's essay, is in direct line with Freud and stands very far from his alleged heir, not only because of his pessimism, but more because Eissler convincingly emphasizes how *unadapted* is that representative of the species to which we belong, supposed to be at the crowning of all others, thanks to his supposed capacity for adaptation.

Could it be that during the period of the Hartmann era one had to make a tragic choice? Either to oppose openly Hartmann's ideas at the risk of falling into oblivion, as was the case with many valuable thinkers among which I will only mention a favorite of mine, Bertram Lewin; or, in order to have a chance to be heard, to adopt, willy-nilly, the official language of the mainstream of American psychoanalysis during that period.

The question could be more political than any else. Until now it is not easily accepted to express critical opinions on the influence of Hartmann (see my controversy with Schafer[2]). It seems that an argument to get away with it is to declare that Freud was the inventor of ego psychology! For sure, an invention about the inventor.

NEUTRAL ENERGY, A STILLBORN IDEA

Let us go back to the unique passage of Freud mentioning a neutral energy (Bergmann, this monograph, pp. 10–11). As in many other instances, Freud is here thinking aloud, considering the reader as a witness of the unfolding of his thoughts and making at one point the hypothesis of this "indifferent Energie," which was labeled by Hartmann as "neutral energy." At this point Freud is trying to find an answer to a puzzling enigma: the transformation of love into hate. The main emphasis is on the displaceability of the energy from one affective pole to its opposite one. The "neutrality" that is hypothesized here is related to desexualized Eros, of narcissistic nature. Neutrality is the result of desexualization as a way of explaining the transformation of love into hate. A primary neutral energy supports the idea of the autonomous ego as safe, escaping the primary influence of the body needs, affects, passion, and desire. I see here the influence of Piaget, who had little understanding of psychoanalysis. Could it be that Hartmann's theory itself is not subjected to these factors, being a scientific deduction? Never in Freud can be found elsewhere the idea of a primary nonsexual, neutral energy. In the quoted passage, like in many others, Freud is testing an idea, considering different possibilities provisionally. The fact that he never took it up again is not only an indication that the idea remained isolated but as an evidence that the hypothesis was stillborn.

ON AN OXYMORON

I have the feeling, considering the contributions of the Hartmannites, of a basic misconception (I realize that it is difficult to find a translation for the French *malentendu*, which is literally "mishearing"). When Peltz

2. Schafer, R. (1992). Response to André Green. *Psychoanalytic Psychology* 12:1.

(1989), quoted by Bergmann, states about Hartmann: "His greatly expanded view of the ego and its functions put that agency of the mind on a par with the id (and the superego) without diminishing psychoanalysis as a depth psychology" (p. 2), I feel as if I was in front of an oxymoron. I take this opinion as representative of the contradictions the answers to these problems can raise. The shift of emphasis from Freud's first topographical model to the second was because he was no longer satisfied with the concept of the unconscious descriptive, dynamic or systematic. Many psychoanalysts considered that much of what he said about the unconscious was simply repeated, in many similar terms, when he described the id. If it is true that many features are present in both descriptions, why change the theory? In fact there is one major modification. When Freud described the id in the XXXIst Chapter of the *New Introductory Lectures* in 1933, any mention of "representations" has disappeared. Freud only speaks here of "instinctual impulses" seeking discharge. He had already made reference to impulses in the papers on metapsychology of 1915; still, his main focus was on representations and affects. Moreover, in 1923, he seems to imply that representations (even unconscious ones) can only occur in the ego. So, on one hand, in gathering all the representations in the ego, he may seem to have reduced the gap between the unconscious, preconscious, and conscious ones, as they appeared in the first topographical model; on the other hand, the gap is reinstated and even increased between the id, devoid of representations, and the ego. This gap constitutes the basis of *depth psychology*, in other terms psychology accounting for not only what is in the depth of the ego, but even "lower" in the depth of the body—in the id.

The dynamic quality, which is the typical attribute of the impulses, an essential characteristic of the id, has to be considered according to its impact on other more differentiated and stable agencies (ego). It needs two conclusions. The first, of course, is that the whole construction of the psychic apparatus is built on the foundations of the id. The second is that the id is, at the bottom, unthinkable. It seems that a paradox is present here, but this is different from an oxymoron. In making no room for representations (which remained a specificity of the unconscious as long as the first topographic model was in use), Freud emphasizes that our conceptualization of the id is inevitably uncertain and probably distorted because of the lack of intellectual tools to give faithful idea of what it is. Putting the accent on the id's anchorage in the somatic, though being, even at that stage of a psychic nature, *"in a form unknown to us,"* Freud wants to increase the differences that he established in the past between the conscious and the unconscious with his new model, most specifically in terms of relationships between surface and depth. The most probable explanation for this is the limitation of the influence of analysis on the patients. Therefore, any effort to reduce this difference in putting the new agencies "on a par" either darkens the functions of the ego in giving a picture of them that overlooks the differentiating power of representation or, more eventually, like here, presents a conception of the id that makes it closer to the ego, that is more structured than in Freud, which is inconsistent or self-contradictory. Hartmann's ego especially distances itself from Freud's. This difference aggravates the situation because Freud's ego was nevertheless in a closer connection with the id than Hartmann's ego. In any way wanting to place them "on a par without diminishing psychoanalysis as a depth psychology" is an internal contradiction.

Many a critic has expressed that last opinion. Hartmann's theory of the ego brought psychoanalysis back in the field of academic psychology which Freud fought. The heir was blamed precisely for having abandoned the dynamic point of view. Long before these criticisms, Fenichel raised objections of that type. It took half a century before the truth that was in them appeared in full light. Though many celebrated psychoanalysts expressed their disagreement, they have not been heard. Again, we must question the interference with theory of influences very far from being the result of a serene "scientific" choice.

A FALSE APPEARANCE: FREUD'S HAMMERING

We may have to accept the idea, in spite of how it appears at first sight and even at many further ones, that Freud's description of the psychic personality should not be confused with a theory of the total personality. This would lead us to build up a picture in which the specificity of the analytic perspective would be drowned among many other considerations that could be valuable seen from another viewpoint. It is my belief that in constructing the model of a psychic apparatus Freud wanted above all to present an articulation of the general principles that, according to him, explained his theory of the mind. He was, I think, not so much concerned with the idea of presenting a complete picture, which could only be seen from the point of view of consciousness. Though his writings sometimes give that impression, I think it may induce us into errors. Instead, he wished to hammer, against skeptic reactions, the strong points of his theory. Mainly, in my opinion, 1) the nature of that part of the mind that is at its roots invisible and almost unthinkable and propels the development,[3] 2) the hierarchy of the structures, not to be seen as a piling up of formations assembled during time, 3) the heterogeneity of the constitution of the organized mind (formed of impulses, representations, affects, language, thoughts, etc., with the related defenses: the "work of the negative," as I call it), which assume various functions in the different types of disorders. This picture is not a realistic one. It is supposed to help us to think what is so strange and so puzzling in our exchanges with the inner world of the patients that are analyzed. Hartmann's view, though wanting to extend and modify Freud's concepts, departs from what I consider to be the true inspiration of his work and inclines to give a more sound image of the mind *from the viewpoint of the ego*, so as to start from a more secure source of knowledge. But it is precisely the kind of knowledge that is at risk of missing the point. As far as I am concerned, it is not possible to defend the idea of an ego that would be, in the beginning, in a position to have its own existence aside from the id. The idea of a differentiation of the ego from the id through the influence of the external world is not an observable fact; it is an axiom to account for the considerable strength of the unconscious and the many compliant aspects of the ego that persist in adult life, including splitting and the absence of awareness of its defenses. The explanation of the limitations of the power of the ego, even when one has to start from its teaching, has to be considered as the scars of his ancient relationship to the id or to its derivatives.

The other axiom is about the nature of the id. I said the id is unthinkable. Here the paradox is that we have to say what the id is challenged by in the absence of any proper instrument to know it. Freud writes: "What little we know of it we have learnt from our study of the dream work and of the construction of neurotic symptoms, and *most*

---

3. Which does not mean that is all that includes development, or that other factors do not play their part too.

of that is of a negative character and can be described only as a contrast to the Ego."[4] What Freud emphasizes is that what he is trying to talk about can only be reached through a negativization of our ways of thinking belonging to the ego. Therefore also maybe the idea of the drive or the instinct, according to the translation, as a concept "at the limit" of the somatic and the psychic. This expression is more a figure of style than a fact; it needs to be clarified. The psychic can be "thought," not the somatic, which can otherwise be known by objective methods. Freud is here struggling with the cradle of thinking. The *Grenzbegriff* may allude to something that is hardly conceivable. To admit the irrational aspects of it is insufficient. This should not lead us to indulge in "mystic" modes of communication. It only calls for new intellectual modes of apprehending the specificity of its functioning. This is Freud's boldest attempt to define the originality of psychoanalytic thinking, which can easily be overlooked in trying to master its obscurities. The unique characteristics of his presentation of the id are reinterpreted by his followers either by discarding the concept or by replacing it by others more handy, in conformity with the requirements of a more "workable" body of knowledge, more close to our current rational exigencies. It is very frequent to observe a preference for the unconscious, denying Freud's arguments to abandon it as a concept.

FROM REPRESENTATIONS TO ACTING

When I agree with Freud that the id is the ground of the psychic apparatus, I do not only imply that the id stands as the foundations of the whole building; the assumptions are different. What Freud proposes to our understanding is that the presence of the id will still be marked, though sometimes unnoticed or misapprehended in the other agencies appearing later: the ego because it is originally a portion of it and the superego that still communicates with it by its roots. There is also another assumption about the emphasis on instinctual impulses. In the first topographical model one could think that Freud's attempt to know was to start from unconsciousness and progressively try to reach the unconscious (through representations and affects). This could account

---

4. *Standard Edition*, XXII, p. 73, italics mine.

for what went on in the session consistently with the theory. For example, this sequence: dream narration, associations, unconscious meaning through guessed latent thoughts and fantasies, giving a picture of dream work, interpretation. Since *Remembering, Repeating and Working Through* (1914) we know that Freud met at one point his most unwelcome difficulty: the patient acts instead of remembering. This is the main reason for me why Freud changed his theory: because of the tendency to act out repetitiously, or to refuse to accept the interpretation of transference as a form of remembering. He started then with the potentially "acting" structure:[5] the drive that he deduced from the resulting representations at play, which repeated themselves. After the disappointments of practice due to the frequency of repetition compulsion, the unconscious representations were not anymore the firm basis of the investigation. Instead the point of departure in the mind (the so-called drives) gave rise to them in favorable conditions and to acting in the unfavorable ones. It was only in the first instance that one could assume that the ego took hold partially of what they originated from. In the old topography and in the favorable cases one could translate its contents in terms of "psychology." In the new topography, psychology was not adequate as a general characterization; it was subordinated to other processes of obscure nature. There is something misleading in the expression "depth psychology," as the more Freud changed his ideas the less depth was compatible with psychology. "Id mythology" was the truest expression in spite of its pejorative intention, in the sense that only myths can express psychic contents that can't be spelled out clearly, openly, rationally. Here the id stood for a psychic activity characterized by its constant change and transformations throughout internal pressures and seeking an outlet.

CONSTRUCTS

Hartmann and other critics of a "personification" of the agencies have to be clarified. Not only is it enough to defend the idea that they are metaphors. Even if this interpretation can be sustained, Freud was not

---

5. There are many observations to the replacement of acting (out) by enactment in contemporary psychoanalysis. I have to leave them out of my contribution.

so much inclined to make deliberate use of metaphors for explanations. It is more true to think of them as *constructs*. In trying to describe more precisely the situation, we will not avoid coming up against aporias. For instance, it is obvious that these constructs arise from psychoanalytic experience. Is it possible to grasp their meaning out of this specific initiation? Their delayed appearance in the body of theory is the reflection of what Freud observed in his practice related to the positive results of psychoanalysis *just as of its failures*.[6] Is the understanding of the new concepts not severely limited by this reference to the unreachability and nonmodifiability of some parts of the human mind that can be grasped only intuitively? Speaking of personification is short-sighted. What can be said from this point of view is that to grasp the meaning covering the field of the agencies needed some identification to the other—even also some projection but not projective identification—to get to the heart of the matter. The other was seen less as a person than as the representation of a field of conflicting organizations in a sort of abstract way. Freud, being aware of the difficulty of giving up the centrality of the reference to the ego, when approaching the matters of the mind, decided to accept, in a strategic move to consider the possibility, that point of departure in order to facilitate our sensitivity to the unheard. But he did so to underline the shortcomings of the ego and explain them by their relationships to the other agencies.[7] The acceptance to start with the facets of the mind that are familiar to everyone is here fully aware not to expect too much from the ego's lucidity or reliability. Freud saw that he must not distract his attention from what he had postulated with the construction of the apparatus, clearly showing the limited power of the ego. It is obvious that those who disagreed with Freud would oppose the results of other psychoanalytic experiences that will deny his discouraging statements about the failures that are reflected in the theory. In that sense, Martin Bergmann is right to underline the optimistic thread running through the new theory. Freud's pessimism could be explained by his own shortcomings, limitations, or mistrust of the ego. This objection is acceptable in theory. In practice we have consider the knowledge we have acquired

---

6. And maybe more from the negative results than the positive ones.

7. This is the way he starts his exposition in the XXXIst Chapter, *predicting that he will raise skepticism when he will introduce his readers to "the psychical underworld which preceded it"* (*New Introductory Lecture* 1933).

with other different experiences of psychoanalysis. I am thinking here of what we have learned from the work of the British Society (mainly from the Kleinians and the Independents) on the treatment of borderline personality disorders. In the States, Kernberg's work is along a similar line. It is very difficult to accept either Hartmann's ideas or his optimism when we read the contributions based on this conception of the ego. In any case, one can observe that the major contributions to the field today do not use Hartmann's ideas, specifically about the image of the ego that appears in these nonneurotic structures, in spite of Hartmann's wish to explain schizophrenia through his concepts. Time will prove, if not that Freud was right, almost surely that Hartmann was self-deceiving in defending so large an autonomy. Otherwise, the findings of psychoanalysis in non-Hartmannian perspectives oblige us to consider them as defects, bridging the gap between the general conception of the mind and the occurrences of these psychically disturbed disorganizations. Whereas, in Freud's view, the general model helps to understand its deviations without compelling us to draw a line that would reject "pathology" definitely out of the borders of the ordinary functioning of the mind.

DOUBTS ABOUT PSYCHOANALYSIS AS PSYCHOLOGY

Do I mean that we have to give up any attempt to "understand" what we call the id? On the contrary, to remember the hypothesis of the id safeguards us against the possibility of building theories that are based on rationalizations. If I ask myself where is in my opinion my basic disagreement, I will answer that it lies in the idea of building a *general psychology*. Hartmann was not the only one who wanted to realize this project. To me, many other thinkers whose ideas are very far from Hartmann follow the same inspiration to keep psychoanalysis within the limits of psychology. I consider this view as at the other extreme to those who, like myself, wish to distinguish and even oppose what is "psychological" from what is "psychical." Space limitations do not allow me to justify this difference.

Freud left us with a central question he hoped the future would solve: What is the nature of what he defined as "the dark, inaccessible part of our personality"? Have we helped to clarify Freud's attempt to go beyond his hypothesis? Do we have to move back to the first topographical model, being disappointed with the application of the second? Will it be enough if we use both according to our cases? Or do we have to give up both of them to turn to other models that have appeared later and better account for the problems we meet? The absence of consensus in the analytic community indicates that we have to wait for a satisfactory answer.

A REASONABLE EXPECTATION

To end this discussion I shall state my agreement with Martin Bergmann, arguing that many of the ideas defended by Hartmann depended on hidden motives. "The unknown unconscious needs that determine the point of view of the psychoanalyst" (pp. 61–62) are overshadowed by the pretense of the theory of being grounded on observation. I object less against such a situation than to its denial. I would even prefer that the thinkers of psychoanalysis openly express their axioms or postulates before developing them, and I do not think that psychoanalytic theory can develop in a totally objective manner. To me, Hartmann's contribution appears with its fate as a disillusionment to reshape a psychoanalytic theory in an attempt to clarify it and purify it from its ambiguities. The outcome in such an attempt should be closer to observation, more scientific in its spirit and its style, more balanced in its judgments, more in agreement with a developmental point of view, and more realistic. The concepts would be less "symbolic" and could be used with a maximum of clarity, more in view of the whole personality, not minimizing its achievements. No gap should be left unfilled between clinical practice and theory. In other words, psychoanalysis would become more acceptable to the academic world and to the general public. The new theory should have given up Freud's romanticism and speculation; it would help psychoanalysis to progress, and even flourish. Half a century later, we know that this *aggiomamento* missed his goals. Are we going to react to it by asking for more realism and more reasonable concepts? I doubt that giving up audacity will, by any means, lead to success, or even more modestly to survival at a period where our future is threatened.

5
The "Hartmann Era": On the Interplay of Different Ways of Thinking

WILLIAM I. GROSSMAN

INTRODUCTION

In a sweeping survey of the more than two decades that he has called the "Hartmann era," Martin Bergmann offers a perspective providing balanced analysis and personal outlook. He has presented a remarkable overview of a period in psychoanalytic history that is thought-provoking and challenging. This comprehensive review reveals the broad range of his erudition and experience. In his illuminating summaries of the work of Hartmann and his contemporaries, as well as of their interrelations, we become aware of the depth of his immersion in the thought of that time and place. In effect, his paper presents the starting point, if not a nucleus, of a history of psychoanalysis in the latter part of this century.

Consistent with his previous consideration of psychoanalytic history (Bergmann 1993), Bergmann describes three interlocking but relatively autonomous aspects of Hartmann's place in an ongoing story of the development of psychoanalysis. One aspect is Hartmann as an intellectual and sometimes political leader of the psychoanalytic movement. Another is Hartmann's theories as an influence and a foil for other contributions to theory at that time, as well as a stimulus to research. A third aspect is Hartmann's contribution to psychoanalytic technique.

Throughout, Bergmann shows the role of E. Kris and Loewenstein in all three areas, as well as the part played by others closely associated with them. He concludes that Hartmann was both an extender and a modifier of Freud's work.

In this paper, I shall be modifying and extending Bergmann's contribution by looking at Hartmann's ideas from a somewhat different perspective. It is based on the idea that designating that period of time as the Hartmann era reflects one possible centering of interest from within psychoanalysis. This is certainly a desirable, even necessary, perspective for any history of psychoanalysis. However, it is not the only possible perspective from within psychoanalysis of that time and, more to the point of my paper, Hartmann's work can be profitably considered from a long view of its place in the development of psychoanalysis and its intellectual setting in society. From this point of view, Hartmann's ideas and the psychoanalytic story of the Hartmann era, and since then, are the psychoanalytic version of intellectual and social processes on a larger scale.

Obviously, the perspective I have chosen can receive only a suggestive treatment here. And, in sketching my perspective, I shall have to mention a number of well-known ideas and generalizations because of their relevance here, in spite of their familiarity. What I have in mind are some of the divisive currents in psychoanalysis and ideas about theory and clinical observation that border on philosophical currents of a wider significance. In recent years, these concerns occupy much of the psychoanalytic literature as the divergences of psychoanalytic thought have become increasingly the focus of attention, discussion, and debate (Wallerstein 1990).

These issues are to some extent old issues that have come out in the open. They have taken new forms and are being considered from new angles. Hartmann began *his* work by addressing a number of issues that were controversial at that time. He faced the resistance to the introduction of the theory of the ego, the "structural theory" or the "second topography." The theories of Melanie Klein had begun to pose challenging alternatives to some cherished views. Neo-Freudian revisionists (Fromm, Horney, Sullivan) challenged basic tenets of psychoanalytic theory while some psychoanalysts sought harmonization of psychoanalysis and Marxism. These are only some of the issues that Hartmann's work addressed, both implicitly and explicitly. It is my view that post-Hartmann psychoanalysis continues to deal with these issues, as has an intellectual world that has had to deal with Freud's contribution to their elaboration.

In this paper, I shall take a first step in looking at some of these developments. First, I will be mentioning some intellectual currents in Vienna and elsewhere in the decade or so leading up to *Ego Psychology and the Problem of Adaptation* (Hartmann 1939). Then I shall outline some key concepts in Hartmann's theory, touching on their significance for the reorienting of theory and for interdisciplinary research. Third, I shall mention a couple of points about Hartmann's ideas and technique. Finally, my focus will shift to considering some changes in philosophical and social outlook, beginning in the "Hartmann era," that have been reflected in psychoanalytic thinking and debate today.

HARTMANN'S CONTEXT

In a certain way, every point of view about psychoanalysis carries a kind of interdisciplinary orientation. I refer to the fact that everyone brings to the study of people some presuppositions and ways of looking at the field. These ideas are, at first, based on personal development and experience, then on training. One's background in particular areas of interest and study provide a framework and context for psychoanalytic knowledge.

For example, Winnicott as a pediatrician seems to have seen the clinical situation in terms of mothers and children, and pathology in terms of the mother–infant relationship. Lacan was interested in language and Hegelian thought, which played an important part in his views.

These different areas of personal experience and interest provide those who possess them with a context within which their psychoanalytic thinking takes place and to which the language of psychoanalysis—as they come to understand it—also refers. Although we might be inclined to think of the influence of such backgrounds merely as a bias, it nonetheless sensitizes those with these interests to special aspects of human experience. The interests in other fields and their ways of thinking also help to illuminate psychoanalytic work and to alert those who are knowledgeable to particular aspects of psychoanalytic theory and its problems. In fact, E. Kris (1952), speaking of his own training in the humanities, went so far as to say: "The study of art and of creative processes in the broadest meaning of the word seemed to facilitate contributions to psychoanalytic psychology itself and to crystallize certain impressions gained in clinical work" (p.9).

I believe that the point of view given here helps to account for some of the argument about psychoanalytic theory, technique and the question of what is "really" psychoanalytic and what isn't, and what is "really" of relevance to "real" psychoanalysis. In the background of such debates, there are unspoken differences in frames of reference and, therefore, in the interpretation of psychoanalytic concepts and observations.

The influence of Freud's neurological background has been well documented, as have his interests in other branches of knowledge. Freud (1926) thought that, in addition to biology, "the history of civilization, mythology, the psychology of religion and the science of literature" (p. 246) should form the background of the psychoanalyst because of what such a background could bring to an understanding of people, not because they had a clear place in psychoanalytic theory or technique. No doubt his interest in anthropology, literature, science, and history, among others, fostered his efforts at interdisciplinary studies, hazardous as he knew them to be (Freud 1913, Grossman 1997).

From these considerations, I conclude that Hartmann's interdisciplinary interests followed Freud's, as do those of psychoanalysts whose interests lead them to discussions of art and literature. Those interests provide a scaffolding as well as metaphors and other content for the psychoanalytic ideas of the psychoanalyst.

Hartmann's background was in biology, and he found it to be a powerful organizing system. For this reason, his use of a biological model and his treating psychoanalytic psychology as part of it is an important and obvious feature of Hartmann's theorizing. In this, too, he continued in Freud's track (Grossman 1992, 1993). I have the impression that his discussion of Karl Mannheim (Hartmann 1939, 1964; see also Friedman 1989) shows that he saw a connection between the biological/psychoanalytic way of thought and sociological/social psychological thought. Any serious discussion of Hartmann's interdisciplinary thinking would have to take note of the fact that his approach was not at all crudely reductionistic. As shown in his sophisticated discussion on the relationship between psychoanalysis and social sciences, he was interested in the recurrence of similar patterns of organization at different levels of complexity in the individual and in groups.

In Vienna, in the years prior to the publication of *Ego Psychology and the Problem of Adaptation*, there were other sources of encouragement for interdisciplinary explorations. Academic psychologists, led by Karl and Charlotte Bühler, had become interested in psychoanalysis and were applying psychoanalytic ideas to their research in child development. Hartmann was aware of their work and cited it. Their student, Else Frenkl-Brunswick, also cited by Hartmann, was later associated with the psychoanalytically oriented researches of members of the Frankfurt school (Heiman and Grant 1974).

While Hartmann was still in Vienna, other groups applying psychoanalytic ideas to their own work generated controversies in their own fields about applying psychoanalysis to their disciplines. Because psychoanalysis was a subject for other areas of study, and because of the claim that psychoanalytic ideas were being tested outside the clinical setting, those applications of various versions of psychoanalysis had to be addressed by psychoanalysts.

The interest in psychoanalytic ideas of the members of the Frankfurt Institute of Social Research has had a role in the development of some present-day movements in psychoanalysis. Among those who were associated with that group, some names have become familiar to American psychoanalysts: Nathan Ackerman, Bruno Bettelheim, Erich Fromm, Marie Jahoda, Herbert Marcuse, and Ernst Schachtel. Fromm and Schachtel were prominent in the interpersonal school that gave rise to the currently popular relational point of view in psychoanalysis. Some members of the Frankfurt group had direct contact with psychoanalysis and with Freud. Karl Landauer and Heinrich Meng of the Frankfurt Psychoanalytic Institute associated with the members of the Frankfurt Institute of Social Research, although they were not members (Jay 1973).

By the middle thirties, Fromm had begun his critique of instinctual drive theory and of the Oedipus complex, at the same time engaging a social critique of Freud's thought. In the light of this and related critiques, Hartmann's effort to place psychoanalysis, biology, and sociology within a unified framework has special significance. In 1946, Adorno gave a critique of the sociological revisionism of psychoanalysis by Fromm as well as by Horney, who had also published in the Institute's *Zeitschrift* in 1935 (Jay 1973). His argument was a defense of Freud's instinctual drive theory as a flexible view of strivings for pleasure and self-preservation with many variations. He rejected the charge of the revisionists that it was mechanistic. However, in his defense of Freud and the drives, Adorno also criticized the revisionists for their emphasis on the importance of the ego. This began to come perilously close to the kind of criticism from analysts to which Hartmann had already been subjected (A. Freud 1966) and would continue to have to answer. Clarification of an ego psychology clearly anchored in a theory of instinctual drives was an important agenda in two areas, theoretical and clinical.

Another intellectual current that Hartmann addressed was the thinking of the school of "understanding psychology." The work of that group of thinkers, especially Dilthey and Jaspers, was influential in German psychiatry and psychology. As Hartmann (1964) explained Dilthey's ideas, the latter rejected the possibility of going beyond description, experience, and understanding mind, that is, rejecting causal explanation in studying mind. He quotes Dilthey: "We explain nature, but we understand the mind" (p. 373). Hartmann adds that a sharp distinction is drawn between "natural and mental events" (p. 373) and the approaches used to gain knowledge of them. Hartmann's statement of the position of psychoanalysis might be considered a credo:

> Psychoanalysis advocates, as opposed to Dilthey's overestimation of mere description, the right of psychology to explain and construct hypotheses. It maintains that the task of psychology, as of other natural sciences, is the study of mental processes and of the laws regulating mental activity. . . . Furthermore, psychoanalysis claims that phenomenological research is only one condition, though an essential one, for the fulfillment of its task. [p. 374]

Thus Hartmann in 1927. What Hartmann called "understanding psychology" came to be referred to as "meaning psychology" and is conceptually related to the recent debates over the hermeneutic as opposed to the scientific view of psychoanalysis. Hartmann's clear insistence on the scientific status of psychoanalysis has, I believe, contributed not only to the eclipse of his former importance but to some extent initiated it. However, critics overlook the fact that Hartmann was rejecting the dichotomy of scientific and hermeneutic/phenomenological. Instead, he was including the latter as a part of what was to be treated scientifically.

Finally, for this discussion, at least, is the related conflict between the biological and the humanistic constructions of psychiatry and psychoanalysis. In a complex, admiring but critical discussion of Freud, Binswanger (1936) described the biological foundations of Freud's theories, showing their advance over the theories of Meynert and Wernicke. Binswanger understood the importance of Freud's work *On Aphasia* (1891) for the development of his theories, as well as the role of the historical dimension in biological concepts of development. However, he criticized the fact that what for him were aspects of an existential dimension in human experience were reduced by Freud to biological origins. Where this reduction was not possible, it seemed to Binswanger that Freud was looking forward to the time that it could be. He noted that in the theory, the ego was reduced to mechanism, and that in speaking of love, Freud lacked "a phenomenological description of what he understands by love . . . and this is even more important—what is missing is any interpretation and description of what he understands by 'self'" (p. 200). While speaking of the depersonalizing of man to "ego" by theory, he observed the fact that Freud also recognized the "dialogical character" of conflict. He added that when Freud wants to present the dialogical character of conflict, he leaves theory and tells a fairy tale to illustrate it. Binswanger acknowledged that "Freud has contributed more to the understanding of inner life history than any single person before him. We, however, distinguish our position from his in that we see the life-*historical* element as the fundament of 'anthropology,' "[by which he means, literally, the study of man] "while Freud sees therein only a 'pictorial language' for biological *events*" (p. 199n).

With regard to the psychoanalytic process, his criticism of Freud's medical-plus-research account of it sounds remarkably like the criticisms with which the Hartmann era ended. Of Freud's view he said; "He saw in the 'attitude' of the patient to the doctor only the regressive repetition of psychobiologically earlier parental 'object-cathexes' and eliminated what was *new* in the patient's *encounter* with him. Insofar as he did this he was able to keep the physician as a person in the background and allow him to pursue his technical role unencumbered by personal influences" (p. 202). The relationship to the current critiques of the objectivity of the psychoanalyst is evident (see Gabbard 1997).

I have gone into Binswanger's discussion at some length because his critique is at times so similar to recent critiques of Freud and of ego psychology. At the same time, Binswanger understood the origin, dimensions, and value of Freud's biological orientation. It appears that he did not so much think that it was wrong as that it was incomplete and one-sided. What it lacked for him was an existential view rooted in an "understanding psychology" dealing with "matrices of meaning" (see also Schafer 1970 on Binswanger). His essay also traces back to Griesinger the division in psychiatry between neurological and experiential views of pathology. He made the important point that much of what passed for neurophysiological explanation of mental activity was, in fact, simply the translation of experience into the language of physiology.

ON THE SIGNIFICANCE OF EGO AUTONOMY AND THE CONFLICT-FREE SPHERE IN HARTMANN'S WORK

My view is that the ego autonomy and conflict-free sphere make explicit something that most people take for granted: that there are inborn functions, such as memory and perception, that play a role in the development of the mind and that they may become involved in conflict, as in motivated forgetting and hysterical blindness, but that conflict may not be relevant to all their activities. We ordinarily take for granted that much memory and perception are reliable for practical use if nothing interferes with their development. In other words, these mental functions are independent variables in conflict (Hartmann 1964). As Hartmann noted, this does not mean that the functions and the contents produced by these functions do not have unconscious meanings. It is simply that under some circumstances those unconscious meanings are not relevant. When people are behaving rationally, he says, their behavior is predictable. This predictability does not depend on unconscious meaning for its explanation, but on its rationality. Of course, he also notes that, for this reason, such behavior may be of more interest to sociology than it is to psychoanalysis, whereas the unconscious meaning may be of no help to sociology. For the areas of overlap of interests, the development of a common language may be desirable.

Despite Hartmann's repeated efforts to the contrary, his critics continued to refuse to recognize the role, or perhaps meaning, of independent variables involved in conflict. It was as though the relativity of autonomy in the layered hierarchy that Hartmann, like Freud, described referred to absolute separation of functions, and "conflict-free" meant "purified of conflict." Although Hartmann (1939) took pains to explain interdependent thinking (Friedman 1989), and the difference between genesis through conflict and involvement in conflict, these other interpretations persisted. So, too, did the misreading of adaptation as adjustment on a social level.

Traditionally, psychoanalysis became interested in these ego functions only when they were involved in conflict, but it never assumed that they didn't exist unless there was conflict. For example, the normal functioning of memory and perception were assumed to obey their own laws, but this was studied by other disciplines whose data was useful for some purposes. In 1895, Freud described an organization of memory that he formulated on the basis of his work with patients (Breuer and Freud 1895). By 1901, having begun to understand the role of various mental mechanisms in motivated forgetting, Freud began to formulate the role of those and other mechanisms in normal forgetting. Freud was, in fact, often at pains to determine the borders of psychoanalytic interest in such functions and the place at which questions could be answered only by other methods. He saw this as an important aspect of demonstrating the value of psychoanalysis to other fields.

From another angle, to speak of the involvement of a function, like vision, in conflict seems to imply that *in some sense* it doesn't have to be. This type of issue is a recurrent one in psychoanalytic discourse. We can recognize the presence of conflict when vision is impaired by it. We know that it can also be involved in conflict even when it is not impaired, but merely guided by conflict in certain directions and to certain contents preferentially. This leads to a consideration of the different ways—often referred to as levels—that conflict is involved in ordinary and pathological use of a function. How to describe these relationships is a theoretical question at what Hartmann considered a more abstract level.

Hartmann answered it by regarding such functions as ego functions that were a subject for a psychoanalytic psychology of the ego. In other words, Hartmann began to examine explicitly and systematically what was assumed by psychoanalysis implicitly: the existence of mental functions, such as memory, whose presence could be taken for granted but became the focus of psychoanalytic interest when they were disturbed—as in forgetting the name of Signiorelli—or when they were subject to special vicissitudes of development—as in infantile amnesia.

One theoretical option, not favored by Hartmann, although I like it, would be to consider the processes of adaptation as being inherently a matter of conflict, at first organismic in relationship to environment and internal in the regulations needed for the external adaptations. In that case, intrapsychic conflict would be another instance of these processes on the level of mind.

The consideration of a concept like infantile amnesia, a "normal" or at least common phenomenon, joins the psychoanalytic interest in development with other developmental considerations of the same phenomenon. Freud, and other observers, have noted that independent factors in the development of cognition influence the nature of memory in early, as compared with later, childhood. It is obvious that the same considerations apply for many developmental phenomena, such as those having to do with the sexual function. The psychosexual functions depend on the development of bodily functions having their own timetable. Freud at times offered formulations of developmental sequences and explanations about them that involved incorrect or questionable assumptions and generalizations that mingled biological and psychoanalytic observations with "common knowledge" and assumptions (Grossman and Kaplan 1988). He often used the observations from other fields when it suited him, but gave those observations a psychoanalytic interpretation, or used them to bolster a psychoanalytic thesis (Grossman 1997).

In interdisciplinary studies, Freud (1913) noted that the result is often unsatisfactory. However, he felt that the mutual understanding that it fostered was worth the effort. Psychoanalysis needs something from other fields, he thought, and they can learn something from psychoanalysis. In the case of boundary problems, when a phenomenon is looked at from two perspectives, such as biological and psychological, a new discipline develops to study the subject by new methods and concepts (Kaplan 1988). This is what has occurred with the development of a number of fields that study unconscious mental processes or development in a different sense from psychoanalysis. Nevertheless, Freud took it for granted that there were relationships between psychoanalysis and other fields on many levels, including the need for psychoanalysts to know something about them.

Hartmann's efforts to clarify issues at the borders of psychoanalysis were thus more in line with Freud's aims than many of his critics recognize. In Bergmann's terms, he was an extender of Freud's ideas in this area. He attempted to explore the way data from many sources, including clinical psychoanalysis, could be brought together to construct a picture of mind. Since this effort involved bringing together observations obtained by different methods, it also involved assimilating to one another different ways of thinking about any psychological phenomenon that could be observed in different ways. I believe that there is a relationship between this use of construction and construction in the clinical situation. The role of construction in the clinical situation, in science and in other areas, such as history and detective work, has been discussed by Waelder (1939, 1970).

Hartmann's work, therefore, was in part an effort to develop a framework that would permit a systematic utilization of observations and concepts from outside and within the psychoanalytic setting. By showing how such extra-psychoanalytic sources could be used and how psychoanalytic concepts could guide useful research in other fields, he tried to replace the common *ad hoc* and *unexamined* mingling of ideas from various sources. Again, it was a matter of making explicit and focusing on processes that ordinarily go on in clinical work and theorizing, where *Weltanschauung,* personal background or special interests, and life experience outside psychoanalysis provide the context for the psychoanalytic ideas that guide the psychoanalyst (see also Grossman 1995b, Sandler 1983).

However, making these issues of integrating different perspectives the focus of attention does not simplify matters. It brings to light problems and difficulties that go unrecognized even if their troublesome consequences are evident. Once the overlapping interests of various disciplines are discussed, the question of confirmations and correlations arise. It is often difficult to know whether analytic concepts studied by methods other than analysis are relevant to analysis, and whether they are, in fact, the same concept. Hartmann discussed these problems in terms that were elaborated by others.

The discussion of boundary problems suggests that some clarification of the boundaries of psychoanalysis is desirable. This is so in any case since the question of whether some consideration or another is psychoanalysis raises the same issue. This is another place where a person's preferences come into consideration. An analyst may decide that biology or philosophy or even an examination of the basis of the psychoanalytic ideas he holds to be correct or useful may not matter for his work.

Recently, the IJPA Discussion Group on the internet had a debate on the relevance to clinical work of some philosophical ideas about the meaning of objectivity, reality, and relativism in the clinical setting. Some felt that the current literature on the psychoanalyst's objectivity and subjectivity was muddled by the misuse of language, while others felt that such considerations had nothing to do with their work. The point I wish to make is that psychoanalysts decide to include and exclude some aspects of theory, and take interest in various other fields and disciplines whose point of view they take. This, in effect, creates a type of interdisciplinary boundary within psychoanalysis and among psychoanalysts.

Hartmann's choice of both the biological framework and the biological concepts, translated into the terms of ego psychology, as Freud had done, serves in a sense to represent biological function in the psychoanalytic picture of the mind. From this point of view, the autonomous ego functions and the conflict-free sphere are borderline concepts, like the instinctual drives, both representing the body's functions in mental functions, and creating demands for mental function. In a sense, Hartmann, in his integrative efforts functioned as the ego of psychoanalysis, integrating the various demands on analysis both from outside and from within.

HARTMANN'S CONTRIBUTION ON THE APPLICATION OF THEORY TO TECHNIQUE: THE PROBLEM OF SCOPE AND STYLE

Bergmann's discussion of Hartmann's ideas and those of his associates on technique provides a valuable introduction to the subject. It seemed that Hartmann could not, on the basis of his writings, convince psychoanalysts that his work was relevant to their clinical concerns. A. Freud (1966) wrote about the "extraordinary opposition" that met his ideas because of the degree to which he turned away from psychopathology and "the clinical concerns of the analyst in practice" in favor of theoretical thinking. She added: "But, above all, there were many who feared that the explicit introduction of an ego psychology into psychoanalysis endangered its position as a depth psychology, a discipline concerned exclusively with the activity of the unconscious mind" (p. 17). An alternative to the idea that Hartmann's ideas were not psychoanalytic was that they were obvious and had always been known (Benjamin 1966). Either way, many readers remained unconvinced that those ideas could help them clinically.

Equally problematic was the fact that some therapists and analysts attempted to treat metapsychological formulations as directly applicable to interpretation. Loewenstein (1970) addressed these issues as follows: "Some believe that Hartmann was *a theoretician only*. But . . . there were always data of observation underlying his generalizations. On the other hand, he was well aware that even ordinary clinical observation tacitly includes theoretical assumptions and hypotheses. What was characteristic of Hartmann's thought was that he would formulate his ideas in general or abstract terms, without mentioning the observations related to them" (p. 14).

Just as Hartmann's theory at the most general level presented a framework for considering the full range of psychoanalytic concepts, his comments on technique provided a framework for considering its relationship to theory. He wrote that "Theoretical concepts helped at various stages and in various ways to facilitate the organization of the data observed (actually also to seeing the facts), and to advance the exactness and effectiveness of technique" (1964, p. 142). Incidentally, we can see here the balanced interactional view and the "modern" view of theory-laden observation in a single sentence. This, too, is characteristically Hartmann.

Expanding these remarks, Hartmann considered the relationship of theory and technique, the *varying influences* of one upon the other, in more detail. He wrote: "While proceeding along these lines from psychology to technique, we are of course aware of the fact that psychoanalytic technique is more than a mere application of psychological theory. . . . To characterize the present, we may say that we know some general technical principles that help us to avoid some typical mistakes, and in the summarized experience of skilled analysts we have at our disposal a huge potential reservoir of specific technical knowledge, which, in the course of training analysis and supervision, is transmitted to students of analysis. . . . we are trying to develop some rules somewhere in between the generality of acknowledged technical principles and the specificity of clinical experiences, some *principia medica*, to choose a term used by J. S. Mill. That is to say, we study variations of our technical principles according to each patient's psychological structure, clinical symptomatology, age level, and so on" (pp. 143–144). His further discussion considered the interplay of the rational and unconscious elements in our work and the consequent need for flexibility. In these comments, we can see Hartmann's attempt to provide a plan for the way to proceed from theoretical generalities to immediate clinical specifics.

However, the scope of Hartmann's framework presents a problem in itself. In a sense, a theory can be too big and do too much. Because Hartmann tried to encompass so much, to reorient and reconceptualize the implications of Freud's framework, his work suffers from considerable compression. In a manner similar to Freud's way of writing, Hartmann attempts to outline an entire hierarchy and its variations in a few paragraphs. For example, in the few remarks just quoted, Hartmann begins with the role of theoretical concepts in organizing observations and in recognizing the data as data—the influence of theory on observation that has become a contemporary slogan. By the end of a couple of paragraphs, he has mentioned the means of teaching the application of technical principles and the role of both rational and inevitable unconscious factors in clinical work.

The scope and depth of Hartmann's theorizing makes discussion difficult, as in the case of Freud's work. In both cases, there are widely different readings in which it is difficult to know whether what we say adds something, corrects something, or discovers implications that become clear only when they are spelled out. Shaw (1989) writes about this dilemma in her discussion of *Ego Psychology and the Problem of Adaptation*. She concludes that Hartmann's work serves to provoke reflection that leads to better understanding, rather than providing a logical explanation and clarification of concepts. Schafer's (1970) comments on perspective from above in discussing Hartmann, as Hartmann takes a perspective from above Freud's ideas, is a response to the need for an all-encompassing overview in order to evaluate the significance of the component parts of the theory.

I believe that these difficulties contribute to the reactions to Hartmann's work, though obviously they are only a part of the story. Hartmann clearly saw the need for ways to join clinical thinking and understanding with theoretical thinking and insight; he did not deal in detail with the conceptual links that he mentioned except to note the linkage provided by teaching and practice. Consequently, the effort to describe those links and to conceptualize those processes was left to others.

Subsequent developments in psychoanalytic theory in the direction of finding experience-near language and theory can be viewed as carrying out that program. In that sense, Hartmann's formulations and their limitations stimulated closer attention to the psychoanalytic process and its conceptualization. By the mid-1950s, the added stimulus to studies of technique provided by the treatment of personality disorders was evident in Stone's (1954) paper on the "widening scope" and in panels devoted to borderline patients (Rangell 1955, Robbins 1956), variations in analytic technique (Loewenstein 1958) and ego distortions (Waelder 1958). By 1970, at the time of Hartmann's death, Kernberg had laid the foundations for a theory and treatment of borderline personality disorders that integrated ego psychological conceptions with aspects of Kleinian and related object relations theories.

My point in repeating these well-known facts here is to indicate their place in filling a gap in Hartmann's work, continuing the development of the fundamental conceptions while elaborating them in novel directions. Hartmann believed that there had been a lag in the application to technique of a highly developed theory. However, I believe that the developments I've mentioned involved important modifications in both theory and technique.

COUNTERCURRENTS IN THE HARTMANN ERA AND AFTER

I have subtitled my paper "On The Interplay Of Different Ways Of Thinking" because this is one way to characterize the subject matter of psychoanalysis and its boundaries, as well as its history and its controversies. So far, I have tried to outline the way Hartmann's ideas were a response to some different ways of thinking. In the process, he evidently thought it was important to formulate psychoanalytic theory in explanatory terms and to establish its scientific position in psychology. He asserted its scientific status and the possibility of precision in applying psychoanalytic knowledge to the description of and progress in the clinical situation. In my view, he did an excellent job of this to the extent that it can be done. However, it was ultimately flawed, as later discussion has shown, partly because of his idea of what a science should be. What seems really valuable to me is the extent to which he discerned the relationship between clinical and experimental observation and theory, and the process of theory formation in psychoanalysis. With this contribution, he stimulated vigorous reconsideration of these issues, as well as greater efforts at clarifying various aspects of the clinical situation. His authoritative and knowledgeable assertions of his positions helped to bring out the assumptions underlying them. Many of these assumptions have been challenged and recast in the nearly thirty years since his death. In the following pages, I shall mention some of the social and intellectual developments, both in and outside of psychoanalysis, that have influenced its recent history.

Many analysts have commented on the rejection of logical positivism and of the myth of the scientific method in the history of science. These and other critiques were applied to metapsychology with the charge that it is not psychology at all. Freud's and Hartmann's metapsychologies, in particular their reliance on the economic point of view and the tendency to reification of structural concepts, were the focus of particular criticism. Most recently, Brenner, a former supporter of the structural theory, has rejected some parts of it. A variety of forms of "person psychologies" have been offered as a substitute for Hartmann's ego-plus-self agencies.

Another line of critique, not unrelated to the above, is the rejection of Freud's and Hartmann's claims for the scientific status of psychoanalysis. At various times, this point of view has been associated with the positivistic critique by Hartmann's philosopher and psychoanalyst contempories. Later, the ascendance of the both the hermeneutic interpretation of psychoanalysis (Habermas, Ricoeur) and the post-modern critique of science rejected the claims of both Freud and

Hartmann. The claim that psychoanalysis is a science stirred controversy that is still very much alive, although to some extent the arguments have changed (e.g., Shevrin 1995). I have discussed some of the problems in thinking about the question even if it is agreed that the usual criteria for scientific *proof* can't be met by clinical psychoanalysis (Grossman 1995a).

Hartmann, Klein, Lacan, and Kohut were the pinnacle in psychoanalysis of what has been called "grand theory." During the Hartmann era, "grand theory" came under attack. The goal of having an all-encompassing theory began to give way in many fields, and in psychoanalysis, too. Hartmann had noted in passing the influence of theory on observation. Greater attention to that fact contributed to the realization that the line between theory and observation was being blurred in psychoanalysis. Hartmann's insistence that psychoanalytic concepts were explanatory and not descriptive was seen as problematic and was the subject of debate. In fact, the clarity of this distinction began to be questioned. It was gradually recognized that the line between explanation and description that Hartmann had been at pains to emphasize might, on principle, not always be as sharp as he had wished. In anthropology, for instance, the idea of "thick description" as an aim replaced the goal of making observations in order to demonstrate existing theories, on the idealized model of physical science.

Investigators in other fields—anthropologists, historians, linguists, and students of animal behavior, to name a few—began to question the basis for existing theories of human nature, explicit or implied, and challenged assumptions that their predecessors had accepted as fundamental. With new perspectives, they began to accumulate a wealth of new observations. This was, in fact, a broad social trend, as well. In other fields, as in psychoanalysis, changed attitudes toward authority in society at large led to reconsideration of all theories relating to women, and in animal research to the place of females in animal societies. In our field, these changed attitudes were also expressed in efforts to reconsider the basis for psychoanalytic thought and practice. While stimulating and productive in many ways, this trend seemed also to support the growth of antitheoretical sentiment in psychoanalysis. In addition to the problems of theory, technique, and exposition that fostered these changes, I believe that the authoritarian and elitist tendencies of psychoanalytic training and treatment played a role as well (see also Kernberg 1996). This was the target of the more general social trends noted above.

These developments were combined with the increasing application of psychoanalytic treatment in cases of borderline and narcissistic personalities. The ego-psychological versions of the self and of object relations, as well as the emphasis on the exploration of the psychic surface were regarded as too theoretical and too removed from the necessary modifications of psychoanalytic technique. Although Hartmann had mentioned the necessity for flexibility in technique because of the gap between theory and technique, he hadn't explored the significance of this necessity. The fact that many observations of the ordinary variability in technique (e.g., A. Freud 1954) were not accounted for theoretically was recognized as a problem, and has been the object of greater interest in recent years. The result was a greater diversity of approaches.

These changing approaches dealt with greater attention to factors that had been summarized by Hartmann and those associated with him under the heading of timing and tact. This apt characterization had to be spelled out and expanded explicitly, since timing and tact were not accounted for theoretically or in relationship to specific problematic encounters in treatment. In a sense, they were left to mature judgment born of experience. The need for greater specificity regarding these concepts led later writers to concentrate on the frame of psychoanalysis, on narcissistic vulnerability, regard for the patient's point of view, and greater attention to the patient's capacity for understanding as this capacity was related to the transference and to character. The so-called "widening scope," greater attention to working with psychotic regressions during psychoanalysis, and the problems of analysis of borderline personalities when using so-called standard technique were associated with a broader conception of analysis and the analysis of transference and countertransference. Attention to the psychic surface and the patient's narcissistic vulnerability took on a wider meaning as well.

The changes in technique necessitated by the treatment of severe character disorders had come about through practical rather than theoretical reasons and could be justified theoretically only in general terms. I believe this was a stimulus to the special formulations of the treatment and theory of borderline and narcissistic disorders by Kernberg and Kohut. Among European psychoanalysts, such as Fairbairn, Winnicott, Guntrip, Rosenfeld, and Balint, the treatment of these patients led to major revisions of technique and theory.

Bergmann has noted the roles of both Stone and Loewald, and from a different angle Kohut, in shifting psychoanalytic treatment into an *apparently* less metapsychologically formulated conceptualization of the therapeutic relationship. Perhaps it would be more accurate to say that it was a metapsychology whose aim it was to explain that area to which Hartmann had referred as somewhere in between the generality of acknowledged technical principles and the specificity of clinical experiences along with variations of our technical principles according to each patient's psychological structure, clinical symptomatology, age level, and so on. In Kohut's case, the technique was significantly modified, but his theory of the self seemed to bog down in a new metapsychology.

The associated emphasis on person-language rather than ego-language, and on hermeneutics, has been to some extent derived from the gradual infiltration into American psychoanalysis of European philosophical-psychoanalytic thought along these lines, especially since Hartmann's death. In part, the interest in the hermeneutic interpretation of psychoanalysis was stimulated by the interest that Lacan's work had for students of literature (e.g., the Yale French Studies publication called "French Freud") and the English translation of Ricoeur's book on interpretation in Freud's work.

The growing interest in language, semiotics, structuralism, and literary analysis found fertile ground in the mounting dissatisfaction with the yield from metapsychological reformulations as their limitations as general and clinical theory were recognized. Rapaport's students were an important source of dissent from metapsychological thought as science and support for psychoanalysis as a nonscientific system of meaning. The development of Schafer's ideas as they took shape in his paper on Hartmann's work was a special case of that line of changing thought (Schafer 1970).

Another powerful group of influences countering the Hartmann influence was the British middle school, especially the work of Winnicott, Fairbairn, and Guntrip, as noted above. Although rarely cited in this country, Brierley (1951) had addressed the problems of "metapsychology and personology." In reference to the theories of Melanie Klein, she offered a sober understanding of what it means to have a "scientific attitude" rather than a "creed" in regard to new ideas. Her work was in part commentary on the problems of analysts dealing with integrating theory and practice, as well as their difficulties with novelty and dissent.

Those varied points of view retained their relationships to Freud as a reference point, whether they saw themselves as critics or supporters of his views. During that period, it became evident that whatever point of view a psychoanalyst took regarding Freud, a different Freud could be found in each one's opinions. It was during this period, partly in response to Hartmann's work and the reactions to it here and abroad, that the problem of "many Freuds" began to be recognized and discussed.

Of course, everyone knew that the Kleinians read Freud differently than allegedly mainstream Freudians, or that the so-called dissident schools "misread" Freud. However, it had seemed reasonable to assume that there was one correct reading of Freud's work. If there were uncertainties, it might be that Freud was unclear. But even given these possibilities, there was something else as well. It was the growing recognition that the American Freud was different from the English and French Freuds, and the problem was put in these terms. André Green (1986), among others, has referred to this fact, and his own discovery that with a "return to Freud" advocated by Lacan he discovered that, in addition to the fact that Lacan's Freud was different from the American Freud, his own discovery of Freud was different from Lacan's. So in fact, there were many French Freuds, English Freuds, and American Freuds, and so on. This discovery of the late Hartmann era was a part of the expanding pluralism in psychoanalysis, paralleling similar phenomena in other fields. There was a growing realization that different cultures and different translations were contributing to different interpretations of theory and its conversion into practice. Furthermore, this intergroup phenomenon is visible among the members within the group, as I indicated earlier, and as exemplified by Green's experience noted above. It is also evident that multiple readings are inevitable for Hartmann and for any thinker of great range or system. (Schafer has written extensively on the significance of multiple readings.) Incidentally, this development in psychoanalytic history is an illustration of the recursive structure of thought processes in individuals and groups.

CONCLUSION

This selective overview of certain aspects of Hartmann's work and the Hartmann era has necessarily omitted a detailed examination of the issues noted. I have not mentioned a number of people, such as Gedo and Gill, whose contributions have been important since the Hartmann period. In addition, I have devoted little attention to what I believe have been the productive continuations of the work of the group associated with Hartmann. This neglect has to do with the limitations of a paper and my own greater interest in the ways that controversies develop and evolve. Psychoanalysis as a field of study has confronted the many divergences within its societies and the broader social pressures to which it has been subjected during and after the Hartmann era. This process is still going on. As I have tried to show, the scope and depth of Hartmann's work and that of his contemporaries was a powerful stimulus to the extension of psychoanalytic interests and the examination of its fundamental concepts and outlook. The many differences of point of view that mark the current psychoanalytic scene reflect differences in thinking that have been around, although muted, for a long time. I believe that Hartmann's work still provides a starting point for the consideration of many issues, particularly those having to do with the integration of psychoanalytic thought with other fields of interest. The interdisciplinary stimulus Hartmann's conceptions provided are now finding expression in the current efforts of analysts to integrate ego psychology with neuropsychological and psychopharmacological discoveries and thought (e.g., Marcus 1992).

This having been said, the clinical relevance of Hartmann's thought is still exerting its influence in less obvious ways. His keen awareness of the subtleties of the interplay of theory and technique may yet provide a framework for their integration.

SUMMARY

Martin Bergmann's comprehensive and searching exploration of the Hartmann era has provided a stimulating opportunity to consider again the work of Hartmann, and his close collaborators, Kris and Loewenstein. Bergmann's work raises many interesting questions, not only about Hartmann but also about the development of psychoanalytic ideas and controversy.

In my paper, I have tried to explore and clarify some of Hartmann's ideas without defending them or offering my own critique. The former would be pointless and the latter would involve a kind of conceptual analysis of limited interest on this occasion. Instead, I have suggested that an understanding of Hartmann's contributions and limitations can be usefully approached by a consideration of the intellectual currents of his time and prevailing ideas in psychoanalysis. The latter included various attitudes, positive and negative, regarding Freud's ideas, as well as attitudes toward clinical psychoanalysis and to relevant research. In addition, problems of terminology and the meaning of metapsychological concepts in Freud's work occupied considerable attention in a way alien to current thought. The clarification of Freud's metapsychology along the lines of Hartmann and Rapaport reached a peak with them and ceased to be of widespread interest.

A point to be made about Hartmann's work: More than anyone I know, Hartmann attempted to explore the ways in which psychoanalytic clinical observation and findings could be integrated with findings obtained by other means of observation. Psychoanalysis could be informed by them, as Freud frequently indicated, as exemplified by his recommendations for the psychoanalyst's background. And psychoanalysis could inform other fields, as Freud had indicated in his paper on the claims of psychoanalysis to interests of other fields. Hartmann was in this way constructing a framework in which a more complete understanding of human mental function could be obtained. This involved detailed consideration of the relationships of psychoanalysis to other fields. He also attempted to provide rationales for integrating diverse kinds of information and theories. He pointed to critical issues associated with his own and other people's efforts of this kind. This integration also involved him in detailed thinking about the complex and variegated nature of psychoanalytic ideas, as well as outlining the complexities of the psychoanalytic situation, including problems of the analyst's objectivity and subjectivity. In summary, he was attempting to contribute to the systematization of psychoanalytic ideas, which the field lacked and still does. I think that this is what Hartmann meant by saying that psychoanalysis was a general psychology. I don't think he meant that psychoanalysis explains or includes everything. His various comments say that psychoanalysis is a general psychology in that it is not simply about psychopathology. Instead, it had something to contribute to and learn from any other kind of study of people's mental function however expressed (e.g., behavior, biology, group behavior). In this respect, he was the ego of psychoanalysis, and like the rest of us his vision of psychoanalysis reflected his own interests. He attempted to locate psychoanalysis in relation to the intellectual currents of the time.

These interests of Hartmann's are relevant to the question of why Hartmann's work has been disregarded and rejected. Many if not most analysts, especially clinicians, have limited interest in Hartmann's kind of conceptual analysis and critique. Since Hartmann did not have a gift for simple and elegant presentation of complex thinking, I think the neglect of his work has as much if not more to do with the difficulty of his writing style and exposition as with the content of his ideas. The relevance of his thinking to daily experience of the practicing psychoanalytic clinician was difficult to grasp and probably served as a rationale for some distant and pseudoscientific approaches to analytic work.

In my paper, I have tried to supplement Martin Bergmann's excellent summaries of the work of Hartmann's contemporaries, especially within the Hartmann circle, with indications of some of the other currents of thought to whose ideas Hartmann sought to respond from a psychoanalytic viewpoint. Even when he did not specifically offer rebuttals to antipsychoanalytic criticism from phenomenological psychiatry, hermeneutic approaches, interpersonal and other post-Freudian schools, it is possible to discern in some of his formulations the hidden opponents to whose views he addressed himself.

References

Benjamin, J. D. (1966). Discussion of Hartmann's *Ego Psychology and the Problem of Adaptation.* In *Psychoanalysis—A General Psychology. Essays in Honor of Heinz Hartmann,* ed. R. M. Loewenstein, et al. New York: International Universities Press, pp. 28–44.

Bergmann, M. (1993). Reflections on the history of psychoanalysis. *Journal of the American Psychoanalytic Association* 41:929–955.

Binswanger, L. (1936). Freud and the Magna Charta of clinical psychiatry. In *Being-in-the-World: Selected Papers of Ludwig Binswanger,* ed. J. Needleman. New York/London: Basic Books, pp. 182–205.

Breuer, J., and Freud, S. (1895). Studies on hysteria. *Standard Edition* 2.

Brierley, M. (1951). *Trends in Psycho-Analysis.* London: Hogarth.

Freud, A. (1954). The widening scope of indications for psychoanalysis. *Journal of the American Psychoanalytic Association* 2(4): 607–620.

———— (1966). Links between Hartmann's ego psychology and the child analyst's thinking. In *Psychoanalysis—A General Psychology. Essays in Honor of Heinz Hartmann,* ed. R. M. Loewenstein, et al. New York: International Universities Press, pp. 16–27.

Freud, S. (1891). *On Aphasia,* tr. E. Stengel New York: International Universities Press, 1953.

———— (1901). The psychopathology of everyday life. *Standard Edition* 6.

———— (1913). Totem and taboo. *Standard Edition* 13:1–161.

———— (1926). The question of lay analysis. *Standard Edition* 20:183–250.

Friedman, L. (1989). Hartmann's *Ego Psychology and the Problem of Adaptation. Psychoanalytic Quarterly* 58(4):526–550.

Gabbard, G. O. (1997). A reconsideration of objectivity in the analyst. *International Journal of Psycho-Analysis* 78:15–26.

Green, A. (1986). *On Private Madness.* London: Hogarth.

Grossman, W. I. (1992). Hierarchies, boundaries, and representation in a Freudian model of mental organization. *Journal of the American Psychoanalytic Association* 40(1): 27–62. Reprinted with additional material in *Hierarchical Concepts in Psychoanalysis: Theory, Research, and Clinical Practice.* ed. A. Wilson and J. E. Gedo. New York: Guilford, 1993, pp. 170–202.

———— (1995a). Commentary: "Psychoanalysis as science" by H. Shevrin. *Journal of the American Psychoanalytic Association* 43:1004–1015.

———— (1995b). Psychological vicissitudes of theory in clinical work. *International Journal of Psycho-Analysis* 76:885–899.

———— (1997). Freud's presentation of "the psychoanalytic mode of thought" in *Totem and Taboo* and his technical papers. In press.

Grossman, W. I., and Kaplan, D. M. (1988). Three commentaries on gender in Freud's thought: a prologue on the psychoanalytic theory of sexuality. In *Fantasy, Myth, Reality: Essays in Honor of Jacob A. Arlow,* ed. H. P. Blum, Y. Kramer, A. K. Richards, and A. D. Richards. New York: International Universities Press.

Hartmann, H. (1939). *Ego Psychology and the Problem of Adaptation.* New York: International Universities Press, 1958.

———— (1964). *Essays on Ego Psychology.* New York: International Universities Press.

Heiman, N., and Grant, J., eds. (1974). *Else Frenkel-Brunswick: Selected Papers. Psychological Issues* 8 (3) Monograph 31.

Jay, M. (1973). *The Dialectical Imagination: A History of the Frankfurt School and the Institute of Social Research 1923–1950.* Boston and Toronto: Little, Brown.

Kaplan, D. M. (1988). The psychoanalysis of art: some ends, some means. *Journal of the American Psychoanalytic Association* 36(2):259–293.

Kernberg, O. F. (1996). Thirty methods to destroy the creativity of psychoanalytic candidates. *International Journal of Psycho-Analysis* 77:1031–1040.

Kris, E. (1952). *Psychoanalytic Explorations in Art.* New York: International Universities Press.

Loewenstein, R. M. (1958a). Remarks on some variations in psychoanalytic technique. *International Journal of Psycho-Analysis* 39(2):202–210.

———— (1958b). Variations in classical technique: concluding remarks. *International Journal of Psycho-Analysis* 39(2):240–242.

———— (1970). Heinz Hartmann 1894–1970. *International Journal of Psycho-Analysis* 51(4): 417–419.

Loewenstein, R. M., et al. (1966). *Psycho-Analysis—A General Psychology. Essays in Honor of Heinz Hartmann.* New York: International Universities Press.

Marcus, E. R. (1992). *Psychosis and Near Psychosis: Ego Function, Symbol Structure, Treatment.* New York: Springer-Verlag.

Rangell, L. (1955). Panel: the borderline case. *Journal of the American Psychoanalytic Association* 3(2):285–298.

Robbins, L. (1956). Panel: The borderline case. *Journal of the American Psychoanalytic Association* 4(3):550–562.

Sandler, J. (1983). Reflections on some relations between psychoanalytic concepts and psychoanalytic practice. *International Journal of Psycho-Analysis* 64(1):35–45.

Schafer, R. (1970). An overview of Heinz Hartmann's contributions to psychoanalysis. *International Journal of Psycho-Analysis* 51(4):425–446.

Shaw, R. R. (1989). Hartmann on adaptation: an incomparable or incomprehensible legacy? *Psychoanalytic Quarterly* 58(4):592–611.

Shevrin, H. (1995). Is psychoanalysis one science, two sciences, or no science at all? A discourse among friendly antagonists. *Journal of the American Psychoanalytic Association* 43:963–985.

Stone, L. (1954). The widening scope of indications for psychoanalysis. *Journal of the American Psychoanalytic Association* 2(4):567–594.

Waelder, R. (1939). The criteria of interpretation. In *Psycho-Analysis: Observation, Theory, Application: Selected Papers of Robert Waelder*, ed. S. A. Guttman. New York: International Universities Press, pp. 189–199.

——— (1958). Neurotic ego distortion: opening remarks to the panel discussion. *International Journal of Psycho-Analysis* 39(2):243–244.

——— (1970). Observation, historical reconstruction, and experiment: an epistemological study. In *Psycho-Analysis: Observation, Theory, Application: Selected Papers of Robert Waelder*, ed. S. A. Guttman. New York: International Universities Press, pp. 635–676.

Wallerstein, R. S. (1990). Psychoanalysis: the common ground. *International Journal of Psycho-Analysis* 71:3–20.

6
The Hartmann Era: Reflection on an Overview by Martin S. Bergmann

Otto F. Kernberg

Martin Bergmann's comprehensive, profound, and challenging essay brings back to us a major development in the history of psychoanalysis, the Hartmann era, that began in the United States in the late 1940s and reached its maximum development in the 1950s and 1960s, to gradually come to an end in the 1970s. The richness of some of the contributions of the Hartmann era includes, among others, Rapaport's revolutionary contributions to psychological testing, the technical implications of Otto Fenichel's contributions to ego psychological character analysis, Ernst Kris's description of the "personal myth" and the "good psychoanalytic hour," and the contributions to early pathology of object relations pioneered by Erikson and continued by Jacobson and Mahler. In highlighting this era's strengths and weaknesses, its contributions and flaws, Martin Bergmann's essay covers a broad spectrum of ideas ranging from theory to technique, and from the application of psychoanalytic thinking to other scientific fields to the institutional implications of the extraordinary dominance of a coherent set of theoretical and technical principles. Hartmann's approach to ego psychology constituted, for a time, almost a monopoly within American psychoanalytic contributions. The very comprehensiveness of Martin Bergmann's overview lends itself to highlighting some particular issues touched by him, and I shall make use of the structure of his own essay to raise questions and convey my viewpoint regarding his historical analysis.

The first point regarding the contributions of the Hartmann group mentioned by Bergmann is the Hartmann group's effort to systematize psychoanalysis. Bergmann states: "The truly great discoveries of psychoanalysis, such as the Oedipus complex, transference and free association, are behind us, but, like a conqueror who rushes forward leaving unexplored territory behind him, Freud did not stop to systematize his findings. Trained clarifiers are needed to coordinate various propositions. Psychoanalysis is in dire need of systematization." Here may lie a major problem with Hartmann's approach: Freud indeed "rushed forward leaving unexplored territory behind him," but these territories themselves demanded further exploration, and had not yet been explored in all their richness. From a methodological viewpoint, the effort to systematize Freud's conclusions rather than to explore psychoanalysis further utilizing his methodology may have been a major limiting factor in Hartmann's contributions.

From the perspective of work carried out contemporaneously to Hartmann in the British schools, in the developments of French psychoanalysis, and in Latin America, the complexity of the Oedipus constellation was gradually explored, and the Oedipus situation as a basic structure of the experience of the reality—in contrast to conceptualizing it only as a phase of development—was gradually clarified. The condensation between oedipal and preoedipal conflicts under the dominance of primitive aggression; the nature of the archaic oedipal structure in contrast to advanced oedipal fantasy and constellation; the nature of the transference, its manifestation as an indissoluble condensation of internalized object relations and drive derivatives expressed in affective communication, and the intimate connection between transference and countertransference; the vicissitudes of free association as distorted by severe character pathology, the importance of the linguistic style of communication as an expression of character defenses; all of these crucial areas still remained to be explored, in terms of their clinical relevance as well as their theoretical implications. In contrast to this explosion of new psychoanalytic discoveries elsewhere, a systematic integration of Freud's conclusions represented the danger of a premature closure, a premature fixation of psychoanalytic theory and technique, an implicit resistance to the development of new psychoanalytic knowledge.

The second point regarding the contributions by the Hartmann group mentioned by Bergmann (1920) refers to the "cherished beliefs of Freud that no longer meet the test of science (and that) have to be weeded out. The two prime examples were Freud's acceptance of the Lamarckian view that acquired characteristics are inherited and Freud's belief in the death instinct." Obviously, theoretical assumptions that, in Freud's writings, reflected the developments within sciences at the boundary of psychoanalysis at that time and that no longer corresponded to new scientific developments, needed corrections, and a reexamination of Freud's views. Freud's intuitive shying away from a too-close linkage with dominant neurophysiological principles of his day, his developing a purely psychoanalytic science with the expectation that eventually new linkages would be established between psychoanalytic science and boundary fields, provided him with the freedom to develop new psychoanalytic formulations, as well as challenging later generations of psychoanalysts to reexplore these boundaries.

However, the rejection of the death drive—as not meeting the test of science—was only the major manifestation of a general tendency in Hartmann's theoretical formulations, namely the deemphasis on primitive aggression and sexuality. Whatever one may think about the relationships between the psychoanalytic theory of drives and the biology of instincts, the clinical manifestations of drives in the form of primitive destructiveness and self-destructiveness, in fact, the overpowering nature of primitive aggression as it infiltrates sexuality and reveals itself in sadomasochism, in the self-destructiveness of individuals and groups, organizations and nations was practically neglected by Hartmann. And that also affected the exploration of primitive sexuality and perversion. The "sanitized" nature of his presentation of Freudian theory may have been one reason for its easy acceptance within the conventional American culture of the day.

The "optimism" implied in Hartmann's stress on the adaptive principle and ego functions, at a time when the history of mass murder in Nazi Germany and Communist Russia became widely known dramatically illustrates, I believe, Hartmann's underestimating Freud's discovery regarding the profound self-destructive nature of human beings, the enormous potential for primitive hatred and cruelty underneath the veneer of civilization and the importance of further exploration of what almost derisively, during the Hartmann era, in the United States, was designated as "id psychology." Here the concepts of primary autonomy, secondary autonomy, and particularly neutralization constituted, I believe, major "breaks" in the consideration of the unconscious infiltration of conflicts around sexuality and aggression into conscious functioning. Hartmann never really explained the concept of neutralization in any way that would convincingly be related to clinical experience, while subordinating the clinically meaningful concept of sublimation to neutralization. The fact that the Kleinian school, at the same time, had proposed that the integration of loving and hateful, idealized and persecutory internalized object relations would bring about their mutual toning down and lead to the depressive position might have merited at least a thoughtful discussion rather than the institutional suppression in the United States of the study of the British schools. In all fairness, however, it needs to be stated once again that the intolerance of the study of alternative theoretical formulations was a general institutional characteristic of the psychoanalysis of the 1950s and 1960s, both in the ego psychological and in the Kleinian camp.

The third point mentioned by Bergmann is Hartmann's emphasis on developmental psychology and on infant and child observation. While the controversy regarding the relevance of infant observation for psychoanalytic theory and practice still continues to occupy our attention, I believe that, on principle, Hartmann's proposal—that the correlation and integration of direct infant and child observation with the findings from the psychoanalytic exploration of children and adults might enrich our knowledge and confirm our hypotheses regarding earliest development—is eminently reasonable. In practice, however, the enormous methodological difficulties implied in such an endeavor were clearly underestimated by Hartmann, and perhaps even by the work of Margaret Mahler, a profound and astute observer (whose contributions unjustifiably, I believe, have been neglected in recent times.) The problem here lies in the natural tendency to observe infants at relatively quiescent or "low affect activation" conditions, to underestimate the importance and early development of unconscious fantasy, and to condense prematurely the empirical observations regarding neuropsychological functions and structures such as affects, perception, and psychomotor integration with the nature of primitive unconscious fantasy. I believe that, in principle, this is a rich field that sometimes is underexplored by the descriptive naïveté of infant observers. What is of particular interest here is that Hartmann, while attempting the development of a general theory linking the biological substrate of behavior with intrapsychic development and the social matrix of human experience, practically neglected all concrete reference to psychoanalytic data, as well as other data indicating the nature of the interchange at the boundaries between the intrapsychic, the psychobiological and the psychosociological. His theory became an integrative system mostly devoid of empirical evidence . . . or curiosity.

The fourth point referred to by Bergmann is Hartmann's theory "that the ego was the organ of adaptation." Here the issue of the individual's relationship with an "average expectable environment," particularly emphasized by Rapaport, conveys the impression, at least from hindsight, of an idealized view of the psychosocial environment, the impression of the viewpoint of a privileged class rather than of a generation haunted by the experiences of two world wars, brutal dictatorships, and totalitarian regimes, not to speak of racial and religious persecutions.

The fifth point, what Bergmann refers to as Rapaport's expression of a "moral fervor that lies behind the idea of ego autonomy," complements the view of a harmonious interrelationship between optimal capabilities of the individual and a facilitating environment, further limiting the impact of the drives and unconscious conflict.

Bergmann's sixth point is Hartmann's "change in function" and, as a consequence, "As the function changes in its new form it belongs to the autonomous part of the ego. It is therefore neither necessary nor desirable to analyze those parts of the personality that have undergone this change. As a result psychoanalysts became much more careful in what they analyzed and what they left unanalyzed." Here emerges another aspect of the emphasis on ego functions and adaptation, and the relative deemphasis on unconscious conflicts' influences on ordinary mental functioning. The corresponding implications for psychoanalytic technique are explored further in Bergmann's point 18, where he examines the specific contributions to psychoanalytic technique derived from Hartmann's, Kris's, and Loewenstein's ego psychological approach.

I agree with Bergmann's statement that the most important ego psychological contribution to psychoanalytic technique was, in fact, Otto Fenichel's *Problems in Psychoanalytic Technique* published in 1941, perhaps to this date the most important single contribution to the theory of interpretation. Fenichel provided the conceptual frame underlying *The Technique and Practice of Psychoanalysis* (1967) by Ralph Greenson, that provided a richness of clinical illustrations of Fenichel's approach. Bergmann points to the ego psychological approach of analyzing from surface to depth, the respect for the layering of ego defenses and impulse/defense configurations, and the need for adequate timing of interpretations.

The interpretive approach from surface to depth, from what is available to the patient's conscious and preconscious awareness to its unconscious roots, is eminently reasonable, and, by the way, was painfully discovered by the Kleinian analysts as well in their radical changes of their technical approach in the last twenty years. However, in practice, this approach during the Hartmann era also tended to remain relatively on the surface of the patient's material, to expand the technique of defense analysis at the expense of interpreting in depth the unconscious expressions of libidinal and aggressive drive derivatives, and the cautious timing of interpretations practically meant an enormous slowing down of analytic work as well as contributing to staying on the surface of the material. It was only Merton Gill's radical critique of the prevalent ignoring of early transference manifestations that changed the ego psychological attitude toward interpretation developed during the Hartmann years, pointing to the early manifestations of defenses against the awareness of the transference as well as against the development of transference proper, and bringing ego psychological technique closer to the British schools. Bergmann convincingly discusses the advantages and disadvantages of Kurt Eissler's concept of "parameters of technique," and the important function of Leo Stone's "Widening Scope of Psychoanalysis" to counteract the rigidity of the technical approach that had evolved within the ego psychological orientation.

In this connection, it is of interest to point out how both in the ego psychological approach and in the Kleinian approach in the 1950s and 1960s, the recognition of the importance of countertransference, and the breakdown of the phobic taboo of the analysis of its importance, paradoxically led to a reemphasis of the analyst's technical neutrality and, in addition, the stress on the anonymity of the psychoanalyst. In fact, the persistence of the traditional concept of the countertransference as the transference disposition of the analyst—to be overcome rather than to be technically utilized in the understanding of the transference—persisted in the ego psychological approach practically two decades beyond the shift toward the modern concept of countertransference as the total emotional reaction of the analyst in the British and Interpersonal schools, and the parallel emphasis on the mutuality of unconscious messages of patient and analyst within French psychoanalytic thinking.

The understanding that the emphasis on the analyst's anonymity is related to an unconscious institutional tendency to protect the idealization of the training analyst has only recently become a more generally shared concern. It may be an ironic and unexpected consequence that the stress on the analyst as a "mirror" that permeated the traditional Hartmann era technique in the United States should have given rise, at this point, to a sharp reaction and repudiation of that formulation on the part of the intersubjectivity approach, which tends to privilege the patient's experience of the psychoanalytic situation, and to both exaggerate the importance of the countertransference and to reduce the importance of its control in the psychoanalyst's behavior.

Bergmann's seventh point, Hartmann's consideration regarding schizophrenia, illustrates once more the pervasive use of the concept of neutralization and deneutralization of psychic energy as an umbrella concept to explain severe types of psychopathology. I do not know whether Hartmann analyzed schizophrenic patients, but the generalization of formulations regarding psychopathology in the absence of clinical data that characterizes most of his writings illustrates the highly speculative nature of Hartmann's formulations. In contrast, Edith Jacobson's careful theorizing about levels of severity of depression from the neurotic to the borderline to the psychotic based upon painstaking clinical observations illustrates what a careful observation of clinical phenomena within a psychoanalytic setting can contribute to the understanding of development, psychic structure, and psychopathology.

It is interesting that in his eighth point, in referring to the contributions of Hartmann and Loewenstein to superego formation, Bergmann should not mention Edith Jacobson's fundamental clarification of the development and layering of the superego. Edith Jacobson and Margaret Mahler, both very interested in the study of patients with severe psychopathology, were aware of the important contributions from the British school, as well as the danger of explicitly utilizing Kleinian concepts in the restrictive atmosphere of the Hartmann era in the United States. While sharply critical of the Kleinian developmental model, the telescoping of all development into the first year of life, the rigidity and indoctrinating quality of the then-dominant Kleinian technique, Jacobson and Mahler recognized the importance of the primitive object relations and defensive operations described by the Kleinian school, and used the concept of early splitting and later integration of aggressive and libidinal strivings in their developmental model. One may say that the "underground" introduction of contributions from the British school by these two authors generated a most creative contribution to the psychoanalytic understanding of severe psychopathology within an essentially ego psychological approach.

I was curious about Bergmann's presentation of Edith Jacobson's concepts under point eleven, "the development of a complex metapsychological vocabulary." Here I would separate the abstract generalizations proposed by Hartmann, such as neutralization, secondary autonomy, and the rarefied employment of the term "cathexis" from Jacobson's clinically relevant concepts of self and object representations, ideal and real representations of self and object and their function as "building blocks" of ego and superego. However, Hartmann's clarification of the concept of the self, contrasting it to the concept of the ego, was an important contribution, one that opened the possibility for Jacobson's and Mahler's introduction of an object relations frame into ego psychological metapsychology. Jacobson's and Mahler's conceptualizations, it seems to me, were always closely linked to clinical observations, "experience close," we might say, but at the same time particularly Edith Jacobson's work provided a framework for an integrated conception of development, structure formation, and psychopathology on a psychoanalytic basis that is relevant for present psychoanalytic understanding.

The twelfth and thirteenth points in Bergmann's essay summarize Hartmann's effort to transform psychoanalysis "into a general psychology with significant implications for all social sciences." In Bergmann's words, "Hartmann's concepts of neutralization of both the sexual and aggressive drives and his concept of the autonomous ego and its conflict-free sphere are the main bridges that lead from psychoanalysis as a theory of neurosis to psychoanalysis as a general psychology." Here we come to what may be called the most ambitious aspect of Hartmann's system, the incorporation of the entire field of psychology under psychoanalytic principles, in contrast to Freud's more circumscribed view of psychoanalysis as the science of the unconscious aspects of the mind and their influence on psychological functioning of individual, group, and culture.

What is most striking in Hartmann's effort is its generally theoretical nature, the almost total absence in his arguments of direct references to clinical observations of the nature of the unconscious, and also the lack of reference to any concrete evidence from boundary sciences that would strengthen the linkages between psychoanalysis and, say, the theory of perception, affects, or cultural influences on character formation. Hartmann's system would seem to neglect both the clinical psychoanalytic roots of his theory and the actual interface between psychic experience and biology, on one hand, and psychic experience and social and cultural structures, on the other. For example, the analysis of character structure, the modeling of character defenses following cultural modes and biases would have been a natural area for illustrating the application of psychoanalytic theory to the broader field of psychology and social psychology, such as the molding of sadomasochistic traits in terms of predominant cultural patterns. The fact that narcissistic pathology, for example, was explored mostly within the British schools, object relations theory, self psychology, and French psychoanalysis illustrates the lack of practical application of Hartmann's system to this fascinating area of psychoanalyst's exploration. Or else the lack of the application of psychoanalytic theory to mass psychology and ideology, a dramatic feature of life in Europe during the first half of this century, also points to the splendid isolation of the general system developed by the Hartmann group. Of course, no efforts evolved to clarify further the still-mysterious nature of the drives. It was as if this theoretical system would have to be accepted on faith by other disciplines, while in practice becoming gradually uninteresting to a new generation of psychoanalysts dealing with the increasingly severe psychopathology of patients approaching analysts' practices, and with psychoanalytic implications of the severe social and cultural conflicts affecting even the advanced democratic countries that emerged victorious from WWII. However, Bergmann appropriately points to the important contributions that ego psychology, particularly Erickson and Eissler, made to psychobiography, and to the analysis of art, especially with Kris's specific contribution to the study of regression in the service of the ego.

In reviewing the contributions of other leading theoreticians of the Hartmann era, Bergmann points to the importance of Spitz's approach to infant observation, and regrets the lack of utilization of complementary observations regarding early development from the British school. Because Winnicott seemed close to Melanie Klein, he was practically ignored in the cultural atmosphere of the Hartmann era in the United States. Bergmann convincingly focuses on the contributions of Jacobson and Mahler as providing an important clinical counterpart to Hartmann's abstract theory, and on the shift that Jacobson's and Mahler's work indicated toward preoedipal conflicts, in contrast to the stress on the centrality of the Oedipus complex in Hartmann's approach. The influence of the study of the early mother–infant relationship and of severe psychopathology of the first few years of life shifted the focus of analytic theorizing to preoedipal conflicts, defenses, and object relations.

In fact, both the British schools and the newly emerging object relations approach of Mahler and Jacobson (that, in passing, fundamentally influenced my own work with borderline and narcissistic pathology) contrasted with newer ego psychology (as represented, for example, in Arlow and Brenner's work) and with the French psychoanalytic renewed emphasis on the archaic manifestations of the Oedipus complex. Clinically, even in the most severe types of psychopathology encountered in adult psychoanalysis, I believe, one never finds cases in which preoedipal issues are not intimately condensed with primitive oedipal pathology.

The conception of linear models of development in contrast with hierarchical models that include synchronic/diachronic modes of functioning constitute an important contemporary controversy of psychoanalytic work. Here contemporary psychoanalytic theorizing has moved beyond the traditional linear ego psychology model of the Hartmann era. The study of earliest development now involves not only the study of the early relationship between symbiosis and separation, on one hand, and castration anxiety and the archaic oedipal constellation, on the other, but also a reexamination of the nature of psychic drives, their relationship to biological instincts, or rather to affects as hypothesized psycho-biological substructures of the drives.

The concept of drives and cathexes, their neutralization and deneu-tralization, their shifts, fixation, and displacements within Hartmann's system gave rise, as a violent reaction to the experienced rigidity of Freud-ian metapsychology in this country, to the antimetapsychology move-ment of Rapaport's disciples, and, from different quarters, to self psy-chology. I believe that these developments in the United States may be considered unexpected, almost ironic consequences of the Hartmann era, probably throwing out the baby with the bathwater in a questionable rejection of Freudian metapsychology. At the same time, particularly in the work of André Green and Jean Laplanche, French psychoanalysis, in close connection with the analysis of the vicissitudes of aggression and sexuality in the psychoanalytic setting, has made important contribu-tions to the contemporary study of libidinal and aggressive drives, and this work is also enriched, I believe, by the study of affect theory and its relations to drives developed in the contributions of Joseph and Anne-Marie Sandler and Rainer Krause.

The final section of Bergmann's essay, the passing of the Hartmann era, beautifully describes the changes introduced by Arlow and Brenner, the recent loss of interest in Hartmann's work, and the key functions of Loewald's classical paper in introducing, as part of his technical approach, object relations theory into ego psychological technique, opening the interest in the work of Winnicott and Balint, and beyond them, Fairbairn, Melanie Klein, and their main coworkers. It is of in-terest to wonder, in following Bergmann's thoughts, to what extent the certainty, comprehensiveness, and categorical nature of Hartmann's contributions reflected the ascent and triumph of psychoanalysis in the receptive scientific and particularly psychiatric ambiance of the United States at the end of the WWII. An overarching theory may have re-flected a triumphant institutional system. Perhaps the definite end of the Hartmann era came with Heinz Kohut, not because of the intrinsic content of his theory and clinical approach, but because he and his disciples courageously stood up to a large and highly critical majority, and were able to maintain themselves within the American Psychoana-lytic Association and the International Psychoanalytic Association without suffering the destiny of "dissidents" of earlier generations whose separation from the mainstream of psychoanalysis impoverished psychoanalytic dialogue. Self psychology, in its radical critique of ego psychology, opened the road for other alternative theories to be studied and tolerated in the United States, and for a creative dialogue to be initiated that, in one of its inspiring illuminating moments, is expressed in today's conference. This seems a good moment to keep in mind what we have learned within the Hartmann era, as a consequence of it, and to continue exploring the challenging and still-mysterious world of the psychology of the unconscious opened by Sigmund Freud. A premature effort to systematize psychoanalysis may not have done justice to its revolutionary, still-evolving nature, but it generated significant findings that will need to be incorporated in our advancing science.

7

Response to Bergmann's Assessment of the Hartmann Era

ANTON O. KRIS

Martin Bergmann's wise and comprehensive appraisal of what he calls the Hartmann era in psychoanalysis—more elegy than eulogy— tells a complex story. His justification for calling it the Hartmann era, although both Anna Freud and Ernst Kris made contributions to ego psychology before Hartmann, seems sound to me. *Ego Psychology and the Problem of Adaptation* (Hartmann 1939) presented a programmatic introduction to the contributions of the subsequent two decades in psychoanalytic research, theory, and technique for the group of Hartmann's close colleagues.[1] Bergmann's use of his own distinction between modifiers and extenders of theory proves especially helpful in demonstrating that Hartmann was clearly a modifier of Freud's theories, not extender alone, as he himself might have preferred to see it. The strands he identifies in the Hartmann era fabric seem to me well chosen, though I believe I may see them from a slightly different perspective. In my view, for example, the aim of *systematizing* psycho-

---

1. "It was quite clear," Loewenstein (1970) wrote of the joint work with Hartmann and Ernst Kris, "although never expressed, that our future work would build on the ideas formulated in *Ego Psychology and the Problem of Adaptation.*"

analytic theory, because it was linked too closely with logical positivism, proved to be a two-edged sword. I shall return to this topic shortly.

It would serve no useful purpose to comment on every point made in Bergmann's monograph, which ranges widely beyond the area of technique in its title. The orchestration and the rich coordination of voices, not the individual notes alone, create his music. Stimulated by his opus, I offer some additional comments on the same developments. Considering a few other threads in the fabric, I do not share the cited negative view of the promotion of child development investigation outside the analytic situation (pp. 12, 82), and, I believe, neither does Bergmann. Nor do I share the view that Hartmann "sought to reduce the role of conflict in psychic life" (p. 76). The "subject matter" of psychoanalysis "is human behavior viewed as conflict," Ernst Kris (1947) wrote in a paper that spoke for Hartmann and Loewenstein, as well— a paper cited favorably by Bergmann. Until 1926, as Loewenstein (1972) pointed out, Freud had formulated all ego development as the result of conflict. In presenting the developmental phase-specific anxieties, however, "for the first time, Freud described an aspect of ego development which, although it is involved in conflict, is not the result of conflict" (p. 2).[2] In following this line in Freud's work, Hartmann did not seek to reduce the role of conflict. He sought to reduce some excesses of Freud's prestructural theories.

I agree most thoroughly with Bergmann's emphasis on the unfortunate political aims of the Hartmann group, directed against the work of Melanie Klein and her followers on one side, and against the interpersonal school of psychoanalysis on the other. The banishment of Jacques Lacan, however justified by his provocativeness and however much in keeping with the authoritarianism of the times, lost them his powerful reading of Freud. These political aims closed off too many avenues to the preoedipal world as it influences the psychoanalytic situation.

Many of the faults that Bergmann attributes to "optimism," "enthusiasm," and "confidence" I would attribute to a regrettable, and re-

---

2. From early on, Freud had formulated development that was not the product of conflict on the *instinctual* side, in the epigenetic sequence of phases in infantile sexuality.

grettably still continuing, tendency among psychoanalysts to assume the establishment of facts and "evidence" where none exist. The Hartmann group and particularly their followers promoted their brand of psychoanalysis as if a large body of data supported the conclusion that their theories were truly superior. (I shall come to another root of the optimism shortly.) Intolerance of uncertainty and premature closure, despite public acknowledgment of the limitations of knowledge, have dogged psychoanalysis from its beginnings. And the beat goes on. The Hartmann era cannot be awarded special credit on that score.

From today's vantage point, I see the most significant innovation in Freud's listening to have been the recognition that his own unconscious processes were essential to the analytic dialogue. To cite the Specimen Dream, was the infiltrate in his own body or in Irma's? Having started with a position of radical subjectivity, Freud attempted throughout the rest of his life to regain a position of objectivity. Repeatedly, he asserted that psychoanalysis was a "scientific" procedure of quite a different sort, a straightforward, observational science, and that his therapeutic method was free of suggestion (Collins 1980). So he recognized the role of the analyst's unconscious as a "receptive organ" in listening to his patient's unconscious, but he demanded "psycho-analytic self-purification" in regard to countertransference (1912). Both points of view persist in his writings. His *inconsistency*, however, much of it expressed in *metaphors*, protected him from totally surrendering one side of this divergent conflict for the other. I have shown on an earlier occasion (1994), that the *political* aim of making psychoanalysis palatable *as science*, contributed to his insistence (1923) that the analyst's personality must not be employed in the analytic procedure, although he himself made excessive use of his own personality. Hartmann and his colleagues, I believe, drove this side of his message home. In doing so, however, they closed the door on an ingredient essential for the treatment of narcissistic patients. The clinical record is plain enough. North American psychoanalysts failed remarkably in their treatment of narcissistic patients, including those narcissistic patients whose difficulties were primarily neurotic rather than borderline, until the revolutionary work of Heinz Kohut and his followers in the late 1960s (A. Kris 1989, 1994).

In the aims of Hartmann and his colleagues I see the last gasp of nineteenth-century idealism, a commitment to technocracy, an adherence to positivism. They believed in Science, and they believed in Progress. Systematization and positivism go hand in hand in their work, and I do not believe that members of the Hartmann group appreciated sufficiently the hidden advantage in Freud's inconsistency. "In psychoanalytic writings metaphors tend to obscure the meaning of statements," Ernst Kris wrote in 1947 (p. 4). It would have been better, hindsight reveals, to say that metaphors coordinate multiple, often contradictory messages. The dialectic between subjectivity and objectivity seems to me an essential component of psychoanalysis, one that remains a lively and fruitful topic of psychoanalytic theory and discourse (A. Kris and Cooper 1995).

The optimism and confidence of the Hartmann group, to which Bergmann refers, comes, in part, I believe, from the extension of Freud's wish for a "scientific" psychology and the strength they drew from an enduring connection with Freud and what they saw as his ambitions for psychoanalysis.[3] It would be hard to overestimate the importance of that connection for those analysts at that time. So they failed to realize the loss entailed in their aim of producing a "general psychology" composed of hierarchically framed testable propositions.

The technical stance of the Hartmann group has been deplored by many, perhaps most brilliantly by Merton Gill (e.g., 1994), erstwhile adherent and later consummate critic. His emphasis on the proposition that "every interpretation is an action" profoundly influenced North American analysts in the 1980s, as they strained to come to terms with new analytic ideas from home and abroad. Although they had gained a subtle understanding of the ego and its development, freeing psychoanalysis from the limitations of prestructural technique, the Hartmann group was caught at the starting gate as other schools (followers of Ferenczi, Melanie Klein, Lacan, and, from a different direction, Sullivan), more open to ambiguity and contradictory meanings, focused on countertransference and handily won the race to the current finish line. Further, as Bergmann (p. 84) points out so clearly, Hartmann and

---

3. The intolerance of uncertainty that I mentioned earlier and the sense of close connection with Freud's aims contributed also to the moralistic tone to which Bergmann refers. For example, he notes "the development of a complex metapsychological vocabulary," (p. 22) "just being conceptualized, and yet those who did not understand them were accused of confusion" (p. 24).

his colleagues tended to treat only a restricted group of patients, because they failed to grasp the essentials of the preoedipal world. Limited in their use of their own personalities, and limited even more in understanding their own countertransference (under the impact of Freud's early view that countertransference must be analyzed away), they could not offer help in the form in which it was needed.

Bergmann's monograph is written at a particular moment. The members of the Hartmann group are now, with one exception, dead. From the period of social restraint in which they started, we have come to a remarkably different social condition. In our field, alternative theories have taken all the prizes. One must look carefully in Bergmann's account to find detailed references to the contributions to *technique* of the Hartmann period, although that is one of the two subjects of his title. He is so familiar, so at home with all those changes in technique that it is enough for him to mention the aim of gaining "double autonomy" from the drives and from the environment (p. 14), without spelling out the technical innovations entailed. He does, however, give a more complete account of the late clinical work of Ernst Kris (p. 63f). Bergmann concludes that with the cultural changes of the 1960s, others were more in tune with the new generation (p. 80).

My own objection to the work of the Hartmann group is that their overstatement of their theoretical position and their "political" motivations have resulted in the loss of much that is valuable and, I believe, even essential to psychoanalytic work. My own solutions to the problems they failed to solve have centered on an expanded concept of conflict. The concept of conflict employed by all psychoanalysts, following Freud's, was too narrow. It encompassed only what I call convergent conflict (1985, 1988, 1992), omitting divergent conflict altogether. At first, I thought that divergent conflicts[4] were identical with intrasystematic conflicts, which played an important part in Hartmann's thinking (1950) and in Anna Freud's (1966). But later I came to see that intrasystemic conflict was formulated as the dominance of one function over another, the exclusion of one tendency by another, on the model of intersystemic conflict. This created no place for conflicts in which an individual feels torn between two desires, for example, pro-

---

4. Initially, I referred to these as conflicts of ambivalence in distinction to conflicts of defense.

gressive and regressive tendencies. Those are the divergent conflicts. I have tried to demonstrate that an understanding of the two kinds of conflict, with their differences of form, resistance, process of resolution, and resulting insight, and their interaction offers a means of access to the tension between the oedipal world and the preoedipal world that is closed to a convergent-conflict-only approach. As Bergmann shows, the failure to address that tension and to be able to work effectively with patients whose pathology has very early roots proved to be the undoing of the Hartmann era.

Today's marching slogans lead to a curious result. Holding a much more benign, egalitarian attitude to their patients, and admirably open to the preoedipal world, many beginning analytic candidates have virtually no shame in revealing countertransference enactments and errors that, 40 years ago, would have driven some candidates from the field in traumatic humiliation. On the other hand, they feel theoretically adrift, unable to formulate the elements of psychoanalytic work. In his balanced assessment, Bergmann reminds us that "When one era passes its contribution is not erased" (p. 81). Loewenstein's (1972) illustrations of the technical applications of the concept of ego autonomy remain a masterful example of the archival riches to be mined. It remains to be seen, however, whether this generation will be able to restore the precision in formulating clinical situations that was the hallmark of the best of the Hartmann era. Martin Bergmann's monograph offers them a powerful start.

Bergmann returns, once more, in closing, to the question of child observation outside the analytic setting (p. 81f). Here, I part company with his even-handed presentation. It has taken over sixty years to develop a tradition of psychoanalytic research, against the opposition of Freud and, initially, Anna Freud (1958), against neglect by the vast majority of psychoanalysts and the major psychoanalytic organizations, and, except for a brief interval in the 1950s and 1960s, against repudiation by funding agencies. At a minimum such research, which includes work both inside and outside the analytic setting, will set boundaries on the uncontrolled speculations and assertions that have passed for theory, and I believe that this *can* and already *does* make a difference in the clinical situation of the analytic setting. New studies of infancy contradict earlier theoretical assumptions. Those who believe that research outside the analytic setting cannot contribute to work inside that setting seem to me to make the same kind of error that the

Hartmann group made in regard to countertransference and the preoedipal world. It is not either/or. True, unfortunate errors have been made in the past, and surely will be again, confusing levels of discourse. That hazard is hardly best dealt with by eliminating one category.

Finally, I want to join Martin Bergmann in personal disclosure. I feel honored to have been invited by Sidney Furst and the Psychoanalytic Research and Development Fund (who are, of course, aware of my close personal connection with several of the major participants in the Hartmann era) to engage in the discussion of Martin Bergmann's deeply thoughtful monograph. An early tendency to slavish partisanship has given way, in my case, for whatever reasons, to an interest in a widening scope, in many senses, in either/or conflicts, and in balanced resolutions. I gave up on formulating my own findings in terms of psychoanalytic metapsychology twenty years ago, choosing instead to use the method of free association as my point of reference.

Three personal observations seem me particularly relevant. First, the astonishing number of causalities in our field, among our own colleagues, at the hands of their teachers and their Institutes (or the Institutes that would not have them, or would have them only under demeaning conditions) has been a powerful influence on my development as an analyst and teacher. So far as I can tell, those casualties have been produced quite independent of theoretical persuasion and occurred as much, for example, among the followers of Melanie Klein as among those of the Hartmann group. I share Martin Bergmann's view that this unfortunate aspect of the Hartmann era was not essential in its failure to survive.

Second, the experiences of undertaking roughly 25 second or third analyses over the past twenty years, even when modified by the important corrective to those experiences of having a number of my own patients return for additional treatment after an interval of years, have led me to reappraise for the worse the analytic work of the generation of my teachers, who came to maturity during the Hartmann era. On the other hand, I think that Hartmann himself, owing mainly to his proclivity for theoretical formulation, but perhaps also for the limitations of his clinical stance, has taken something of a bad rap. "During the years of our collaboration I was also impressed by Hartmann's remarkable clinical acumen," Loewenstein (1970, p. 419) wrote in his obituary. "Nevertheless, in his writings clinical data were usually neglected or only alluded to. This was in accord with his belief that clinical observations per se were of secondary significance, that they acquired primary importance only as a part of a conceptual framework or by illustrating a general theory. This approach rested on his rare ability to formulate general concepts without ever losing the implicit tie to observable data" (Loewenstein 1970, p. 419).

Third, on a happier note, about ten years ago, in a situation of evaluating the clinical work of a number of analysts, chance placed me side by side with a leading analyst, perhaps twenty years older than myself, whose geographical origins, theoretical persuasion, and even personal connections could hardly have been better designed to create my polar opposite. The uncanny coincidence of our findings and evaluations, both positive and negative, of the clinical work of analysts neither in his group nor in mine, began a friendship that fortunately continues. The way we use our theories in our work does not depend on the written account of the theories alone. I do not believe that the theorists of the Hartmann era took this sufficiently into account in presenting their work, although I recall vividly my father making just this point to me in the early 1950s.

In sum, there is much to regret in the outcome of the Hartmann era. Much, too, has been successfully achieved. The relay race is not yet over, and I believe that the fellow with all the arrows in his back will hand off to a fresh runner in due course.

References

Bergmann, M. (1997). The Hartmann era and its contribution to psycho-analytic technique. Unpublished manuscript.

Collins, S. (1980). Freud and 'the riddle of suggestion.' *International Review of Psycho-Analysis* 7:429–437.

Freud, A. (1958). Child observation and prediction of development: a memorial lecture in honor of Ernst Kris. *Psychoanalytic Study of the Child* 13:92–112. New York: International Universities Press.

Freud, S. (1912). Recommendations to physicians practising psycho-analysis. *Standard Edition* 12.

——— (1923). The Ego and the Id. *Standard Edition* 19.

——— (1926). Inhibitions, Symptoms and Anxiety. *Standard Edition* 20.

Gill, M. M. (1994). *Psycho-Analysis in Transition*. Hillsdale, NJ and London: Analytic Press.

Hartmann, H. (1939). *Ego Psychology and the Problem of Adaptation*. New York: International Universities Press, 1958.

Kris, A. O. (1985). Resistance in convergent and in divergent conflicts. *Psychoanalytic Quarterly* 54:537–568.

———— (1988). Some clinical applications of the distinction between divergent and convergent conflicts. *International Journal of Psycho-Analysis* 69:431–441.

———— (1989). Helping patients by analyzing self-criticism. *Journal of the American Psychoanalytic Association* 38:605–636.

———— (1992). Ambivalence is divergent conflict. *Common Knowledge* 1:123–139.

———— (1994). Freud's treatment of a narcissistic patient. *International Journal of Psycho-Analysis* 75:649–664.

Kris, A. O., and Cooper, S. (1995). Objectivity and subjectivity in psychoanalysis. *Common Knowledge* 4:174–196.

Kris, E. (1947). The nature of psychoanalytic propositions and their validation. In *The Selected Papers of Ernst Kris*. New Haven and London: Yale University Press, 1975, pp. 3–23.

Loewenstein, R. M. (1970). Heinz Hartmann—1894–1970. *International Journal of Psycho-Analysis* 51:417–419.

———— (1972). Ego autonomy and psychoanalytic technique. *Psychoanalytic Quarterly* 41:1–22.

8
Evaluation of the Hartmann Era

PETER B. NEUBAUER

Martin Bergmann's comprehensive and clear paper permits me to add a few notes to this era of psychoanalysis. A review of the history of the development of psychoanalytic theory and practice, not surprisingly, reveals that there is not a straight developmental line. There is progression in one direction, often to the neglect of another; there are deviations from the central core of psychoanalysis and then there are attempts to propose or to prepare precociously an extension of psychoanalytic theory without the appropriate data to translate these propositions in the context of present reality of practice. When we select one period, as we do there, namely the ego psychological factors, it is useful to see it within these generally occurring fluctuations, the unevenness of the development of psychoanalytic theory and practice.

When we examine the range of Hartmann's work, it may be useful to remind us of the position that he defined in his pivotal contribution, *Ego Psychology and the Problem of Adaptation*: "Psychoanalysis alone cannot solve the problem of adaptation . . . it was fostered by our increased interest in the total personality." And furthermore, there was his recognition that "In general, characteristics which are relevant in a broader theory may be irrelevant in a more limited context. . . . I believe it is an empirical fact that these (other) ego functions are less decisive for the understanding and treatment of pathology," and then "Many of these lengthy, but still incomplete, considerations are not psychoanalytic in a narrow sense, and some of them seem to have taken us quite far from the core of psychoanalysis" (p. 3).

The quotes are Hartmann's assessments and therefore a critique of his work must take these into account and we must decide whether we wish to maintain the narrower place of psychoanalysis or whether to follow Hartmann's outline of a general theory of psychoanalysis and development, or at least his psychoanalytic theory of psychology and psychoanalytic theory of development.

Hartmann's ego psychology has been criticized on both accounts: that it abandons the psychoanalytic arena of investigation and that he has failed to create a general psychology that will bridge psychoanalysis with psychology and sociology. I shall examine both positions and point out that, since Hartmann, no other investigation has achieved a systematic way to build these bridges.

In order to assess his work, it is useful to place his monograph on *Ego Psychology and the Problems of Adaptation* in the context of his collective contributions. Did he and others continue to explore his concepts of the undifferentiated phase, the conflict-free ego sphere, conflict-free ego development and primary and secondary autonomy, and his emphasis on the inborn ego apparatus? These concepts are on different levels of theory formation. Some are not verifiable by psychoanalytic methods of investigation. These propositions led to the need for observation of children, particularly from infancy to 3 years of age. Ernst Kris, and later Anna Freud, accepted the significance of observation in order to confirm psychoanalytic propositions and clinical data arrived at by reconstruction, and to add to knowledge about maturation and developmental processes.

When I review Hartmann's papers after *Ego Psychology and the Problem of Adaptation*, I find the following of interest:

1) He never fails to introduce his papers by placing them within the context of psychoanalytic history. This helps the reader to understand how deeply his work is anchored on Freud's and it allows an assessment of the nature of his extension.

2) Hartmann does not elaborate further the concepts he has introduced, but uses them as a given and as a reference.

3) His later elaborations are more closely tied to the usual province of psychoanalytic concerns, focused on the many functions of the ego, but not on adaptation.

In his "Mutual Influences in the Development of the Ego and Id" (1952), Hartmann studied both the normal and pathological development and he stated clearly that developmental issues transcend often what is accessible to the psychoanalytic method. Here he explored the core of the spheres of the ego, inborn characteristics, and the impact of reality. He offers the postulate that neutralized aggression still retains characteristics of the original drives. The stability of the ego to regression to their genetic antecedents allows the assumption of a secondary autonomy. Thus he offers criteria that can measure aspects of autonomy.

Hartmann continues his ego oriented approach in his paper on "Notes on the Theory of Sublimation" (1955). Here he follows Freud's concept of deinstinctualization in contradiction to Freud's earlier assumption, which explains sublimation as being a derivative of the libidinal drive.

It is noteworthy that Kris applies the notion of neutralization and sublimation (1955) to the observation of children in a nursery in an attempt to prove that ego concept can be applied usefully to the observation of development.

Hartmann's examination of ego psychological propositions is clearly demonstrated in his "Notes on the Reality Principle" (1956). As usual, he starts his investigations by quoting Freud's two principles of mental functioning. Hartmann questions the possibility that the tendency for pleasure again and the avoidance of unpleasure cannot fully explain the evolution of the reality principle. He postulates that ego functions must enter the process. He discusses the complexity of Freud's notion of objective reality based on magical thinking and intersubjectivity, and he ends his paper by suggesting that the variety of realities depends on the variety of ego functions involved.

One can demonstrate Hartmann's intention to base his propositions on Freud's work, and on the clinical requirements to pursue "the logic of theory formation." Those psychoanalysts who studied children from infancy on, and child analysts in general, responded to the proposals that ego functions emerge early; that intentionality, engage-ability, and particularly the ego apparatus from the beginning of life on, can be observed side by side with the drive expressions.

It is noteworthy that Lustmann, in his paper on "Rudiments of the Ego" (1956), was one of the first psychoanalysts who undertook research on neonates to verify inherent autonomous endowment with its conflict-free sphere of the ego, while recognizing and profiling the individual differences. With similar intentions, Annemarie Weil much later (1970) formulated the important concept of the *basic core*. Here she observed and proposed the precursor of the organizing and integrative function of the ego that regulates the threshold and discharge of tension. Moreover, she observed the channelization of the aggressive drive, fused with libidinal strivings. She speaks of an energy reservoir and intensity of pleasure–unpleasure.

These authors found Hartmann's propositions useful for the understanding of development, but beyond it, they formulated the earliest conditions that help to predict normal or pathological structure formation. They do not consider their inquiries to be outside the basic tenets of psychoanalysis or to be an application based on a general theory of development.

When one reads *The Selected Papers of Ernst Kris* (1975), it is most useful to note that Kris, who stayed closer to clinical observation than Hartmann did, integrates Hartmann's propositions into the observable data arrived at by either analytic investigation or by child observation. He applies his knowledge to the mode of interpretation, to the changes that have occurred in the scope of psychoanalytic theory and the technique of the therapy of neurosis. He stressed, in this context, the significance by the change in the understanding of resistance of defense analysis. Kris gave the study of the ego apparatus an important impetus in the paper "Recovery of Childhood Memory" where he stated that reconstructions tend to encompass more details, have become more specific, and are better equipped to learn how various levels of genetic interpretations dovetail. He offers examples of three levels of interpretation. One addresses the influence of the id, the mechanisms of defense, and how identification can by itself be a defense. He states that "the situation allows for and ultimately requires all three interpretations."

This short review of papers from this period leads me to formulate these points:

1) There is no impetus today to explore further Hartmann's concept of adaptation. References in the literature employ it mostly
in order to consider environmental influences or responses to
it. This was not Hartmann's primary proposition.

2) Hartmann's emphasis on the ego apparatus is also not pursued.
Perception, language, and motor development were not studied by psychoanalytic investigation based on the psychoanalytic
therapeutic process. The study of memory by Kris informs us
more about its role in reconstruction and free association rather
than exploring the maturational sequences.

3) Hartmann's proposition of the evolving conflict-free sphere from
the undifferentiated states with the logical extension to primary
and secondary ego functions became important for those child
analysts who observed children's normal and abnormal development. These led to important diagnostic considerations. Some
precursors of pathology were understood to be related to primary disorders of the ego apparatus and other ego functions.
These were not always the result of phase-related conflicts, but
seem to be based on dispositional characteristics. Later on, Anna
Freud suggested similar considerations when she elaborated
developmental pathologies, particularly those factors that contribute to uneven development.

4) Thus, Hartmann influenced the emphasis on the function of the
ego. He strengthened Freud's ego psychological position and
contributed to a shift in psychoanalytic technique, and reformu-
lated the meaning of resistance and the defense maneuvers. He
never failed to point out all aspects of the structural point of
view, while his attention focused more on drive rather than
superego components. The resolution of conflicts and other
pathologies was strongly tied to the integrative and organizing
function of the ego.

Such assessment leads inevitably to the conclusion that Hartmann's
work cannot lead to a general judgment of whether his role was positive or negative in the history of psychoanalytic theory and practice. We
would rather have to assess the various areas of Hartmann's contributions in order to know which of these has an enduring usefulness.
Martin Bergmann's excellent paper addresses the contributions of Hart-

mann, but also asks us to reevaluate the Hartmann era and, more specifically, its contribution to the technique of psychoanalysis. There is the general assumption that theory and practice mutually influence each other; that a change in one effects a change in the other. I do not think this balance always exists. It may at times take decades before new theoretical propositions can either be verified or translated into clinical application. Similarly, new clinical findings have to wait before they can be incorporated into a new set of theoretical propositions.

As I have stated before, and as he has done so himself, some of Hartmann's contributions are distant from our clinical work; other areas are more clearly related to it. Therefore we have to determine the place of each in psychoanalysis. We could pursue the same path when we review Freud's work, his metapsychology, or Anna Freud's metapsychological profile, or her proposition of developmental lines.

There is another point. When I listen to or read case presentations, I am aware of how the nature of psychoanalytic data collection appears to be unchanged, but the discussion of the data reflects the prevailing psychoanalytic theoretical propositions. Thus, for instance, influenced by Mahler's outline of the first three years of life, the analyst will see the data in the context of her separation–individuation sequences, emphasizing the rapprochement phase, or those who follow Anna Freud's development point of view will refer to the developmental lines. But, throughout the years, neither the steps of separation–individuation have been filled in since Mahler, nor has it been done—in spite of Anna Freud's encouragement—for the developmental lines. The latter meant to bind together drive, structural, and maturational factors in order to follow the sequences of the developmental process and to locate the fixation and regression and, side by side, the progression. After all, her yardstick of health was the capacity to maintain or to regain developmental progression.

If we were to follow Hartmann's and Loewenstein's emphasis on the autonomous functions, intactness of memory, and reality testing, then one might expect that Anna Freud's focus on the expected changes of structure will lead to the assumption of an autonomous development. But we are reminded that *intactness of memory* or *reality testing* are terms that can only be seen as relative due to areas of conflict invasion, or, in Hartmann's terms, to the secondary autonomy.

In order to assess Hartmann's era and its contributions to psycho-analytic technique, we have to ask the question: Why we have not extended our knowledge of the ego apparatus, of the developmental changes, of those technical interventions that support the neutralization of the libidinal and aggressive strivings? From the economic point of view, the technical question arises: How do we achieve the fusion of the drives—Nunberg's synthetic function—and how do we differentiate our intervention either to promote neutralization, or the integrative and organizing function of the ego?

Ego psychologists raised the question of how the ego responds to the profoundly internal, the unconscious fantasies, the omnipotence the primary identification and to the internal in the external world. How does the ego function in order to maintain its regulatory influences? Hartmann, and others, have studied its anatomy, its apparatus, its defense systems, which make it possible to transfer primary process to secondary process thinking in response to the reality principle.

These studies do not explore the inner experience, the symbolic meaning of the history of conflicts, but are we therefore to exclude these studies from our field of interest? The studies of the anatomy of the ego allow one to find the location of ego pathology, whether there is a fault in integrative or organizing function of ego or whether there are disorders in the ego apparatus, either perception or motility or language, and thereby one can assess more clearly the primary ego disorders and contribute to our understanding of borderline conditions.

In addition, the focus on developmental and maturational changes provides us this factor that contributes to conflict and conflict resolution and helps us to understand the ascendance of secondary process thinking.

There are other propositions that immediately affected the technique of intervention for reasons that may be of interest to pursue but are outside the topic of our discussion. Melanie Klein's theoretical frame of reference had a direct influence on technique. Similarly, some aspects of Kohut's work on narcissistic disorder or Kernberg's study of the borderline conditions have immediate technical consequences. But we should not neglect the pressure for change that derived from the clinical need to improve the achievement of our treatment aim, particularly of conditions outside the neuroses.

But this was different in my experience. During the early fifties I had not observed a significant shift in the psychoanalytic technique; it was conflict oriented; the unresolved oedipal pathology was in the foreground of our interest; so was the recovery of the repressed, a favored pursuit in the context of transference. Hartmann's supervision of a case of mine did not differ from other supervisory experiences or case seminars during this period. The change occurred slowly, as Kris has pointed out, based on the experience that the recovery of memories did not reveal a single event, a trauma, but continues to influence what may later become condensed into a single experience.

Martin Bergmann has given us a most comprehensive and valuable review of Hartmann's contribution and of those who influence the ascendance of ego psychology. I would like to raise a few questions for further discussion: I suggest that the ego psychology area of psychoanalysis should be evaluated in the context of the history of the development of psychoanalytic theory and practice. When do we locate the reason why the early drive-trauma focus period and the topographical model was then changed to the structural point of view? When do we understand the causes, theoretical and clinical, that led from there to the attention to object relationships, with its further elaboration on intersubjectivity? Then we may be able to understand whether each period fulfilled its expectation; then we can judge the comparative place of each. Do we dare to predict where the next shift will occur? Each new focus has contributed to our understanding of the complexity of the mind, the multiple determinants of its function, and each had reached limits or overemphasized some factors to the neglect of others.

It seems that Freud, and others since then, have given us the reasons for the shift to the understanding of the function of the ego, after decades of exploration of the power of the drives, of pre- and unconscious determinants of mental function, after trying to read the language of the unconscious, its timelessness, condensation, and symbolism. The study of the ego's struggles against undue influences from the drives, the superego, and the environment enlarged our knowledge both of theoretical and clinical interventions. The extension of the investigation to establish a general psychology, to explore the ego apparatus, seemed to have reached a territory beyond this.

The shift to object relations was influenced by the widening scope, by the study of early development. It increased our view of mental functions. It is of interest that with it there is an emphasis on preoedipal pathology; rarely do we find today a contribution to our knowledge of the vicissitudes of oedipal conflicts and their solutions, the primary interest of early psychoanalysis. During this period the explanation of pathology is seen in the context of object interaction. Primary structural deficiencies, dispositional factors, and core constellations are neglected as the dynamics of the objects' interactive processes appear to explain pathology and normality.

The analyst's behavior as a new object will interfere with the patient's neurotic expectations and will therefore lead to a widening of the patient's awareness of his pathology and interfere with his enactment of the neurotic conflicts. Implied in this proposition is the notion of the conflict-free ego and the analyst's alliance with it. Hartmann never considered such a position to be in harmony with the unconscious repetition of conflicts, which is never avoided in treatment. The working-through, as the alliance with the observational capacity of the ego in response to the continuous presence of conflicts alone, has not been the position of the ego psychologists. The present-day analysts pay primary attention to the object relations of their patients and to the psychoanalytic dyadic relationship between patient and analyst.

It was inevitable that, with the introduction of the structural point of view, attention became focused on the ego. The emphasis on drives had preceded it. The Hartmann era explored function, as Anna Freud did with her outline of the ego and the mechanisms of defense, on theoretical and clinical grounds. Hartmann attempted to create a general psychology, beyond the borders of clinical psychoanalytic evidence. Here then, as usual, his era found its limits.

It seems impossible to maintain a balanced view of the interaction of all mental agencies as one explores new territories. Let me quote Goethe (xxxx): "Nature forms man, then man transforms himself, and this transformation is, in turn, natural. He who finds himself situated in the vast world creates another one inside himself, a little world enclosed and protected by walls, and fitted out in his own image" (p. 33).

It is clear where psychoanalysis situates itself.

References

Goethe, J. W. (xxxx). *Nature Forms Man*. Ans Lavaters Physiognomisher Framenten. In *Werke*, vol. 13, p. 33.

Hartmann, H. (1958). *Ego Psychology and the Problem of Adaptation*. New York: International Universities Press.

—— (1952). Mutual influences in the development of the ego and id. *Psychoanalytic Study of the Child* 7:9–15. New York: International Universities Press.

—— (1955). Notes on the theory of sublimation. *Psychoanalytic Study of the Child* 10:9–15. New York: International Universities Press.

—— (1956). Notes on the reality principle. *Psychoanalytic Study of the Child* 11:35–40. New York: International Universities Press.

Kris, E. (1955). Neutralization and sublimation: observations on young children. *Psychoanalytic Study of the Child* 10:37–42. International Universities Press.

—— (1956). The recovery of child memories in psychoanalysis. In *The Selected Papers of Ernst Kris*.

Lustman, S. (1956). Rudiments of the ego. *Psychoanalytic Study of the Child* 11:89–90. New York: International Universities Press.

Weil, A. (1970). The Basic Core. *Psychoanalytic Study of the Child* 25:405–456. New York: International Universities Press.

9

Some Comments on "The Hartmann Era: An Evaluation"

ALBERT J. SOLNIT

At the outset, I wish to express my admiration and gratitude to Martin Bergmann for his lead paper for this symposium, "The Hartmann Era and Its Contributions to Psychoanalytic Techniques."

I have attempted to evaluate the contributions of Hartmann in previous presentations. Although my past evaluations have been elaborated in my thinking and work, the central issues raised in the previous evaluations are as valid and challenging to me now as they were in 1964, 1972, 1994, and 1995. By referring to the Hartmann era, we call attention to several perspectives—Hartmann was an original thinker who found it useful to relate his ideas and contributions to Freud's original concepts and revisions; in other words, Hartmann had no need to create a separate territory or school of thought. He enlarged, elaborated, and revised earlier work but resisted the notion that new ideas become dogma for a different or separate school of thought. Secondly, he provided new perspectives especially in ego psychology that were related to drive theory, to development, to social reality, and to adaptation, both pathological and normative, and finally, he presented views of that complex mosaic of the personality that moves in the direction of what constitutes health. His approaches to what constitutes a healthy personality were productive formulations that have facilitated my own work as well as that of many child analysts and those interested in psychoanalytic child development.

Heinz Hartmann provided crucial guideposts in his theory-building contributions, as well as critical suggestions about the sources and directions of future developments in the science of psychoanalysis. It is now appropriate to survey, from the peaks he surmounted in his own work, some of the perspectives provided by the range of his psychoanalytic views, especially in ego psychology. At every point in his pioneering work he also demonstrated his competence as a historian of science by [fully] documenting Freud's creation of psychoanalysis and relating its history to elaborations and contributions by others who have helped to develop psychoanalysis into the general psychology that Freud had envisaged. Hartmann's contributions to this developing science are of such a range and of such basic importance that it is impossible for anything short of considering all of his work, as Martin Bergmann has done, to do justice to the advances he contributed, to the questions he raised, and to the many facets of human development and adaptation he insisted we keep in mind. Over the years his work emphasized the dynamic, changing influences of the simultaneous inner-instinctual and outer-reality demands in individual development. The balance of these demands yields a focus on adaptation through which Hartmann sought to make possible the establishment of a general psychology of human behavior within a frame of psychoanalytic theory. Hartmann's earlier experimental work set the stage for his later accomplishments, in which he critically clarified and advanced psychoanalytic theory, formulating and applying the synthesizing criteria through which he sees all human adaptation (Hartmann 1939a).

All of his work is a blending of psychoanalytic clinical observation, developmental illumination, and theoretical abstraction. Hartmann's intellectual vigor and astuteness enabled him to reach clarifying theory-building constructs with a comprehensive vision of what lay ahead and a precise memory and knowledge of the clinical observations, the hypotheses involved, and the pathways required to force into view the appropriate theoretical abstractions. Thus, much of Hartmann's published work had a tentativeness indicating openness to revision and refinements. By titling his papers "Notes on" or "Comments" or "Problems of" or "Selected Problems in" Hartmann also indicated his aversion to dogma.

Using his paper "Notes on the Reality Principle" (1956) as an example, I shall focus on how Hartmann's concepts have enabled many of us to approach applications of psychoanalytic theory in usefully conservative ways.

Hartmann in his Freud Lecture (1960) spoke of using psychoanalytic insight [for] its application to practical ways of dealing with human behavior. In that same lecture as he examined continuities of his own thinking with Freud (Hartmann 1939b), with special attention to the interests and limits of psychoanalysis as a science and as a clinical method, he stated, in agreement with Freud, that it was not appropriate to deduce a *Weltanschauung* from analysis. In that instance, he quoted Freud, "Psychoanalysis is not in my opinion in a position to create a philosophy of life" (Hartmann 1960, p. 20).

It may fit into my comments regarding Hartmann's perspective on applications of psychoanalytic theory to quote Freud, again (Solnit 1967):

> You know that the therapeutic effects we can achieve are very inconsiderable in number. We are but a handful of people, and even by working hard each one of us can deal in a year with only a small number of persons. Against the vast amount of neurotic misery which is in the world, and perhaps need not be, the quantity we can do away with is almost negligible. Besides this, the necessities of our own existence limit our work to the well-to-do classes, accustomed to choose their own physicians, whose choice is diverted away from psycho-analysis by all kinds of prejudices. At present we can do nothing in the crowded ranks of the people, who suffer exceedingly from neuroses.
>
> Now let us assume that by some kind of organization we were able to increase our numbers to an extent sufficient for treating large masses of people. Then on the other hand, one may reasonably expect that at some time or other the conscience of the community will awake and admonish it that the poor man has just as much right to help for his mind as he now has to the surgeon's means of saving life; and that the neuroses menace the health of a people no less than tuberculosis, and can be left as little as the latter to the feeble handling of individuals. Then clinics and consultation-departments will be built, to which analytically trained physicians will be appointed, so that the men who would otherwise give way to drink, the women who have nearly succumbed under their burden of privations, the children for whom there is no choice but running wild or neurosis, may be made

by analysis able to resist and able to do something in the world. This treatment will be free. It may be a long time before the conditions may delay its arrival even longer; probably these institutions will first be started by private beneficence; some time or other, however, it must come.

The task will then arise for us to adapt our technique to the new conditions. I have no doubt that the validity of our psychological assumptions will impress the uneducated too, but we shall need to find the simplest and most natural expression for our theoretical doctrines. We shall probably discover that the poor are even less ready to part with their neuroses than the rich, because the hard life that awaits them when they recover has no attraction, and illness in them gives them more claim to the help of others. Possibly we may often only be able to achieve something if we combine aid for the mind with some material support, in the manner of Emperor Joseph. It is very probable, too, that the application of our therapy to numbers will compel us to alloy the pure gold of analysis plentifully with the copper of direct suggestion; and even hypnotic influence might find a place in it again, as it has in the treatment of war-neuroses. But whatever form this psychotherapy for the people may take, whatever the elements out of which it is compounded, its most effective and most important ingredients will assuredly remain those borrowed from strict psycho-analysis which serves no ulterior purpose. [Freud 1919, pp. xx–xx]

In his 1956 article, "Notes on the Reality Principle," Hartmann briefly (but strikingly) states: "We should also consider what is, I think, a necessary assumption that the child is born with a certain degree of preadaptiveness; that is to say, the apparatuses of perception, memory, motility, etc., which help us deal with reality, are in a primitive form, already present at birth; later they will mature and develop in constant interaction, of course, with experience; the very system to which we attribute these functions, the ego, is also our organ of learning." He then added, "Sooner or later, though not every step has been clarified thus far, the child unlearns and outgrows the distortions inherent in the purified pleasure position. . . . The impact of all stages of child development—the typical conflicts, the sequence of danger situations, and the ways they are dealt with—can be traced in this process. The problem has been most extensively studied in relation to the development of object relations. Perception, objectivation, anticipation, intentionality, neutralization of energy—all participate on the side of the ego in this process. One may well ask why this whole development of the reality principle (or the corresponding ego functions) shows such a high degree of complexity in man, a complexity to which there is hardly a parallel elsewhere, except perhaps for some higher mammals. No doubt, one reason is that in the human the pleasure principle is a less reliable guide to self-preservation. Also, self-preservation is mainly taken care of by the slowly developing ego with its considerable learning capacity. But pleasurable conditions for the ego on the one hand and the id on the other differ significantly, while the instincts of the animals represent at the same time what we would call in man ego functions and functions of the drives. Also, probably as a result of the differentiation of the human mind into systems of functioning, the id is here much farther removed. . . . In those situations in which pleasure in one system (id) would induce unpleasure in another one (ego), the child learns to use the danger signal (a dose of unpleasure) to mobilize the pleasure principle and in this way to protect himself. He will not only use this mechanism against danger from within but also against danger from without. The process is directly guided by the pleasure principle; it is really the pleasure principle that gives this move its power. What interests us in this connection is that through a special device an aspect of the pleasure principle itself (avoidance of unpleasure) is made to serve one of the most essential aspects of the reality principle" (Freud 1926).

One of the many contributions that this paper on the reality principle makes is contained in the idea that the young child, while still predominantly under the domination of the pleasure principle, learns to use the danger signal (a dose of unpleasure—i. e., of the reality principle) to mobilize the pleasure principle in the service of the ego to protect himself. The failure of this function to develop or operate would appear, from our observations, to be one of the major factors in explaining a leading threat to child health and survival, the possibility of serious "accidents," in the second and third years of life. From the time a child can walk independently, certain expected risks or dangers become inherent in the "average expectable environment." In Hartmann's efforts to establish the groundwork for a theory of human behavior, observations and formulations are based on normal as well as on abnormal phenomena.

Children in the second and third year of life who are "safe" in their growing up have the assistance and guidance of the maternal figure in using their survival tendencies. The protective presence of the parent is felt through identifications that are grounded in object constancy. The parent supplements the child's capacity to avoid danger and to depend increasingly on painful danger signals emerging from the developing ego when an id-determined pleasure impulse threatens to endanger the child. The capacity to feel ego discomfort and to respond to it in the situation of dangerous id temptation depends on early learning experiences in which the parent's perception of reality as safe or dangerous is available as a guide to the child in the intimacy of sound object relationships, that is, of the dawning of the capacity for object constancy. Such early learning experiences are constituted by the same mechanisms that later enable the child to take care of his body as the parent has, and to sense from the parent what is prohibited in the context of the early object relationships. These mechanisms include also the earliest ego identifications, especially the protective parental object constancy that is so essential for adaptation. As Hartmann explained, it is a situation in which the child learns to use the danger signal (a dose of unpleasure in the ego) to mobilize the pleasure principle to protect himself from dangerous consequences of pleasure in the service of the id. This mechanism is used against danger from within as well as against danger from without. Where this mechanism fails to operate, the child in the second and third year of life is in need of extraordinary environmental protection from such things as gravitational forces in certain situations (stairs and other heights), objects that are excessively hot or cold, the ingestion of noxious substances, and many other everyday situations. Obviously, the well-developing child is in need of and thrives on a large number of appropriate opportunities to explore and experiment with the aid of external and internal safety factors. Since the cognitive resources of the ego are not yet sufficiently developed for the understanding of causal relationships, the prelogical child relies on a balance or combination of environmental safeguards provided by parents (auxiliary ego) and the unpleasure danger signal from his own ego when the demands of pleasure from the id in the usual environment threatens the child's safety or well-being.

It is not a matter of excessive environmental safeguards or none, since the environment of the healthy 2-year-old child must have built-in safety factors. However, if the child is not capable of cooperating with the love object or the love object with the child, early learning mechanisms may be jeopardized. These would include those mechanisms through which the ego's functions become experienced as pleasurable when they are harmonious with the directions and influences of the parental figure. A paucity of such early learning mechanisms interferes with the ego's ability to develop unpleasure in the face of danger and the child is then less well protected from the necessary—and desirable—risks of the average expectable environment. Conversely, the child's average expectable environment can be safe for and stimulating to development when the confluence of id, ego, and environmental influences promote adaptation and survival rather than danger and destruction. Thus, a 2-year-old child whose ego development has lagged in establishing a capacity for unpleasure created by id demands that are dangerous is more likely to stumble to a fracture, ingest aspirin or a toxic household agent in a life-threatening way, or walk into a swimming pool where only ordinary precautions have been taken. The reasons for this developmental lag in a physically normal child are most likely to be found in the pattern of the early experiences with the mother, that is, in the area of object relationships.

Although much of the above is a working hypothesis derived from Hartmann's work, it is also derived from studies of children who have accidentally ingested a noxious substance. In these preliminary studies of children under the age of 4, cognizance was taken of the fact that over 400,000 children were seen by physicians in 1962 for "accidental" poisoning (National Health Survey 1962). However, the most impressive fact is that so many more children do *not* ingest noxious agents ranging from aspirin to ant poison, and from cleaning agents to heating fluids, such as kerosene.

Hartmann's formulations are unusually fertile in the critical suggestions and predictions they offer in the applications of psychoanalytic theory. Thus, in our study (Lewis et al. 1966) of 14 children under the age of 4 who had accidentally ingested poison, Hartmann's psychoanalytic investigation of the pleasure and reality principles enabled us to approach an understanding of those children who do *not* ingest poison as well as those who do. In each of the 14 children studied, for a variety of reasons, the mother–child relationship was deficient because of the mother's state of depletion. In those children under 2 years old, the mother's lack of psychological and emotional resources was re-flected by an environment that was less safe than an average expect-able environment should be for mobile, grasping children of this age. For example, kerosene was left where an 18-month-old child could easily move toward it and drink it. One might say in this youngest group that the environment created by the depleted mother offered invitations to ingest noxious substances (id temptations) without the expected protection of the mother, and before the child's ego devel-opment could provide the danger signal of unpleasure or the protec-tion of understanding.

In older children studied, between 2 and 4, there were a number of influences that sapped the resources of the maternal figure, rang-ing from unexpected pregnancies to the disapproval and rejection of the mother by her own mother (the child's maternal grandmother), or by inadequate supportive interest and care from her husband. It became clear that the withdrawal of such crucial psychological sup-port of the mother impaired the mother–child relationship to the det-riment of those ego capacities of the young child (2 to 4) that enable him to learn from and identify with the protective mother, and which stem from libidinal ties of a satisfying and soothing nature. In these situations it appeared that the child was unable to develop or use effectively the unpleasure signal of the ego to ward off the impulse to ingest a tempting noxious substance, even in those instances in which it had been put away with ordinary precautions. In a child in whom the object relationships were sound and in whom ego devel-opment was not impaired, we assumed that such impulses stemming from the id (to open the bottle and eat the aspirin) would probably have been warded off by the danger signal of unpleasure from the ego based on early learning mechanisms and on partial identifications of the child with a libidinally satisfying love object. This formula-tion received support from our comparative study of 14 children of the same age and sex who did not ingest poison. In this comparison group, factors of maternal depletion or deviant ego development were absent.

Thus, the physical and psychological presence of the parent con-stitutes a protective influence when toddlers are exploring environ-ments in which there are risks of physical injury (falls, burns, ingestion of noxious agents, etc.). In healthy development, one could say that each parent–child pair develops a sense of how, when, and where the protective physical or/and psychological presence of the parent is available to facilitate the dynamics of the pleasure principle being in service of the reality principle. The absence or depletion of this protective presence, physical or/and psychological, constitutes a risk of injury to young children. As Ernst Kris pointed out (personal communication) many mothers are confident that their young children are safe in the average expectable environment because they know the radius and effectiveness of their protective presence even when their child is out of sight in the next room.

Hartmann's formulations enable us to understand not only why so many young children do not ingest poison, but also underscore the necessity to avoid simplifications that explain "accidents" mainly or only on the basis of carelessness in the environment.

This study is an example of the productivity of Hartmann's insistence that theory, clinical observation, and developmental considerations be viewed as related aspects of psychoanalysis, a general human psychology. Thus, Hartmann's conceptualization of the pleasure principle in the service of the reality principle is on a developmental continuum, enabling us to approach the study of accidents in early childhood with fresh and promising hypotheses that relate normal or healthy development to deviant development.

Hartmann's published work is filled with fruitful suggestions and direction indicators for the uncovering of new knowledge and the refinement of areas of understanding that have been staked out previously. Many psychological vistas have been made possible by his theory building, a unique form of theoretical illumination that, because of its closeness to clinical realities, is replete with suggestions for research, involving applications of psychoanalysis that, in turn, have the effect of sharpening or refining theoretical formulations.

It is also characteristic of Hartmann's comprehensive views that they increase our knowledge of psychic health and indicate pathways to the prevention of mental illness. His many contributions have provided sufficient well-designed questions and suggestions about future studies that could keep psychoanalysts and other behavioral scientists busy and productive for many years to come.

References

Freud, S. (1919). The ways of psycho-analytic therapy. *Standard Edition* 2:400–402.

——— (1926). Inhibitions, symptoms and anxiety. *Standard Edition* 20.

Hartmann, H. (1939a). *Ego Psychology and the Problem of Adaptation.* Monograph Series of the American Psychoanalytic Assn., #1 (translated by David Rapaport 1958 and 1995). New York: International Universities Press.

——— (1939b). Psychoanalysis and the concept of health. *International Journal of Psycho-Analysis* 20:308–321.

——— (1956). "Notes on the reality principle." *Psychoanalytic Study of the Child* 11:31–53. New York: International Universities Press.

——— (1960). Psychoanalysis and moral values. (Freud Anniversary Lecture Series of the New York Psychoanalytic Institute.) New York: International Universities Press.

Lewis M., et al. (1966). An exploratory study of accidental ingestion of poison in young children. *Journal of the American Academy of Child Psychiatry* 5:255.

Solnit, A. J. (1964). A tribute to Heinz Hartmann. *Psychoanalytic Quarterly* 33:475–484.

——— (1967). The psychiatric council: applied psychiatry in an antipoverty program. *American Journal of Orthopsychiatry* 37(3):495–506.

——— (1972). Aggression: a view of theory building in psychoanalysis. *Journal of the American Psychoanalytic Association* 20:435–450.

——— (1994). Heinz Hartmann—psychoanalysis and health values unfolding. *Psychoanalytic Study of the Child.* New Haven: Yale University Press, 49:36–45.

——— (1995). Heinz Hartmann, 1894–1970. (An Essay.) *American Journal of Psychiatry* 152(1358).

10
A Contribution to the Discussion on the Significance of the Hartmann Era

CLIFFORD YORKE

There is every reason to be grateful to Dr. Bergmann for his extensive and very clear survey of the work of Heinz Hartmann, his associates and collaborators, and others whom he regards as contributors to the Hartmann era. I do not agree with everything he says, but some of the questions he raises are decidedly difficult and do not lend themselves to easy resolution.

For me, Dr. Bergmann's assertion that Hartmann's extensive influence was essentially an American phenomenon has the ring of truth. One can only speculate on why this should have been so.[1] But it may

---

1. Hartmann's extensive essay, *Ego Psychology and the Problem of Adaptation*, though published in German in 1939 and read, in shorter version, to the Viennese Society two years earlier, did not appear in English until 1958—an astonishing gap—when Rapaport translated it, so its English-speaking readership may, before that time, have been somewhat restricted. It is true that Rapaport had published an abridged translation in 1950, summarizing omissions in footnotes, as well as adding informative comments; but if London was anything to go by, not many people in England read the massive collection of papers in which it appeared, put together and extensively annotated by Rapaport under the title *Organization and Pathology of Thought*. Hartmann had of course written a good deal in English before 1958, either by himself or with Kris and Loewenstein, but nothing gives quite such an overall picture of his

be of interest to turn to some personal observations of the state of affairs in the British Psychoanalytical Society at the time.

As far as that organization was concerned, I never noticed a "Hartmann era." As a student, I was surprised that Hartmann was rarely mentioned by my teachers, and almost everything I knew about his work came from my own reading. As for the main body of the Society, it would stretch credulity to claim that the principal propositions of so-called ego psychology were widely, let alone universally, known. At the Hampstead Clinic, as I soon discovered, the position was certainly different; but within the ranks of the British Society, Hartmann's psychoanalytic status was, at best, equivocal. The Kleinians, to be sure, were united in their opposition; but Kleinian trainees were taught no more about Hartmann than the rest of us. In any case, from Mrs. Klein's point of view, intrapsychic conflict raged fiercely from the very start of life; and since no one—*no one*—overcame, without Kleinian analysis, the tortured dilemmas that, at best, ended in the depressive position, the very idea that anything psychological could be conflict-free was unthinkable. So you didn't need to know much more about Hartmann than that particular proposition. An equally negative view was taken by those members of the Independent Group, whose thinking was closely attuned to the Kleinian tradition. But even among those members whose persuasions lay elsewhere, interest in Hartmann—or for that matter Kris, Loewenstein, and most certainly Rapaport—was less than widespread, and even then a matter of indifference rather than articulate opposition. And where that was not the case, Hartmann's acceptance was often as uncritical as his rejection was sometimes ill-considered. Furthermore, inasmuch as there *was* any controversy about him, a number of misconceptions clouded discussion and impeded constructive assessment.

So I can't be said to have been born, psychoanalytically, into the Hartmann era, even if his existence, and many of his ideas, were acknowledged at Hampstead. But when, some years later, Hartmann died, it was difficult for the British Society to ignore him. His death was formally lamented at a Society meeting, and a little later a memorial evening

---

thinking as the original work, even though these later papers added much. But I doubt if these facts can account for European neglect.

was arranged. I was invited to open the meeting by giving a brief summary of Hartmann's ideas, and the fact that the organizers thought this necessary speaks for itself. I didn't find it easy to be succinct, but I found room for a few criticisms, knowing that memorial speeches were usually sufficiently laudatory to make such comments permissible. Perhaps I was influenced by the fact that, a few years before, I had spoiled part of a summer holiday by reading, or rereading, one after another, the papers in Hartmann's collection of *Essays on Ego Psychology* (1964) as part of an undertaking to review the book for one of the journals. I felt it only right to do all this, but whatever may be said for a sense of duty, the method had serious disadvantages. It was not just a matter of getting through 450 pages of theoretical exposition without any clinical illustrations, though that was certainly tiresome. But collections are notoriously repetitious, and one became uncomfortably aware that Hartmann was often forced to repeat, in furthering his arguments, what Freud and others had already said, sometimes with greater eloquence, before the kernel of a paper's point was finally reached. Reading some of those papers subsequently for reference purposes, and as occasion demanded, was a less frustrating and irritating experience.

There was an interesting, and perhaps curious, sequence to the memorial meeting at the British Society. Anna Freud asked me if I would read my brief talk again at a similar meeting at the Hampstead Clinic. But I was more than a little surprised when she sent it to Hartmann's widow. In due course I received a letter from Dora Hartmann seeking to put me right on a few points. Whatever else, the episode seems to say something about Anna Freud's attitude toward ego psychology that is not spelled out in her address on the occasion of Hartmann's 70th birthday (1966).

It occurred to me that, although Dr. Bergmann's review of the concepts that characterized the work of Hartmann and his colleagues was impressively extensive, it might be worthwhile to restate briefly some of Hartmann's principal tenets and to express some personal views about their significance. But I shall not seek to examine, other than incidentally, the work of many of those whom Dr. Bergman has called "Hartmannites." Even if I liked the term, which is surely not meant to be as pejorative as at first it seemed to be, I would have thought that many people so characterized would have made substantial contributions to psychoanalysis even if they had set aside Hartmann's work. That, surely, is true even of close associates like Kris. So, for present purposes, I shall mostly restrict myself to some key propositions put forward in *Ego Psychology and the Problem of Adaptation*, and in a few papers enlarging on or adding to the concepts set out there. I hope this approach will prove of value. Please bear with me in referring to many matters you know so well.

What appeared to be so decisively revolutionary in 1937 was Hartmann's assertion that there were important influences on ego growth and development that were neither subject to conflict nor sprang from its resolution. In this view, the ego had important in-born roots that significantly influenced its development and maturation. Important ego functions that could foster adaptation, such as "perception, intention, object comprehension, thinking, language, recall phenomena, productivity, [as well as] the well known phases of motor development, grasping, crawling, walking, and . . . the maturational and learning processes implicit in all these and many others" (1958, p. 8) could develop *outside of conflict*. This seemingly cardinal point of departure led Hartmann to postulate, firstly, a conflict-free ego sphere, and secondly, ego-apparatuses that served the adaptive processes already exemplified. Closely linked with these concepts was Hartmann's further belief, shared with others and largely derived from Freud's statement in the *Outline* (1938), about the formation of the ego in an *undifferentiated matrix* in which the ego apparatuses developed. Insofar as the "apparatuses" were not intrinsically engaged in conflict, they were said to have "primary autonomy," and it therefore follows that, if these assumptions are granted, adaptation may *precede* conflict and not necessarily derive from it.

Since, in following Hartmann only this far, we have already dived into what in the context of the time, must have seemed very deep water, it may be as well to draw breath, to pause and take stock, before proceeding. Although we have the advantage of a long period of acquaintance with Hartmann's ideas, certain questions will still trouble the minds of the uncommitted, however decisively they may have been settled, one way or another, in the minds of others. But it is surely important to recognize at once the qualifications with which Hartmann, in the very first chapter of his essay, introduced his concept of a "conflict-free ego sphere":

> I certainly do not imply that the childhood activities I have enumer-
> ated . . . remain untouched by mental conflict; nor do I imply that
> disturbances in their development do not in turn give rise to conflicts,
> nor that they do not get embroiled in other conflicts. On the contrary,
> I want to stress that their vicissitudes play an important role in the
> well-known typical and individual developments and conflicts of in-
> stinctual drives, and in facilitating or hampering the individual's at-
> tempts to master these. [p. 8]

Hartmann's added that his use of the term "ego sphere" was *not* intended to imply a topographical area of conflict-free activity.

Unfortunately, Hartmann did not always write in the spirit suggested by these disclaimers, which may in part account for the fact that
they are so easily overlooked. But if they are kept in mind, it could
with reason be asserted that Hartmann's qualification of his initial
proposition was so substantial that much of its novelty was lost. I would
have thought this criticism ungenerous if what we are dealing with is
less a question of novelty than an area of potential neglect. For all these
ideas were, at the very least, anticipated by Freud, and it can be argued that the relevant passages in his writings are among those that
are so readily forgotten or set aside. But, among other references to these
matters, Freud wrote, in 1937:

> The next question we come to is whether every alteration of the ego—
> in our sense of the term—is acquired during the defensive struggles
> of the earliest years. There can be no doubt about the answer. We
> have no reason to dispute the existence and importance of original,
> innate distinguishing characteristics of the ego. This is made certain
> by the single fact that each person makes a selection from the pos-
> sible mechanisms of defence, that he always uses a few only of them
> and always the same ones. This would seem to indicate that each ego
> is endowed from the first with individual dispositions and trends,
> though it is true that we cannot specify their nature or what deter-
> mines them. Moreover, we know that we must not exaggerate the
> difference between inherited and acquired characteristics into an
> antithesis; what was acquired by our forefathers certainly forms an
> important part of what we inherit. When we speak of "archaic heri-
> tage" we are usually thinking only of the id and we seem to assume
> that at the beginning of an individual's life no ego is as yet in exis-
> tence. But we shall not overlook the fact that id and ego are origi-
> nally one, nor does it imply any mystical overvaluation of heredity if

> we think it credible that, even before the ego has come into exist-
> ence, the lines of development, trends and reactions which it will later
> exhibit are already laid down for it. [p. 240]

Ignoring, for present purposes, the Lamarckian tendencies on which
Dr. Bergmann has commented, statements of this kind by Freud have
indeed been pointed out by many, including Rapaport himself (who
quoted this very passage—in an earlier translation—in his book on
thinking) in a footnote to his abridged version of Hartmann's 1937 paper
(p. 365). But it could, I believe, be legitimately claimed that Hartmann
had drawn attention, and given greater emphasis, to matters of proper
concern for psychoanalysts, and ones that hitherto had not received
sufficient consideration.

Nevertheless, the use of terms like "conflict-free sphere" and "ego
apparatuses" has been a source of difficulty for many. In this connection, Glover, writing in 1950, had insisted that it was necessary "to
define" with some precision the concept of *conflict*. He continued:

> Some years ago Hartmann suggested that this term is applied too
> exclusively to the process of adaptation and that there is a "sphere
> without conflict" which nevertheless records clashes between the or-
> ganism and its environment. In the writer's opinion, Hartmann might
> have developed the idea further. Clearly, if such spheres exist they
> indicate that, at some stage of development, stress without conflict
> must have been a characteristic feature of mental activity which, later
> on, manifests itself in more limited "spheres." Stresses due to the
> opposing aims of instincts existing before the ego is organized can-
> not be labelled "conflict" without making nonsense of the concept
> of the Id, to say nothing of the primary processes which take no cog-
> nizance of contradictions. [p. 370]

If, with prescience, Hartmann had taken this step, and pointed out
that, to begin with, everything psychic is, in a general sense, "conflict
free" (rather than *outside of conflict*, which is not at all the same thing),
his initial pronouncements would have been less controversial. But it
would not, to my mind, have been sufficient to restrict his concept to
what many people have called a preconflictual phase of development
or to what Glover called a "primary functional phase." As Glover himself suggests, such "spheres" manifest themselves in later mental activity, after the ego is sufficiently well formed to make the concept of

intrapsychic conflict meaningful. But Glover puts the word "sphere" in inverted commas: it is, to my mind, a very unfortunate term. For if, as Hartmann says, no topographical area is designated by "sphere," why use the word at all? And "ego-apparatus" is likewise a misleading expression. It has undoubtedly caused trouble for a number of reasons, one of which was that Hartmann used it in a way that did not always make clear the difference between physiological and psychological "apparatuses," and though he himself was aware of that difference, there has always been a danger of conflating the two.[2] It is questionable whether Rapaport helped matters by repeatedly using the term "apparatus" in the sense of "structure," and in some respects Hartmann's concept of "apparatuses," even within the ego, are dangerously close to, if not identical with, structures.

And here again I want to refer to Glover (1968), who pointed out that "Hartmann seems to have been uncertain of his own terminology." Speaking of the conflict-free sphere, Glover continues:

> . . . he goes on to define this "sphere" as an ensemble of functions which at any given time exert their effects outside the region of mental conflicts. It is not, he adds, a "province" but rather an ensemble of "processes." But why, one may ask, employ a static structural image for activities that are best described dynamically and economically? Why use the term "ego apparatuses," as Hartmann does, to describe processes and functions? [p. 109]

I would want to add two further points. First, precision about the term "conflict" demands that we specify the *kind* of conflict to which we refer. Variously stated in the literature, the different types were brought together by Anna Freud (1962) in her diagnostic profile schema in the following orderly fashion:

(a) external conflicts between the id–ego agencies and the object world (arousing fear of the object world);
(b) internalized conflicts between ego–superego and id after the ego agencies have taken over and represent to the id the demands of the object world (arousing guilt);

---

2. It is precisely such a conflation that has been responsible for so much confusion in some contemporary affect theory (see Yorke 1995).

(c) internal conflicts between insufficiently fused or incompatible drive representatives (such as unsolved ambivalence, activity versus passivity, masculinity versus femininity, etc.). [p. 56]

The type of conflict indicated under (b) should perhaps be extended to include superego precursors (see Kennedy and Yorke 1982). The expression "unsolved [unresolved] ambivalence" referred to in (c) is preferable to "love versus hate," which is too readily, though wrongly, thought of as a conflict within the id—a concept which, as Glover pointed out, is a contradiction in terms.

Second, "conflict free" is not to be equated with "freedom from pathology." Conflict can exist without pathology, as it does in the normative, and pathology can exist that is not derived, at any rate initially, from conflict. Anna Freud's concept of *developmental disharmonies* (1979) is of first importance in this respect. And in terms of the young child, pathology can exist *before* organized ego functioning is established. This was acknowledged by Glover, when he discussed the nature of infantile traumata and functional disorders, including in the latter "interference with oral, gastric and intestinal disturbances, which at first carry the main load of libidinal excitation," and adding "feeding difficulties, anorexia, constipation, screaming, kicking and convulsive seizures," and reminding us that "psychic tension can be discharged in *any* bodily or mental activity or give rise to *any* form of mental inactivity or bodily inertia" (1968, p. 82). These comments will also serve to remind us of the very close links between body and mind in the early phases of development. Anna Freud repeatedly emphasized this matter, and put the point very well in her classic paper on "The Symptomatology of Childhood" where her first heading in her preliminary classification of "symptomatology proper" was *Symptoms Resulting from Initial Nondifferentiation between Somatic and Psychological Processes: Psychosomatics*. By way of clarification, she added:

> Before somatic and psychological processes are separated off from each other, bodily excitations such as hunger, cold, pain, etc., are discharged as easily via mental pathways in the form of unpleasure, anxiety, anger, rage, as mental upsets of any kind are discharged via disturbances of the body surface, of intake, digestion, elimination, breathing, etc. Such "psychosomatic" disturbances are developmen-

tally determined at this time of life. It is important for later events which particular bodily outlets[3] are given preference by the individual since this choice gives rise to increased sensitivity and vulnerability in the organ system concerned, i.e., the skin, the respiratory system, the intestinal system, the sleep rhythm, etc. [1970, p. 164]

And she pointed out that "this easy access from mind to body (and vice versa) diminishes with advancing ego development and the opening up of new, purely mental pathways of discharge by means of action, thought, speech. Where it remains more than usually open, on the other hand, it accounts directly for the range of *psychosomatic symptomatology*, i. e., for *asthma, eczema, ulcerative colitis, headaches, migraine*, etc." (p. 164).[4] Here again we have pathology that does not stem from conflict, though conflict may well become involved in a secondary way.

As this passage and innumerable others indicate, Anna Freud followed her father in his (1923) statement—rarely challenged—that the ego is first and foremost a bodily ego; where the biological givens are concerned, almost everyone agrees that, as they develop, the somatic pathways subserving visual, auditory, tactile, kinaesthetic, and other perceptions, as well as motor discharge pathways, play an enormous part in fostering ego growth. To this extent it is perfectly legitimate for psychoanalysts to take into account the origins and maturation of *biological* structures, the impact of the stimuli they *mediate* on the developing psyche, including the promotion of adaptation (or maladaptation), and the way in which the functions they subserve are brought under the executive control of the growing ego. But it seems to me that the passages I have quoted from Glover and Anna Freud point to a clearer and less misleading picture of early life (and its consequences for the future) than Hartmann's survey of the role of "conflict-free spheres" and "ego-apparatuses," as these are held to be operative in early childhood, conveys. And, for all their recognition of the importance of biological factors, they do not confuse them with psychologi-

---

3. i.e., of what would otherwise be dammed up discharge, to use an unfashionable expression but one which seems to me indispensable.

4. I have suggested elsewhere that the term "psychosomatic" is open to misunderstanding unless, as in this case, it is given precision (Yorke 1985). Further, the italicized passage is quoted without prejudice to other aspects of etiology.

cal ones, while rightly recognizing their mutual influence. Indeed, in using Anna Freud's profile, the Hampstead Clinic came to refer to "apparatuses *subserving* ego functions," to avoid any confusion of biology with psychology. This designation allowed the diagnostician to consider the effects of both sensory and motor impairment on *the child's mental functioning* at the stage of assessment. That, after all, is what matters. Admittedly, the change in wording in this section of the profile schema differs only slightly from the published version, and though I think it would have been better to avoid the word "apparatus" altogether, the emphasis on ego *functioning*, always present in the schema, at least makes it clear that the diagnostician is not meant to think in terms of *static mental structures*. But since what is laid down at the very beginning of life is a developmental *program*, a good deal may happen later (trauma or illness, for example) that interferes with that program (or pattern for development) and affect the child's functioning, often in a detrimental way. Psychosomatic disturbances, for example, may arise long after early childhood is passed.

Anna Freud's approach to psychoanalytic diagnosis did not make her a "Hartmannite," honorary or otherwise. It is hard to believe, in any case, that even without Hartmann's contributions she and her colleagues would have failed to take account of sensory and motor impairments or, for that matter, *exceptional endowments* on the child's psychological development. When the Clinic first began its studies of blind children, partly on the grounds that a knowledge of the role of sight in psychological development is best approached through psychoanalytic observation and study (including, where indicated, psychoanalytic treatment) of those who do not possess this capability, or who only possess it in part, or who have acquired it and then lost it, the staff engaged in the project were concerned with the effects of the incapacity on *all aspects of psychic development*. And the same goes for the deaf, and other children we studied with other handicaps or chronic illnesses that impaired sensory input or motor discharge. For it is not just a matter of the effects of psychic *structure*, let alone specialized psychic structures, that is in question. When Freud first used the term *mental apparatus*, he did not mean "mental structure," but used a way of referring to a mind in which the interplay of structure, dynamics, and economics all played an indispensable part. As long as these considerations are kept in mind, however, the enormous difficulties posed for ego development in the congenitally blind child will serve to remind us of the importance of Hartmann's general reflections, however much we may disagree with some of them in detail.

Some further comments on autonomous "functions and processes" seem called for, and I will refer briefly to some of Hartmann's own examples. Perception has been mentioned in relation to the blind, and we can agree with Hartmann that perception in all its modalities has an important part to play in ego development and, inter alia, the capacity for reality testing. But few faculties are more susceptible to psychological interference, and minor misperceptions are, for almost everyone, an everyday occurrence. Hysterical blindness is rare, but time and time again we find that a second glance shows that the first gave a false impression. Many of these misperceptions are self-evidently in line with a wish: the recently bereaved or the rejected may repeatedly find that the reappearance of the loved one seen in the distance or passed in the street is a painful illusion; perception, and with it reality appraisal, has been momentarily outwitted by a desperate longing. And the fleeting triumph of the wish over reality occurs in a great many less overtly painful and more routine states of mind. Admittedly, it is the prompt reinstatement of the reality ego, through a *relatively* independent perceptual system, that reestablishes the painful reality or the real states of affairs in matters of seemingly everyday trivia. So the "autonomous" function of perception, however stable, is at least subject to temporary interference; we are all familiar with the more serious instances when less stable functioning permits the distorted perception of illusions in deliria or the delusions of psychoses.

The notorious unreliability of perceptual recall (Hartmann's autonomous "recall phenomena") has made many a judge in the criminal courts acquainted with at least some superficial aspects of the psychology of testimony. Different witnesses of the same incident, of whom there is no reason to suspect bad faith or mental impairment, give accounts that differ, at least in detail, in matters of import. However honest the witness, some id derivative may silently interfere with his accuracy of recall. And interference with recall phenomena can occur from preconscious sources. Anxiety in court may interfere as readily as any unconscious wish to aid defense or prosecution. And speaking of anxiety, we all know that, in many other circumstances, anxiety may interfere not only with recall but many other "autonomous" functions mentioned by Hartmann, including intention, object comprehension, and think-ing. If you cannot find your car keys at a moment when you need them urgently, and *panic*, the capacity to retrace your steps in a few moments of rational thinking goes by the board. And in many instances of se-vere *fright* brought about by a totally unexpected trauma, we know, as Freud (1920) pointed out, that the ego is briefly knocked out, and *all* ego functions, autonomous or not, cannot for the moment be brought into service, however effective their work has been carried out hitherto. The ego, as Freud said, is flooded with the excitation of *fright*.

But "thinking," in any case, is not a good example of an activity that derives from the ego alone. Rapaport (1950, 1951) has laid the foun-dations for a metapsychological view of its development and one that needs to be restated in terms of Anna Freud's (1963) concept of devel-opmental lines. Rapaport sketches its development from "hallucinatory wish fulfillment," through the "drive organization of memories," through the superimposition of a more sophisticated memory orga-nization, and through further steps until the capacity for abstract think-ing is reached. (It is of some interest that Rapaport put forward the ker-nel of these ideas in footnotes to his abridged version of Freud's paper on *The Two Principles of Mental Functioning* [1911] and that he referred, in so doing, to the "*id-psychology* of thought" [1950, pp. 311, 324–325]). That, at least, was a corrective to the one-sidedness of the term "ego-psychology": there may, indeed, be "ego-psychologists" but it would be a little surprising to meet an "ego psychoanalyst." At the higher levels of thinking, the past played by the id may not be detectable, but it would be wrong to assume that an element of primary process men-tation cannot unwittingly guide the thinker at moments of seemingly spotless logic.

When we come to speech, which in its development is so closely linked with a growing capacity for thought, we have no doubt about its built-in maturational capacities, even though the language in which it finds expression has to be learned. When fully developed, it seems to provide a good example of *relative* ego autonomy: unless something is seriously amiss, almost everyone acquires the capacity to speak, ir-respective of upbringing, and in doing so to use at least a primitive form of grammar that recognizes subjects, objects, and verbs, however im-perfectly these are strung together in violations of syntax. But we can *love* words, and *hate* them, too, and we recognize those moments in childhood when nothing is real *as long as it isn't said.* And the ease with which both words and thoughts can be instinctualized is familiar, at least to every analyst. The autonomy of language is by no means self-evident.

Perhaps we should also ask ourselves what happens to ego autonomy under operations of large group conditions as first described by Le Bon (1895) and amplified and expanded in psychoanalytic terms by Freud (1921). When the superego loses its effectiveness or is willingly loaned to a charismatic leader; when rational thinking is so readily set aside; when hatred is so massively projected and, so often, put into action; when a group *knows it is right* and cannot listen to or consider any other point of view—under all these conditions, it is hard to speak of ego autonomy. It may be said that, in such cases, we are not speaking of an "average expectable environment," but it is an environment and way of regarding the world to which many otherwise seemingly sane people dedicate a substantial part of their lives.

I have tried to indicate how questionable an unqualified view of "autonomy" can be. It seems to me that psychoanalysis can manage perfectly well with the concept of the preconscious and the *relative, if sometimes fleeting, autonomy of some of its operations.* Indeed, Hartmann (1958) himself recognized that the preconscious was in need of greater study. It is one of the great contributions of Ernst Kris to have embarked on that task in 1950, in a paper of permanent value, and one that is, in my view, highly pertinent to these discussions. Perhaps this matter will be raised in our further deliberations this weekend.

It may assist the discussion of some of Hartmann's other observations if we first turn to the concept of the mutual development of ego and id from an undifferentiated matrix. Many will be familiar with statements made on this matter by Anna Freud, Hoffer, Melanie Klein, and others in the 1952[5] symposium; and Hartmann himself emphasised the difficulties in introducing such a complex and wide-ranging subject. So perhaps it should be said that nothing lends itself more readily to speculation than the earliest phases of mental organization and functioning, infant observational research notwithstanding. We have no direct access to the minds of the very young, and it is all too easy to

---

5. See *The Psychoanalytic Study of the Child* 7:9–68.

attribute to the early phases systems of functioning that are derived from the later analytic study of older children. The simplest formulations may be the best, but there can be no certainty attached to them. Like many, I have always thought of the drives as active from the beginning. However, it seems important to remind ourselves of Freud's dictum that the drives as such can never be known; they can be inferred only through their representatives or derivatives. In this sense they are, as Freud said, "our mythology," which does not mean that they are, as some psychoanalysts would like to think, dispensable constructs. We accept that they take up a place somewhere between psyche and soma, and although we have to be content with that limited assumption, we do not question a connection between drives and bodily sources. As Freud (1938) said: "There can be no question but that the libido has somatic sources, that it streams to the ego from various organs and parts of the body . . . though in fact the whole body is an erotogenic one of this kind" (p. 151). Nor can one doubt the bodily roots of destructiveness, and the dichotomy between bliss and murderous rage characteristic of early life.

But, at the very start, with the memory trace, activated and reactivated in the energic ebb and flow of drive activity (to paraphrase Glover 1950), it seems reasonable to speak of an undifferentiated state out of which id and ego develop. Freud was very clear about the matter. In *An Outline of Psychoanalysis* (1938), he described the id as the "oldest of these psychical provinces" and added that it contained "everything that is inherited, that is present at birth, that is laid down in the constitution—above all, therefore, the instincts, which originate from the somatic organization and which find a first psychical expression here [in the id] *in forms unknown to us*" (p. 145, emphasis added). And in a footnote he states that this, "the oldest portion of the psychical apparatus, remains the most important throughout life."

And so: What of ego? Freud (1938) went on to assert that, under the influence of the "real external world, from what was originally a cortical layer, equipped with the organs for receiving stimuli" and with what elsewhere he called a protective shield against them, "a special organization has arisen which henceforward acts as an intermediary between the id and the external world" (p. 145). This is the ego. It has a "pre-established connection between sense perception and muscular action" and can store experiences about them (in the memory)" (p. 145) (i.e., through the organization of memory traces). Freud then mentions briefly the bearing of all this on other ego functions in relation to the external world. But the ego also looks *inwards*, and Freud describes how the id is (gradually) brought under its control, though he is clearly no longer restricting his account to the earliest phase of development.

Does this amount to a concept of an ego developing out of an "undifferentiated ego-id"? In a later revealing passage Freud (1938) has this to say:

> There can be no question of restricting one or the other of the basic instincts to one of the provinces of the mind. They must necessarily be met with everywhere. We may picture an initial state as one in which the total available energy of Eros, which henceforward we shall speak of as "libido," is present in the still *undifferentiated ego-id*[6] and serves to *neutralize*[7] the destructive tendencies which are simultaneously present. (We are without a term analogous to "libido" for describing the energy of the destructive instinct.) At a later stage it becomes relatively easy for us to follow the vicissitudes of the libido, but this is more difficult with the destructive instinct. [pp. 149–150, emphases added]

So there cannot be much doubt about the origin of the concept of an undifferentiated ego-id, even though Freud had begun by describing the ego as arising out of the id. Personally, I think that to distinguish the *ways* in which the formulations were couched would not amount to a point of much substance. Nor did Anna Freud (1966), whose observations on the concept seem well worth quoting:

> Hartmann reminds us of the concept of an "undifferentiated ego-id" (Freud 1940) from which the id-ego differentiation arises on the basis of inner and outer perception, motility, preconscious memory traces, experience, and learning. [p. 237]

It is quite clear that Anna Freud considers it Hartmann's merit to have emphasized and developed what was in all essentials her father's concept. It allows us to see that ego development is no mere matter of the influence of the external world alone, and to avoid what she called

---

6. In a footnote, Freud says that "this picture of the basic forces or instincts . . . still arouses much opposition among analysts."

7. It is of interest to compare Freud's use of this word with that of ego psychology.

"the mistake of treating the two agencies in the mind as two different personalities altogether" (p. 237). As for the inborn roots of the id, its underlying physical correlates can foster atypical development that has profound psychological consequences. We would understand facts of this kind better if we knew more about the links between body and mind—perhaps the oldest and most intractable philosophical problem of all. I am thinking of a child who showed remarkable physical precocity by the age of 3 and who was menstruating at the age of 5. Her id development, and not just her physical maturation, was premature, and its consequences for ego development correspondingly atypical too.

Hartmann, in extending his list of primary ego-autonomous functions to include *synthesis* and *self-preservation*, also conceived them as activated by instinctual energies—libido and aggression—that become increasingly *neutralized* as their functions are put at the service of reality adaptation rather than instinctual needs. I would regard the "neutralization" as relative rather than absolute. Since people differ in important respects, its stability is more readily maintained in some people than it is in others. But even the strongest ego may succumb to fatigue, illness, and other misfortunes so that executive control (even of self-preservation) is put at risk. And, for children in particular, the outside world can exercise irresistible pressures. To take an example, ambitious parents may send an intelligent child careering to the bottom of the class by inordinate demands for academic success at all costs, neglecting the child's other needs in the process. If, for instance, this comes about by mobilizing the child's powerful (if unrecognized) aggressive forces against the parents, or—via the superego—against the child's feelings of self-worth, a high I.Q. born of inheritance may do nothing to save *that* situation.

Hartmann further contended that certain ego-structures and functions (even defenses such as *reaction formation*) could, in the course of time, become so modified that, by a process of "change of function," they are freed from involvement in earlier conflict and may therefore be said to have acquired "secondary autonomy" (Hartmann 1951). The original drive connections no longer survive without modification and gradually take over a wealth of other functions in the framework of the ego. The greater their stability in these circumstances the more they may contribute (for example) to character formation. Intellectualization, for instance, may arise as an important defensive maneuver in adolescence; and if it continues to function defensively—as in some obsessional people—it may lead to personality defect in the form of emotional impoverishment or inhibition. In rather a different way, something similar might be said about altruistic surrender. But in the course of development, intellectualization and altruism may lose their defensive status and so change their function that they become important autonomous factors in adaptation. (In these last examples, I have deliberately chosen mechanisms described by Anna Freud in 1936— the year preceding Hartmann's presentation and a work that was very much in his mind at the time. They have the merit of demonstrating that "change of function" may be the enemy of healthy adaptation, and character formation may lead to a personality that may satisfy its possessor but may be remarkably unattractive to others and maladaptive to their needs.)

In Hartmann's thinking, the concept of autonomy, and with it neutralization, is extended to include *automatization*. Special mention may be made of *preconscious automatisms*. Walking, for example, may be an enjoyable activity undertaken for its own sake. It can also be almost wholly automatic (which is not to say without purpose) if it facilitates a more impelling intention. And a child may use it in a conflictual way in defying or complying with the mother's wishes. Likewise, shaving is a rapidly acquired and, as a rule, conflict-free skill, though there may at any moment be a breakthrough of aggressive force when the shaver "inadvertently" cuts himself and roundly berates himself for doing so. But it is quite clear that relative freedom from conflict for functions such as these is of immensely adaptive value in routine everyday life. If they never were, or no longer are, driven by unmodified instinctual forces it is equally true that they may receive little attention cathexis when carried out habitually. Preconscious activity is freed for other purposes such as thinking and planning ahead. In these respects preconscious automatisms differ from the pathological automatisms of compulsions and tics. But Hartmann has in mind more than this. Following Freud, he reminds us that the development of the reality principle may involve the progression from mere motor discharge to *adaptive action*. In well-established and habitual achievements, motor "apparatuses" not only function automatically, but their mental correlates and related mental acts are automatized too. And automatic response is a vital acquisition that may be self-protective when meeting sudden and realistic danger. That, at any rate, is how I understand the usefulness of these concepts, while stressing the readiness with which they may shift from conflictual to nonconflictual activities and back again.

How do neutralized activities relate to sublimation? Dr. Bergmann has raised this interesting point. A spontaneous answer might well be that "neutralization" extends the concept of "sublimation" to include the aggressive drives. Kris (1955), in studying the issue with special reference to child development, underlined the fact that the term comprises both goal displacement and energy transformation, and suggested that the first be designated as "sublimation" and the second as "neutralization." But he did not see the relation between the two as a necessarily simple matter, and spoke of their relationships and sometimes interdependence in artistic creativity as well as childhood (considering child art in the process). I find his paper of great interest, though it does not seem to have had great influence. Incidentally, in reference to a point made by Dr. Bergmann, Kris does not appear to have found the notions of neutralization on the one hand and fusion and defusion of drives antithetical. I can readily identify with this view, and would add that the whole question of binding and delay in preconscious functioning is closely involved in these issues; Kris, above all, cannot be accused of neglecting them in his writings.

Hartmann's psychology also extends the concept of ego synthesis, closely associated with Freud and Nunberg, to what he called "fitting in" or "fitting together," in which he saw Parr's (1926) discussion of the lawful correlation of the organism's individual parts and, in discussing their interdependence, regarded them as the biological underpinning, in the service of adaptation, for the ego's synthetic function. And lest it be thought, again, that in stressing adaptation, Hartmann was indifferent to psychic conflict, it is only fair to emphasise that he did make contributions to, and put considerable stress on, intrapsychic conflict. Within the id, "intrapsychic conflict" would be a contradiction in terms, as Glover (1960, 1961, 1968) observed. Within the superego conflicting identifications have long been recognized; and the "two-faced" superego of one of his drug addicts was graphically described by Simmel many years ago. But, as Anna Freud (1964) pointed out, Hartmann's main concern was with conflicts within the ego. Denial, for example, may have a defensive function that fosters internal har-

mony, but in certain cases it may, by interfering with reality perception, impose a substantial handicap on a different, but equally important, adaptive ego function. Lastly, any precis of Hartmann's views on
the psychology of the ego must indicate his concern, not only with the
relationships between intrapsychic structures and their integration with
the demands of social reality, but also with biological and maturational
factors, and with the recognition that ontogeny cannot be regarded as
the sole arbiter in development, but that due place must be given to
phylogeny in adaptation to an "average expectable environment" as
well as to an "average expectable conflict."

Dr. Bergmann has already indicated that broad sweep of Hartmann's
interests, and I, too, would like to point to some of his further contributions. I have in mind his paper on the metapsychology of schizophrenia, to the distinction between the ego as a mental apparatus and
the ego as a self-representation within that structure (in an extremely
useful clarification of Freud's applications of the term), to his important contributions to the understanding of "infantile neurosis" (a term
I always thought unfortunate), to his views on mental health, and to
his searching essay on psychoanalysis and moral values. Finally, every
psychoanalytically trained observer of children will recognize what
Hartmann (1950) called the "sign and signal function of behaviour" as
indicators of "structurally central and partly unconscious developments." As Anna Freud has emphasized on more than one occasion, it
has long been legitimate to make deductions (outside formal analysis)
from symptomatic acts, daydreams, and children's dreams, as well as,
at a later date, from certain character traits.

Hartmann's name became so closely linked with the *adaptive* point
of view that, for a long time, it became almost necessary to say that he
did not invent it. The same may be said of the developmental point of
view. Hartmann and Rapaport added these viewpoints to the other
metapsychological ones. I have questioned this before, and will do so
again. In the very first phase of psychoanalytic thinking, up to 1897,
adaptation to the internal or external world could be interfered with
by the psychic damage occasioned by a traumatic event. It could properly be said that adaptation was always a major consideration for psychoanalytic thinking, and this was true throughout the many modifications that shifted the focus of psychoanalytic attention in any given
historical period. In 1923, the drastic changes in the view of the ego

and its functioning especially emphasized the view of the ego as an executive apparatus of the mind that tried to meet the often conflicting claims of the id, the ego, *and external reality*. Any lingering belief in the ego as the helpless rider of the id horse was formally and finally dispelled by 1926, in spite of the fact that, under certain circumstances, its power can be seriously weakened. The ego, in its executive capacity, was *first and foremost an adaptive organ*. As for a developmental point of view, psychoanalysis always was, whatever else, a developmental psychology. Anna Freud was once rather irritated when, in discussion, she felt obliged to make this point. But Hartmann and Rapaport repeatedly added to the points of view of metapsychology an adaptive and a developmental one.

As you are all aware, Freud formulated three metapsychological points of view—at first, the topographical and dynamic, adding the economic one later. With the advent of the structural theory, it became customary to replace "topographical" by "structural." Hartmann and many of his colleagues, including Kris and Rapaport, continued to speak of a topographical point of view to stand alongside a structural one, and I have always considered the thinking behind that assumption sound. Anna Freud never gave up the topographical point of view, as she once told me in the course of a long discussion, and her father used the term in the *Outline*, even though he considered the terms *Ucs.*, *Pcs.*, and *Pcpt. Cs.* as depicting qualities of psychic content. I find no difficulty in this, and no doubt many of you share this opinion. But to speak of a developmental point of view, or an adaptive point of view, as on all fours with the others seems questionable; after all, adaptation and developmental shifts at every level depend above all on the operational relationships between the structural, topographic, dynamic, and economic *points of view*, not *systems*.

I would not lose any sleep over this matter, let alone go to war about it, but the danger of psychoanalytic theorizing has always been the emphasis of one or other aspect of metapsychology to the exclusion or relative neglect of the rest. The problem, in Hartmann's case—as I see it—is that sophisticated and organized ego structures are attributed to the earliest, dynamic phase of the functioning of the mental apparatus to the detriment of serious attempts to establish the orderly, sequential developmental stages of early infancy. Had that not been so, many of his formulations could not so easily be called into question.

I would regard Hartmann's ego psychology as one that over-emphasises the structural point of view at the expense of the dynamic and the economic one—a one-sidedness, perhaps, to be detected in a good deal of theorizing since the appearance of *The Ego and the Id* in 1923. I have suggested elsewhere (Yorke 1996) that, although that book was a watershed, *in the way it was subsequently misused by some psychoanalysts* it was not altogether an unmixed blessing. At that time I had in mind the so-called "object-relations" schools; but the observation is relevant in the present context—and perhaps in others.

To my mind, Anna Freud undersold herself in the 70th Birthday Hartmann address. She never found it easy to be publicly critical, and on an occasion of that kind she was understandably generous, though she never said anything she knew to be untrue. But at least she did refer, in the context of her talk, to her concept of *developmental lines*, and for me that concept is of the greatest value in the detailed study it affords both of adaptation and maladaptation. It is less overtly metapsychological than the developmental profile, but it is shot through with metapsychology in that it brings together the *results* of the interplay of id, ego, and, where established, superego, in the form of way stations that are the result of their interaction, and "also age-related sequences of them, which in importance, frequency and regularity are comparable to the maturational sequences of libidinal stages and the gradual unfolding of the ego-functions" (A. Freud 1963). And she allows for premature attainments, arrests, and reversals along the lines (A. Freud 1965). In an earlier discussion I added:

> In effect these lines put together what the profile takes apart: they *synthesize* rather than *analyze* (in an everyday or chemical sense). Examples will readily spring to mind: they include such closely scrutinized lines as the one which leads from dependency to emotional self-reliance and adult object-relations via various stations on the way; from irresponsibility to responsibility in body management; from wetting and soiling to bladder and bowel control; from ego-centricity to companionship; and many more. [Yorke 1980, p. 598]

In that respect she has, I believe, been more successful than Hartmann, though her study of the ego was less extensive than his.

In spite of the reservations expressed in this paper, there is no doubt that Hartmann has been responsible for some very rich and rewarding observations, some of which still await integration with the main body of psychoanalytic theory. Take, for example, his comments on fantasy. We all know that withdrawal into fantasy can be pathological. But is is also true that fantasy, insofar as it involves the bringing together of different mental content in a form that corresponds neither to a past or present reality, can point to a future goal and act as a spur to bringing about a new reality. In this connection I am reminded of a little boy, reported by Lussier, who was born with a severe congenital shortening of both arms, and whose mother was so ashamed of him that she dressed him in a coat that hid his arms from public view. The boy's fantasies were that, in spite of his severe handicap, he would learn to play the trumpet; he would learn to swim; he would learn to be an angler; and he would ride a bicycle. None of these fantasies remained fantasies; he learned to swim, to dive, to ride a bicycle, to fish, and to play the trumpet sufficiently well to teach it professionally.

The paradoxical fact seems to be that Hartmann would have agreed with many of the criticisms made in this paper. Most of them can be found, at least in embryo if not more fully developed, at various points in his writings. But he had the rather maddening habit of giving with one hand and taking away with the other. That doesn't make for easy reading, but it has to be allowed for in arriving at any assessment of his achievements.

Lastly: a point related to Dr. Bergmann's paper. I really can't see Hartmann's stress on adaptation as conformity, or as necessarily running counter to the views set out by Freud (1930) in his masterly *Civilization and Its Discontents*. Perhaps it is the stress laid on the "average expectable environment" that is in part at the root of the trouble. Adaptation is adaptation to external and *internal* surroundings, we agree; but it has to be said that, these days, the environment itself is far from expectable. Family structure is everywhere changing, and changing unpredictably; anything and everything goes. Adaptation involves the capacity to adapt *as best one can* to anything and everything. And it isn't just a matter of family structure. To take a different kind of example, one may have to adapt to being put into prison, and some will do this more easily than others. Nelson Mandela's survival is indeed the remarkable achievement of a remarkable man, but lesser yet still remarkable achievements can be found in others.

Finally, I would add this. Whatever is to be said about the Hartmann era—and I don't view it in the almost global terms of Dr. Bergmann—when I look around at the contemporary pluralism that is somehow collectively called psychoanalysis, I can only feel sad about its passing. There was plenty to disagree about, but even within an I.P.A. that accommodated highly controversial and often clear departures from some basic Freudian principles, it was, on the whole, possible to see what was psychoanalysis and what was not. That was an advantage that, sadly, is rapidly being lost.

References

Freud, A. (1936). *The Ego and the Mechanisms of Defense*. Writings, II. New York: International Universities Press.

———— (1952). The mutual influences in the development of ego and id. *Psychoanalytic Study of the Child* 7:42–50. New York: International Universities Press.

———— (1962). Assessment of childhood disturbances. *Psychoanalytic Study of the Child* 27:149–158. New York: International Universities Press.

———— (1963). The concept of developmental lines. *Psychoanalytic Study of the Child* 13:245–265. New York: International Universities Press.

———— (1966). *Links Between Hartmann's Ego Psychology and the Child Analyst's Thinking*. Writings, V. New York: International Universities Press.

———— (1970). *The Symptomatology of Childhood: A Preliminary Attempt at Classification*. Writings, VII. New York: International Universities Press.

———— (1979). *Mental Health and Illness in Terms of Mental Harmony and Dis-Harmony*. Writings, VIII. New York: International Universities Press.

Freud, S. (1911). Formulations on the two principles of mental functioning. *Standard Edition* 12.

———— (1920). Beyond the pleasure principle. *Standard Edition* 18.

———— (1921). Group psychology and analysis of the ego. *Standard Edition* 18.

———— (1923).The ego and the id. *Standard Edition* 19.

———— (1930). Civilization and its discontents. *Standard Edition* 21.

———— (1937). Analysis terminable and interminable. *Standard Edition* 23.

———— (1938). An outline of psycho-analysis. *Standard Edition* 23.

Glover, E. (1950). Functional aspects of the mental apparatus. In *The Early Development of Mind*. New York: International Universities Press.

——— (1961). Some recent trends in psychoanalytic theory. *Psychoanalytic Quarterly* 30:86–107.

——— (1968). *The Birth of the Ego*. London: Allen & Unwin.

Hartmann, H. (1939). *Ego Psychology and the Problem of Adaptation*. London: Imago.

——— (1951). Technical implications of ego psychology. *Psychoanalytic Quarterly* 20:31–43.

——— (1952). The mutual influences in the development of ego and id. *Psychoanalytic Study of the Child* 7:9–30. New York: International Universities Press.

——— (1964). *Essays in Ego Psychology*. London: Hogarth.

Hoffer, W. (1952). The mutual influences in the development of ego and id. *Psychoanalytic Study of the Child* 7:31–41. New York: International Universities Press.

Kennedy, H., and Yorke, C. (1982). Steps from outer to inner conflict viewed as superego precursors. *Psychoanalytic Study of the Child* 37:221–228. New York: International Universities Press.

Kris, E. (1950). On preconscious mental processes. *Psychoanalytic Quarterly* 19:540–560.

——— (1955). The recovery of childhood memories in psychoanalysis. *Psychoanalytic Study of the Child* 11:54–88. New York: International Universities Press.

Rapaport, D., et al. (1950a). *Organization and Pathology of Thought*. New York: Columbia University Press.

——— (1950b). On the psychoanalytic theory of thinking. *International Journal of Psycho-Analysis* 31:161–170.

Yorke, C. (1980). The contributions of the diagnostic profile and the assessment of developmental lines to child psychiatry. *Psychiatric Clinics of North America* 3:593–603.

——— (1985). Fantasy and the body-mind problem: some preliminary observations. *Psychoanalytic Study of the Child* 40:319–328. New Haven, CT: Yale University Press.

——— (1995). Freud's psychology: Can it survive? *Psychoanalytic Study of the Child* 50:3–31.

——— (1996). Diagnosis in clinical practice: its relationship to psychoanalytic theory. *Psychoanalytic Study of the Child* 51:190–214. New Haven, CT: Yale University Press.

III

CONFERENCE PROCEEDINGS

OPENING REMARKS OF THE CONFERENCE

Bergmann: In the tradition in which I was brought up, I should open with the benediction that my maker has kept me alive, sustained me, and brought me to this day, for surely not many 84-year-olds can say that much. In more secular terms, I want to thank the participants of this conference, and particularly André Green and Clifford Yorke for crossing the Atlantic to be with us at this conference. Each of them brought a perspective to bear on the Hartmann era that could not have been obtained within the continental limits of the United States. One of the pleasures of this conference for me was that all those who were asked to attend did in fact want to participate, a rare event in life. I also want to thank the Psychoanalytic and Research Fund for unanimously agreeing to support and fund this conference, and in particular I would like to thank Sidney and Eleanor Murphy for having taken over its administrative burdens.

The book we are planning will consist of three parts: my monograph, your discussions, and a record of our deliberations of today and tomorrow. Two-thirds of this work is done, and I want to express my gratitude and happiness at the level of the presentations. They have enormously broadened and deepened my work in many directions. The future reader of this section will be amazed to discover how little redundancy there was in your presentations. This reader, like myself, will learn much that is new but it will not always be easy reading.

I hope that our deliberations this weekend will throw light on some of the dark spots, if not the dark continents, of our presentations. What remains to be done is to have a discussion that does justice to your contributions.

Harold Blum wondered whether the Hartmann era is still sufficiently alive among psychoanalysts today. I believe that reading your presentations will convince everyone that Hartmann's thoughts and the Hartmann era come back to life if approached on the level of this conference. However, I would like to stress that we were not aiming for a best seller, nor should we be interested in consensus, but in demonstrating that when senior analysts meet they talk with each other rather than at each other, and what emerges from their deliberations is more than just the sum total of the individual contributions.

I shall now enumerate the issues that emerged for me from the presentations.

(1) My decision to speak of the Hartmann era was challenged by Yorke, who pointed out that Anna Freud's book, *The Ego and the Mechanisms of Defense*, preceded Hartmann's monograph; Ernst Kris and Jacobson also made major contributions before they became Hartmann's co-workers; Anton Kris, Kernberg, and Blum dealt with the issue of whether there was such an era, but came down on my side. The question of "eras" is controversial in history. Erwin Panofsky, the distinguished art historian, entitled one of his books *The Renaissance and Renaissances in Western Art* (1960).[1] His opening sentence reads, "Modern scholarship has become increasingly skeptical of periodization." We should not be surprised if there is no unanimity on this question. It would enrich our conference if we could shed light on this issue. There is more at stake here than meets the eye. If we accept the fact that there are eras in the history of psychoanalysis, we have to acknowledge that psychoanalysis is not necessarily undergoing a linear development.

(2) I feel grateful to Grossman's presentation for suggesting that the Hartmann controversy may be seen as a boundary problem. From his discussion psychoanalysis emerges as a discipline with flexible and often vague boundaries. He traces it back to Freud's (1913) "The Claims of Psychoanalysis to Scientific Interest." I am inclined to go further back to the differences between the *Studies on Hysteria* and *The Interpretation of Dreams*. The former had firm boundaries in that it was a work of specialists writing for other specialists interested in treating hysterics. The *Interpretation of Dreams* reached into normal psychology and laid the foundations for psychoanalysis as a depth psychology. Be-

---

1. Panofsky, E. (1960). The *Renaissance and Renaissances in Western Art*. Stockholm: Almqvist & Wiksell.

cause of its wider scope, it did not have firm boundaries. I have pointed out elsewhere (Bergmann 1997) that the question of what is and what is not psychoanalysis erupted for the first time when Freud announced, to the astonishment of the Vienna Psychoanalytic Society, that Adler's views are not psychoanalysis. The significant differences between Green, Kris, and Kernberg on one side, and Neubauer and Grossman on the other, can profitably be approached as a boundary problem. Neubauer has asked us to arrive at a decision whether we wish to maintain the narrower place of psychoanalysis, or whether we follow Hartmann's outline of a general theory of psychoanalysis.

I would like to free us from the word "must." I would be satisfied if we could succeed in saying something on this subject that has not been said before.

(3) Blum and Kernberg raised the troubling question of the silence of the members of the Hartmann era about the real events that took place in their lives—their exile from Europe and the Holocaust. They emphasized an average, expectable environment when in fact all around them nothing was average. It would enhance the value of this conference if we could throw light on this phenomenon. Blum also raised an issue that is significant, the idealization of psychoanalytic theory during the Hartmann era. Idealization leads to disillusionment.

Hale (1996) in his recently published history of psychoanalysis in the United States made it clear that the spectacular growth of psychoanalysis after World War II began in the armed forces.[2] Military psychiatry during WW II was under the influence of Freud's ego psychology. It humanized army psychiatry by the insight that every person has a potential breaking point. The psychoanalysts who presided over this expansion were William and Carl Menninger, Kubie, Alexander, and others. The Hartmann group reaped the benefit of this expansion, but it did not bring it about.

(4) Kernberg observed: "The rejection of the death drive—as not meeting the test of science—was only the major manifestation of the general tendency in Hartmann's theoretical formulation, namely the deemphasis on primitive aggression and sexuality." Hartmann underestimated Freud's discovery of the destructive nature of human beings. This deemphasis also led to the neglect of the exploration of perversions. On the other hand the "sanitized" Freud was more readily accepted by American culture. Blum's and Kernberg's observations complement each other.

---

2. Hale, N. (1996). *The Rise and Crisis of Psychoanalysis in the United States*. New York: Oxford University Press.

(5) From André Green's perspective the gap between Freud and Hartmann is great. He brought us to Chapter 31 of the *New Introductory Lectures* (pp. 73–74), emphasizing that in the id any measure of representation has disappeared. There is always something breathtakingly radical in Green's writings and we find it again in this presentation. His citing of Chapter 31 made me reread this passage in the English translation as well as in the German original. The German original conveys a greater sense of awe about the mystery of the id. But in my reading of Freud, Green's emphasis on the absence of representation in the id may be implied but is not explicit in Freud's writings. For in that chapter Freud also speaks of: "What little we know of it (id) we have learnt from our study of the dream-work and the construction of neurotic symptoms, and most of that is of a negative character and can be described only as a contrast to the ego" (p. 73).

In the outline, Freud (1940) returned to what seems to me his more habitual way of discussing the id, namely as having a language of its own, the language of the primary processes: "We have found that processes in the unconscious or in the Id obey different laws from those in the preconscious Ego. We name these laws in their totality the primary process, in contrast to the secondary process which governs the course of events in the preconscious in the Ego" (p. 164).

Here, Freud practically equated id with unconscious and ego with preconscious. It is not clear to me whether Green regards the primary processes as governing only the unconscious and not the id. On a clinical level, it seems to me that when we analysts are doing our best work, we are in direct contact with our patients' id and superego. When we speak to the ego, we usually uphold in one form or another the reality principle. I would appreciate a discussion on this clinical point.

(6) Green raised the valuable question of whether Freud's id was put aside or even eliminated by Hartmann's ego psychology. It reminded me that in 1966 Max Schur published a monograph entitled "The Id and the Regulatory Principles of Mental Functioning." It appeared as a monograph of the American Psychoanalytic Association. It therefore carried official imprimatur. There it stated: "The concept of an undifferentiated phase involves the assumption that the id is a product of development" (p. 69). "The emergence of the 'wish' marks the beginning of the functioning of what we call psychic structure" (p. 68). I propose that this transition from functioning on the level of a reflex apparatus to that of a wish represents the developmental model for the transition from "somatic needs" to instinctual drives as mental representations of stimuli arising within the soma, and for the development of the structure id from the undifferentiated phase (pp. 68–69).

The editors of that monograph expressed appreciation to Schur because he broadened the concept of the id and saw it as a constantly developing structure that has adaptive and survival functions. If we understand the logic of history, we can conclude that someone during this era had to write such a monograph, for the undifferentiated phase demanded a reevaluation of the id and a considerable diminution of its power. I was remiss in not giving this question the space that it deserves in my essay. Green also called "neutral energy" a "stillborn idea." On this point there seems to be unanimity. No one seems to have written in favor of the idea of neutralization.

(7) Anton Kris and Grossman raised the interesting question of the relationship between the Hartmann group and logical positivism. Kris saw the effort at systematization as the "last gasp" of nineteenth century idealism. If I understand him correctly, he considers logical positivism and psychoanalysis to be incompatible. In Green's terms, this attempt also went counter to Freud's spirit, and should be designated as antipsychoanalytic. I would like to raise the question of whether systematization is inimical to the psychoanalytic enterprise, or whether it was only undertaken prematurely.

(8) The relationship between Anna Freud and Hartmann was raised by Yorke, who warns us not to take Anna Freud's congratulations on Hartmann's 70th birthday as reflecting her real attitudes. Since I approached Hartmann from an historical point of view, I was fascinated by the fact that the 1939 monograph came to life in Yorke's discussion as if it were a contemporary document. Vividly Yorke showed that all autonomy of perception and memory, as well as speech, is only a relative autonomy. This autonomy may disappear under stress. He drew our attention to the fact that psychopathology takes place in early infancy and it therefore antedates, and is independent of, psychic conflict. By so doing, he highlighted basic differences between Anna Freud and Hartmann that their friendship tended to obscure.

Not unexpectedly, Kernberg made a similar claim for the relative independence of Jacobson and Mahler from Hartmann. These are welcome corrections of my attempt to create a Hartmann group. It seems to me now that it would have been better if I had differentiated between an inner circle consisting of Kris, Loewenstein, and Rapaport and a more independent group, Anna Freud, Jacobson, and Mahler, with Spitz and Eissler occupying an intermediary position.

Yorke's two quotes from the late writing of Freud (1937, 1940) assumed added significance because I quoted only one instance where Hartmann was rooted in Freud and Green took it to be the only anchor for Hartmann in Freud's work (from *The Ego and the Id*, p. 44). I realize that at this point we are in danger of becoming Talmudic.

(9) Grossman and Blum made me take another look at Hartmann's collected papers, and indeed, neither Hitler's name nor the term World War II appear in his index. I remember conducting a similar experiment with the *International Journal of Psycho-Analysis,* and I came to a similar conclusion: if that journal alone had survived, one would hardly know that World War II had been fought. Ernst Jones is the one exception,[3] with papers like "The Psychology of Quislingism" (1940). Since Grossman mentioned Eric Fromm and the Bühlers, Charlotte and Karl, I consulted the index of Hartmann's collected papers as well as the 1939 monograph. Neither Fromm's nor Adorno's name appears, but the Bühlers are quoted a few times. Nevertheless, one cannot say that Hartmann is actively engaged in a discussion with them. The only dialogue I found in Hartmann's writing is with phenomenologists: Dilthey, Jaspers, and Binswanger, and that was in 1927 in his very first publication.[4] In the rest of his work, Hartmann is reflecting but not engaging in any dialogue. I was thus forced to confront the question of Hartmann's style, a topic I did not address in my monograph. The difference between his and Freud's styles is striking. Ilse Grubrich-Simitis reports how when Freud was working on *Totem and Taboo,* he described how an idea "suddenly came together a few days ago, almost snapped in with an audible 'click,' and since then I am practically giddy" (p. 76). In a similar vein, Freud recorded the moment in which he was struck by the relationship between little Hans's phobia and the Oedipus complex. He exclaimed: "As I saw the two of them sitting in front of me and at the same time Hans's description of his anxiety horses, a further piece of solution shot through my mind, and a piece which I could well understand might escape his father" (p. 42).

No such moments are found in Hartmann's writing. Everything is secondary process. Small wonder that Yorke had a miserable summer reading Hartmann cover to cover.

(10) I am also grateful to Grossman for enlarging the horizon of my presentation by the discussion of the social forces that were active in Vienna when Hartmann's 1939 monograph was written. What emerges is the realization that many of the problems that we now struggle with were already active *in nuce* on the eve of World War II. They were only postponed by the war, emerging fully after 1945. These problems go to the very essence of what psychoanalysis is, as well as to its vulnerable structure.

---

3. Jones, E. (1940). The psychology of Quislingism. In *Applied Psychoanalysis,* vol. 1. London: Hogarth Press, pp. 276–283.

4. Hartmann, H. (1927). *Die Grunglagen der Psychoanalyse.* Leipzig: Thieme.

(11) Neubauer and Kernberg emphasized the close connection between the Hartmann era and infant observations. This issue may ultimately decide the place of the Hartmann era in the history of psychoanalysis. If infant observations will contribute markedly to the clarification of psychoanalytic theory, the place of the Hartmann era in the history of psychoanalysis will remain significant. At the present moment it seems difficult to have a productive discussion on this question. The opposing lines seem sharply drawn.

(12) Solnit's approach, as well as some of Neubauer's and Yorke's observations, made me aware of an aspect of the Hartmann era I failed to notice in my monograph, that the impact of Hartmann on child analysis and child therapy may be of greater significance than his contribution to adult analysis. If this is so, then Hartmann's role in child analysis will be a more lasting one.

I also would like to ask Solnit to tell us something about Hartmann's style as an analyst. My wife and I owe to the Hartmanns a hotel in Sils-Baselgia that we often visited. The Hartmanns are buried in a small churchyard near there and on their grave is a quote from Nietzsche, "Weh sagt vergeh, aber lust will alle ewigkeit" ("Pain says pass on, but desire yearns for eternity").

(13) As to the relationship between Hartmann's work and technique, Neubauer made the point that in the 1950s psychoanalytic technique was conflict-oriented, and centered on the Oedipus complex and the recovery of repressed memories, and that Hartmann himself as a supervisor was not significantly different from other supervisors. I assumed on the basis of the 1951 symposium on technique, Eissler's parameter paper, but particularly on the basis of Ernst Kris's last three papers in 1956, that the impact of the Hartmann era on technique was considerable. I learned from Kris and have taught my students to conduct psychoanalytic sessions in such a way that they give maximum chance for the good hour to emerge (Bergmann 1993). The number of people that Hartmann could supervise was necessarily small by comparison to the number of students who read his writings during their training period. What was the impact of Hartmann's thinking on them? The monographs of the Kris study group should offer testimony. I have not consulted them in writing my monograph, but I realize now that they are a mine of further information.

(14) Neubauer raised the question of what fuels the history of psychoanalysis, and what makes an era come and go. I read a note of anxiety into Neubauer's observation that every period carries a point to excess and that every line of inquiry, be it that of Mahler or Anna Freud, at a certain point comes to a halt. As we meet there is considerably anxiety about the future of psychoanalysis. We are therefore faced with the question whether psychoanalysis, like a ship

buffeted by storms, has no clear direction or whether, diversions notwithstand-ing, we can say that our discipline maintains a steady course towards a dis-cernible port. These are difficult questions, but they cannot be evaded. These question were implicit in my monograph, and hopefully we can find some-thing significant to add.

(15) I appreciated Arlow's reference to the Sidney Hook Symposium. For this symposium was also important in my own personal development. Together with Thomas Kuhn's (1962) *The Structure of Scientific Revolutions* it affected my view on psychoanalysis. Although Kuhn spoke only about the natural sciences, the application of his ideas to psychoanalysis was easy to make. My differentiation between heretics, modifiers, and extenders (1993) was stimulated by him.

As to the Hook Symposium, it took place in New York on March 25–29, 1958, and was published in book form in 1959. It was entitled *Psychoanalysis, Scientific Method and Philosophy*. The main psychoanalysts participating were Hartmann, Kubie, Kardiner, and, of course, Arlow himself. The philosophers of science were Ernst Nagel, Morris Lazerowitz, and Phillip Frank. Some soci-ologists also participated. What became evident to us younger analysts was the fact that the psychoanalysts were no match for the philosophers of sci-ence. The series called *Psychological Issues*, which began publication in 1958, as well as the *Journal of Psychoanalysis and Contemporary Thought*, were in part responses to the Hook Symposium.

In 1962, Waelder, reviewing the Symposium, divided psychoanalysis into various levels. The first level deals with all the facts of observation that an analyst makes about his patients. It was called the level of observation. Orga-nizing this data yields the level of clinical interpretation. This is, in turn, fol-lowed by a more abstract level, that of clinical generalization. On a further abstract level is psychoanalytic metapsychology, and the last level constitutes Freud's personal philosophy. Waelder made it clear that Freud's personal phi-losophy need not be adopted by other psychoanalysts. I recall vividly how Waelder's classification helped me to organize my thoughts and my teaching. However, soon metapsychology was found by George Klein not to be a higher clinical approach, but parallel and obsolete. When I think back to Waelder's classification today I am struck by the fact that it did not reflect the history of psychoanalysis, and it was another attempt at systematizing psychoanalysis.

(16) When I wrote my monograph, I set out to show that there was a Hartmann era in the United States, and that that era had come to an end. I also wanted to show that the Hartmann era is not synonymous with ego psychology in gen-eral. Your contributions have shown that to answer this question, sociologi-cal and cultural factors have to be taken into account in addition to strictly

psychoanalytic considerations. I treated Hartmann's 1939 monograph as background to the Hartmann era. In many presentations, however, Hartmann as a person returned to the center. It seems that Ernst Kris, Mahler, Spitz, Jacobson, and Anna Freud all made contributions that may survive independently of Hartmann. Even Rapaport, so very closely associated with Hartmann, may survive if psychological testing will continue to have a place in the mental health field. It is the captain himself who may go down with the ship. But, many of you have struck a more optimistic note. Thus

> Kernberg: "A premature effort to systematize psychoanalysis may not have done justice to its revolutionary, still evolving nature, but it generated significant findings that will need to be incorporated in our advancing science."

> Grossman: "The interdisciplinary stimulus Hartmann's conceptions provided are now finding expression in the current efforts of analysts to integrate ego psychology with neuropsychological and psychopharmacological discoveries and thought. . . . His keen awareness of the subtleties of interplay of theory and technique may yet provide a framework for their integration."

> Blum: "Hartmann remains an enduring influence upon psychoanalytic thought, internalized in the continuous evolution of psychoanalysis."

If we during this conference end on such an optimistic note, it seems to me that we would have to spell out as clearly as we can, how the Hartmann heritage will continue to be fruitful.

(17) You have read each other's contributions. If it meets with your approval, I would suggest that we first give every member of this group a chance to speak freely about whatever touched him and appeared significant in the readings. By this method I hope to prevent a purely "secondary process" discussion. Green has suggested, and I agree with him, that the personality of the analyst can never be eliminated from psychoanalytic discourse. We have your papers. We now wish to establish contact with you as a person. We will then proceed to a systematic discussion of the prepared contributions and hopefully, before we close, return once more to a general discussion. I am keenly aware of the fact that the number of questions I have raised by far exceeds the time at our disposal. On the other hand, I am also painfully aware that I have left much that is valuable out of my discussion. My aim was not to summarize, but to initiate a discussion. I hope I have succeeded.

Hospitality demands that those who have crossed the ocean, André and Clifford, speak first.

Green: I'm very happy to have been invited to participate in this conference. This is the ideal type of conference that I wish to be established in the analytic community, selecting a topic and asking a few people chosen for their competence, holding divergent views, to express their opinions and then organize them in a publication that would be available to everyone.

My position may be a surprise to you because you may have not had a precise idea of what has been going on in Europe in comparison to what happened in the same period in the United States. For us, there is no doubt that there was a Hartmann era. The way it appeared in Europe, and especially in France, is that Hartmann's time was not only an era, but that he was dominating American psychoanalysis. Of course, I later realized that Hartmann's was not the only voice, that he had opponents. For some of us, these opponents were respectable, for instance, Bertram Lewin, whose influence was belittled. But there are also others. Martin emphasized that there were many important people whose names were connected to Hartmann, but in fact much of what they wrote was independent of Hartmann's core of ideas. Many are classified as Hartmannites, but their way of thinking was not Hartmann's. For instance, I was not surprised to see that Otto could easily transfer Edith Jacobson's findings into the framework of object relations theory. She was supposed to belong to Hartmann's stream. I enjoy reading her writings and have no reservations about her ideas, as I always have towards the fundamentalist Hartmannites. From a European point of view, there was a considerable isolation of American psychoanalysis. Maybe because it all started during the war. We can now retrospectively consider the total failure of psychoanalytic congresses since the end of the war because they did not succeed in establishing a real communication within the IPA. There were discussions between Europeans and North Americans during these meetings but they hardly had an influence on anyone's thinking *even in the absence of any language barrier*. In Europe there was the feeling that the Europeans were not understood by the fraction of the I.P.A. that stood at the side of Hartmann. Let us not forget that the American Association outnumbered any other society. They were the only group to have the status of a Regional Association. The representation of the USA in the Executive Council was largely predominant. The situation was quite different in England, but in the British Society there was a connection with Hartmann and his followers. The connection was Anna Freud and, needless to say, the very important links of Anna Freud to American psychoanalysis. Their support included financial assistance for her institution. Anna Freud found assistance in the States in her conflict with Melanie Klein and her followers. Though, as Clifford rightly emphasized, it would be exaggerated to think of Anna Freud as belonging to the Hartmannites. She had her own point of view. But, apart from the Anna Freudians, not only the Kleinians but the Independents as well were speaking in the desert, as far as North America was concerned. It took a long time for Winnicott, for instance, to be heard, read, and studied in the United States. He was considered in England as an opponent to Melanie Klein; not in the States.

Another point I would like to make is that the French position about Hartmann should not be confused with Lacan's criticism. Lacan was infuriated with me when I wrote in 1970 that, contrary to what is usually thought of, Lacan and Hartmann were much closer than one would think. The autonomous ego and the signifier are more compatible than wished for by Lacan. But, on the whole, we had no Hartmannites, just as we had no Kohutians later. The Kleinians crossed the channel, they lectured, they supervised, and raised a lot of interest but they did not succeed in converting the French into Kleinianism. Does that mean that the French are orthodox Freudians? Not at all. We value very much the exegesis of Freud's work, because we make the difference between Freud and the other authors of psychoanalytic literature. We assume that to evaluate the changes proposed in theory nowadays we have first to know Freud's work, because it all started from there. We have different readings of Freud. The main reason for our inclination to study Freud in detail and in depth is to reinsert his ideas in their epistemological context. Based on the text, concepts have to be worked through.

A few years ago I had given an interview to two candidates of the Boston Psychoanalytic.[5] During this interview, expressing my thoughts in a rather free association way, I said I thought that Hartmann did a lot of harm to American psychoanalysis. This statement was strongly opposed by Roy Schafer, who replied accusing me of displacing my ambivalence toward Freud on Hartmann! He argued that it was Freud who invented ego psychology! And finally that my opinions reflected French "colonialism"! He came back to that topic, showing that it was not only a sudden change of mood.[6] We have here a fundamental disagreement. Is there anything in Freud that can support the ideas expressed by Hartmann and labeled as ego psychology, or is there a real gap between Freud and Hartmann? My opinion is that there is a real gap, and I'll try to show it during our discussion.

For me, there is no mention in Freud about an independent origin of the ego from the id, no autonomy for the ego functions, no neutral energy of its

---

5. Now published in *The Inward Eye*, edited by Laurie W. Raymond and Susan Rosbrow-Reich, Analytic Press, 1997. Roy Schafer, "Response to André Green," *Psychologist Psychoanalyst* 12(1):7, 1992.

6. Schafer, R. (1995). "In the wake of Heinz Hartmann." *International Journal of Psycho-Analysis* 76:223–235.

own, on the contrary, the differences between ego and id are sharpened and the ego's dependence on the id from which it is originated is very marked. Freud even says that the ego never frees itself entirely from his origins in the id, bearing, so to say, its trademark. This is why he considers the ego as hypocritical, unreliable, cheating, and such.

I believe there is a major issue. Is psychoanalysis a psychology? I shall come back many times to that question in our discussions because I think this is a very important issue. We know Hartmann's intention to arrive at a general psychology. This is debatable as such, but the second question, which is also debatable, is: If yes, what kind of psychology? We have opponents coming from every side today, the neurosciences, the cognitive sciences, and many arguments from anthropologists and sociologists, so eventually we have to say where we stand within the field of psychology. Depth psychology, even if Freud used the expression, is not a clear enough definition. There is a great difference between the psychical and the psychological, a point that did not escape C. S. Pierce. The points that Martin raised in his paper, in which he finds himself in disagreement with me, are linked to this issue.

Yorke: I'll follow André's lead. I'll say something about psychoanalysis in England. We have to remember that, even before the war, the situation, as far as London was concerned, was quite extraordinary. In 1927, Melanie Klein came to England, joined the British Society at the invitation of Ernest Jones, and quickly established her authority—authority that, within a few years, bordered on supremacy. The fact that she was a psychoanalyst of children, at a time when few could claim such experience, may well have contributed to the conviction she carried. Until 1932, when her book on child analysis[7] was published, it was, evidently, generally accepted that what she was saying was entirely in accord with Freudian thinking (even Glover shared this view at the time). It's a very interesting exercise to look at her papers published between 1919 and 1932. It's possible to trace, in that period, a succession of very subtle changes in her basic assumptions, changes that allowed her to arrive, almost unnoticed, at the position she did—a position that began to cause some dissent among a minority. Glover was the best known of this small body, he was the most vocal, but there were others who began to question at least something of what she said. They were not numerous.

At that time—and indeed for many years afterwards—London was not greatly interested in what was happening in the United States, either before or after Hartmann. It was sufficiently insular not to be too interested in what

---

7. Klein, M. (1932). *The Psycho-Analysis of Children*. London: Hogarth.

was happening in Europe, either, except in Vienna, and it was Anna Freud who received attention on account of the type of child analysis she was promoting. For their part, the Viennese began to realize that something very different was happening in London. There were exchange visits, but Robert Waelder was not well received in England, and the visits failed to solve anything. Hartmann's ideas were starting to develop, but were formally brought together only in the later part of the decade and met a good deal of opposition even in Vienna. Anna Freud had trained at roughly the same time as Hartmann, and he was active, together with Schilder, at Wagner-Jauregg's psychiatric clinic in Vienna when Anna Freud was attending ward rounds (grand rounds) there on a regular basis.

Later, dramatic events soon made London feel justified in considering itself the center of the psychoanalytic universe. Indeed, that attitude was detectable long after the war, after all the intervening controversies. I sat at a number of Training Committee meetings when, as happened often, an applicant from abroad had applied to be trained in London. Should he or she be accepted or not? "Well," someone was apt to say, "if we don't take him he'll train in————[the country he happened to come from], and unless he comes to London he's not going to get the best training in the world." That was the kind of arrogance that could be expressed in the privacy of the confidential meeting.

As you know, from the mid-1930s, following the ascendancy of Hitler, analysts began to emigrate from Germany. Some had the foreknowledge and the foresight to see what was inevitable; all this is well documented in the splendid account of the "controversial discussions" edited by and Pearl King and Riccardo Steiner.[8] That book makes clear that Melanie Klein was very hostile to the reception in London to Anna Freud, and was critical of Jones for arranging Freud's coming to England instead of the United States, and it was for this reason, among others, that the new immigrants felt somewhat isolated from the rest of the British Society, in spite of warm welcomes from many individual members. Naturally, the hostility—where it existed—was covert rather than overt.

The formal discussions ended without scientific conclusion but with major political consequences: the Society was divided into three groups. There were those who stood by Melanie Klein and strongly supported her views. There were those who could not wholly commit themselves either to Klein or to the Viennese; these formed what was known at the time as the "Middle"—

---

8. King P., and Steiner, R. (1991). *The Freud–Klein Controversies 1941–1945.* New York: Routledge.

later the "Independent"—Group. There was a small group of British Freudians (and some German Immigrants) who joined the Viennese in forming the Freudian Group, though they were not accorded that designation at the time. Hartmann's work attracted little attention (though it is true that Anna Freud and Hoffer took notice of it); the alignments for or against Klein remained the central interest. Hartmann came into view only gradually, if at all. The "Kleinians" were contrasted with the "Anna Freudians," though the "Middle Group" were more numerous than the others.

During these difficult times Anna Freud strongly took the view that "we are visitors here; we haven't come to make ourselves nuisances; we haven't come to be contentious." This didn't mean that she was willing to agree with views she thought incorrect, but she did feel that discussion should be conducted with consideration and politeness. At times, it led her to put matters more delicately than she otherwise might have done. As far as I know, she never criticized Melanie Klein in person, and when I knew her she always spoke of Klein politely, though on points at issue she made her own views clear. She criticized Klein's ideas, circumspectly, and those of you who have read the account of the controversial discussions will know that the person who spoke out most strongly and uncompromisingly was Edward Glover. It's possible that Glover's eventual resignation from the British Society failed to have the effect he hoped it would because Anna Freud was not going to desert the Society to which she felt she and her father owed their existence in England. There were other reasons why Anna Freud wanted to remain in that country: it was the second time she had been there; she had loved England when she first visited many years before, but that visit was interrupted by the outbreak of World War I. She felt a very strong allegiance to England, matched, it may be added, by a later adherence to and love of Ireland. She once said, tongue in cheek, that it was a matter of regret that she could not found a psychoanalytic society in Cork.

If one reads carefully the paper that Anna Freud read at the 70th birthday celebration for Hartmann, one will see that she matches, all the way through, whatever she felt was positive in Hartmann with what other psychoanalysts were already thinking and trying to deal with. For all her tact and diplomacy, and though apparently favorable to Hartmann, she was not, in fact, deeply convinced by some of the ideas in ego psychology. Over the years when I was working closely with her, she almost never referred to Hartmann's work, though she had considerable personal regard for him. On one occasion, she said he was rather patrician, and that, when he makes statements, he behaved as if he didn't care whether or not listeners agreed with them. He expected acceptance and, if didn't get it, that was that. I don't want to say too much about what, after all, may be domestic matters.

There is, however, something in Martin's paper on which I would like to comment. It has to do with the question of the diagnostic profile and Anna Freud's use of the phrase "ego apparatus." I dealt with that in my paper so I won't repeat it here, but I will say that she strongly believed, as her father did, that whatever the connections between biology and psychology, one should never confuse the two. One should never mistake the one for the other, and she thought that the concept of the "ego apparatus" was perilously close to confounding the idea of the physical apparatus and the psychical functions that were mediated by that apparatus. Hence her ready agreement to the change of terminology to which I referred in my paper.

As a whole, the British Society never, to my mind, really warmed to Anna Freud, let alone Hartmann. She was formally respected. She was treated with courtesy; but even today I still search in vain for her influence on child psychology outside Hampstead and in the Society as a whole, though there is an official training in child analysis. The Independents continue to respect Winnicott, but if they undertake a child training it is more likely to be Kleinian than Freudian. Hartmann, of course, never had the slightest influence on Kleinian school, and if he had penetrated more deeply into Anna Freud's ideas his influence on the Society would still have been exiguous.

Certainly, the British Society is very good at *formal* compromise that still allows dissent. But there is a current tendency in that Society that Anna Freud and Hartmann might equally have deplored. It is the notion that, although we use different languages, fundamentally *we all share the same views*. It's like accepting that conflict exists *while calling the Society conflict-free*. I once took part in a discussion, at a Society meeting, with Betty Joseph. We exchanged copies of our papers beforehand. After she had received my contribution, Betty rang me up and said, "Cliff, I've just read your paper. No one would think we belonged to the same Society!"

Incidentally, Edward Glover's name (until the King/Steiner book appeared) was almost never mentioned in the Society by *any* of the groups. As Martin mentioned, he was critical of Hartmann, but it was his outspoken repudiation of Klein that made him a permanent outsider for so many other members. Yet it was Klein's theory of child development—just as it was Hartmann's—to which Glover objected. Perhaps it's worth remembering that Edward Glover was a founding editor of the *Psychoanalytic Study of the Child*.

Blum: I want to pay tribute to Martin for the extraordinary work he's done, for the contribution of his monograph on this whole period, for the many stimulating questions he raised, and also for championing the idea that we don't need consensus. In fact, we do better without it because it sharpens our thinking and allows us to go further than we were able to go before. Perhaps the most enduring contribution of the period might be infant observation. This brings me to the question of whether observations outside of psychoanalysis became that important at that time, are still considered important, or are peripheral. It also raises the debate to a different level about the importance of analytic data versus nonanalytic data. One of the consequences of the Hartmann era may have been the idealization of analysis that occurred at that time, the idealization of clinical analytic data and an esteem on the part of some analysts for data originating outside of the analytic situation. The influence of developmental psychoanalysis really began during this period. Hartmann was the stimulus for Spitz, for Mahler, and for others, although they emerged quite independently of Hartmann in their own contributions. There was an over-reliance on such data, especially as there was quite a difference at that time as to what they could contribute on infant observation. Infant research was really in its infancy. That contributed to this whole idea in which analysis was idealized and everything it touched, including the study of infancy, could be so enriching.

Neubauer: Do you speak about infant observation or observation in general in childhood?

Blum: I address the point Martin brought up about infant observation. Kris, in his paper on the recovery of childhood memories, contributed to the rapprochement between the observational studies of early childhood and infancy and reconstruction from adult analysis. The picture is mixed because we still hadn't emerged in the 1950s or even in the 1960s from Freud's emphasis on the central role that recovery of memory plays. The very title of Kris's paper is on memory recovery. At that time, there was an important shift occurring toward a major emphasis on transference analysis and much less attention to the direct recovery of childhood memories and the lifting of infantile amnesia.

The discussion has already highlighted, in a way that didn't come out clearly in Martin's monograph, the differentiation of Hartmann from the Hartmann era. The contributions of Spitz, Jacobson, Mahler, and even of Kris and Loewenstein, who tried so hard to unify Hartmann with clinical work, really stand on their own, quite independent of Hartmann. With the idealization, there was also a special problem that arose and, to some degree, continues and that is the role of authoritarianism. There was always a nod to Hartmann. Of great interest to me is Martin's raising the Hartmann era to a new level of consciousness. Prior to this discussion and Martin's stimulating monograph, the Hartmann era had in many respects receded in relative eclipse. Perhaps no other person in psychoanalytic history had such a dominant position, was cited so regularly, was perhaps the most cited author of his day, and then virtually disappeared from the psychoanalytic literature. Hartmann became conspicuous by his absence. This is an important question for us to consider how Martin has, in a sense, resurrected an entire era as well as Hartmann's own personality and contributions.

Jack referred to the cultural change, the new generation that arose, as one of the reasons for Hartmann's relative eclipse. The new generation was not interested in looking inward. They were not soul-searching. They were more outwardly directed and more interested in the so-called "quick fix" that resulted in rapid change, immediate symptom relief. Another aspect had to do with the authoritarianism of the period that, in America at least, was an analytic orthodoxy. It was very difficult to challenge ideas, to raise new ideas. Consensus was not only sought, it was sometimes demanded. Those who raised questions were considered to have heretical tendencies. Analysis itself had not only been overidealized, it came to be considered part of the establishment. The new generation then revolted against the establishment. It was related also to the Vietnam War and to an antiestablishment, antiintellectual, antianalytic bias, which still in some respects persists.

I'd also like to say something about forces within analysis and some of the ramifications and reactions to Hartmann and the Hartmann era. Although Jack has sometimes been considered to be on line with the Hartmann era, the work of Arlow and Brenner really is vastly different. It has persisted and continues to influence psychoanalysis today in a way that Hartmann's didn't. Jack's emphasis on unconscious fantasies and the interplay of reality and fantasy is very different from the question of ego autonomy and the conflict-free spirit. Perhaps no one else in psychoanalysis has taken such a sharply different, really opposed point of view, to Hartmann as Brenner. For Brenner, everything is conflict and compromise formation. Nothing is autonomous.

Solnit: He admits that he doesn't know much about children or child analysis.

Blum: In time, although Brenner overlaps chronologically with the Hartmann period, we can look at his work and see that this is an influential voice in psychoanalysis in sharp opposition to the Hartmann point of view. We need to look at the reactions against Hartmann, as well as the ways in which his influence continues to be elaborated and amplified, leading not only to new questions but influencing the direction of analysis. I'll mention two of them. One of the reactions against Hartmann was intersubjectivity: the analyst himself may not be outside the conflict; the analyst is subjectively drawn into intersubjective discourse with the patient. It was a reaction to ego autonomy, the role of the conflict-free sphere, including the energy issue, which was still abstract and far removed from clinical work. Intersubjectivity seemed to be very human: two human beings interacting with each other and having a conversation. Hartmann positively influenced analysis and helped to move it into American psychoanalysis, and throughout most of the world toward object relations. This was a counterbalance to some of the previous views. Not that object relations theory was entirely overlooked by Freud or Anna Freud or the pioneers, but rather Hartmann gave it a special stress and emphasis that continues to the present day.

Kernberg: You said that Hartmann gave a special emphasis to object relations theory. That is a big surprise to me.

Blum: Particularly, Otto, in the emphasis on the environment. With all the controversy and my own criticism of the average expectable environment, the attention to the environment, and to the earliest environment, gave a new emphasis to the primary object relation.

Solnit: He also applied it to the need for object constancy.

Kernberg: Here we clearly disagree, because it seems to me that he was emphasizing the influence of the ministrations of the real object and the need for the real object, which is very different from object relations theory, the building up of an intrapsychic dyadic experience of relation between self and object influenced by drive and conflict.

Blum: Object constancy is at the root of self and object representation.

Kernberg: But this doesn't come from Hartmann. It comes from Jacobson. Hartmann differentiated ego from self, but the transformation of these concepts into clinical conflict theory was Jacobson's contribution.

The most important issue for us is to relate Hartmann's influence on the basic thrust of Freudian theory, the influence on drives, the dynamic unconscious, or the id to human existence. There was a consistent deemphasis by Hartmann on the drives, the dynamic unconscious, or the id. One question is to what extent are there advantages in what he did in other areas to compensate for this problem, or to what extent this meant a slowdown, a kind of putting a stop to the development of psychoanalytic thinking? This is the major critical issue. Here, I find myself very close to André Green's view that the emphasis did damage to the development of psychoanalytic theory, slowing it down. When I say damage, I don't mean destroying, but putting a stop to things rather than developing them. The authoritarian quality of Hartmann and his group was enormous, and perhaps I'm the only one here who experienced it as a victim rather than part of the establishment.

Kris: It was not only in New York. We had it in Boston, too.

Kernberg: I trained in Chile. I started out my training in 1953 when the Institute was mostly ego psychological. We started out ego psychological and gradually, under Argentinean influence, became more and more Kleinian. By the time I graduated, the Institute was Kleinian and I got worried, feeling one of these two had to be right. I was very naive and I thought maybe I'm too far away from where the action is. Anyway, I went to the States for one year to work in Washington, where they were interested in Sullivan, and got myself immersed in the Sullivanian experience. Then, feeling again that they were throwing out the baby with the bath water, I decided I really had to learn ego psychology and went to Menninger's. There I rapidly felt at home with Jacobson and Mahler, and technically with the contributions of Otto Fenichel and Ralph Greenson. Otto Fenichel wrote his fundamental work in 1941.[9] I also thought that Reich's contributions to technique, in spite of his unfavorable developments, were very important. I was impressed with how indirectly Reich had been taken up by Herbert Rosenfeld.

Second, the group psychology of German Jewish refugees, who unconsciously identified with the aggressor and became totalitarian. They tried to adapt to the environment desperately and exert control, German Prussian control, whenever possible. In the United States, the German Jews who came stopped speaking German; they started speaking English the day they came here. I don't know whether you're familiar with the book by Jacqueline Amati-Mehler on the Babel of the unconscious, where she very scholarly studies the fact that, for 20 years, nobody discussed the implications of polylinguistic capacity for the theory of the id. Is there one unconscious? Does every language have its unconscious?

Green: That was the reason for the silence.

Kernberg: In Chile, where I emigrated, the German Jews all spoke German for years because they looked down on these inferior Indians.

---

9. Fenichel, O. (1941). Problems of psychoanalytic technique. *Psychoanalytic Quarterly* 2(2):1–158.

Bill Grossman has made very strong points about the potential importance of Hartmann in linking psychoanalysis to philosophical thinking. Did he really help, or was that an illusion because he operated in a vacuum? Did he seem a philosopher only to us and not to the philosophers?

Grossman: It would be more correct to say that I thought that is what Hartmann was trying to do. I did not say he did it.

Kernberg: They tried to do the same in linking psychoanalysis to other sciences, but they did it in ways that really ignored that. There is a curious contradiction there, opening up to biology and at the same time not to practical biology, to sociology and not to practical sociology. It's giving us an illusion that we were a universal science when we were in fact totally isolated. We were talking about the importance of infant observation, while a totalistic attitude operated against concrete research that might lead to findings different from our theoretical assumptions.

Another major controversy is: Is infant observation important or not? It seems to me that infant observation illustrates a general problem with psychoanalytic research. We observe infants from the outside under relatively benign circumstances, which usually corresponds to laboratory conditions, not at a moment of intense excitement nor terror nor where issues have developed that are much more important for the unconscious functioning of the mind. The methodology of infant observations may have enormous difficulty in reaching what is essential to psychoanalysis. That doesn't mean that it cannot be done. I'm just saying that methodological difficulties have been ignored, and there has been a naiveté that has made many people react against research altogether. Hartmann was in favor of research, but in practice he ignored what he could have studied, the shortfalls, the dangers, the traps. The methodology to study the unconscious is in its infancy. I'm doing research on psychotherapy. The methodology of psychotherapy research, let alone analysis, is evolving since 1950 and we are slowly able to relate process to outcome, after 40 years. There are still no important findings from research that have influenced psychoanalytic work. In medicine, people do research, and five years later it changes the treatment. In psychoanalysis the effect is zero. This is because we are at the beginning of the process, not because in principle it is impossible. I'm criticizing his approach to research and yet trying to reaffirm the importance of research.

Kris: You fault Hartmann for not sticking to facts, and yet you say there were no facts to stick to.

Kernberg: That is correct.

About technique, Hartmann, of course, never talks about concrete clinical cases. Hartmann did not contribute to psychoanalytic technique. Fenichel did. The question is: Is that really ego psychology? Let me put it differently. Metapsychology can be applied by anybody, by French psychoanalysts, by Kleinians, by ego psychologists. It transcends particularly theoretical orientation. The statement that one had to go very carefully, respect the defenses, in practice reduced the depth of analysis. Clinically, when I'm thinking of the average clinical case presentation in this country, it did not have the depth that I would see in the analysis of the work done in London by any of the three groups. But I was particularly impressed by some of the Kleinian work, although in their interpretation of what happens the first year they were rather fantastic. As the Kleinians have evolved in recent years, they have changed the bath water without throwing out the baby. The Hartmann approach superficialized the technique, ignored the theory, the drives, and made timidity the technical approach to patients. While we saw sicker and sicker patients with the most primitive sadomasochistic, aggressive things going on, the optimism of Hartmann regarding drives and adaptation ignored that clinical reality. Fundamental changes were made at the same time in this country regarding severe psychopathology and psychosis by the Washington group, by Frieda Fromm-Reichman and Lewis Hill. Their theories were weak, but their clinical observations matched the borderline cases that already were being seen more and more frequently and led to discussions in New York. One of the damages that was caused by the authoritarian nature of our approach was the rejection of psychoanalysis in the scientific segments of the universities, in psychiatry and neurology, while Hartmann seemed triumphant. When I came to the United States, first in 1959 and then in 1961, and I had a Rockefeller Foundation fellowship, I visited universities all over the country. There was indeed resentment within departments of psychiatry and the mental research institutes against psychoanalysis, while psychoanalysis was still triumphant. IMH was spending millions giving the psychoanalysts chances to do research, and much of that was wasted.

There is no doubt that some of Hartmann's co-workers were some of the most creative contributors: Jacobson, and Mahler, and the enormous importance of Rapaport regarding psychological clinical testing (in spite of the rigidity of his thinking, which led to a rebellion among his students). At Columbia we teach Hartmann, Kris, and Loewenstein. It's the tradition. Nobody is very interested in doing that, yet you have to teach the basics. I'm asking you, do we really need it and, if not, what do we replace it with?

Green: One remark on Otto's remarks about object relationships: I think we must be careful not to mix up everything. Every analyst has written about

the object. This does not mean that all agree with the viewpoint of object relationships, more or less extensively. To speak of object relationships involves
three conditions. First, to emphasize the predominance of the internal object.
I say the predominance, not exclusiveness. Needless to say Klein's internal
object is not Freud's. Second, that the object exists from the beginning of life,
which is Klein's idea, not Anna Freud's or Hartmann's, and not many others.
Three, that the term *relationship* has a very specific meaning. Relationship is
really linked to the relation with the internal object in terms of Melanie Klein's
basic ideas, which involve the archaic fantasies, the primitive defense mechanisms, and the early anxieties. Let us observe that the expression does not say
relationship to what? Here we have also to assume the existence of an ego from
the beginning. In Melanie Klein, object and ego exist independently from the
start of psychic life. This is what object relationships mean. Of course, relationship is a term that belongs to everyday language and everybody can use it
but, if you want to put things in context, we should be careful not to use the
expression *object relationship* without discrimination as it is done sometimes
today. One must also be aware that an emphasis on object relationships will
bring, one day or another, a parallel emphasis on "subject relationships." It
can take the form, after ego psychology (Hartmann having introduced the self)
of self psychology, followed today by intersubjectivity. In fact, as I observed
in 1975,[10] a new metapsychology was on the way on the basis of subject–
object relationships. Are we ready to accept this change? I am not sure we have
any advantage to it, as it draws us back before Freud.

Ostow: I have a little story about an old woman who won a contest in the
Soviet Union, which gave her the privilege of speaking to Khrushchev. When
she arrived there, she said, "Comrade Khrushchev, I have to ask you a question." He said, "What is it?" She said, "I was wondering, is Communism a
science or a philosophy?" Khrushchev thought and he said, "I don't know. I
think it's more of a philosophy." She said, "That's what I think, because if it
were a science they would have tried it on rats first."

I disagree with Otto. He was far from the only one to have suffered from
the authoritarianism of the times. Most of us were students in the late '40s and
early '50s and the authoritarianism was really quite devastating. I remember,
as a student, one was not permitted to ask any questions. We learned that the
outcome of analysis was to permit the patient to be able to think clearly and
independently, without being influenced by the unconscious or by external

---

10. Green, A. (1986). The analyst, symbolization and absence in the analytic
setting. In *On Private Madness*. London: Hogarth.

authority. But we were trained to be completely orthodox, completely compliant. If any student asked any question whatever, he was put down and told that he was resistant. Jack, do you remember that? It was really a religious orthodoxy complete with a scripture and with ideas of heresy. It would tolerate no other religion. Klein was never mentioned in my training. I learned about her only incidentally. Lewin and Kubie were barely tolerated. I remember when Nunberg got up to speak he was often harassed while he was speaking and interfered with because he didn't quite go along. Now, I'm not saying this is to be attributed to Hartmann as a person or to his associates, but it certainly happened at that time and we have to ask ourselves why.

Otto brings up the issue of Jewish German refugees. They not only repudiated their Germanism, but they also repudiated Jewishness. I don't know to what extent that was a change. They may have done that in Europe itself, but certainly, when Abraham Blau went to Yom Kippur services one year, that became a subject of great gossip within the Society and one wondered what was going to be done about it. I myself suffered from two issues of orthodoxy. One is that, at the time, I was teaching at the Jewish Theological Seminary, and secondly I had begun to experiment with medication. That was the middle '50s and early '60s, both of which, incidentally, were encouraged by my analyst (Nunberg), but at the same time that was anathema elsewhere. People would call me after hours to ask me for consultation about patients of theirs whom they had in therapy. They made it clear that these were not analytic patients, they were only in therapy, and I would give them advice. The advice never worked out. They never did what I told them to do. There was tremendous resistance and the effort was to demonstrate that it couldn't possibly work. I think that this kind of orthodoxy had deleterious effects on analysis for many years, and I'm glad to see that has changed and I don't know whether it's gone too far in the other direction at the present time. I don't know whether to associate it with Hartmann, but certainly Hartmann and his associates did nothing to oppose it or counteract it.

Arlow: There was a split in the faculty on those matters. As a rule, Hartmann and Kris were on the liberal side. They would not have reacted the way the other people in the group did, for example, Isakower and the people around him. What you say is true, but it's not part of the Hartmann era.

Neubauer: As I listen to our attempts at definitions of Hartmann's contribution, I had a feeling I had to defend Hartmann, both from a viewpoint of theory formulation as well as the implications for technique. I remember my experience with him as a supervisor and the ambiance of the psychoanalytic institute at that time. It was authoritarian; psychoanalytic knowledge was transmitted in an authoritarian way. But, at one time, Hartmann encouraged people in his class to discuss any topic and explore with others in the group. The other teachers wanted to go through Freud in a very strict sense. It was his attempt at extending psychoanalysis without disconnecting himself from basic Freud positions. He explored beyond what could be documented. He knew that he offered propositions that the clinical findings could not substantiate. I remember very well in one discussion in Princeton with the CAPS group, where he presented some of his ideas and the colleagues of my age opposed Hartmann. He said to them, "You know I have, at times, arrived at certain conclusions that were based on the logic of theory formation and not from the clinical data. For instance, when I refer to the function of the ego and assume that such processes are connected with some psychic energy, and if I do not want to assume an additional ego energy separate from the drive energy, which Anna Freud at one time or another also proposed, what are the consequences? I have to deaggressivize and delibidinalize. I have to transform energy into the ego economics, that is to neutralize drive energy in order to maintain the Freudian idea that energy is based on the sources of the drives and the ego does not have its own energy." Most of Hartmann's statements, the conflict-free sphere, or the transformation of energy, or the undifferentiated phase, are propositions that are impossible to prove. Take primary versus secondary autonomy; How does this autonomous system continuously operate in interaction? The primary autonomy is not totally free of influence and the secondary is not totally outside of the primary forerunner. Therefore, if you ask me to make clear the divisions of differentiation, we polarize something that takes us away from the elasticity of our terminology, which we need when we expand it into different arenas. Now, Hartmann was very clear that he has gone beyond the provable, and that his idea of creating a general psychology was one that he hopes that the future will do. I do not even know whether it is possible and certainly whether psychoanalysis alone can do it based on psychoanalytic investigation and exploration.

He was very much aware of it, and there is something else that I think we should take into account. It is Hartmann's style. He was a special person with a very organized style, the way he presented himself and spoke, and he did not engage with empathic interaction. His terminology is mechanistic rather than experiential, more propositional. His style contributed in some ways to the difficulties to work with him. Consider Anna Freud's *Ego and the Mechanisms of Defense*. I always thought it was not a good way of putting it when one speaks about the ego, to speak about a "mechanism" rather than about the various modes of interaction; similarly with the proposal of developmental lines. There are propositions by Hartmann that cannot be clinically verified.

Bergmann: Peter, can you also say something about the issue of infant observation and psychoanalysis?

Neubauer: I think you mentioned in your review that child analysts feel more comfortable with certain of Hartmann's propositions. We should spend some time determining why it is so, whether it is justified for those who observe infants and children until the age of 3. After all, Mahler's findings were not based on psychoanalytic data; they came from observation. We all feel she made a contribution. She herself thought she belonged to the group of ego psychologists, while so obviously the content of her observations were object interactive processes, which she outlines in 6 steps.

Mahler proposed the following stages during the first 3 years of life:

Autism: A normal condition of the first two months when the infant is
   objectless.
Symbiosis: The second stage, six weeks to five months; here there is a
   fusion between mother and infant.
Differentiation: 5 to 10 months
Practicing: 10 to 15 months
Rapprochment: 15 to 22 months
Emotional object constancy: 22 months to 3 years.

When one observes a child, one does not recover the internal psychic experience; one can observe infantile behavior. It is almost impossible, when one looks at an infant and sees how the infant in the first few weeks of life makes an adaptation to receiving the nipple, of taking it in, of knowing how to react to one object, or of knowing how to interpret a social smile at 6 weeks or 2 months, then it is almost impossible not to assume that there are already regulatory mechanisms available that go beyond the expression of drive representation. It is easier for somebody who looks at infants to take the proposition that there is ego at work, in a preliminary way. The drive and ego are so interactive at this moment that I cannot say at the beginning is drive and slowly out of it emerges the ego. It is easier for infant observers to accept the so-called undifferentiated phase. I'm not sure that it is correct to refer to undifferentiation. Today, one would rather speak of nuclei of the ego rather than of an undifferentiated phase side by side with drive representation.

There is good reason why the child analyst and observer of infants, found a certain affinity to some of Hartmann's propositions. Still, one is as yet not able to form a theory that leads to a general developmental psychology. One runs here into a limit. What is the limit of the object relation propositions? There are fashions in theory formation. Where are the limits and why are there shifts over to other theories? We as analysts should raise these questions about the nature of the limitations of theories. I very much hope that we have more time to discuss infant observation and child analysis in connection with Hartmann.

Green: I would like first to make a suggestion and then respond to Peter's defense of Hartmann. In the organization of our schedule this afternoon and tomorrow we should devote sufficient time to topics that recur in the discussion. Infant observation or research could be one, adaptation another, and finally, of course, the conception of the ego in the psychic apparatus, according to Freud and to Hartmann. I think that these three topics have emerged from the present discussion.

About what Peter said, I think that, if we do not want to mix up everything, we have to sort out the different aspects related to Hartmann. One, there is the person, the personality, and Hartmann's personality is one side of the assessment of his influence. The second thing is his theoretical references, the people who have influenced him, as Bill's paper states extensively. Hartmann's theory is the main topic of the discussion much more than his personality. I agree with Peter that we have to judge this content the way Martin did. But there is also another level that we should also specifically deal with. This refers to what Otto said, the institutional influence of Hartmann. You can say everything in defense of Hartmann, but you cannot say that he has been fostering dialogue. Again, I come back to international conferences and their failures. How is it that such an important endeavor can take place, mobilizing so big a machinery to have confrontations of opposite views expressed by psychoanalysts who belong to different geographical areas, appointing for each session or panel: speakers, discussants, reporters, chairmen, with no change at all in the literature? After a congress each one went back home and continued to practice, to lecture and to write, as if nothing happened! In the International Psychoanalytic Library, the only book that has different dimensions from others is Hartmann's *Essays on Ego Psychology*. It is not only the thickest, it is the largest.

Now, to come back to Mahler's work. It is marked by *ambivalent methodology to assess psychoanalysis*. Peter argues that Mahler's findings were the result of observation more than the application of psychoanalytic concepts. Can he really defend the idea that Mahler, being trained as a psychoanalyst, considering herself as a contributor to psychoanalytic theory, addressing psychoanalysts, could observe children independently from a psychoanalytic background in her mind? In Peter's defense of her work there is no real epistemological discussion of what is "Trieb" as a concept, what is adaptation, what the ego is supposed to be, and even what it is to "observe" as far as psychic is concerned. Freud made important remarks on all these topics.

Kernberg: I think the last point is so important that we should have it on the table very clearly. The German *totschweigen* means to silence to death. It is a way in which you deal with thoughts that are not permitted to exist, and it was the technique of the Communist party in the Soviet Union. Even in photographs, they eliminated those who no longer existed. We must confess that there has been such an unfortunate tendency in our literature, and Hartmann certainly participated actively and leadingly in eliminating from his statements anything going on simultaneously in the international psychoanalytic debate about all issues. That, I think, is tragic, and he did it with the Kleinians, and the Kleinians did it with the Anna Freudians. It was a more general problem, but he certainly did not go beyond it.

Bergmann: May I exercise my right as chairman, because I want to make sure that everybody who is participating speak at least once in the morning session.

Furst: I have some general impressionistic remarks. I'm thinking of a paper by Robert Waelder[11] (whom I consider probably the most unappreciated analyst from the beginning) delivered on the impetus for Freud's changes in his theoretical orientation at various times in his career. In a beautiful way, he developed a thesis that Freud changed his mind, first from the topographic to the structural and so on, because of disappointment in the clinical relevance and usefulness of his former positions. I also think of an old medical adage (I believe it's attributed to Ulster) who said that when there is more than one cure or medication for a given disease, it's because none of them works completely satisfactorily. I think this is true to a great degree for psychoanalytic theory and accounts for its diversity. People have raised the question, to what do we attribute the diminution of the passing of the Hartmann era? I suspect it's because its clinical relevance was limited. Hartmann made certain points that were useful, and I think these survived even though Hartmann himself and people who considered themselves Hartmannites are now few and far between. We use a lot of his insights and findings without realizing that they are his.

A number of people have raised the point of authoritarianism, of almost a religious orthodoxy that characterizes various analytic institutes. I believe this

---

11. *Psychoanalysis: Observation, Theory, Application. Selected Pages of Robert Waelder*, ed. S. Gutman. International Universities Press, 1976.

is due precisely to the point that none of them can prove their superiority to any others and this leads to an emotional defense of one's position, because one cannot defend it as one would like on the basis of observable evidence. Where does this all leave us? I suspect that much of the debate between various theories and positions relies these days on what is most intellectually elegant, as opposed to what can induce the greatest amount of clinical observations and other objective facts. This is not true for child development. This is not true for our study of our continued use of defenses and mechanisms of defense. To some degree, it's not true for our appreciation of the operation of drives. But some of the more technical matters that the various theories seem to be concerned with, such as the Kleinian ideas about early life, or Hartmann's conceptions of energy, are not useful, and the debate relies on what appears to be most intellectually elegant. I think, as time goes on, and we do more analytic work and child development work, we will slowly begin to evolve a theory of the mind, a model of the mind that does seem to be compatible with what we can show and adduce from objective observations. Until then, we have to struggle with these things. We also waste a good deal of time with purely intellectual speculations, in which we argue whose intellectual speculation is superior.

Grossman: Let me start by saying that I really am pleased, and I feel honored to be included among this group of people. Some of them have been my most respected teachers, and people that I think are among the most important contributors and discussants of psychoanalytic thought. I have a sort of dual drive version of my approach to psychoanalytic ideas and their development. I believe that you approach them either by destroying the old ones, or synthesizing them into something that's new, or recognizing their own synthetic properties. This approach is evident in my paper, where I try to trace what I see as continuing currents in the development of psychoanalytic thought and some of the influences that render that development dynamic. In his discussion, Martin talked about the relative independence of Jacobson and Mahler from Hartmann. This seemed to me to be a social version of the notion of relative autonomy. It is descriptively and fundamentally the same thing. These people had their own origins independently of Hartmann, but they had to deal dynamically with the force of his presence and ideas. Even so, they managed to arrive at some secondarily relatively autonomous positions. I describe it that way because it's what Hartmann meant by autonomy. It says something about the many levels on which the dynamic concepts of psychoanalysis are really relevant. It's an important feature of psychoanalytic thought.

When I read Martin's paper, I became aware of a number of things that I hadn't considered before. First, I had never thought there was a Hartmann era even though I grew up psychoanalytically in the middle of it. Obviously, my training was considerably after Martin's, and I came from a very different kind of background. I was very interested in his perspective because my association with the literature and thinking of that period was always critical. I think it was my second psychoanalytic paper (Grossman and Simon 1969)[12] that was a direct criticism of Hartmann, Kris, and Loewenstein. We challenged their assertion that the anthropomorphic language of psychoanalysis was not a problem because it could be translated into a much more abstract scientific language. I thought Bennett Simon and I demonstrated in that paper that their argument was really a cop-out. We said that it really couldn't be done without distortion, and that it greatly underestimated the importance of metaphor in the creation of theoretical ideas that were linked to the clinical experience. I saw that as a key problem, and I still do.

It seems to me that a thread that runs through many of our discussions is the relationship between theory and practice. Hartmann left a big gap there, as illustrated in the quotation that I gave in my paper. The other thing that I wanted to say is that in thinking about Hartmann, my goal is really, as it is in reading Freud, to get straight what he is writing. The more they write, the harder it is to get it straight and to know what it is. In this way, I'm very much with André. This is my other dual orientation. I have one foot in Europe and one foot in the States, not because of my history but because of the nature of my interests. The exegesis is extremely important. I notice that whenever I try this either with Freud or with Hartmann, positions are attributed to me that are not mine. That is, I appear to be defending something that I'm not really defending, although I can easily be forced into that position by feeling misunderstood.

With regard to what Otto said about intersubjectivity being a reaction to Hartmann, I think in a certain sense that's true. However, here's where the difference in background is significant as it is with Martin: although Otto has some similar background in interpersonal theory, I see the relational schools, at least the intersubjective part, coming straight out of the Sullivanian background. At an early stage of my career, I was very much involved with some of the Sullivanians. These people were involved with Ferenczi's views, and I think that Clara Thompson had been associated with him. They were involved with Racker's views on transference and countertransference. They were interested in the influences of the patient on the analyst. Now, I don't think that's the only source, but it's an important one in this country and in the context of

---

12. Grossman, W., and Simon, B. (1969). Anthropomorphism: motive, meaning and causality in psychoanalytic theory. *Psychoanalytic Study of the Child* 24:78–111.

the New York scene. Martin is right that Hartmann didn't refer to Fromm. I had the impression that he did, but it really is unimportant for my point. You can see in the nature of his argument to whom he was referring. So even if he wasn't explicit, he referred to an idea that one can identify. He had a battery of people with whom he was constantly in contention.

I remember Freud said in *Totem and Taboo*, "My own contribution is visible only in my selection both of material and of opinions" (p. 75n).[13] That's a powerful contribution. The boundaries of psychoanalysis were very important to Freud. It seems to me inevitable that boundaries would be important because he was coming out of a background that was not at all psychoanalytic. Even so, he had a way of thinking psychoanalytically before the fact.

Harold and Morty have made a strong case for the idea that Hartmann and his associates ignored the Holocaust, and that some of Hartmann's ideas seemed to involve a denial of its real impact. This may be related to what has been said about Hartmann's insularity and authoritarian attitudes. I think that these attitudes characterized psychoanalytic organizations from the '20s to the '70s. In part this was a reaction to emerging dissident groups, in part a function of rivalries among the societies of the IPA and the American. As is evident in our discussion, their was significant rivalry between American and European societies. All of these organizations were insular and to some extent authoritarian, at least in attitude. This helped to keep the position of psychoanalysis precarious in relation to the outside world. When institutions began to crumble in the '60s, when the structure of the universities were under attack, psychoanalysis took a hit. That's what Jack was alluding to.

The idea was that Hartmann had been so involved in the internal workings of the theory that he was developing. He was not even attempting to apply it to the other disciplines whose boundaries he attempted to find. I don't think he made any effort to apply it. I think what he did try to do was to provide a kind of framework that others tried to fill in. He may have provided the wrong framework, but that was its goal. So I would be very careful about faulting him for not having done things that were not his goal, and could only be perceived as worthwhile goals as an outcome of the critique of the Hartmann work.

One of the things a thinker can do is to provide enough of a basis for people to contradict him so something better can emerge. He certainly succeeded at that. He tried to integrate various fields; he tried to talk about the integration; sometimes he made some nuanced formulations about the extent and limits of the overlap. The problem was that he made so many statements about all of these things, many of them buried in the papers where they don't seem to be

---

13. Freud, S. (1913). Totem and taboo. *Standard Edition* 13.

the main point. He didn't deal with the problems of those fields. He invented unfortunate names for what he was talking about. Some of those concepts were really quite simple, that is, the idea of the conflict-free sphere. To call it that already created an entity in which many of the things he said were contradictions of that entity. People attacked him right and left. The literature with which I was involved during much of that period when I was a student was critical. Jack Arlow was orthodoxy to me. I understand in retrospect that Jack had a different opinion and I have a somewhat different opinion but, compared with where I was looking, he was relatively more orthodox.

Ostow: Jack was normative, not orthodox.

Grossman: Normative—very good, because that is really what I mean. As a student in the first-year course on the drives, that was not immediately apparent. The literature I was involved with was very critical of Hartmann. I felt I had to struggle with the problem of where I stood in all that.

In describing Hartmann in this way, I did want to say that he had very broad interests and a broad concern where it came to certain features and boundary problems of analysis. However, these interests are narrow and peripheral from the point of view of the range of problems in applying theory to clinical problems. In this way, his interests were very narrow in the sense that people have mentioned. It's related to the points about intersubjectivity. The most exciting thing in the French literature of the late '60s and early '70s (when I was more involved with that literature) was the fact that there could be a fantasy orientation to the unconscious, which seemed much more alive to me, and had great organizational possibilities in the effort to have systematic ideas in analysis, even though they were very differently centered than ego psychology. So I became aware of the difference in the center from which one starts in the consideration of these issues.

Another point is that Hartmann's distant view of the field, both in analysis and in the contents of analysis, is more like a philosophical view in that he attempted to question and reformulate underlying propositions. His effort to establish psychoanalysis as a scientific theory involved an attempt to formulate clinical observation on the same model of scientific observation as the boundary fields he discussed. Consequently, he spoke about the process of analysis as one involving the collection of data as though it were systematic, and as though the application of the treatment method was systematic, or could become so. The dynamic relationships between the process of gathering data and the nature of the data, and the dynamic relationship between observation and theory were not explored. I believe he was aware of these issues, but his more distant perspective led to more schematic versions of the relationships of data and theory.

This corresponded to the gap in his own description of how one makes a connection between the psychoanalytic theory and the experience of the analytic process. An alternate approach might be to regard scientific theory formation as a dynamic and evolutionary process that integrates ideas and experience. This would make the development of ideas in analysis the model for the development of ideas in science, which is what I think Freud was trying to do. There is a rhetorical issue to be considered in reading Hartmann. Many of the statements that Hartmann makes are extreme because they are the counterpoise to somebody else. For example, in a general way, he is the counterpoise to Isakower, who was a respected educator at the New York Psychoanalytic Institute when Hartmann was, too. Isakower's ideas emphasized one type of experiential relation to the analytic situation which both diminished the emphasis on the application of theory, and seemed closer to an "id psychoanalysis" (for comments on Isakower's work, see Grossman 1992, 1995).[14] I suspect that Hartmann needed to justify his focus on the ego in reply to people with views like Isakower's.

Bergmann: What a great moment there was when the accusation towards Jack that he was orthodox was changed into normative. That happens so often in psychoanalysis. You use a word with slightly different connotations and peace is established.

Arlow: At that time, your evaluation was correct. I was orthodox.

Grossman: I always remember one exchange we had after we read the paper on narcissism. In that paper Freud is arguing with Jung about the possibility of some originally neutral energy that was not related to libido. He says, it could be so, but it's about as important to the theory of drives as the fact that all men are brothers is relevant to somebody who holds an entitlement to certain property. After class one day, I said to Jack, "It sounds to me like in this paper the libido theory is coming apart," and he said, "What's coming apart?" Which I thought was a fair question, but it seemed to me at the time that was the case and I thought that his response was, again, in line with his stance.

Solnit: That was a prediction.

Kris: I feel very honored to be included in this company. I want to emphasize that this is an evaluation of the Hartmann era. Frankly, I think it gets a

---

14. Grossman, W. (1992). Hierarchies, boundaries, and representations in a Freudian model of mental organization. *Journal of the American Psychoanalytical Association* 40:27–62; (1995). Psychological vicissitudes of theory in clinical work. *International Journal of Psycho-Analysis* 76:885–899.

little one-sided when we come to bury Hartmann rather than to praise him. I think we should talk about the Hartmann era in which Hartmann's monograph and ideas were central, as Loewenstein documented in his obituary. It's impossible for this group to give a conflict-free appraisal because there are powerful, personal views in this group. We have all been through that era and most of us weren't so happy with it, but we also are all inconsistent, and nobody is absolutely one way. Jack has just admitted to changing his mind, and that is true for all of us. I was an adherent at one point. I don't think I am quite that way now.

Freud was very eager to have a scientifically acceptable psychoanalysis, and I've written about the place where I found him working overtime to keep things clean in the analysis of Joan Riviere and the famous footnote in *The Ego and the Id*.[15] He was trying to do that through his students, my father and Hartmann and Anna Freud, at the end of his life. Freud always discussed what was on his mind with his students, especially with his analysands. It's quite clear that Riviere got a big dose of what he was thinking about. It is certain that Stratchey and Hartmann did. The Hartmann period was in the end a rather bloodless period. I think that's what everybody is referring to. I'm rather surprised that Martin's monograph, which contains the contributions to psychoanalytic technique in its title, speaks very little of technique and very little has been said about technique here this morning. It is in technique that the whole thing floundered. As I wrote in my discussion, the prizes have gone to the other groups. Our side lost. I believe we lost the race. I do think of it as a relay race and I do think that there is a future. It would be very good if the best of the ideas of the Hartmann era could be reintegrated into the future because I think we are in some danger of having a disorderly and undisciplined era in psychoanalysis. That is a serious concern.

Furst: We already have it.

Kris: I want to point out that one of the reasons it's difficult for us to evaluate the Hartmann era is because it's so recent and we may imagine that certain things are clear about what the influences were. Recently, in the *New Yorker*, I read that Yale students no longer engage in sexual activity in anything like the numbers that they used to. There is, it seems, a sea change in sexual activ-

---

15. The reference is to a famous footnote on p. 50 of the *Ego and the Id*. It is discussed by A. Kris (1994). Freud's treatment of a narcissistic patient. *International Journal of Psycho-Analysis* 75:657–658. In the footnote Freud describes a sense of guilt as the sole remaining trace of the abandoned love relationship.

ity and perhaps even in the attitude towards responsibility. It's not inconceivable to me that in the next decade people will once again be interested in their own responsibility for their development in a way that the revolution of the '60s absolutely stopped the old way of looking at oneself. There has been a period of at least thirty years in which it has not been popular to examine one's own responsibility, and therefore psychoanalysis has not been the mode of choice.

I agree also with those who feel that there was a terrible authoritarian problem. I agree also with Cliff Yorke that Anna Freud was different and disapproved of at least some of the Hartmann, Kris, and Loewenstein views, though it seems to me she was opposed to a lot of work by others, especially when it modified Freud's work. Otto mentioned Victor Calef. Eddy Weinshel told the story of Anna Freud coming to San Francisco, and several of the senior people gave papers. When he discussed his case, she said, "Well, it's good to see that at least Dr. Weinshel knows what analysis is." She left few unspared insofar as I can see, and it was a problem because Hartmann and Kris particularly were so devoted to her, and through her to Freud. This was a powerful influence on what Otto speaks of as the silencing. In deference to her need to oppose Melanie Klein and to shut Melanie Klein out, they controlled it here. That's how I see it. It may not be exact, but I do know that Hartmann was not a close personal friend of Anna Freud. He was very deferential to her when they were together, but that was part of what I believe was their need to relate to Freud and to continue the Freud tradition.

There is one other point that I'm rather surprised about, as a matter of fact, that seems to me wrong, and that has to do with the Holocaust, which is mentioned by Martin, briefly by Otto, and by Harold. I think you may not know how much, for instance, my father was involved with war propaganda. He wrote a book on German war propaganda. He wrote several papers on prejudice, hostility, and mass reactions, but these happened not to be in psychoanalytic journals for the most part. They were not unaware of the Holocaust or of the Nazi phenomenon. As for Hartmann going to Switzerland, it wasn't some chance event. He was a Swiss citizen. That's why he went to Switzerland. He was very proud that his grandfather, perhaps it was his great-grandfather, had been smuggled into Switzerland and made a Swiss citizen. His children are Swiss citizens. It was not a trivial matter for him. As for the reason Hartmann didn't serve in the war, he was about to be made a general in the army, but he had a heart attack and that ended his military possibilities. Hartmann was to have been one of those who would have led the American psychiatric movement. It would be very hard for me to imagine that a denial of the Holocaust had anything to do with Hartmann's theories.

As to Hartmann's idea about adaptation, he's not talking about adapting in a social sense: of being a good boy or a bad girl. I think he's talking about what today is actually taken for granted, that the infant is born with a capacity for object relations, with a capacity for perception, with a capacity for many things that are operative much earlier than Freud ever imagined and that psychoanalysts, following him, imagined 20 years ago. Hartmann saw way ahead that there might be a misreading of his idea about adaptation. There are some methodological encumbrances in our discussion, some of which have to do with simply forgetting history, some of which have to do with how close we are to it. I do think this is an extraordinarily valuable moment and that Martin's monograph is a triumph. He has created a nucleus for a reconsideration, and I'm very pleased to be here.

Bergmann: Thank you very much. I know you are very hungry, but there is something to be said in favor of the fact that everyone has spoken at least once before we have lunch.

Solnit: I'm delighted to be here and I feel deeply indebted to Martin for the reasons that Tony was more articulate about than I can be. I think he has helped to do what we failed to do in the 1994 *Psychoanalytic Study of the Child*, when we celebrated Hartmann's 100th birthday and attempted to have a scientific display of the rediscovery and review of Hartmann's contributions. Martin's paper certainly does capture the spirit of that. I will start with a personal comment because in Martin's paper, he suggests, I'm not sure it's true, that I was the only one here who was analyzed by Hartmann. Maybe there were others here who were.

Bergmann: If there were, I think they would raise their hand. I don't think so.

Solnit: I felt like a member of the extended family in the Kris, Hartmann, Loewenstein group. Tony and I used to travel the train together. In my psychiatric training after being a pediatrician, I was attracted to psychoanalysis by the infant observations made by Spitz and to the theories that were taught to me in my military service. It was the only theory that helped me understand the soldiers who were returning with psychiatric disorders as a result of a severe and sustained trauma. We had a study group in my first military installation where we studied Freud and we had an advanced candidate from Milwaukee who taught it. So I did not have any experience of authoritarianism. Yes, a little with Isakower. I graduated from the New York Psychoanalytic Institute in 1955. I always had the feeling I was with a very special group of people who were friendly, who were communicative, who loved to hear criticism and new ideas. I was insulated from what seems to be the sense of authoritarianism. I didn't even recognize it; maybe I denied it. At any rate, I entered into psychoanalytic training because it showed great promise for helping me understand children. The Hartmann, Kris, Loewenstein papers, and Loewenstein's clinical teaching at Yale, were extraordinarily influential. Later on, I had contact with Anna Freud. In working with her and Joan Goldstein, I never had the feeling that you couldn't argue, you couldn't disagree. In fact, Anna Freud used to say, "Goldstein and I are you, and you try to help us understand what we're arguing about." I'm glad I missed it, if it was there. I did not experience it. Hartmann would have been the first to say he doesn't like the idea of an era or Hartmannites. I never had the impression that was something he sought. Yes, he was austere, he was aristocratic, but I don't think he ever thought of himself as leading or being in charge of a school. He was a free thinker.

Actually, Martin asked me indirectly in his introduction what it was like to be in analysis with him. He didn't say it that way. Hartmann helped me listen to myself. He was very tactful and he was eager to know how I heard myself and then he would help me hear myself better. I think that's the best way I can describe it. I was in analysis with him for five years and we had a New Haven group who were free thinkers. One became a very strong disciple of Edith Jacobson and Sam Levy. We had a seminar before and after on the train coming and going.

The thing that attracted me the most about Hartmann's ideas and why I have found them not needing to be based on clinical observation was for specific reasons. I kept looking to explain health, not psychopathology, how the inner life was reflected when people were functioning well and finding ways of adapting to and overcoming conflict and difficulty. Hartmann's ideas were extremely important. The other attraction was we had a terrifically exciting project that Ernst Kris ran in New Haven together with Marianne and Milton Sand, but Ernst was clearly the leader, in which he kept developing the idea that direct observation can help you be critical of theory, can help you build theory, but you have to test it. You only have to look at his earlier paper on validation of psychoanalytic propositions that indicated he'd never gave up the rigor of his scientific thinking. He kept saying, "Don't be constricted in thinking, you have to fit it into some other scientific mode." Psychoanalysis is a science that comes out of a number of different sources.

Hartmann, it seemed to me, should not be faulted for what he did not address, for what he did not look into, what did not interest him. If there was a Hartmann era, we should look at what he was interested in rather than what he wasn't interested in. This creates an imbalance, but not everybody can be interested in everything. If you look at the range of interests around this table, you'd have to say that none of us could encompass all of the ideas, all of the areas that this range of talented people have put forth on the table. What was so interesting about Hartmann was that he kept trying to understand why things functioned well rather than why they didn't function well.

At least in my work, it was always a help to know why children didn't ingest poisonous substances when they were $2\frac{1}{2}$ to 3 rather than why they did. His theory opened that door. There was no doorman connected with it. That's why his papers always say "comments" on some ideas. These are papers that give you a comprehensive systematic view. Most of his papers suggest that he's got an idea he's following and he did have a goal, not that he was going to achieve it, but psychoanalysis might be able to achieve the status of a general psychology. It's not a bad aspiration if you think about bringing in some of the ideas that he, Kris, Loewenstein, and others had.

The other teacher I had was Larry Kubie, who was quite a free thinker, and Bob Knight. They brought the Topeka influence. They taught at Yale Department of Psychiatry in three- and four-month sessions and we had an immersion in them. They'd come sometimes two days a week. As a pediatrician, I was eager to support healthy development and to find out what interfered with it. Sam Ritvo thought it was very funny when I came to New Haven. I knew out of my work in San Francisco as a pediatrician, that I wanted to be analyzed. I didn't know whether I wanted to be an analyst. I then had my interviews in New York as I was starting my residency, and they told me I should go see Heinz Hartmann. I went to Sam and asked who was he. By that time, he was rather well known and he was the director of the Clinic of the New York Psychoanalytic Institute. So he was a man who was immersed in clinical thinking, although it was his style not to use that in a way in which he built theory.

Nunberg: This is really quite fascinating to hear this from the beginning, where we really heard Hartmann more or less anathematized, and come right around to a point of view which is quite the opposite. It makes me think of my acquaintance with Hartmann, which was really my father's because as I was growing up my father and Hartmann were basically anathema. He thought of Hartmann as destroying analysis because he went away from id analysis.

Kris: I remember your father saying one day, "They will canonize him."

Furst: I have a very interesting personal story. I was in analysis with Herman Nunberg.

Kris: As was Waelder.

Neubauer: Nunberg was against the ideas of Hartmann, but he wanted me to be supervised by him. He did not want me to go to an American analyst.

AFTERNOON DISCUSSION, OCTOBER 18TH

Bergmann: I want to express my happiness at the level of discussion this morning. Many ideas came up. I am still waiting for new ideas to suddenly emerge from the group unconscious. Following the same rhythm, we should start with André Green's paper, and maybe every discussant who speaks about his paper should not try to summarize but verbalize what, in his opinion, are the major issues for discussion. Then we may disagree and say no, your paper raises completely different issues, but we should start on the question of what issues did you address or what issues do you wish to discuss with us, and with these remarks I turn to André Green.

Green: Thank you for giving me the opportunity to explain myself about what I have written. My main point is about the local influence of Hartmann. Seen from European eyes, it looked as if Hartmann was the general representative of American analysts, their leader (as Leo Rangell wrote) or their ambassador in the international community. Of course, this is a generalization that is schematic.

Let us consider the quotation by Peltz that is in Martin's paper: Peltz stated,[16] "His greatly expanded view of the ego and its functions put that agency of the mind on a par with the id (and the superego) without diminishing psychoanalysis as a depth psychology" (p. 559).

I have no special interest in Peltz's writings. I do not know his work, but it seemed to me that it was an oxymoron to write such a sentence. Nevertheless it seemed to state a commonly accepted view. It is theoretically inconsistent to say that one can put the ego "on a par" with the id if one has in mind Freudian theory. Freud seems to confess that we cannot have any precise idea of what the id is because of its nature. In *Moses and Monotheism* Freud returned to the same subject.[17] To some extent, to give a radical formulation, the *id is the unthinkable*. This is why we can only define it negatively, having in mind our usual ways of thinking, which are those of the ego: rationality, without falling into the trap of a superstition or occultism or mysticism. This is our challenge. To say that we can put the ego on a par with the id is inconsistent because it is a major hypothesis of Freud that the id dominates the ego, be-

---

16. Peltz, M. L. (1989). On the origins of contemporary structural theory: an appreciation of "Egopsychology and the Problem of Adaptation." *Psychoanalytic Quarterly* 58:551–570.

17. In *Moses and Monotheism* Freud stated: "What is unsatisfactory in this picture—and I am aware of it as clearly as anyone—is due to our complete ignorance of what distinguishes a conscious idea from a preconscious modification, or perhaps a different distribution, of psychical energy" (1939, p. 97).

yond any superficial examination. Moreover, the ego is supposed to be the differentiated part of the id under the influence of the external world, obviously a very small portion of it. I have always found that *depth psychology* is a misleading expression, even if it is used by Freud. The whole construction of the psychic apparatus is built on the foundation of the id. If you disagree with this principle, then you disagree with the whole description of Freud's psychic apparatus. Our conceptualization of the id is inevitably hypothetical and certainly metaphorical. Clifford speaks of the id's anchorage in the somatic, though even at that stage its already psychic primitive form is unknown to us. This is our challenge, to try to imagine what goes on beyond the point where Freud stopped, feeling unable to present anything consistent further. He confesses that he has not found a serviceable working hypothesis. We will come back to that in detail later. Some other psychoanalysts, feeling that they were also unable to forward the problem, took other paths. For instance, object relations, which does not answer the question of Freud. It changes the cards, and distributes them differently. We shall see later in the discussion why this orientation was chosen.

As time went on, psychoanalytic theory has become a *"theory of the total personality,"* which, according to my idea of psychoanalysis, is wrong. Now, I do not deny that sometimes Freud gives that impression, that the theory he tries to build has an extended scope that would make psychoanalytic theory close to a total personality, as in the *New Introductory Lectures* and more specifically in the title of Chapter 31, *Dissection on the Psychical Personality*, but this, to me, is a superficial interpretation. I was pleased to read in the paper by Martin on the history of psychoanalysis[18] Freud's exclamation to Adler, "This is not psychoanalysis." A very actual question indeed. Freud was aware that there were other ways of describing the personality. He wanted to illustrate his postulate of the primacy of the unconscious and of the id. For a long time the id dominates the situation in development. It does not mean, of course, that other processes are not also at work at the same time. Modern research has shown that the infant, already from the beginning, possesses sets of coordinated reactions that come into play in the relationship with the mother. Anyhow, it is impossible to deny that the infant's needs, which are at the basis of drives, are not over all important in the beginning. This is what is usually called the "prematurity" of the infant, which is here aggravated by the impossibility of using sophisticated tools of communication. Here it is important to link preverbal communication (through signs, signals, indications, all of

18. Bergmann, M. S. (1997). The historical roots of psychoanalytic orthodoxy. *International Journal of Psycho-Analysis* 78:69–86.

which are impregnated with affect) with the further verbal communication (through language). This involves instinctual needs or drives having to find ways of expression to convey the inner tensions within the infant. Here is where the concept of representation comes into play. Two sorts of representations are mobilized. The first are related to representations coming from within the internal body reaching the mind of the infant, and the second, almost indissociable from the preceding, from the helpless child to the helpful and understanding mother, more or less in a symbiotic relation to her child. All the evidence brought from infant observation enriches our picture of the situation but does not change our basic assumptions—at least mine—on the fundamental significance of the reality called "drives." Maternal care is the condition to the survival of the infant, only gradually is it superseded by the ego and then by the superego. The influence of the id still marks the other structures even after more differentiated organizations have appeared. But this is less obvious. That is what Clifford says when he speaks of relative autonomy.

A whole meeting could be devoted to the difference between concepts and metaphors. What are metaphors? They relate to theoretical gaps, between the facts observed—which even at this stage raise lots of debates about their consistency, their significance, and delineations—and the theory we build on them. There is no possibility of joining the two together without leaving a gap in our understanding and between the concepts and what they account for. This is the reason for which a metaphor is needed in order to help establish the workable picture for the conceptual mind. Such are most psychoanalytic concepts. In France we emphasize that theory cannot be drawn entirely from practice; theoretical concepts cannot apply to practice without some distance. This is not only a matter of elegance. We speak of a *practical-theoretical gap* (J.-L. Donnet). David Tuckett[19] asked the whole psychoanalytic community: What is a clinical fact? We cannot say our facts can be entirely separated from our theories because our facts are delineated by some of our theoretical assumptions. The Kleinians, for instance, do not speak anymore of repression. They prefer splitting, in a way different from Freud's concept because their basic assumptions are in fact different. Unless we point them out and spell them out, the debate with them will remain stillborn. Maybe the worst would be to try to find an artificial way of bringing together Freudian and Kleinian concepts for the sake of a patchwork consensus that will sooner or later prove its weakness. But this can be applied to any

19. The reference is to the International Symposium "What is a Clinical Fact?" The symposium was organized by David Tuckett and published in volume 75 of the *International*.

other body of knowledge that opposes Freud's work and the post-Freudians. The task of clarifying the differences, not only between the concepts of each subgroup of modern psychoanalysis, but also about their respective basic assumptions, is the precondition required for a fruitful dialogue. It is illusory to think that we can overcome our divisions if we do not try first to discuss what is in the back of our minds before uttering the words to express our thoughts.

This is a matter about our preconceptions, which help in understanding our conceptions. We should make clear that when we speak of the id, or of the drives, ego, and superego, and even of representations we do not mean that we are speaking of realities but of concepts—concepts are intellectual tools that help to us to grasp what we mean by reality; they are not reality itself. As Freud reminded us, reality is unknowable. Concepts have an indirect relationship to it. They are mediations.

My main objection to Hartmann was that he thought he could provide a sounder image of the mind if he turned his back to the viewpoint of the overpowerful influence of the id. Today, you find in psychoanalytic journals the expression, "From the vantage point of . . ." It is not that I approve of the expression, but I'm sure that you have heard it many times. There is no vantage point from the ego in psychoanalysis, because if you have a vantage point from the ego you lose the essentials of psychoanalysis, even if you are cautious enough to emphasize that you include the unconscious ego in defense of your positions. Take the idea, forwarded by Freud in the *New Introductory Lectures*, that most of what we know of the id is of a negative character and can be described only as converse to the ego; Freud here warns us. We are always tempted to come back to the ego because it is the easiest way for us to look at our data. It is always the trend or the habit to come back to a familiar way of thinking, which means also that we are inclined to think in the language of our defenses against the scandal of unconscious determinism. Martin said the same thing this morning when he observed that we only find secondary processes in Hartmann, concluding that all are secondary processes in Hartmann. This is the consequence of Hartmann's theory built from the point of view of the ego, even if he considers its relationship with the other agencies. It is more a question of the choice of a starting view point than a simple reappraisal of "mutual influences," to quote him.

Now I come to the reason why I question Freud's reformulation of the topographical model, called the *structural point of view* by the Hartmannites. This is my debate with Martin; I assume that the formulation about the id makes no mention of representation in Freud. You may read Laplanche and Pontalis. You will see that Laplanche and Pontalis make the observation that when Freud speaks of the id,[20] there is no reference to representation. It is interesting to compare, in Freud, the formulation about the unconscious and the formulation about the id. They have much in common. What matters are the differences, which sometimes are unnoticed. When Martin, using Freud's words, says that what little we know of the id we have learned from our study of the dream work and the construction of the neurotic symptom, observing that the dream *work* is not yet representation but is on its way to it; he considers that it is a preliminary work on representation, if not a representation already. My understanding is different: the dream work is about thought processes, in this case latent thoughts. It works on representations but is different in nature from them. Condensation and displacement are related to metaphor and metonymy. Lacan has defended this parallel but he was contradicted by Roman Jakobson. So the comparison is only half true. In fact, the fecundity of the processes that come into play in dream work is that they apply all the same to quantities of energy (the flow of the dream), images of the dream (representability), and ideas (latent thoughts). The main difference for me between the first topographical model and the second one, named by the Hartmannites the "structural point of view," is that, in the first topographical model, drives are excluded from the psychic apparatus. Freud explicitly says drives are neither conscious nor unconscious; only their representations can be said to be conscious or unconscious. What he will write later about the id implies that, *at this level*, instead of representations we have instinctual impulses. Freud seems to say that contents—which are so basically linked to representation—are an attribute of the ego. Freud compares instinctual impulses in the id to what would be a representation in the ego. It follows that any theory that will consider the basis of psychic activity as formed by representation of any kind is, even if it differs from Hartmann's, another sort of ego psychology. So the difference between an instinctual impulse and the primary process bound to representations is marked. In the 1915 paper on the unconscious, Freud's descriptions of the primary processes seem to apply primarily to representations (and affects). Though the representations are derived from impulses, they are considered as existing in a figurable way. The question of affects remained debatable. In 1915, Freud wrote that they were more suppressed than repressed, denying the existence of unconscious affects, but in 1923, returning to the topic in the second chapter of *The Ego and the Id*, he expressed the opposite opinion. He had to admit the existence of an unconscious sense of guilt, which could not be thought of in terms of representations.

---

20. The reference is to the item "id" in *The Language of Psychoanalysis* by Laplanche and Pontalis (New York: Norton, 1973).

We can see how, in the 1923 model, Freud proceeded to a major reorganization of his thinking on many important points of his previous theory. Why did Freud change his mind? We have indications of this turning point in the paper *Remembering, Repeating, and Working Through* (1914). It took six more years to write *Beyond the Pleasure Principle* (1920) and you have to add three more years until *The Ego and the Id* (1923), nine years in all!

In the second topographical model, he gives his first description of the id. Two changes have occurred, compared to the concept of the unconscious. The first change is, as I said, that representations are replaced by instinctual impulses. The second change is the introduction of the death instinct. Concerning this second point, I would like to make clear that I will not discuss it from the point of view of the existence of this concept in reality. My aim is to understand what Freud had in mind expressing these views. Nobody will be able to show that there is an id and an ego united or separated. Martin quotes Max Schur. But Schur speaks of a reflex model leading to the undifferentiated matrix. The reflex model is a creation of Schur. When Freud writes on drives, he doesn't refer to the reflex model because the ambiguity in the drive concept is to locate it between the somatic and the psychic. Schur addressed the somatic, which is an expectable idea coming from someone who was essentially a physician. How to imagine something between the somatic and the psychic? What is somatic is understood through physiology. Only the psychic is capable of representation. The Paris Psychosomatic School, led by Pierre Marty, has defended the idea that the psychosomatic patients were not very well organized as far as "mentalization" was concerned. When Marty had to explain himself about the attributes of "mentalization," he found no better criteria than the function of representation but, as we will see, we shall have to consider different modes of representation beyond the traditional opposition of things and words. Nobody also will be able to prove or disprove the existence of a death drive. If we admit that the field of Eros is largely beyond the manifestations of manifest sexuality (genitality), we may admit also that the field of destruction extends largely beyond the manifestations of overt aggression.

We have to understand that what Freud wrote about were *theoretical constructs*. More than ever, he clearly shows the existence of the practical-theoretical gap. When Freud deals with constructs, he is always in an uneasy position. Sometimes he refers to what can be observed, but obviously it is not where his main interest lies. His main interest is in building a body of concepts helping to understand the originality of his discoveries. The constructs reflect usually the positive results of psychoanalysis. Freud wants the failures of psychoanalytic treatment to be part of the theory, also as revealing ideas characteristic of the psychic apparatus. They may be due to the limitations of the psychoanalysts, but one can't exclude the idea that they are limitations of the mind itself. Therefore, his concepts are ambiguous. People have criticized the anthropomorphic, the personification of the agencies. Freud didn't have in mind "persons" when he described the second topographical model. He was caught between a construction and a way of making it accessible to others. When he used anthropomorphic constructions it was his way of fabricating theoretical comic strips to help us understand him, in a way that was deliberately nonphilosophical. He had to recourse, *in his theory*, to modes of communication understandable through figurative concepts. Therefore the anthropomorphism is a way of talking to us anthropoids, which is not a pejorative qualification but one supposed to convey concepts born from a different basis, other than the one that belongs to traditional thinking based on reason, that is, an attribute of the ego.

Maybe we can say that this pictorial image of the mind was in itself a representation of how it would look like. This provisional view was in the expectancy that one day the experience of the psychoanalyst and the findings of science would help us to build a better conception. Unfortunately, the advances in scientific discoveries and the experience of psychoanalysts have not favored the wished-for encounter.

I shall end by again expressing doubts about psychoanalysis as a psychology. I agree that the problem didn't start with Hartmann. All those who objected to drive theory followed the same path. The project of the reformulation of psychoanalysis to arrive at a general psychology was the aim of Hartmann's theory, but it didn't stop with him. After that we had self psychology. Now we have intersubjectivity. What is the subject in this context? Is this Husserl's subject? Is it Descartes's subject? The subject is supposed naively to be just what we "are," and then to describe the interaction between you and me. It is striking how much the reference to interaction does not give us the slightest idea about how it works. It seems to refer to a model combining action and reaction, and such a model buries the reference to representation. The subject is the subject of action. Is thinking a mode of action? What for? We have to decide whether action is in relation to desire (to avoid the reference to drive) or to adaptation, or what else? If action becomes the reference, its aims and goals have to be specified. I prefer to consider thinking as representation, speculation rather than action. Action ends the process. With representation the working through goes on.

I don't know if the intersubjectivists are "extenders" or "modifiers."[21] This is the reason why we have to watch the evolution of concepts. Concepts have

21. Bergmann, M. S. (1993). Reflections on the history of psychoanalysis. *Journal of the American Psychoanalytic Association* 41:929–955.

potentialities, and you have to pay attention to the direction that will develop such and such of their potentialities. Sometimes it can be in a promising direction, but sometimes you will, without knowing it, go in a reductionistic direction that will lead you to impasses. Some people supported Hartmann's point of view, like Kurt Eissler, in the beginning, who wrote later that paper about the relevance and future of psychoanalysis in which Hartmann is criticized.[22]

I want to make myself as clear as possible, and in order to do that I have to lean on Freud's ideas as he expressed them himself. You may agree or disagree with what he said, but at least you will know what is the matter of your disagreement. In a paper written for the thirteenth edition of the Encyclopedia Britannica, in 1926 (Psycho-Analysis, *Standard Edition* 20:263–270), Freud tries to explain his axioms and their development. Considering the *dynamic* point of view, he says "psychoanalysis derives all mental processes (apart from the reception of external stimuli) from the interplay of forces, which assist or inhibit one another, combine with one another, etc. All these forces are originally in the nature of *instincts*; thus they have an organic origin. They are characterized by possessing an immense (somatic) store of power (*the compulsion to repeat*); and they are represented mentally as images or ideas with an affective charge" (p. 265). It follows from this that if one disagrees with the theory of instincts, one dispenses with Freud's basic conception of psychic activity as an "interplay of forces." Would it be possible to keep the reference to forces and try to propose something else instead of drives? The fact is that no one tried to propose that. Because the force without the drive will keep the dynamic dimension but will lose the relationship to representation and meaning. It follows also that if one disagrees with the opinion that mental representations (images or ideas with an affective charge) are *representations in the mind of this interplay of forces*, one dissociates the representations from their supposed roots in the body. In other words, representations will be understood as being the result of relationships to objects and it is this relationship that will be represented. But where to find the source of energy that helps keep systems moving and functioning? We come back here to the traditional view of representation having "beheaded" representations from their sources seen as springing from the body.

The project of transforming psychoanalysis into a general psychology, which implied the rejection of the theory of drives, or the reformulation of psychoanalytic concepts in the language of psychology, aimed at dissociating mental activity from its supposed bodily organic sources. Such a removal from

---

22. Eissler, K. (1969). Irreverent remarks about the present and the future of psychoanalysis. *International Journal of Psycho-Analysis* 50:461–471.

Freud's theory applies also to the concepts of *cathexis* and energy as an expression of the *economic* point of view (in terms of quantity and of transformation), and also to the idea of a mental apparatus as a topographically *heterogeneous* compound. The apparatus is bound to conflict precisely because of the heterogeneity of its agencies, which implies conflicting aims and conflicting modes of functioning. Such a reappraisal, giving up the bodily roots of psychic activity, left the place empty, inviting the neurobiologists to take over. The result was, almost generally, to deny to psychoanalysis any availability, considering it irrelevant in totality.

In *Moses and Monotheism*, Freud, coming back to the dynamic point of view, confesses his "complete ignorance" of its foundations. "We talk of cathexis and hypercathexis but beyond this we are without any knowledge on the subject or even any starting point for a serviceable working hypothesis" (p. 97). This sentence goes at least as far as the most radical criticisms Freud's theory has undergone.

To come back to the 1926 article, Freud proceeds: "The most important conflict with which a small child is faced is his relation to his parents is the 'Oedipus complex'" (p. 268). Confronted with such a challenge, to try to solve the problems of the relationship between the dynamic point of view (that is, its reference to psychic forces), so obscure in essence, and the approach to the "most important conflict" (Oedipus complex), psychoanalysts have chosen to investigate the latter one, which seemed more easily solvable or, as they thought, "workable" by the investigation of development. So they were inclined to *forget the reference to psychic forces* (or instinctual demands from the side of the id and the other "force in the mind," the superego). It is not so easy to understand what implies the idea of force applied to the mind. What was an axiom for Freud, the reference to the drives, was replaced by an alternate conception expressed in terms of observable "relations" between people, children, and adults. Soon the point of view of "relationships" was supposed to be enlightened by the observation of mother–child relationships. The roots of the Oedipus complex were pushed backwards. Child psychoanalysis was not enough. Child and infant observation investigated the evolution from birth till the age of the outcome of the complex in a developmental perspective. In getting rid of the dimension of forces, which implied thinking of their transformation into representations from an intrapsychic point of view, the findings of observations were stated in the language of intersubjective psychology, which stood for the speculative approaches about the intrapsychic. In this new inspiration, observational facts were in fact under the influence of preconceptions that brought back the observers closer to the thinking of pre-Freudian academic psychology, without being always aware of that change. The question of how the observational method could reach the intrapsychic world was ignored. *Id mythology was supposed to be replaced by ego psychology. It was in fact a return to "ego mythology,"* a conception of the psychic internal world governed by an ego freed from its dependence on the id, an idea that goes back to the most traditional thinking.

In fact, the resistance was directed against the id, as a more radical form of unconsciousness than the unconscious. We can assume that the preconscious is the gate of a vast domain extending from the unconscious to the libidinal body and even to the biological somatic. In other words, we can say that the domain of psychic activity is caught between the soma, which is beyond the domain of subjectivity (this can hardly be " located" out of the unconscious), and the external world in which the object stands. *By all means it will prove more easy to observe the relationships between subject (or ego) and object than to speculate on the nature of psychic processes of the internal world, that is, of the mind and the soma, as Freud tried. When they consider the nature of the mind, psychoanalysts will have to fight against the reductionistic conceptions of cognitive science and neurosciences. Both disciplines aim at the suppression of the concept of unconscious psychic activity, according to psychoanalysis.*

To continue, I want to come back to some of the points that have been raised by Bill Grossman. He was right to underline the influence of the origins. There is one origin of Hartmann's work that he may have undervalued, the influence of Paul Schilder. Hartmann had been an assistant to Paul Schilder for 14 years. Paul Schilder was asked by Freud to join the analytic movement even if he wasn't a psychoanalyst himself. Martin said that the only people with whom Hartmann maintained a dialogue were Dilthey, Jaspers, and the phenomenologists. This is quite true, but I think one should emphasize also the influence of Gestalt psychology. He was deeply influenced by this movement in Vienna, by Klaus Konrad, Kofka, and Kurt Lewin, who emigrated to the States. Many of these people were psychologists at a time when psychology was a leading science. Hartmann's theory bears the mark of that conception of structure. I'm not saying that he was not a psychoanalyst above all, but he obviously followed the bent of the psychologists. The second point about Hartmann is the one that Schafer raised, about the use of the metaphor of the government. This was due to the influence of his father, who was a diplomat, an ambassador. His son had been his secretary, for a certain period. Hartmann was very much interested in sociology, and the ideas of Max Weber were important to him ("neutral axiology"). Any serious study of Hartmann's theory must evaluate the situation of the movement of ideas in Vienna in those circles to which he belonged: biology, neurology, psychiatry, psychology, sociology, political science!

Finally, I conclude that Hartmann's effort, and for me, Hartmann's failure was the result of an illusion—and now we have the disillusionment—in the attempt to present a *more reasonable theory of the mind*. Freud's theory is not a reasonable one because it emphasizes the influence of nonrational factors in psychic activity. It strongly emphasizes the role of passion in man, which drive him mad. But this madness is not limited to the patients. One can meet it as well in colleagues and so-called normal people.

Kernberg: I have two interrelated points. First, Hartmann's approach, his basic challenge implied a downgrading of the importance of psychoanalysis as a science of unconscious drives. André Green has been stressing psychoanalysis as the science of human behavior under the influence of the unconscious. I find that convincing. Then André's view of the nature of the id, or our limitations in establishing what the id is, should receive attention. That, I think, is extremely interesting in itself, although it is not at the center of our subject. I personally would be extremely interested in hearing more about this.

I know that André has stated that there are no representations in the id, and I have difficulty with that. It is true that there is one statement by Freud that goes in that direction, but one can also quote a number of other statements of Freud's that imply all that we know about the drives are representations and affects.

Green: In the *New Introductory Lectures* (Lecture 31) Freud writes, "Instinctual cathexes seeking discharge—*that, in our view, is all there is in the id*. It even seems that the energy of these instinctual impulses is in a state different from that in the other regions of the mind, far more mobile and capable of discharge; otherwise, the displacements and condensations would not occur which are characteristic of the id and which so completely disregard the *quality* of what is cathected—*what in the ego we should call an idea*" (*Standard Edition* 22:74–75, italics mine). We notice here that the emphasis is on *energy* and discharge, exclusively. Ideas are supposed to belong to the ego. There are many points in common with what Freud already wrote in his paper on the unconscious in 1915. But, in that same paper, Freud mentions "object cathexes" and "thing presentations" (cathexis of remote memory—images of the thing) (*Standard Edition* 14:201). In German the word is either *Dingvorstellung* or *Sachvorstellung* for thing-presentation. *In the 1933 paper, any mention to Vorstellungen in the id is omitted.* In saying that the processes occurring on instinctual impulses disregard "*what in the ego we should call an idea*," Freud is implicitly denying that one can find in the id what the *Standard Edition* alludes to by the "*ideational representation of the drives*" (*Vorstellung representanz*) in the 1915 paper on metapsychology. Freud presents in 1933 a basically energetic conception of the id, without any reference to the *idea, quality, or representation*. The only possible representations are representations in this part of the psychic apparatus of somatic excitations that force the most primitive forms of psychic activity. One can notice also a shift of emphasis on condensation and displacement: in the *Interpretation of Dreams*, these mechanisms are applied to thoughts *and* to charges. In the 1933 text, they apply *only* to charges, that is, to energy. Freud is almost surely thinking here of the precursors of affects. One should underline Freud's evolution, not only in respect to the last dual theory of instincts, but also towards an energetic interpretation of the basis of the mind. The dynamic point of view may be absent but it still is Freud's main postulate.

Kernberg: I understand that, yet, you remember Herman Van der Waals's contribution[23] to the discussion of the ego and id in which he says, "At the end when we look at our patients, the content of the id, as much as we can get to know, what we find are again and again wishes, affects, representations of primitive, aggressive and sexual wishes" (p. 67). The question that I'm raising is: To what extent may the id be formulated as representations that have a quality of primitivity because of the extreme nature of the affects that they are invested with, so that the basic, the dyadic relation between self representation and object representation in the id takes the form of an overwhelming totalizing relationship that knows no other reality, so that there is a mad constellation of representation of self and object under the impact of primitive aggressive desire or sexual desire? The id is a constellation of primitive wishes that take the form of unconscious fantasies that contain a powerful affect, a self representation, and object representation. The difference between the id and the representational world of the ego is the intensity, the overwhelming, totalistic nature of the aggressive and sexual wishes. They do not respect the boundaries between representations. In other words, metaphor and metonymy, if you prefer, condensation and displacement, are a universal characteristic of such extreme constellations of primitive object relations. That corresponds more or less to my concept of the id. It's very difficult for me to imagine a nonrep-

---

23. In 1951 at the International Congress in Amsterdam, H. G. van der Waals participated in the Symposium on "Mutual Influences in the Development of the Ego and the Id." There he observed: "Ex difinitione, the id is an agency that does not possess any knowledge of the external world and does not keep any direct contact with the outer world. These occur exclusively via the ego. When strictly adhering to this definition, I must state that I have never found a pure id tendency or impulse in my patients. . . . The repressed unconscious thus appears to possess a fairly accurate knowledge of reality and the possibilities existing in it. Ex difinitione, such knowledge is the exclusive view of the ego." *Psychoanalytic Study of the Child* (1952) 7:67–68.

resentational nature of the wish, because I see wishes clinically, always centered in fantasies, wished or feared relations between self and an other with different degrees of fusion.

Green: What is the central point between the wish of a neurotic and the wish of a borderline? Can you even apply the term "wish" to your model?

Kernberg: A wish is always a desired change from a present situation to a different one.

Green: Why don't you say the drive instead of a wish?

Kernberg: Because I see the wish as a concrete manifestation of the drive. I see unconscious fantasies as concrete idiosyncratic individualized expression of wishes that represent the drives. I see drive as the overreaching hierarchically supraordinate motivation, the integration of corresponding sexual and aggressive affects. I see, for example, the concept of the death drive as the most profound need to destroy self and/or other. It's universal and it makes eminent sense to me, but I have never seen a patient who presents a drive that is not expressed as a wish, and a wish that doesn't express an affectively laden fantasy about a situation that needs to be changed.

Neubauer: What about psychosomatic patients?

Kernberg: Before going on to psychosomatic patients, in borderline patients we have this overwhelming wish to destroy, conquer, and sexually possess, the opposite of being castrated and destroyed. In such patients, we see direct expression of the drives and it contains representations. I'm questioning what André said about the nonrepresentational nature of the id. I have a theory of drives that is controversial and probably coincides with that of Sandler's, namely that primitive affects are the biological "building blocks" that get integrated into drives as hierarchically supraordinate systems.

Bergmann: In order for it not to become too much of a discussion between the two of you, I'm going to interrupt now and say, does anybody else want to speak on this particular issue, the question of representation and the id?

Neubauer: I'd like to raise three questions. One, André questioned those who say that the ego has superiority over the id or is more significant. If some people have chosen the ego as a significant point of entrance to get to know the id, because it is available for observation and for study, or for therapeutic reasons with emphasis on resistance and defense, we may get the capacity to strengthen the ego against drive influence, superego influences, and external influences. The ego becomes the point of significance without saying that it is structurally on a par with the id. Moreover, André says psychoanalysis should not pretend that it can speak for the total personality. When Freud made statements at various times in his developmental history, whether about the trauma and the drives or whether it's the later structure, does he say, "I only address myself to one aspect of the mind and never try to understand the overall structure of the mind, superego, ego, and id"?

Green: That's not what I said.

Neubauer: I can understand from where you come and therefore how you judge, for it is outside of what you consider to be the focus of psychoanalysis. When you speak about psychoanalysis and total personality, you stress the limitations about psychoanalysis rather than try at various points to encompass additional areas, encompass agencies of the mind that go beyond the one you have outlined. You speak about the id as being between the soma and the psychic. Would you therefore say that the drive is the biological demand on psychic life?

Green: It is only the first part of the definition of Freud.

Neubauer: The somatic source of the drive aims at discharge and is on different levels of representation and on a different level of discharge. This puts the drive, except for the source, in the realm of psychic function and not in between the somatic and the psychological. Only the source is in between the two.

The next question is, as you so interestingly and stimulatingly explore: How can we as analysts know more about the language and about the mysteries of the id and the drives? Where are the limitations? In all of these years, how far did we go in the attempt to know the drives and where do we have to move in order to understand better ways of doing it? Because those who are primarily oriented toward the id have also faced great limitations.

Blum: What I find enriching and stimulating about André is that he makes us think even about the unthinkable. I would like to ask André the following: How can we think about anything, including the unthinkable, without an ego? Is it possible to conceptualize anything, including the id, without automatically bringing in ego? The second thing has to do with the way in which wishes came into psychoanalytic thought, which is that psychoanalysis is basically an analysis of conflict. I'd like you to clarify, when you are thinking of the id, as Freud once described it, as a seething cauldron; that was Freud's metaphor. We know from recent discussions, and in the media too, that atoms and molecules behave very strangely at radical temperature gradients, whether it's exceedingly high or extraordinarily low temperatures. In the seething cauldron metaphor, it is very difficult to conceptualize discrete, distinct representations as opposed to what Arlow has described, the tendency towards condensation, displacement, and the inability to have stable, discrete representations. The last question is: Would we lose sleep over the question of a differentiation between id and ego, if it were not for the larger question about Hartmann's work and whether or not Hartmann's work is viewed as abandoning the depth psychology of the id so that drives and wishes are set aside, versus the other view, that one cannot conceptualize reality wishes or instinctual impulses without taking into account the fact that they emerge from conflict? From the very beginning, there was not only an id wish, but a defense against the wish—in other words, conflict. One can raise the question whether from the beginning the id and ego weren't introduced on a par with each other.

Arlow: Toward the end of Otto's remarks, he got to the point of making a distinction between wish and drive. The idea is that they belong to two different realms of discourse. Wishes are concrete and can be translated in listening to the patient's productions into verbal and other terms, whereas a drive is a broader concept or a more metapsychological concept. The two cannot be used indistinguishably.

Kris: I curiously hear in André's presentation the voice of my teachers. It's very striking to me; if one doesn't agree with your view, one is not an analyst. This continues to be a serious problem among analysts: we know what is true, the others don't. I hear it in your presentation. For my thinking, it doesn't make a particle of difference whether the id is representational in some sense or not representational. I don't think that that's what Hartmann's theory foundered on. I believe that regression and psychosis were relatively intolerable to his group. So instead of using the fine ego psychology to explore it more, they used it to limit analytic dialogues. If a patient were referred to as borderline or psychotic, that was already a value judgment, and a very negative one. I can recall the intonation: so and so is really psychotic. It was used against colleagues and was said to patients and it meant they were *out*. At the very time that they were elaborating ego psychology, other analysts were trying to get involved more and more with their sick patients, and for good reason. It turned out there were a lot of them, and they needed help. But the tools, as these ego psychologists used them, were limited by not being allowed to examine countertransference, not being allowed to have much regression, not being allowed to be interested in primitive affects, as Otto said. Those were by and large taboo. That's much more what affected Hartmann's psychology. André, you and I spoke during the lunch break and agreed that the critical attitude of these analysts to their patients played a profound role. You imagined that I was Kohutian because I said that the introduction of Kohut's ideas radically revolutionized things. You were surprised that I didn't have these Kohutian tendencies, as you referred to them. We agree on the way in which analysts in that period, belonging to the Hartmann group, shut out crucial matters, but whether those are connected with a representational id strikes me as irrelevant.

I want to add one other point. In the ten years before Freud developed his structural theory, in 1923, he had forgotten a crucial part of his theory. That is, when he invented the notion of repression in his version, adopting Hebart's notion,[24] he gave it two components, a push component and a pull component. Those two components, also called psychic inertia, primal repression—it didn't matter which word you used—lasted until 1915. He had two components for repression, and from 1915 to 1925 the pull component of repression is gone. Its only representative is in the concept of fixation. If you go, as I did, through every example of repression in Freud's writing in that 10-year period, you find it is ego repression, that is, the push component. I believe that Freud (1925) then tried to rescue the concept of the pull component, calling it the resistance of the id, and it seems to me that André does too. I think Hartmann was right, however, to elaborate the ego theory and he had to put it in context. I believe he was wrong in other matters, particularly in the stance toward the patient and that, I believe, is why his views foundered. I do not believe it's a theoretical matter and I do not think that Maury Peltz, when he says they are on a par, has any intention of implying that the two are equal. I'm sure he means, following Anna Freud, that they are on a par insofar as the analyst pays close attention to both.

Yorke: This one point is not so much a response to André but it is raised by Tony's question. I was astonished to hear that the "pull" component of repression had disappeared. I felt at once that I wanted to go and check it out and see what had really happened. I grew up, like many of us, with the notion that, as far as the neuroses were concerned, the return of the repressed was

---

24. Johann F. Hebart developed his theory of the ego in the early nineteenth century. It entered psychiatry through the textbook of Wilhelm Griesinger, with whom Freud was familiar.

all-important and that, in that process, the "push" and "pull" components combined. Perhaps I have misunderstood something.[25]

Kris: It is curious that neither Charlie Brenner in his review[26] nor Anna Freud in hers[27] noted that, but to my way of reading Freud for those 10 years, every reference to repression is repression from above and not the pull component. The place where the pull component is represented is in fixation.

Green: I'm sorry, I don't get your language.

Kris: The pull component of repression. There's a push component and a pull component. The pull component eventually becomes the resistance of the id but, in the 10 years previous, it's missing from Freud's writings.

Bergmann: André, the dream, you said, is not representation. In clinical work, I feel, when a patient dreams about something, I consider that a good sign. I say to myself, he is beginning to dream about something he needs to articulate. That is not a representation yet, but it is on a road towards representation. Where do you put the primary process if there are no representations in the id?

Kernberg: Very good questions were raised. We have a unique opportunity for intercultural exchange, which is wonderful.

Furst: I wonder how many of the questions that have been raised are answerable?

Bergmann: Asking a question is in the direction of representation, and even if the answer isn't there, having formulated the question I consider a step.

Neubauer: It is important for me what you have said, Tony, that the position of André should be discussed. What are its consequences?

Kris: And it is exactly a mirror of the way I hear the New York ego psychologists, the Boston psychologists speaking.

---

25. Tony has since written to me giving support for his view.

26. Brenner, C. (1957). The nature and development of the concept of depression. *Psychoanalytic Study of the Child* 12:19–46. New York: International Universities Press.

27. Freud, A. (1978). A study guide to Freud's writings. *The Writings of Anna Freud* 8:209–276.

Neubauer: One more question. Since André's position is clear and it leads to clear consequences about what is and what isn't within the province of psychoanalysts, I would like to ask you, André, what are the national and international consequences of your position at a time when there is so much ecumenical cooperation, where there are so many positions quite different from André's?

Green: First, I want to thank you all for raising major issues that, I think, are the real ones of my paper and of my summary.

No one has supported my view that there are no representations in the id. To give a convincing argument to this, I have to develop two issues. One is to expand on Freud's concept of representation. Second, if you allow me, I shall try to draw a schema which maps an outline of many of the problems about this specific topic.[28] I shall start with a well-known aspect of the problem and then extend the application of the notion.

What is usually known of Freud's conception of representation speaks of thing or object presentation and word presentation. This is already present in his work on Aphasia in 1891. The first type characterizes the unconscious, the second associated to conscious thing or object representation are only met in the conscious in connection with the corresponding word presentations. The Americans add to this something that is not in Freud, "self representation." As if the ego could only represent the different types of its activity (perceiving or talking or thinking) but not the self. One's image is perceived through a photograph or a glass but these are technical tools that are not part of our equipment. The two main issues are thing presentations and word presentations. In fact, Freud's conception of representation is partly Brentano's.[29]

I shall now mention here without comments the different types of representation that one can find in Freud's conception, which is wider than what I have recalled: 1) The *drive* (the "representative" of stimuli born in the interior of the body reacting to the mind); 2) the *psychic representative of the drive* (not to be confused with the ideational representative; example: the tickling in the throat in case of thirst), so the drive *is* a psychic representation and *has* psychic representatives; 3) the *ideational representative* (also called the thing pre-

---

28. See Figure 1.

29. Refers to Brentano: teacher of philosophy of Freud. A letter to Silberstein, dated March 15, 1875, records Freud's visit to his master, to discuss philosophical problems. Brentano hoped to enroll Freud in the study of philosophy, in vain. *Sigmund Freud Jugend Briefe an Eduard Silberstein, 1871–1881*, Herausgegeben von Walter Boehlich, S. Fischer, 1989.

sentation unconscious and conscious), which will relate to *object or thing presentations* as opposed to *affects*; 4) the *word presentation*; 5) the *representations of reality* ("ideas and judgments representing reality in the ego"). Let us detail the description.

Here you have this map about the first topographical model with the conscious, the preconscious, the unconscious, but it is very easy to translate into the second one. You can, for instance, say that from the vicinity of the somatic to the border of the Pcs, you have the id; from the border of the unconscious near the preconscious to the entire field of the conscious, we have the ego; and from the id to the conscious, you have the superego because the superego is said to have its roots in the id but is the result of a splitting in the ego. The main reason that Freud wanted to break with his former model was the fact that he was obliged to consider the role of repetition compulsion *beyond the pleasure principle*, as even painful experiences are compulsorily repeated. So he had to create an instance that could account for the compulsion to repeat instead of remembering through representations. I believe that Freud was wrong. Remembering is not the aim of psychoanalytic process. Patients who recover do not recover through remembering. Freud confused the awareness of what is psychical with something that antagonizes the awareness of what is

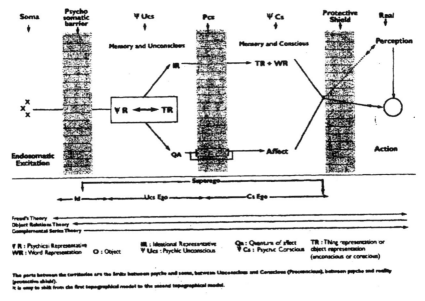

Figure 1.

psychical. It is repetition, automatic repetition through acts or repetitions overwhelming representations, like in hallucinations. This is why I consider that the basic drive activity lacks representation in the sense we have been using till now. If representations can be said to be present in the id it is only in the form of representations of stimuli born in the somatic that are represented at this lowest level of the psychic apparatus. Martin says that the dream work is on the road to representation. I am not sure that with the dream work we have to arrive at a representation. Representation can exist prior to dream work or after it. There are other theories that have dealt with the same problem without the help of representation, for example, Bion's alpha function or Winnicott with the difference between the subjective object (not always a representation) and the objectively perceived object. Winnicott asks us not to overcome the paradox, to accept it as impossible to solve. This is another way of expressing the subjectivity and objectivity. I believe that Freud wants to emphasize that the dream work is characterized by processes rather than contents. Processes can be related to energetic charges, affects, and/or representations. Here the accent is on nonfigurative features.

The French psychosomatic schools emphasize that there is a disturbance of the function of representation in the psychosomatic patients. They speak of an irregular functioning of the preconscious. These are debatable findings, but there are many evidences that, I think, support Freud's views. Drives are only seeking for discharge, says he. But discharge is different from acting out. Think of psychosomatic symptoms, hallucinations, and acting out. They share common features. They can be considered short circuits bypassing elaboration. They are precipitates.

Freud said that the drive is the psychical representative of the stimuli arising in the body and reaching the mind. This is his first approach in the definition of the drive in the paper on "Instincts and Their Vicissitudes." In metapsychology,[30] Freud uses implicitly a topographical reference, he defines the drive as a concept at the limit "between the somatic and the psyche." He also refers to a dynamic point of view, speaking of stimuli born within the body and "arriving" to the mind, which involves not only the idea of a journey but also, in defining two domains, a topographical reference too; finally we have also an economic point of view, the measure of the demand made upon the mind for work, in consequence of its connection with the body. What I want to emphasize is that the reference to representation in 1915 has different meanings to which I will come back later.

---

30. The reference is to Freud's 1915 paper, "Instincts and Their Vicissitudes," *Standard Edition* 14.

In his paper on *"The Loss of Reality in Neurosis and Psychosis,"*[31] in 1924, he speaks of the repression of reality, a negativization of reality in the mind that suppresses the representations of reality.

Three areas of "work" are here distinguished; the body, the external world, and the other (through language). All have in common their task to differentiate between inside and outside and between what is in the mind only and what is also in reality.

For the id, there is no access to reality. The ego has to go through representations of reality. The ego is attached to reality through the function of perceptions and through the judgment (of existence). So we have defined the five kinds of representations.

In fact, these different types of representations can be grouped, according to two models that seem to contradict themselves. The first model is expressed in terms of *internal communication*. It is based on the idea of a delegation of power, for instance, as an embassy. This is about the drive as representative of the body. The drive is the ambassador of the demands of the body in that other (country) domain: the mind. As such, it has to express itself (to "speak," so to say) in the language of the country to which it is sent: the mental, in order to ask for help. The drive has to speak the language of the object (the language of signs in communication, from cry to word), which can be decoded by the object. This is the first model. The second model is what I will call the *optical* model. The representation refers here to the relationship between an image in the mind and an object present in the external world. The object is the means by which the demand can be satisfied. This is what happens in wish fulfillment. The mirror (mind) produces an image that is related to the mnemic trace of an existing object out of reach. Psychoanalysts have overlooked the fact that these two conceptions are contradictory and it is Freud's task to make them compatible. How does he do it? Let us go back to my schema. We have the psychosomatic barrier here, between the somatic and the psychic unconscious. What we have to understand is that this is not a clear-cut frontier, as between two lands; it is a "no man's land," a territory, an area of transformations (somatic → psychic). Let's have here the unconscious, and between the unconscious and the conscious another "no man's land": the psychic activity named the preconscious, also a domain of transformations from unconscious to conscious. Finally we have here the real, with the protective shield separat-

---

31. In the 1924 paper "The Loss of Reality in Neurosis and Psychosis," Freud writes: "In a psychosis, the transforming of reality is carried upon the psychical precipitates of former relations to it—that is, upon the memory traces, *ideas and judgments by which reality was represented in the mind*" (*Standard Edition* 19:185, italics mine).

ing the conscious from the external world, a shield to protect psychic activity from being overwhelmed by excessive excitations. Four territories—the somatic, the unconscious, the conscious, and the real—and three no man's lands— the psychosomatic barrier, the preconscious, and the protective shield—that regulates the relationship with the outside world, where the external object stands, perceived and acted upon.

Let us come back to the source of the drive: Freud, in defining it as the excitation born within the body and reaching the mind, emphasizes the mobility or, if you prefer, the internal dynamics of drive expression. In the middle of the somatic, it is not yet the drive, but at the limits of the mind it is already the drive, as the inchoative forms of manifestations of psychic activity that acts as a stimulus on the mind, waiting for an elaboration. At the frontier of the mind, he calls it the psychical representative of the drive. What happens when some need or urge appears, hunger or anything else, that will give birth to a desire? The messages arrive from the body to the mind and it is as if, excuse my very imaginative language, the discourse sounds like, "I am calling the mind, something is going wrong in the body, you should do something about it." You can translate this abstract conception in the concrete terms of an infant–mother relationship, the infant asking help in his helplessness. This is the *psychical representative*. What the psychical representative does is to bring forward the object representation in the first instance. The mnemic traces of a previous satisfactory experience stimulated and evoked in hallucinatory wish-fulfillment. A matrix of the combination of the psychical representations born from the body in quest of an object and the object presentation of an experience of gratification is formed. *This matrix marks the difference between our conception of representation and that of philosophers.* For us psychoanalysts, representations are always dynamic. They are always carried *by forces that become representations* or *give birth to them.* I think it is inappropriate to speak of wishes at this stage because we are dealing with the most primitive expressions of mind functioning, which lack the sophistication of wishes and are filled with energetic tensions (affects). They deserve to be considered *impulses*, or drives if you prefer. The impulse aspect is stronger than the figurative aspect, which is derived from the psychic work on memory traces of perceptions. The wish is not a raw, primitive material. The wish is something that is elaborated, but the drive is connected to primitive objects and to their sketches of representations. A unit is formed combining psychical representatives of the drives (their stimuli) and the traces of the perception of the objects as representations in the most elementary raw material with which we deal that can be mobilized through the memory of the experience. This matrix will split further into *affects* and *ideational representatives* (contents). In the metapsychology, Freud states that each (representations and affects) can have a separate fate. When

Freud speaks of separate processes, he has in mind neurosis, not psychosis (see the paper on Repression, *Standard Edition* 14:152). The ideational representative will try to cross the barrier of the preconscious under the pressure of the "Trieb." A conflict takes place between push and pull. The content is repressed until it succeeds in taking a disguised form that is unnoticed; it crosses the border of the preconscious.

When the disguised content has crossed the barrier of the preconscious, object representation occurs, but this time it is conscious and, being conscious, it is associated with word presentation. This of course relates to the analytic situation. To come now to affects, they are present in both domains, unconscious and conscious. What is the difference? Affects are quantitative in the unconscious; they have no quality. They express themselves as tensions at this point. Becoming conscious, they acquire their quality. The work of the preconscious comes here into play, and gives birth to thoughts, conscious and preconscious thoughts, derived from the linkage of thing presentation with word presentation. But words are not always necessary to thought processes. Think of the latent thoughts of the dream processes. Words favor the perception of thought processes. Near the end, between conscious and real stands another no man's land: the protective shield that separates the psychic frontier from the external world. In the conscious, perception and action regulate the relationship to the external object. Now, modern neurobiologists call them *representactions*, condensing representation and action. This total overview gives an idea of what I've been trying to talk about. You can evaluate in this conception the radical imbalance between the unconscious and the id on one side, loaded with heavy energetic charges (affects), and what belongs to consciousness and preconsciousness. You can also evaluate the weight of the body through all the psychic productions.

Kernberg: I would like to comment on this briefly because it seems to me that André's presentation contains an extremely original concept that goes beyond Freud, but at the same time synthesizes Bion and other theories, and it's compatible with my view that is based mostly on Jacobson, and I would like to test it.

When I speak of object representation, it is within the context of a relationship between object and self. The object representation often contains the projected impulses. What André has added is that in extreme regression the primitive affect itself is the representation. These affects have psychic and somatic qualities. They operate under the impact of extreme aggression. Self-destructive wishes bring about somatization or take the form of acting-out. Working with borderline patients means retransformation of somatic feelings and acting-out into psychic representations. The absence of representation is not the cause but the consequence of the destructive power of the primitive destructive drive on the self and object representations. With these changes, I think that your viewpoint is compatible with both Bion and Jacobson.

Bergmann: I'm going to ask you to shift gears and to go to Clifford's paper.

Yorke: I felt very honored to be so invited. My first thought was that I had nothing to say about Hartmann, and just digging out a few notes written at the time of his death hardly seemed to offer enough to build on. But I quickly became caught up once more when I read Martin's splendid paper.

I was very interested to hear what Tony Kris had to say about his father and about Hartmann, about the Holocaust, and about the whole of that terrible period. At first sight, it does seem strange that Hartmann and his colleagues had so little to say about it, and there is a certain incongruity between the notion of an "average expectable environment" and Hitler's extraordinary domination of Europe and his policy of mass extermination of Jews, not to speak of Gypsies, homosexuals, and mental hospital patients. Nothing "expectable" in all that!

On that note, I'll begin with a personal story, although I'm neither Jewish nor have any Jewish relatives by birth or marriage—as far as I know. I was involved in the uncovering of the concentration camp at Belsen, and I worked there for some time until it was finally burned to the ground. But it is a striking fact that, after I left there and returned to England, I had no further thoughts about it, except for a short period when close friends and colleagues wanted to hear about it, and I was asked to make it the subject of a talk to the medical school. I had a large number of photographs depicting so many horrors—at the time "top secret" documents—which I took home but have never been able to find since. I never thought about it (even when the Holocaust was discussed, I never said anything), until about twenty-five years later when someone read an article in the Army Medical Journal that referred to the presence of some of us in Belsen while the war was still continuing. The article listed our names, and the reader of it, who worked for television, wanted to interview some of us for a program. I said to the would-be interviewer, "I don't think I can be of much help to you because I haven't thought about Belsen since I left." (I had never done so consciously or deliberately, and never talked about it.) Much to my surprise, she said, "Everybody I've spoken to says the same thing." So whatever was behind the suppression of those memories, we must all have shared it, irrespective of different personalities. There certainly wasn't any true repression; as soon as I started to talk, things came back and I was able to give quite an articulate account for the television program. It did strike me that the defensive reaction to that particular horror had shown itself in a number of ways. My former analyst told me later, when I asked, that the frightful event appeared only through dreams and not through direct reporting or free associations. My wife told me she didn't even know I had been to Belsen. I mentioned all this to suggest that it may have some bearing on the way in which people deeply involved in such matters may respond later on, though, if one had been a victim, it is hard to see how *that* could have been put out of mind. Funnily enough, as I speak I realize that I often tell people I know no German, but I remember that the first German I learned was in Belsen, and I picked up a lot of words, through sheer necessity, from the prisoners. I've never tried to learn German since, and when I was learning another language Anna Freud said to me, "Why do you spend so much time on that? Wouldn't German be much more use to you?" I didn't have a ready answer at that time, but I do have one now. I mention all this for what it's worth. I don't think we should criticize Hartmann too much for seemingly ignoring the Holocaust, though I can't pretend to know what his reasons were.

As for the optimism of the Hartmann era, of which Martin spoke, I recall an incongruous note struck by Eissler on the occasion of the celebration of the 20th birthday of the Anna Freud Clinic. There was a general celebratory atmosphere: people were saying, "Isn't it great, this place has been going for twenty years, look what it has accomplished." Eissler didn't look too moved by it. He gave a talk that cast doubt on whether psychoanalysis had any future at all, quite irrespective of the achievements or otherwise of the Anna Freud Centre.

Furst: He didn't think man had any future. Why should he think the Centre had any?

Yorke: That's right, but a lot of us wonder where psychoanalysis is heading.

A point raised in several papers was the relevance of psychoanalytic theories and clinical work. It seems to me that, in addressing this problem, one has to tread warily. There are many psychoanalytic theories today that are purely *clinical* theories. They are based entirely on clinical practice. Any idea or notion that seems to make the clinician's task easier will be seized on as something important or worthwhile. Its relationship to a consistent, coherent, and comprehensive *theory of mind* may not come into question. If it works in clinical practice, does anything else matter? Now if Freud had taken a similar view in regard to his patients and to his self-analysis, he would have provided us with a clinical theory, with a method of procedure, but not with a firm and consistent theory of mind. Consider *The Interpretation of Dreams*. The first six chapters are entirely adequate and sufficient for the clinical practice of dream interpretation. But Chapter 7 starts with a cautionary note. You will remember that Freud gives an account of a dream told to him, though not by the dreamer. Before the dream occurred, a father had been sitting beside his child's bedside for days on end, but the child died. The father went to lie down in the next room, but left the door open to see into the room where the dead child was laid out, with candles standing round the bed, and a watchman in charge. The father fell asleep and dreamed that the child was standing beside his bed, caught him by the arm and said, reproachfully, "Father, don't you see I'm burning." The father awoke, rushed into the child's room, found that the watchman had fallen asleep, and that a lighted candle had fallen and burned the child's arm.

Freud pointed out that, hitherto, the central problem discussed in his book was that of interpretation, of what the dream *meant*. But here, the *meaning* of the dream was obvious. Here was a dream the meaning of which was obvious, but which raised two questions that had nothing to do with interpretation: Why did the dream take an hallucinatory form; and why did it have all the vividness of actuality? And Freud then took a path, with no maps to guide him, and embarked on the body of the seventh chapter in which, for the first time, the basis was laid for the first comprehensive model of the mind. It was, as Freud conceded, only provisional and could be modified whenever further experience demanded. But without that daring excursion, we would be without the concept of a mental apparatus and without a theory of the way the mind works—without, that is, a coherent and comprehensive one, even though we all know, as Freud knew and acknowledged, that there is so very much we do not know and are still not within sight of knowing.

I was captivated by Chapter 7 when I first read it; it seemed to me that I had never come across anything in psychology quite so exciting, and that feeling has persisted ever since. The metapsychology that was born there gave us insight into the way the mind worked in sickness and health. So I cannot myself have much sympathy with those who produce clinical theories quite unconnected with an idea of how the mind operates. What the student of Hartmann finds, however, is that he writes as if clinical work didn't count—the common error in reverse—as if the speculative armchair could do without the couch. I am not saying he believed that, of course; I don't see how *that* could have been the case. Lastly, it seems worth adding that Freud was tentative in putting forward his model of a mental apparatus. He saw no harm in a model of this kind "as long as we don't mistake the scaffolding for the building." This struck me as a comment in impressive contrast to the cocksure attitudes of so many people today who want to tell us what psychoanalysis is about, how it works, how it is best revisited or revised.

One question that has been raised is: Was there such a thing as a Hartmann era and, if there was, what was its significance? I never thought in terms of a Hartmann era, and in England that was perhaps understandable, for reasons I have mentioned, and very little was said about it. It was easy enough to read his work and that of many analysts who approved of it. But many of the people I most admired have been mentioned today, and I would not, without hesitation, have called them "Hartmannites." Edith Jacobson was one. Mahler—up to a point—was another. Incidentally, she once told me how very much she minded Anna Freud's failure (as she saw it) to appreciate her work. Many others mentioned today, including Ernst Kris, are high peaks, and not what someone called high peaks of a secondary range. He and others were major figures for me. I still feel their contributions are immensely important, and that they would have been made, perhaps not altogether in the same form, if they had been unacquainted with Hartmann. Recently, as a result of reading the papers written for this conference, I took another look at some of Kris's work. I think his paper on preconscious mental processes is an outstanding contribution, and its hard to see now how it's possible to manage without some of the concepts put forward in it. Another example is his work on childhood memory and the recovery of memory in child analysis—to my mind another beacon, and a high point in the development of psychoanalytic thinking. He pointed out, for example, that you cannot remember every time your mother walked past the foot of your bed without looking at you, every time she ignored you, or every time she passed you on the stairs without saying anything or even recognizing your presence. Instead, all these innumerable occasions can become condensed into a single event so that, if you happen to have been in hospital or sent to stay with a relative, it is *that* circumstance that becomes the trauma and stand for all the other minor traumata that happened before or after. It seems to me that Kris cannot be regarded solely as a member of the triumvirate that wrote about ego psychology.

I want to say a word about the question of mind and body, a matter that has repeatedly arisen. Anna Freud's name came into the last comments of André's and the subject of the drives, and how and in what way they link psyche and soma. In considering psychosomatic disorders it seems important to recall the contributions of Anna Freud and Edward Glover and the concept of preconflictual development because, in infancy, pathology can exist without conflict. The root of future psychosomatic disturbance may sometimes rest there. I won't try to say here what has been said so well elsewhere by Glover and Anna Freud, but I want to add a personal note. Although I still greatly admire the figures from the Hartmann Era to whom I referred, the people who influenced me most in my own psychoanalytic development were Edward Glover and Anna Freud. It was Anna Freud who directed me to my personal analyst. The first thing I read and clearly understood (or thought I did) about psychoanalysis was the second edition of Glover's book on the subject.[32] I've

---

32. Glover, E. (1939). *Psychoanalysis: A Handbook For Medical Practitioners and Students of Comparative Psychology*. London: Staples Press.

felt grateful to that book ever since; it greatly simplified, for me, the task of reading Freud himself. It doesn't speak well of psychoanalysts that Glover's book has been out of print for at least thirty-five years. Glover has been what, in a different field, has been described as the necessary antidote to everything. That was said in relation to the modernists writers—James Joyce, Ezra Pound, and their contemporaries. It was said by Wyndham Lewis (himself a modernist), who strongly criticized these writers in a book called *Men Without Art*.[33] Lewis, whose outspoken style was somewhat reminiscent of Glover's, criticized so many generally accepted views that many who disagreed with him still thought him "a necessary antidote." Although, in some ways his criticism can be seen as destructive, it raises questions that demand answers. Martin mentioned Glover's 1961 paper[34] in which he criticized Hartmann at considerable length and with a certain force. Glover's theoretical critiques attach considerable weight to Freud's metapsychology, which he puts to good effect, even when his style borders on the polemical. In my view, he uses it to better effect than Hartmann, who doesn't always see its full implications for some of his theoretical constructs.

I know that the metapsychology is repeatedly under attack. For one thing, it seems, to many, too remote from clinical practice on account of its high level of abstraction. I find it indispensable. It can of course be argued that there are many forms of metapsychology but I don't know of one other than Freud's that successfully addresses so many of the issues we have to face. This again links for me, as I have just hinted, the relationship between clinical theory and the theory of mind. The latter cannot address itself simply to what happens on the couch or what happens with a 3-year-old in a playroom. It also has to look at everyday life, at the way we think and feel when we relate or fail to relate to others. When teaching students, I find it helpful to encourage them to extend their interests beyond clinical practice, to look at what happens outside the consulting room, and to try to understand it all in terms of *the working mind* (to adapt an expression of Luria's[35]), in Freudian terms.

We have considered, in our discussions, the "failure" of the Hartmann era, and have spoken of its collapse. But if one believes, as I do, that there was less a Hartmann era than an era in which Hartmann's influence was felt (in some part of the world), is it a matter of the collapse of that influence, or is it that psychoanalysis itself began to collapse at that time? Was it, perhaps, some-

---

33. Lewis, P. (1934). *Men Without Art*. London: Cassell. Reprinted with notes, 1987. Santa Rosa: Black Sparrow Press.

34. Glover, E. (1961). Some recent trends in psychoanalytic theory, *Psychoanalytic Quarterly* 30:86–107.

35. Luria, A. R. (1973). *The Working Brain*. London: Penguin.

thing more general that was happening in the sixties? Was it the time when people began to notice that the adolescent rebellion was ever more easily recognized in young adults—and not only in patients? The protest against parents was not confined to parents and their traditions but to all kind of authority, and the rebels had plenty of older supporters, particularly in the universities. Family structure began to collapse, and much else with it. It may be worth just thinking about whether or not psychoanalysis, too, started to lose authority and bring about its own downfall.

Long before the time when Hartmann was so influential, there were major schematics within the psychoanalytic movement. I made no secret of the fact that I always regarded Melanie Klein as one of those schismatics, and Hartmann, as we all know, was strongly opposed to the Klein system. But one of the major differences between Klein and earlier schismatics was surely this: in the time of Adler and Jung, people whose views departed in radical ways from psychoanalysis *left* the movement. They founded their own, and that was fine. That didn't happen with Klein's case, and in that respect she set a precedent. It seems to me now that, in psychoanalysis, anything goes. I will just remind you that my criticism of Hartmann is not that he directed attention to an area in psychoanalysis which badly needed to be addressed, or even that he said many things that had already been said by others in different ways. I regard his viewpoint as excessively structural. Something of the kind is happening today with the use by some contemporary theorists of the word *representation*. I would have preferred André, where it was applicable, to have used a word like *representative* instead, because so many people are using *representation* in a way that is almost entirely structural. When Edith Jacobson[36] used the term, she couldn't be accused of *that* misconception. But when it's used today, dynamics and economics have so often disappeared. Even at Hampstead I've heard people say that they're "changing the patient's representations," not changing the patient. This is not a matter of confounding the clinical with the metapsychological (a forgivable error that's easy to commit), because there's not metapsychology in it, anyway. Many today would say it doesn't matter: What use is economics, after all? But how can you say that the relative strength of contending forces is of no account, or the rise and fall of drive forces doesn't matter, unless you throw out psychoanalytic theory altogether?

In the course of my paper, I tried to address the fact that a lot of adaptive behavior is only relatively adaptive. It is transient. It is easily overthrown, and that is something that we need to keep in mind. But it hasn't been possible to listen to the discussion so far without picking up new ideas, without

---

36. Jacobson, E. (1965). *The Self and the Object World*. London: Hogarth.

wanting to think them over afresh, and I think any meeting that does that is adaptive to our needs and can claim real success.

Bergmann: I would suggest that we first take the question that was raised by Clifford, namely, the question of the Hartmann era, the question of whether or not the co-workers would have gone their own way and made their own contribution even without Hartmann, and the question of whether the Hartmann period came to an end or psychoanalysis itself was in jeopardy. Does anybody have something to add to what we have said?

Solnit: This may sound a little parochial, but if you look at the history of the *Psychoanalytic Study of the Child*, you'll see that Hartmann and Kris and Loewenstein and Anna Freud really have the idea that they needed each other in order to bring together a body of knowledge and become a repository in which the psychoanalytic contribution to child development and the learning about the developing child as applied to adult analysis. In that sense, I have the same reservation about calling it the Hartmann era. It might just as well be called the Hartmann, Kris, Loewenstein, Anna Freud era in that sense, even though they didn't each of them agree with the other. There were many lacunae in the discussion today. Ernst Kris did a great deal about the war. He was a consultant on propaganda to the British government. What I'm getting at is, as a matter of convenience, to refer to it as the Hartmann era is fine so long as you go on to explore the nucleus of a transatlantic group, especially the American immigrants from Vienna and the one in England, who said that an addition to Freud's contributions was going to come from understanding children and understanding child analysis and what you can learn from it. The part that we are trying to concentrate on is what Hartmann contributed, but you notice how irresistible it is to bring in Ernst Kris and Anna Freud. In fact, Loewenstein deserves a very strong representation as well, because he was the clinician. He and Kris were particularly sensitive to clinical issues, although neither of them were child analysts. They understood the excitement and the wonder, as did Hartmann, of child development, to enrich and to stimulate and to provoke psychoanalytic theory and its practice.

Kernberg: Just two points, the Holocaust and concentration camp. That is indeed a striking phenomenon all over the world for all of us who have been interested in reading the literature. I think that point is very well taken. It was a universal denial.

Ostow: Not just the Holocaust, Otto. Throughout Jewish history, after every catastrophe, after every persecution, a period of 25–50 years elapsed before there was any written record.

Kernberg: The best book ever written about the Holocaust, an incredible book published about half a year ago by a young German sociologist, which I had the good fortune to read in German, which has been translated and is available for a month now, is called *The Order of Terror* by Wolfgang Sofsky. I think it overshadows everything else we read about the Holocaust. For those who read German, he also has a treatise on violence that's extraordinary. It is devoid of any psychoanalytic thinking, which is good in the sense that it leaves open what we as psychoanalysts can contribute. It is a major challenge to psychoanalytic thinking because it brings together data from sociology, politics, history, and personal memories. It has not a drop of sentimentality and it is the most devastating document I've ever seen.

The other thing I wanted to mention is that this kind of denial operated not only during the Holocaust, but also the terror regime in Soviet Russia. We are forgetting that one-sixth of humanity has been submerged for 70 years in a terrible regimen and that's still going on in China, of course, with millions of people having been killed. It still maintained the quality that during the Hartmann era was already known in this country. When you remember the Slansky trials, the Moscow trials, there was an enormous amount of information. Yet, in all the liberal, progressive left, there was a complete denial of what this implied for the messianic thinking involved in Marxist ideology. I've referred to this as the thin veneer of civilization. In this regard, the one thing one can criticize, notably Hartmann, within psychoanalysis, is that the optimism that took over in the 1950s neglected the capacity for massive regression that existed at all times. The task of psychoanalysis is to deal with social issues. In this regard, I think the French psychoanalysts were much more courageous, as far as I could see, in dealing with social and cultural issues, and benefited from that activity in that psychoanalysis maintained itself as a cultural, viable science while, in this country, psychoanalysis restricted everything to be seen from the position of the couch rather than the application of the psychoanalytic instrument to other settings. There is a risk of seeing the psychoanalytic instrument as only an instrument geared to the couch.

Blum: I want to follow Otto and continue with what Cliff brought up before. I do think that there's a difference between an appreciation of the potential for massive and destructive regression present in human beings that is worldwide and universal, and the actual cultural setting in which a particular theory first appears. The historical cultural setting has to be taken into account. We've learned that from Freud, and as we hear about all the influences on Freud and Freud's own development and Freud's own theoretical development, it seems to me that we really have to take a look at the fact that although the ultimate test of the theory is independence and autonomy, to use Hartmann's term, relative autonomy from the creation, we also know that there is a relationship. We know that from the first studies of psychoanalysis, beginning with Freud, there is a connection between life and work. The theory of the conflict-free sphere, the theory of the average expectable environment, and the theory of the importance of adaptation are occurring in a setting of massive conflict, massive regression, an environment that's not average, that's not expectable, on the verge of chaos. People were at great risk since, on the one hand, they were aware of the reality, and on the other hand, including Freud himself, there was an attempt to deny it so that escape became very tenuous. As we know, Freud stayed until virtually almost the last moment, and Ernst Jones and Marie Bonaparte and others had to practically extract him or a very different outcome would have occurred. The same thing was true about the triumvirate in certain ways, that differed for Kris and Loewenstein. Tony is right. Not only was his father a consultant, he actually wrote papers on the role of propaganda in an attempt to analyze propaganda. Loewenstein subsequently wrote a book called *Christians and Jews*, an attempt to analyze in very profound ways anti-Semitism through the ages. It was a contribution not only to the Holocaust, but to the whole history of anti-Semitism, in terms of social stereotypes, social unrest, and finally persecution. I think that it's not really anything we can prove. It's a particular point of view, but it's one that we have to take into account, not that Hartmann overlooked certain facts but that he was living within them. They were facts and realities that were overwhelming, and that may have been part of the problem. It is certainly true that all massive trauma tends to have a latency period, after which it can then be reflected upon, contemplated, and written about. The Holocaust is only one example of that. It's probably true of most catastrophes; there tends to be some latency, some period of time before which there is an opportunity for real reflection, especially by those who are not directly involved in the catastrophe. What's unique about the Holocaust and World War II is the fact that over one hundred analysts left Vienna, founded new institutes, developed psychoanalysis in our country, and hardly wrote a word about it as analysts. These were not just other people, columnists, chemists, and so forth. One would have expected that they would have been able to have been more reflective and more introspective about what happened, and it took another generation, exactly as you described, Clifford, the very people interviewed about the event often overlooked it. Furthermore, most of the cases at that time, including supervised cases, if you take a look at the supervision and look at cases of patients who were either directly involved in the Holocaust or with the second generation, you find that the supervisors, who were often very senior analysts who themselves were refugees, in many ways overlooked the significance of the entire experience in the clinical work. I discussed such a case at the American.

I want to shift to psychosomatics, which, I think, is important. I just want to raise a different dimension. We have been mired in early psychoanalysis and, you know, Freud never gave up any point of view. They really coexisted side by side. We can say that Freud was inconsistent to that degree, but he had a way of holding onto points of view long after he appeared to have given them up, including the seduction trauma, including actual neurosis. I think the idea of the drives being so closely related to psychosomatic phenomena is very important, but by no means the whole story, especially if one thinks of it in terms of the toxic effects of repression, or in terms of the earliest period of development, when psyche and soma are poorly differentiated. Another reference to an undifferentiated phase is the lack of differentiation between psyche and soma, but it is also true that psychosomatic phenomena are probably not entirely related to the earliest phase of life. The soma changes, the psyche changes, and there are all kinds of neurobiological suggestions now to indicate that in the course of life.

There are other reasons and other explanations for psychosomatic trauma other than regression or fixation to this earliest phase and the influence of the earliest phase of life. I'll give just one example, and that is massive trauma in adult life. Almost all people who have been massively traumatized have psychosomatic disturbances, not just nightmares, but also psychosomatic disturbances. The psychosomatic disturbances of adult life may be related to the kind of affect explosion of traumatic anxiety, the overflow of anxiety and rage and other affects and internal responses that we can't exactly define right now, but that are not directly a replication of or directly traceable only through the influence of the earliest phase of life. Our conception of *psychosomatic* today is more complicated and in some ways more sophisticated than Freud's early formulations, or to the theory of the actual neurosis, although there is much to be said for it. I think that repression, repressed drives, probably in some way are more likely to result in a psychosomatic proclivity, and we're much more aware today too, on a somatic basis, of organic genetic predisposition.

Green: I think that the problem is not only that Hartmann did not talk about some topics, but that his theory is massively contradictory with obvious facts. We find more in *Civilization and its Discontents* about facts that Freud could not know of because they happened after his death (the atomic bomb) than in Hartmann about facts that he did know of because he witnessed them. So it's not only a question of not talking about it but about the choice of daring to think along psychoanalytic lines radically or compromising with academic disciplines.

The second point is again about the Hartmann era. I think that some of you gave very good reasons to define it as such. For instance, Martin's observation that there was hardly a list of references that did not include the work of Hartmann in a certain period. These lists exclude very often other authors who did not agree with him. When Martin compares the references of the later literature and the present situation, he sees that the name of Melanie Klein is quoted today more frequently than Hartmann. *Sic transit gloria mundi.* Another reason is the one that was presented by Clifford. Many of the Hartmannites, Jacobson, Mahler, and I could add Annie Reich, and even Loewenstein sometimes developed their ideas in the shade of Hartmann's dogmatic conceptions. If they were compelled to seem in agreement with Hartmann's thinking, it means that Hartmann's thinking imposed itself as a model that had to be followed. It's not necessarily that Hartmann was a dictator who obliged people to agree with him. His influence was so powerful that people went to him spontaneously because they thought that he was the strong thinker. What idea do we have of theory? Do we really think that we are all pure spirits? No, we are very frequently subject to emotional pressures; we want to be on the right side; the right side is represented by the great man who has many followers. It will maybe be easier to be able to be known if you are on the right track. I can compare the American situation to what happened in France with Lacan's tremendous success. There also was a Lacan era in France. It took us many years to realize how much he was wrong. He also wronged psychoanalysis.

There is also a Hartmann era, in my opinion for other reasons that were beyond Hartmann's work. Hartmann focused on questions that extended beyond the scope of his own work. Maybe the Hartmann era was characterized by the challenge of psychology to psychoanalytic theory. I think that even outside the name of Hartmann, works such as Rapaport's[37] or George Klein's[38] are indicators of this tendency to question and even to reject Freud's metapsychology because it was too much biologically rooted in his speculations. Freud wished to anchor psychoanalysis in the natural sciences. His "psychology" (depth) was a natural science. "What else could it be?" he asked.

How about the present era? I think that it's not only because adolescents don't want to look into themselves that we are going through a different era. The present era is characterized by the overwhelming power of technology. It is this omnipotence of technology that questions the attitude towards the mind as we see this now. The attitude towards the mind that is considered the most interesting is the one that is conveyed by the neurosciences and the cognitive

37. Rapaport, D. (1960). The structure of psychoanalytic theory: a systemizing attempt. *Psychological Issues* 2(2):1–168.

38. Klein, G. (1976). *Psychoanalytic Theory: An Exploration of Essentials.* New York: International Universities Press.

sciences, with their oversimplifying tools used as weapons against psychoanalysts: computers and artificial intelligence. This is a challenge for us, because, unless we get acquainted with these theories and oppose their views as they deserve to be fought, we shall disappear as old-fashioned. Though this fashion will be dethroned by some other one, maybe worse. On one hand, we can assume the biological hypotheses have won over. But, on the other hand, this is untrue because what is characteristic of this kind of biology is that it does not want to have to do in any manner with Freud's hypotheses: drives, energy, unconscious as a system of wishes or beliefs, repression, and so on. We will have to watch the reactions of the residents in psychiatry. They may be seduced by the claims of the neurosciences, but they will surely discover how short they are.

Neubauer: The question is not what Hartmann's co-workers would have done without him, but how such very different people formed as a group. I saw them as quite different. They formed a unity over decades of collaboration. What interests me is the underlying dynamics that made it possible. Was it the power of Hartmann's theoretical mind that enchanted the others, or was Hartmann supported by Kris and Loewenstein in his ideas, giving him the fervor to continue to explore it? It seems that Kris attempted to link Hartmann's theory to clinical theory and Lowenstein to the clinical intervention.

I don't think they have developed a clinical theory, but offered propositions of genetics and metapsychology. Therefore, when one speaks about an era, do we really mean an era of a theory that gained dominance over a period of time, or do we mean an era of clinical intervention that became important? Do we really have any measure that those who believed in it and discussed their papers from a metapsychological point of view conducted a different kind of psychoanalysis? Or did they just use the same data to explain it on the basis of the fashion of a new theory? This is always a question when I listen to clinical case material. We very often give much too much dominance to theoretical propositions and do not see or adequately study the penetration of these positions into the daily clinical work in the office.

They devoted themselves to explore one structure, the ego, not only its defenses, but Hartmann focused on the ego apparatus. How do we understand their genetic dimensions? How can we understand its intersystemic conflicts? What kind of conflicts do we see? They really put the microscope on the ego in order to find out what else one can do in understanding the mind and new possibilities. It is true, it wasn't dynamic. It is true, it was not economic, except for his attempt to desexualize and deaggressivize the drives in order to make it appropriate to the ego but, all in all, the ego was the focus of the interest and we can ask why.

Except for the genetic point of view, the Hartmann era was not particularly interested in the study of development. The developmental point of view came from Anna Freud, namely the transformation and changes over a period of time, changes of conflicts and of the conflict resolutions. New stages of the mind allowed us to observe perception, the ego apparatus, and adaptations.

It was specifically Anna Freud who really gave it the impetus for the developmental exploration. Freud introduced the developmental point of view with the three phases of psychosexual development.

This is different with Mahler. While she spoke about separation individuation being sort of a depressive state, her stages in the first 3 years of life are stages of developmental sequences not coordinated to the conflict at each phase of the conflict. She stated that separation and individuation are not attainable without loss. There is loss involved, and this was to her an unavoidable conflict. Autonomy can only be attained by a loss of the caring object. She did not really follow the original model of Freud, and the developmental lines, mentioned by Martin, are lines in which there are coordinates of various ego function and drive function in a package. Her steps in independence, independence from body, are not organized around each stage of conflict on the way to maturity to filling in the profile and the developmental lines of Anna Freud, who wanted to avoid becoming one-sided by establishing the profile, which was not very successful. It was not considered to be a useful psychoanalytic instrument by the world at large, but rather it was sort of an organizational attempt at data collection without the preferences for what is significant. I had the impression from Martin's statement that Hartmann underplayed the developmental aspect.

Solnit: I disagree with Peter, in that when Kris and Sam Ritvo put their heads together and did longitudinal studies at Yale, that was a deliberate attempt to look at the multidetermination of development and to compare it to analytic data of children and parents undergoing psychoanalysis at the same time. It was a small sample, but it was a way of opening up the awareness. Ernst Kris insisted that their predictions be checked out. They were useful, not because they were accurate or not, but to see if they were useful to generate better theory in regard to the way in which the application of psychoanalytic theory could be put into research, could be put into child development.

What I find really not sufficiently emphasized so far is the so-called Hartmann era, which I always think of as the group. It really opened up, as a result of the heroic work of Anna Freud in Hampstead; the aim was to make more valid, more reliable analytic theory for adults and children, and that, it seems to me, has not had sufficient emphasis in our discussion so far. In fact, Peter Neubauer is another pioneer in this endeavor in his child development studies.

Kris: I think our topic is the question: Is there a Hartmann era? It's a heuristic fiction. It's Martin's genius that invented the Hartmann era. Supposing he had written a paper on ego psychology or psychoanalytic psychoanalysis in America from 1940 to 1970, we wouldn't be here, or certainly we wouldn't be here with the enthusiasm we have. The creation, the invention of the Hartmann era, directs our attention to Hartmann's monograph, to Hartmann as president of the International, as the most quoted analyst and so forth, and gives us a framework for all these discussions. But asking whether there is a Hartmann era or there isn't doesn't quite appreciate Martin's genius in inventing it. I want to say again, I think that there are incidental matters that are more important in the fate of that group. Otto mentioned their not paying attention to groups, and that if you worked on couples you were suspect. Hartmann himself was much more liberal, as Jack said, but something happened. There was a limitation of what was allowed to be discussed. That, I believe, caused trouble. A second matter that caused trouble is that the results of treatment were not as good as the claims. There was a double claim. One claim was that the field was only at the beginning, "we really don't know very much," and the other was, "we damn well know everything and we have the best treatment." And that caused a lot of trouble. We are still at a very great disadvantage when people say, "Why should we invest in treatment of that kind when you have no evidence of its being successful?" In fact, we have tremendous evidence of how many failures we have, and certainly we have no evidence that it's any better than anybody else's treatment. We don't have the evidence, and that is a serious problem from the point of view of the outside world, and that has influenced the fate of this very high-powered inner group that dominated the field. One of the things that Cliff said was that there is trauma that is preconflictual. Well, I think that there's another view that one can hold and that is that the concept of conflict that this group used was wrong.[39] I say that because I do not believe that it was a simple matter of approaching things from the ego that was the problem. In fact, I still think they were on the right track. I really believe that the Hartmann era invented by Martin is a very fruitful area for the discussion.

---

39. Those aspects of conflict that I have subserved under the term *divergent conflict* (whose prototype is found in the relationship between an unconscious element seeking expression and the pull component of repression) may better account for the trauma that Cliff speaks of than the assumption that it is pre-conjectural. The trauma may only precede conflict of the *convergent* kind (whose prototype is the relationship between an unconscious element and the push component of repression).

Bergmann: Trauma before conflict is a very important subject that we need to return to.

Furst: The Hartmann era and the main people in the Hartmann era are criticized for failing to appreciate the significance of a more regressed stage of primitive affective states, particularly negative ones. Otto has been talking and writing about that for a couple of decades now. I think the reason for that is simple: the people in the Hartmann era, and especially the leaders, never had any experience with patients of this kind. At that time, when there was a plethora of patients, you had to qualify as being analyzable and by the time you qualified as being analyzable, you usually didn't need analysis, to say nothing of not being borderline or occasionally psychotic. They were afraid of such patients. We were lectured that you're not to take such a patient for treatment because they are going to regress and become psychotic because of the treatment. All because of this, can any of us imagine Hartmann, Kris, or Loewenstein analyzing a borderline? I think that's a big reason why the Hartmann era has taught us so little about this broad area.

The other thing that keeps coming up, about the analysts and the Holocaust, there are many answers that are not so complicated. I think they intellectually appreciated it, but at that time one had very strong ideas of what one's identity as a psychoanalyst was going to be. The psychoanalyst was supposed to be a dispassionate neutral observer who sought to understand, and they took that role. Analysts were not supposed to take an activist role, not just in regard to the Holocaust, but in regard to anything in politics. So I think that was why they didn't like to have more active roles.

Kernberg: I think that there is such a thing as the Hartmann era because there were common features to theory, to technique, to development. The developmental schemata were all linear, in this country as well as in Great Britain. Nobody had the conception of the alternation between synchronic and diachronic stages of development, and that therefore to think that first came oral, then came anal, then came oedipal, was the fiction. You see that in the sickest patient. You don't have only oral conflicts, but you have a condensation of primitive, archaic, oedipal, and preoedipal issues that were not conceptualized, a serious limitation in focus.

Second, regarding technique, the stress on the dispassionate analyst led to a technical approach in which technical neutrality was expanded into anonymity. The concept of the anonymous analyst was rationalized as necessary in order not to influence the transference. In fact, sociologically, it protected the idealization of the analyst and reinforced particularly the power structure of the psychoanalytic institutes. I think the concept of anonymity is one of the authoritarian concepts of psychoanalysis, totally contrary to Freud's thinking. Also, by the same token, they held onto a classical concept of countertransference as something that had to be eliminated to avoid its regressive features, and therefore prevented themselves from seeing the activation of primitive object relations that did not show up in the context of free association but were enacted in the transference and countertransference. The fact that we are now using the term *enactments* as if Freud had not talked about this is a funny consequence of the Hartmann era.

Third, the so-called *preconflictual trauma*, the concept that structure depended on the interaction between ego, superego, and id, as if there were not primitive psychic conflict from the beginning of life before the consolidation of ego, superego, and id. We talk about preconflictual trauma, prestructural conflict, as if it were within a given environment, neglecting the concept of psychic conflicts from the beginning of life. Unconscious conflicts predating the interpretation of a normal tripartite structure are typically illustrated in narcissistic pathology. On the surface, the narcissists look like healthier patients. They were treated with this limited technique and it didn't get anywhere. It required the Kleinians to draw attention to these cases, and then, of course, Tartakoff[40] and Jacobson and others developed it further.

Bergmann: Let me call your attention to some things that we are going to discuss tomorrow. The question of the relevance of child observation to psychoanalysis itself is an important topic and I learned that André Green wrote a paper on that subject. The question of whether psychoanalysis ought to be systematized or not is also an important question. The question of opening and closing of the mind is important because the discussion today brought up that Hartmann and the era closed their minds to the contemporary Holocaust, closed their minds to borderline psychology. To the question about whether the Hartmann period should be called Hartmann or not, I'm not sure that we can say much more. That Jacobson, Mahler, and Anna Freud would have been productive without Hartmann is not the question. The question is whether they would have written in the way they have written. The man Hartmann, who was relatively noncommunicative, who was writing on a theoretical level, nevertheless stimulated a whole group of creative people to write and to give

---

40. Tartakoff, H. (1964). The normal personality in our culture and the Nobel prize complex. In R. Loewenstein, L. Newman, M. Schur, and A. Solnit, eds. (1964). *Psychoanalysis: A General Psychology: Essays in Honour of Heinz Hartmann*. New York: International Universities Press, pp. 222–252.

psychoanalysis a certain period of life. Whether it came to a tragic end or not, it was exhilarating to live through that period.

MORNING DISCUSSION, OCTOBER 19TH

Bergmann: We want to make sure that everybody who has presented has a chance to have his paper discussed. The issues that seem to me to require further elaboration are the following: the role of infant observations and its effect on psychoanalysis; the question of systematization of psychoanalysis, what we mean by it and what we think about it; connected with that is the relationship between logical positivism and psychoanalysis; finally, our estimation of the impact of the Hartmann era on psychoanalytic technique. Clifford will be our first speaker.

Yorke: I will attempt to address the questions that were raised yesterday. Harold emphasized that a great deal that contributes to the formation of psychosomatic symptoms does not occur in the first weeks (or, for that matter, months) of life. I never intended to imply that it did. I simply wanted to underline the fact that pathology *can* precede conflict. (On this point, I disagree with Otto.) Anyone who speaks of a conflict-free "area" must take this early period of life into consideration. I didn't mean to convey more than that. The points made by Glover and Anna Freud about this early phase were very important and easily overlooked. *Pathology* is not synonymous with *pathology stemming from conflict*. Anna Freud also talked about *developmental disharmony*—another widespread form of pathology, and I don't know any of her formulations that have been so easily misunderstood and perhaps misused.

Many people will realize that the id, the ego, and the superego may develop at different rates and have different strengths within the same personality. It is generally recognized that ego development can be premature, and superego formation can certainly advance ahead of its time, so that the child may be unduly tormented by guilt at an early age. But Anna Freud meant more than that. She meant not only that these different macrostructures sometimes develop unevenly in relation to each other, but that they do so under the influence of the *synthetic function of the ego*, and that, for better or for worse, the disharmonies *remain* out of step with each other. In the ordinary course of events this state of affairs is refractory. I'll give an example that may be of interest because it involves pathology that's comparatively conflict-free but may lead to pathology that's conflictual. It's well known that, in the obsessional neurosis, the ego and superego develop prematurely and are unduly strong—so strong indeed that anality seriously lags behind, delaying the development of more advanced drive organization and invoking the condemnation of a harsh superego. And that, we know, is a major factor in the development of the obsessional personality. But it may also lay the ground for a later obsessional neurosis through the customary processes of regression, return of the repressed, and compromise formation. We know that treatment of the neurosis may be difficult, but if we are able to bring about a substantial improvement in the neurosis, the underlying personality organization may still be difficult to change. But disharmonies often exist without subsequent neurosis or conflict leading to pathology in the conventional sense.

The question has been raised about the extent to which other disciplines can cast light on issues that have long been considered the province of psychoanalysis. Neuropsychology is having its own internal troubles, just as we are, with the cognitive often studied at the expense of other aspects of the discipline. Many of you will be aware that Luria and his colleagues in Moscow virtually founded neuropsychology. Luria's approach to the subject was similar to Anna Freud's approach to psychoanalysis. Luria never thought that a particular psychological function could be studied without regard to any other. In one of his popular books, *The Mind of a Mnemonist*,[41] he wrote about the man who had the most extraordinary memory, who could reproduce endless amounts of information given to him. But Luria declared himself incapable of considering memory in isolation from other psychological abilities. He had to think of it as a part of a whole and look at its relationship to the other mental functions. There's a striking similarity there with the profile in which pathology is not studied in terms of isolated disabilities. It has to be understood in relationship to the whole personality, to what is right with the child as well as what was wrong, in the context of as complete a picture as possible, within the limits of available information, of the child's mental functioning. It has to consider all the assets and endowments as well as the deficits, the developmental failures, the physical illnesses, and so forth. If anyone hasn't read Luria's autobiography[42] I can strongly recommend it; he has some very wise things to say about the nature of science that are relevant to analysis and neuropsychology. He discusses the distinction between romantic science and classical science—a distinction many people fail to draw. The distinction can be equally well expressed in terms of the science stemming from Newton on the one hand and the science stemming from Goethe on the other. At the end of the 19th

---

41. Luria, A. R. (1969). *The Mind of a Mnemonist*. London: Jonathan Cape.
42. Luria, A. R. (1979). *The Making of Mind: A Personal Account of Soviet Psychology*, ed. M. and S. Cole. Cambridge, MA: Harvard University Press.

century, the two approaches to psychology were called the *nomothetic*[43] and the *ideographic* respectively. It was Vigotsky, Luria's friend, who said that the resolution of these differences was the greatest task facing psychologists this century. Luria clearly believed that remark to be true, though we still hear much less about the distinction than perhaps we ought. He says that, in the course of his own work, he's been obliged to study science from both points of view. The nomothetic involves, numbers, calculations, comparisons, and so on—the kind of research that so many psychologists tell us today is the only legitimate one. The ideographic approach rests on the awareness that the intense study of the individual can lead to very important conclusions, as it did when Goethe studied the skull of a sheep and drew fresh and important understanding from it. I emphasize all this because of the tendency among some psychoanalytic researchers today to insist that the ideographic must increasingly give way to the nomothetic, and the low regard that is held for the clinical research that has so often served us well.

There are some very interesting links between Freud and Luria, who did in fact correspond with each other. When Luria was a very young man he wrote to Freud saying that he was thinking of setting up a psychoanalytic organization in Central Asia. Freud, in reply, wished him good luck and said, with good humor, that if he could set up a psychoanalytic institution in Central Asia he could set one up anywhere, adding that he hoped he'd do well. Of course, in those early days of the Soviet regime there was great optimism, especially among the Jewish people. Luria used to say that his father would never have become a doctor had it not been for the Soviet system. It may be that for reasons of this kind that he remained loyal to the system, even in the years after he was thought to have been banished to the study of mental defect. Oliver Sachs wrote to him at some point, saying how terrible it was to study nothing but mental defect. Luria replied, saying that his years at the "Institute of Defectology" were among the most rewarding of his life, and that he had learned a great deal about the brain and the way it worked. Nothing narrow about that approach.

---

43. "According to Aristotle, poetry, like theoretical science, is 'more philosophic and of graver import' than history, because poetry is concerned with what is pervasive and universal but history is addressed to what is special and singular. Aristotle's remark is a possible source of a widely accepted distinction between two allegedly different types of sciences: the *nomothetic*, which seeks to establish abstract general laws for indefinitely repeatable events and processes; and the *ideographic*, which aims to understand the unique." Nagel, E. (1961). *The Structure of Science*. New York: Harcourt, Brace & World, p. 547.

To return to Freud: we know that when he deserted the neuroscience current in his day—that is, in the Viennese and German tradition—and turned to Hughlings Jackson, he made a major move with neurology. Many people said later that he, like Jackson, was at least a quarter of a century ahead of his time. I went back to Hughlings Jackson and read some of his key papers.[44] There was a wonderful paper in 1884 that outlined his general approach, and the very impressive *Factors of Insanities* (1894)—a marvelous account of what were then called *insanities* from a neurological standpoint. Freud was deeply impressed by Jackson's work and acknowledged it in his own work on aphasia (1891). He pointed out that Jackson reminded that, for all the importance of the connections between the brain and the mind, we mustn't confuse the two. They must be looked at separately, not confounded. In Hartmann's discussion of *ego apparatuses*, he comes uncomfortably close to doing just that. He fails to draw a clear distinction between "apparatuses" subserving ego functions and the psychological correlates and consequences of bodily processes. Psychological operations are not identical with their substrates: brain is not mind.

Jackson considered the structure of the brain from the standpoint of a hierarchy, and arrived at the notion of positive and negative symptoms. Some symptoms stemmed from the loss of higher structures and the functions served by them; others were due to the release of the activity of lower structures when no longer kept in check by the higher controls. Freud was deeply impressed by this. Indeed, the concepts of fixation and regression rested on these ideas of Jackson. We can only wonder what he would have felt about the development of neuropsychology in the last twenty years or so. I envy the fact that many of you in New York are actively engaged in discussing the relationship between contemporary neuroscience, neuropsychology, and psychoanalysis. That seems to me a purpose well worth pursuing. In this company at any rate, there isn't much danger of confusing what belongs to the brain with what belongs to the mind.

Lastly, Peter made the point that Hartmann's primary concern was with the study ego and he ought not, perhaps, to be criticized for what he did *not* study. I did not want to suggest that he failed to make important studies of ego development, or that he did not draw attention to matters of moment in psychoanalysis that had hitherto been neglected. My point was that, in doing all this, his viewpoint was excessively structural and that he failed to give

44. Jackson, J. H. (1884). Evolution and dissolution of the nervous system; and (1894). The factors of insanities. In *Selected Writings of John Hughlings Jackson*. New York: Basic Books.

adequate attention to the other metapsychological dimensions. I don't think he was unaware of that. Indeed, he might well have accepted some of the criticisms that I made. Perhaps it wasn't a question of what he himself believed, but of what happened in practice.

Grossman: There were three major interests that I had. One was to place Hartmann in a context of the history of ideas. This means finding Hartmann's place in psychoanalysis, and the place of developing psychoanalysis within a development in the history of ideas, in psychology, in relation to philosophy, in relation to science in general. I felt that these were not only Hartmann's concerns, but Freud's concerns. This may be simply my bias because those are my concerns. I like to think that they were Freud's concerns and that I'm influenced by them.

Second, much of what was said in criticism of Hartmann's ideas was not really addressed to what the ideas were, but rather to what they evoked in people when expressed by some of Hartmann's alleged followers or others who claimed to apply these ideas. I wanted to point out what I thought were the directions of Hartmann's thoughts.

Third, it was important to address the characteristics of the Hartmann era, so named by Martin. What was important was the powerful countercurrents to Hartmann's ideas and his whole approach. I felt that that was something that was very powerful from a number of directions, from those who Anna Freud described as being at pains to protect the idea of the id and the unconscious, as they understood it, from ego psychology.

One of the most interesting of those people was Wilhelm Reich, who regarded Freud's introduction of the ego, and *The Ego And The Id*, as a total betrayal of his original insight. In fact, it was around 1923–1925 that Reich began his experiments with sex economy as a return to his understanding of what was the basic discovery in Freud. When people were talking about dissensions, I recalled a book in which Eissler interviewed Reich.[45] It's a wonderful, fascinating book for the politics and ideational developments in psychoanalysis. Reich says in this book that after he had presented his ideas at a meeting, Freud said to him as they were leaving, "Either you are completely wrong or you will have to carry the heavy burden of psychoanalysis alone" (p. 178). I thought that was a great response to a paranoid defense.

I think that, in a way, it states a core problem in the field that Cliff really alluded to. André has alluded to it and addressed it in most interesting ways.

---

45. Eissler, K. R. (1967). *Reich Speaks of Freud*, ed. M. Higgins and C. Rafael. New York: Farrar Straus & Giroux.

I'm referring to the relationship of how we are to deal with the reality of the brain and its appendages, to psychic life, and how we can think about the gap that separates these two, which André puts very nicely in his distinction between the psychic and psychology. Freud stated this very clearly in many places, but notably in the *Outline* as a kind of final statement. This gap was really never to be closed. There could be only some notion of what link could be constructed. Finally, these tensions within psychoanalysis, as such, and in relation to Hartmann, had to be addressed, including the fact of the social context, which was very powerful because it necessarily has an influence on the history of ideas in our field. The social forces have a great deal to do with what's happening to analysis today. It is partly due to the fact that there were certain problems in analysis that were not addressed. Among these were problems having to do with its relation to the society at large and to the need for a clear presentation to others that it was not merely our authority and special knowledge. We were not simply the subject who was supposed to know everything and, therefore, were the final arbiters. We had in some way to respond to the requirements of the community. So I tried to at least allude to those forces in analysis and outside. That's the essential conceptual outline of my paper.

Cliff just touched on the dichotomy between the romantic and the classical, which is just one version of what I see as the contrast between the nomothetic and the ideographic, which is now continued into our present computer conceptualizations in the form of the digital and the analog. I think that this is an interesting problem in human thought and in the development of our thinking about the human mind. We have many versions of this. The mind–body problem is another instance of this problem. As Edith Jacobson once said to me, "We live and die with the mind–body problem." I think that's true, but the important thing, as Freud said, is that we are all born and we die and we know the outcome, but how we get there is also interesting.

Bergmann: Does anybody have anything to ask?

Neubauer: Let me go back to what we had discussed yesterday. André referred to it by his definition of drive. Is the cleavage between the somatic, the brain, and the psyche, not bridged to a certain degree when we say the drive is a biological demand on the psyche? If we speak about ego apparatus (which is criticized because it is not in the foreground of psychological phenomena: memory, language, motility) then we must be aware that some still equate the function of the apparatus with physiological, anatomical factors. The ego apparatus is differentiated from other functions such as judgment, reality assessment, the synthesizing and integrative functions of the ego. When Hartmann speaks of the secondary autonomy of the ego, does he mean differentiation, integration, or reality assessment? The term *conflict* would have to be defined when we extend it to other meanings than those given it on an oedipal level of organization.

Green: I found Bill's paper very useful and informative. I would like to discuss some of the issues he raised, which cannot be separated from what had been said yesterday. For instance, we are now discussing again the body–mind problem. Freud was influenced, in finding his own solutions, by Griesinger, as Bill recalled. There is evidence that he really studied him very closely because we have Freud's copy of Griesinger annotated by him. To explain the gap or the difference between something happening in the brain and something occurring in the mind, Griesinger says, "Even if an angel came down from the sky to explain it to us, we wouldn't be able to understand it."[46] This is not only an historical question because of our present debate with the neurosciences, which is about the same topic. There is a complete misunderstanding, not only between the neuroscientists and the analysts but among analysts also. For instance, Peter Fonagy does not mention the psychic apparatus anymore; he speaks of the brain,[47] and he is a psychoanalyst doing infant research. He contends that the concept of psychic apparatus is not useful anymore and that we should speak of the brain. This raises the question of the use of metaphor in psychoanalytic theory. You can't dispense with it and, on the other hand, if you use it too widely you lose the contact with the facts. This is a basic problem for psychoanalytic theory.

It is an epistemological task to clarify the difference between the brain (or the central nervous system) and the psychic apparatus. Freud himself called it "a fiction." Can we say that the time has come when the recent discoveries about the brain do cover the field of the psychic apparatus? Fonagy's position is ideological. He wants to end with theoretical "fictions" just as the Hartmannites wanted to get rid of "mythology" (id). The discussion should not stop with these opposite statements. We have to start with clinical facts—or on what we agree labeling as such—and ask ourselves what are the theories—with their inevitable part of speculation—that better account for these facts. That is what makes them intelligible to us. Intelligibility can be paraphrased.

---

46. Wilhelm Griesinger, 1817–1869, was the first director of the Berghölzli in Zurich. He was known for his exclamation, "Mental diseases are brain diseases." He expected that a better knowledge of the pathology of the brain would solve the problem of mental illness.

47. Griesinger, W. (1845). *Pathologie und Therapie der Psychinschen*. Stuttgart: Krankheiten.

Paradoxically, both phenomenological and neuroscientific explanations do not go beyond this.

About the relationship to biology: in my own work, I always try to keep informed of what the discoveries in science are and how we can use them, or how they can contribute to theory, because we can't ignore them, but it is the use of these concepts in the debates that is important. Take, for instance, the problem of adaptation, which is of some importance in Hartmann's work. The notion comes from evolutionary biology, obviously, but see what is written today by the geneticists about adaptation. They do not use that concept anymore because they find it is approximate (if not wrong). Read François Jacob, the French biologist, or Stephen Jay Gould. Adaptation is an obsolete concept and there are lots of modifications in the evolutionary processes that do not obey any adaptational aim or task. Ideology is not absent from biology, just as with psychoanalytical ideas and theory, and it is this ideology that I criticize personally in Hartmann's work. There are so many indications in normal people failing to prove their adaptational value that they will be overlooked in order to defend this seemingly optimistic viewpoint.

This is a matter of debate with Peter. It is impossible to say that Hartmann's theory and Hartmann's followers focused on the ego alone, or on some ego functions like memory, because this limited portion of theory depends on the conception of the ego you follow and of the place given to the ego in the general system you defend. The problem with Hartmann is that he had a different conception of the ego from Freud, contrary to the attempt of Roy Schafer[48] to bring them close to each other. From this different starting point and from the gap that follows in consequence, the conclusions are totally different. For instance, to argue about memory, language, or attention depends on what facts you are going to promote in these fields. For Freud, dreams have a function of memory, and repetition compulsion is a substitute for it. Otherwise, he alludes to an "organ language" in the metapsychology and defends modes of thinking that he compares to instinct in animals, but only in an analogical way. What kind of activity in language are you going to consider as important and others as secondary? How will you prove that these functions escape the influence of drives? You can say the same of many other ego apparatuses.

Also, it is impossible to say, like Sidney said yesterday, that in those times borderline cases were unknown or that you were not even allowed to treat them. They were quite known by the British Society and even by some Ameri-

---

48. Schafer, R. (1970). An overview of Heinz Hartmann's contribution to psychoanalysis. *International Journal of Psycho-Analysis* 51:425–446.

cans (R. Grinker, R. Knight, R. Bak, etc.). What is the usefulness of psycho-analytic literature? The main paper on the metapsychological and clinical use of regression by Winnicott is 1955.[49] Paula Heimann's paper on countertrans-ference is 1950.[50] Do psychoanalysts read each other? Even when they write in the same language? Why couldn't the findings about borderline cases be taken into account in the way that calls for a modification of the theory since the fifties in the USA or, more precisely, in the mainstream of North American psychoanalysis at that period? The answer could be that the Americans con-sidered all the contributions from the British Society—except of course those of Anna Freud and her group—as bearing the print of the devil of those times, Melanie Klein. Even the independents were seen as marked by the same mor-tal sin.

Finally, I would like to raise a question from Bill's paper: the opposition between the hermeneutic and the scientific. One important task of psycho-analysis is to overcome this opposition, and to say that we are neither narrow-minded positivists nor hermeneutics, because this gap is not only between the body and the mind, but also between practice and theory. We cannot derive all theory from practice only. It is also impossible to apply totally the theory in practice. This is not only a general principle but a limitation in relationship with our field: the inner world, about whom we have only indirect knowl-edge, depending on hypotheses that cannot be entirely proven.

Moreover, practice today is not homogeneous anymore. It may never have been, but in the work of Freud the transference psychoneuroses are central to the elaboration of his theory. Today we cannot say that anymore. We see that neuroses are the minority in our practice and that there are many other types of disorders we have to deal with. Sometimes, in practice, you are confronted with patients who, instead of developing a transference neurosis, display a transference depression or even a transference psychosis. The example of the Wolf Man comes to mind in a way that was overlooked by Freud himself, because his aim was to prove the existence of the infantile neurosis and the influence of the primal scene. You have to assume, with Freud and some oth-ers, that there is one technique for all patients, which we know is wrong be-cause we have to make the difference between the various types of indications for psychoanalysis, psychotherapy, and analytic psychotherapy, and even this division doesn't satisfy me. In my practice, I can say that sometimes I have a

---

49. Winnicott, D. W. (1955). Metapsychological and clinical aspects of regression within the psychoanalytic set-up. *International Journal of Psycho-Analysis* 36:16–26.

50. Heimann, P. (1950). On countertransference. *International Journal of Psycho-Analysis* 31:81–84.

face-to-face analysis with some patients, which is very different from psycho-therapy. Even within the limits of psychoanalytical treatment, we have an important variety of structures, which raises problems of mental functioning involving a reappraisal of the classical functions of our "agencies."

Bergmann: If we are looking for an era in the history of psychoanalysis that was alive and came to an end we should remember Wilhelm Reich. It's not compa-rable to the Hartmann era, but there is a comparison. If Wilhelm Reich had not committed hara-kiri by going into orgone therapy, we might have had a differ-ent history. There was definitely a climate of opinion. I still captured one of the last of Reich's disciples in my control work with Moses Barinbaum, who was a Reich disciple of the character analysis period. I have no doubt that the encoun-ter with Reich's character analysis was a major influence on me when I was young.

We are continuously bringing up the question of ego functions, and I would like to suggest that there were specific ego functions, at least what I call ego functions, that are unique to psychoanalysis and were not discussed by Hartmann. The ego function that I am most interested in is the capacity to differentiate fantasy from reality because that is, in my opinion, definitely an ego function, and the absence of that capacity is what plays havoc when you are analyzing seductions of children, where it is impossible to differentiate be-tween fantasy and reality.

Furst: Martin, isn't that what's really conceived simply as reality testing, or do you differentiate?

Bergmann: A clinical case that made me realize that the differentiation between fantasy and reality requires an ego function was a woman survivor. In her first years of life she was cared for by her mother, grandfather, and grandmother. At the age of $3\frac{1}{2}$, her mother and grandfather were deported and her grand-mother died from shock. The patient survived under an assumed name in a Catholic orphanage. Miraculously at the age of 6, the mother returned from the concentration camp and claimed her back. About the period in the orphan-age she could tell me innumerable and often bizarre events, but we were inca-pable of determining whether these were fantasies or real events. I learnt from the case that the capacity to differentiate in the early years of infancy depends on a continuous relationship with the primary caretaker. When this relation-ship is prematurely interrupted this ego function becomes arrested.

Grossman: I'd like to comment on that. I wouldn't think of that as an ego function. I would think of that as the fundamental problem of life. We struggle all the time with the question of what we produce out of our fantasy and what the world is really like. It is related to André's comments about different ideo-logical positions. In fact, the first draft of my paper was about the relation-ship of presuppositions, ideology, theoretical background, and personal background in the formation of theoretical conceptions. It's a question of how we arrive at some understanding of events in a way that makes sense in terms of our experience. How do we apply our thoughts to action is that same question. The patient's difficulty in the present in differentiating the real-ity of memories from fantasy may have to do with the conditions of early experience and the preservation of its memory. It may be a problem of later revision and/or the meaning of recall in the transference relationship. The difference between reality testing and the question you ask is really a very broad one, in the sense that we localize reality testing in some sense as an ego function.

At the time that Hartmann was my teacher, one developing criticism of his work was that the way Hartmann spoke of ego functions was concrete. It sounded too physical, too mechanical, too reified. This was part of the critique at that time. At issue was a functional point of view as opposed to the creation of a bunch of entities that may be or have functions.

I enjoy listening to André and reading his work, because I find that there is such a convergence in overall attitude and orientation, and that we have arrived at similar things from totally different sets of premises. André's re-sponse to Sidney's remark about borderlines touches on the fact that it was a problem within American ego psychology to work with borderline patients. People were really struggling with how to conceptualize this, and they were not happy with the way they were conceptualizing it. This dissatisfaction at-tracted many of my colleagues to the British schools. They were interested in Guntrip and Balint. The New York Psychoanalytic had some sense that there was a way to integrate these views. They were not obviously integratable because the terminology and the conceptualization were so different. André commented about the importance of the transference neuroses in analysis. Freud wrote in 1925[51] in his preface to Aichorn's book: "Children have become the main subject of psychoanalytic research and have thus replaced in importance the neurotics on whom the studies began. Analysis has shown how the child lives on almost unchanged in the sick man as well as in the dreamer and the artist" (p. 273). It's not the content as such, but the principle that informs a number of things for me. The important thing is that "the child lives on," not "the child is replaced by," not "the child is incorporated into," and so on, but

---

51. Aichorn, A. (1925). *Wayward Youth*. Viking Press, 1935. Preface reprinted in *Standard Edition* 19:273–275.

"the child lives on in the sick man, dreamer, artist." "It has thrown light on the mode of forces and trends which set its characteristic stance on the childish nature and it has traced the stages through which a child grows to maturity. No wonder, therefore, an expectation has arisen that psychoanalytic concerns with children will benefit the work of education whose aim it is to guide and assist children on their formative path and to shield them from going astray" (p. 273). He says, "Two lessons may be derived, it seems to me, from the experience and success of August Aichorn. One is that every such person should receive psychoanalytic training, since without it the object of his endeavors must remain an inaccessible problem to him" (pp. 273–274). That's the difference between learning and learning through insight. He goes on to say that the person needs to be analyzed and "when analysis fails to penetrate deeply enough it carries no conviction" (p. 274). He goes on to say that "the second lesson has a somewhat more conservative ring" and that education isn't psychoanalysis, which is not a substitute for education. "The possibility of analytic influence rests on quite definite preconditions which can be summed up under the term analytic situation. It requires certain psychical structures and a particular attitude to the analyst. Where these are lacking, as in the case of children, of juvenile delinquents, and as a rule with compulsive criminals, something other than analysis must be employed, though something which will be at one with analysis in its purpose" (p. 274). This is a very important statement. As I understand Freud, he seems to be saying that the psychoanalytic process requires certain things from a patient. It is possible to be helpful in analytically informed ways even when the conditions required by this process can't be met. However, the use of psychoanalytic understanding doesn't make the process psychoanalysis. This distinction might be helpful in thinking about problems of psychoanalytic technique. In difficult therapeutic situations, it may be a question of developing psychoanalytically informed ways to make analysis possible.

To some extent, it touches on the answer to Peter's question and how I deal with such issues. It's also related to the notion of adaptation. There are a number of important statements that Freud makes that are the organizing nuclei of psychoanalytic theory as I understand it. One of them is related to this idea that the child lives on, and another is that every association is a compromise formation (this is in one of the technique papers) in which both the conscious and the unconscious are expressed. These two are related. Another version of that is in *Totem and Taboo*, in which Freud says that every time an idea is consciously judged you have two new things, an unconscious stream and a conscious stream. Both are infinitely reproduced and it has to do with the continuous life of the child in the adult. The undifferentiated phase is that point from which there are two streams: one is the ego stream, the other is the drive stream. Everything has this structure and there is no escape from this.

If I were to criticize some aspects of Hartmann, it would go something like this: although Hartmann speaks a great deal about the layering that creates structure as a theoretical proposition, in the actual discussion that he provides you don't see him using the recognition, except as a passing comment. It really has to do with what Peter asks about this relationship between *anlage* and the psychic function, because that's again the same fundamental question.

In the quotation that André gave yesterday, and the definition of the *drive*, the form of it is very interesting because it actually begins with Freud. He's taking a biological standpoint. There are three functions for the drive. It's a concept on the border of the mind and the body. It is the representative, the ambassador function that André refers to, in the mind from the body. And, third, a demand for some energetic measure. It defines a relationship and that relationship is the best we can say about it. If we try to give a content to that relationship, we can't because, as André says, it's unknown. Freud attempted to deal with this gap.

What Cliff said is important in this regard. I haven't read Griesinger so I would be in no position to make a serious statement. I was quoting Binswanger, who does make the point. Freud was different from Meynert in this respect because Meynert went so far as to talk about the "ensouling" of the individual cell, that is, the cell contained, the soul or the mind. This was a different view that Freud was really counteracting in "On Aphasia." This is important because it brings up the issue that Cliff raises about the relation to Hughlings Jackson. Freud took organizing principles from these sources, and the real links between psychology and biology, and psychoanalysis and psychology, are to be found in the degree to which the organization of the mental life is a reflection of the organization of biology. This is the importance of Darwin's natural selection, which is Freud's true reliance on Darwin. I don't believe Freud was Lamarckian, although he said he was Lamarckian. As I understand the problem, Freud accepted the idea that he was Lamarckian because he couldn't do without the idea that in some way the behavioral adaptations of the past influenced the biological endowments of the present. However, everyone believes some version of this idea. The point is that Freud never suggested a biological mechanism by which this occurred phylogenetically. Whenever he discussed mechanisms, he described or mentioned explicitly the process of natural selection. The only place I found describing a Lamarckian use-inheritance mechanism is in a letter to Groddeck.

Green: He's right. It's not because you claim that you are a Hartmannite that you are one.

Grossman: Exactly. I think this was an important point because his use of those principles was important. I think Hartmann picked that up and understood that, but again, he had his own interests and, as André said, he also had his own ideology, and many people referred to some of the roots of that ideology yesterday. Hartmann had a very sophisticated knowledge of science, much as Freud did. Freud prepared the total revision of the philosophy of science that took place really starting in the '60s and even in the Hook Symposium. Logical positivists, like Philip Frank,[52] were much more positive about psychoanalysis and understood some of the problems in ways that others didn't. But logical positivism was already going, and Hartmann had some notion of this. He had an ideology and agenda that he was following and that is where the problems came in.

To pick up again on what Cliff said, and André too, about neuroscience, there's an important organizational principle. They are being driven to come out with ideas that, although crude in many ways, provide their notion of the unconscious. They are forced more and more into positions whose organization sounds more and more like psychoanalytic ideas. What most of us are used to from our earlier years, and you still see a lot of it, is the use of biology as metapsychology. It's a form of metapsychology, a very crude one and an inadequate one, but it can be used as one. The same thing can be said about ideas having to do with social forces that are imported into analysis by various people. They create a new metapsychology instead of the old one, and they use these ideas in metapsychological ways. By speaking of biology and ideas about social forces as metapsychology, I mean that these fields generate their own data, whose connection to psychoanalytic observations can only be as systems of thought. Their justification lies elsewhere, and their connection to psychoanalytic observations is speculative. However good these speculations may be, they serve the same functions as the systems of metapsychology created by Freud and other psychoanalysts. In pointing this out, I'm trying to distinguish between the application of a set of ideas and the work of correlation of different kinds of observations in constructing a picture of the mind and its functions. The issue of adaptation was very important in Freud, and I would take some issue with André. It's true that people like Steven Jay Gould point out that not everything that is present can be thought to be an adaptation, that is, in some crude sense, survival of the fittest. A lot of features are not necessarily even good for survival, and they serve other functions. They may also be vestigial, and not directly responses to adaptation. That has to do

---

52. Frank, P. (1959). *Psychoanalysis and Logical Positivism in Psychoanalysis: Scientific Method and Philosophy*, ed. S. Hook. New York: Int'l. Univ. Press.

a lot with the complexity. Gould has done a wonderful job, in fact, in his book, *Wonderful Life*. He has a statement about the return, knowing from the final consequences what the beginnings were, and then, as he says, running the tape in the other direction. It's like Freud (1920), the famous quote. If we look back and we reconstruct, it seems to us there is only one path. If we try to go over the other way, we can imagine many. In Gould's system, it is because of the contingencies of history. Freud leaves out history. It's clear that he has the understanding that history counts, but chance events spur adaptation. That's what natural selection is about. The other part of that is the crucial point, that adaptation is not a result but a process. Here's where English has a problem; Loewenstein used to point that these "tion" words refer to a process and to a result. It makes a difference whether we're talking about process or a result. So adaptation as process is a relationship, and it's an ongoing relationship of the type that I've already outlined. That is, every time there is an adaptation, there are two possibilities or two necessities that derive from it, one of them having to do with consciousness and the other having to do with unconsciousness. Development is a form of perpetuation of this fundamental relationship.

Now, again, I can show you places in Hartmann's work where he makes the statement that adaptation is relationship, but that's not his interest. He goes on and talks about some other things. This is one of the problems with Hartmann. He says a lot of things. They are very good one-liners, but they aren't his real agenda. He goes on to do other things, which then become problematic because he hasn't integrated the principles that he's stating into the work that he's doing. I think that's a major problem and it left him in the position that Jack said, that he really couldn't answer the philosophers. He couldn't answer those who really criticized metapsychology saying that metapsychology is not psychology, but merely protoneurophysiology.

I agree with André. The role of metaphor is really powerful because metaphor is the means by which we always fill this gap. The more I thought about this, the more profoundly important it seems to be because of the fact that we have five senses from the beginning of life. We have to create metaphors that will allow us to integrate the information of five totally different senses. This is known as *cross-modal transfer*. It's what allows us to know that an interval in time in relation to, let's say, the duration of a sound and the interval of time in the duration of pain, have an underlying temporal relationship. As a result of cross-modal transfer, we create what we call time, which unites all of these things in spite of the fact that they are all different. The same is true, as André says, in regard to metaphor. Metaphor does for the construction of concepts what cross-modal transfer does for the construction of the mental representation of an object. In the paper written with

Bennett Simon,[53] we discussed this problem of the relationship of theory to clinical practice in terms of the relationship of observation to the formation of theory. It seemed to me to be crucial that we must create some kind of intermediate space of conceptualization that belongs, at least by its organization, to both realms.

Bergmann: It was wonderful. Thank you very much.

Ostow: Many of the speakers during the past two days have referred to the potential impact of the study of the neurosciences upon psychoanalytic thinking. My own experience with this is far less sanguine. What little I know about neuroscience research reveals that the neuroscientists have yet to be able to fasten on any parameter. There is just no correspondence at the moment; I don't see any movement in that direction. What they are talking about has very little relationship to what we can conceptualize, except if we make some very broad assumptions and hop from one to the other. The drive is the demand of the body on the mind. This is hypothetical biology, not real laboratory biology. There is a discipline at the present time, that began during the Hartmann era, that no analyst aside from Freud talked about, and that is the influence of chemical agents on the mind. Freud, who lived before the age of chemical agents, already made the correlation. He said that when chemical agents will be available, they will work by means of energy. Hartmann became an expert on energy, but he didn't refer to that at all. The fact is that if you study the effect of chemical agents on mental functions at the present time, there is no function, no metapsychologic function, that is more closely related to the concept of energy. At any rate, if you don't want to go that far, it impacts directly upon affect, and, it seems to me, impossible to have a truly metapsychologic discussion nowadays that deals with ego function and affect without referring to the experimental results that are available for everybody to see, as a result of the application of chemical agents. It seems to me impossible to believe that it has not yet been mentioned during the past two days of discussion.

Green: I agree with Mortimer Ostow. In what Bill has shown us, we have to be aware that there are different types of biologists; some of them have open minds. I'm thinking mainly of Gerald Edelman in the United States. There are others, and I know some in France too, who are broad-minded and can be useful people to debate with (Jean-Didier Vincent, Alain Prochiantz, Gabriel Gachelin,

---

53. Grossman, W. I., and Simon, B. (1969). Anthropomorphism: motive, meaning and causality in psychoanalytic theory. *Psychoanalytic Study of the Child* 24:78–111.

Francisco Varela, etc.). I agree with what Mortimer Ostow said that, for most of them, there is very little possibility of having a fruitful dialogue. Still, we have to continue to be informed of their researches, because I cannot think of any theory of mind that would sever itself completely from the study of the brain or from the general mechanisms of biology.

Blum: Freud certainly thought about the possibility of biochemical effects, not only theoretically but in terms of treatment. It's not that he said that mind and brain must forever be separated, but that premature closure should be avoided. He left the possibility open that some day there might be a convergence, but it was a long, long way off, and we were nowhere near it at this time.

Ostow: It was 14 years between the 1939 statement and the first appearance of the psychoactive drug in 1953—not that long.

Blum: Also, Anna Freud supported the use of drugs.

Ostow: I wasn't talking about the use, I was talking about what you learn from it.

Blum: She implied that as well, and she also supported the use, where it was appropriate, of psychopharmacological agents. I was interested, parallel to Bill's interest in the cultural influences on Hartmann, I was interested more in the intra-analytic influences on Hartmann's development. Not so much as criticism of Hartmann, but as the explanatory reach and limits of the theory. By trying to say what the theory offered that might go further than before and at the same time looking at the limitations of the theory.

This led me to view several things. One was Hartmann's own personal analytic development. Another one was the way in which he attempted to create an ideal kind of theory, and one might say here that in some ways his reach exceeded his grasp because he tried, in a monumental effort, to accomplish an extraordinary feat in terms of creating a general psychology and that the crux of Hartmann's effort was to create a general psychology, to look at psychoanalysis in that way, and at the same time systematize a lot of loose ends within psychoanalysis, which had some very positive features and also some negative repercussions and ramifications.

With respect to the Hartmann era, let me begin with the following anecdote, which shows something about an era. I think this conversation convinced me that we both had had a Hartmann era and that there wasn't a Hartmann era. On the occasion of his 70th birthday, Kohut, who had been invited to Hartmann's birthday party, was walking out and he was overheard saying,

"Heinz, Heinz, Heinz. Why does everyone talk about Hartmann?" Everybody was talking about Heinz.

It was of great interest to me to learn that Hartmann's first analyst had been Rado, and this, I think, is of interest historically in terms of the effects of analysts on each other. We'll come to the question of the mutual influence of Freud and Hartmann on each other in a moment. Rado turns out to have been interested in adaptation, and then Hartmann writes about ego psychology and the problem of adaptation. They write about it very differently, in fact, in some ways opposed in their approach, but they use some of the same terminology and there is a degree of interpenetration and overlap as well as differences. Hartmann comes to the United States in approximately 1941. He's at the same institute as Sandor Rado, and Rado promptly leaves and founds another institute devoted to adaptation. In fact, he calls it, I believe, *adaptational psychoanalysis*. I suggest that the problem was probably percolating for a long time in terms of the influence of one on the other.

I think too that one can look at the last part of the paper *Analysis Terminable and Interminable*, where Freud discusses the constitutional endowment of the ego and that the lines of the ego are perhaps laid down constitutionally and innately—we would say today *prewired*. There are two ways to see that. The traditional one has been that Freud was thinking about this kind of problem and the role of endowment and the genetic predisposition for ego development and that this influenced Hartmann. The other way around is that some people think that Hartmann influenced Freud, since Hartmann was then in analysis with Freud and they undoubtedly discussed these issues at great length. In fact, Hartmann indicates that he and Freud discussed all manner of things, including theoretical questions. The whole role of ego development was one of the things that was just incipient at the time in 1937. The point has been made that the genetic viewpoint was already firmly established, for example, in the preface to August Aichorn.[54] The developmental point of view, so allied to the genetic one (looking at it in terms of not looking backwards but looking forwards), was just beginning to be formulated. I believe Hartmann made an important contribution. It has infiltrated analysis, but in ways that are not recognizable today. His distinction between *primary* and *secondary* autonomy implied a developmental transformation. I prefer to consider this in terms of its positive value and the constructive contribution he made; to point out that developmental transformations were occurring, that they might be regressively lost, but that they also represented major changes in the course of development not easily traced back to their precursors. The terms don't

---

54. Freud, S. (1925). Preface to Aichorn's *Wayward Youth, Standard Edition* 19:273.

appear in contemporary literature; we don't talk about secondary autonomy today. The idea of developmental transformation has replaced it. It is a transformation of Hartmann's idea. The change of function and secondary autonomy were already a developmental point of view. He gave a thrust to developmental psychoanalysis, which, I think, persists in many forms and relates to the issue under discussion. He helped to promote infant research even if he himself didn't sufficiently pay attention to the beginning research of that period. I don't think Hartmann particularly cited Spitz and, although Mahler leans a great deal on Hartmann, it's not clear that he was very much influenced by Mahler. Mahler took Hartmann's idea of the development of object relationship from the need-satisfying object to object constancy, put this into a developmental framework far beyond what Hartmann had done with it, and she fleshed out the idea of object constancy and gave it a very significant place in psychoanalysis that it had not had before. I'm not clear, looking in the other direction, what Mahler's influence was on Hartmann.

We need to understand the development of an idealized, all-embracing general psychology, what was going on at the time that would lead to that point of view, because I don't think that it can be found in Freud. Not only did Freud warn against the *Weltanschauung*, he never gave the impression that psychoanalysis was to be the theory of everything, as physicists look for today, that it was to be the theory of the total personality. It was a very specific point of view, oriented towards looking at personality from the point of view of intrapsychic conflict. Considering that and the introduction of a problematic metaphor and concept, the average expectable environment, I asked myself: What was the environment in which Hartmann created this particular set of concepts and began to formulate a theory? This led to the interesting observation that there was a reversal of each major concept in relation to what was going on at the time. Namely that, when he wrote about conflict-free, conflict was raging all around and Freud was talking to him and to others about the fact that he felt the noose around his own neck was being tightened ever more. He was writing about adaptation at a time when adaptation was not talked about because Hartmann used adaptation in many different ways. He also spoke about social adaptation. That's one of the difficult things about Hartmann. There's a shift so often in the framework he's using and you don't know whether he's using a biological, social, even an embryological framework similar to Abraham, but he did, at times, use adaptation in a social sense and clearly it was impossible to adapt to National Socialism. He also spoke about the turning of the drives and the superego. He did not mention at that time the tyranny around him, that he was living under a very threatening persecutory tyranny. So that it looked very much like one impetus, and vastly overdetermined. Hartmann was a very complex figure and there were many influences. One aspect of this was a denial of what was going on in reality, even though there was simultaneous acknowledgment. So it was conflict-free, it was an average expectable environment that was far from anything that could be expectable or adapted to. This became an influence on theory formation. It's not a criticism; it's a way of looking at the way theories are constructed and the components of theory. It is, however, important to understand that when one looks at the government metaphor of the Hartmann approach, the way in which the mind is organized, the different components, one might say the subcities, the towns, the rural and the central areas, and so forth, when one uses that metaphor one can see also not only Hartmann's identification with his father and grandfather, who were involved very much in government (one of whom was an ambassador to Germany, the other was a professor of history), but also the classics were very important. At no point did Hartmann refer to the immediate situation and to current history compared to the history of the past.

It's important to distinguish between Hartmann and Kris and Loewenstein. One can look in terms of the group process at a "ménage à trois" of the three of them, and one can also see them quite individually, relatively autonomous from each other. Kris during the war wrote about prejudice, contributed a significant paper on the psychology of prejudice, and wrote two very interesting papers on the psychology of propaganda.[55] Loewenstein was also interested in some of the social problems. We don't see any of this in Hartmann and we do see a flight into fantasy, and into theory as fantasy and fantasy as theory, I know that Bill's been interested in that too, in his theory construction. One can look at this in terms of two different streams. One is the way in which the theory addressed problems in psychoanalysis, the intra-analytic influences, and attempted to redress problems in psychoanalysis, particularly a minute study of functioning. The "Notes on the Reality Principle" is an interesting paper and a very significant contribution, because he attempted to take the reality principle and show many different important dimensions of it. One of the things that would be of interest in terms of what you brought up before is the inability to separate certain functions from others, that one cannot study any one function totally in isolation.

55. Kris, E. (1941). The "danger" of propaganda. In *Selected Papers of Ernst Kris*. New Haven: Yale University Press, 1975, pp. 409–432; (1943). Some problems of war propaganda: a note on propaganda New and Old. In *Selected Papers of Ernst Kris*. New Haven: Yale University Press, pp. 433–450; (1944), Danger and morale. In *Selected Papers of Ernst Kris*. New Haven: Yale University Press, pp. 451–464; (1946), Notes on the psychology and the study of creative imagination. In *Selected Papers of Ernst Kris*. New Haven: Yale University Press, 1975, pp. 465–472.

The point Martin brought up about the patient who couldn't remember that period in the orphanage and didn't know whether it was false or true memory, fact or fantasy, is not only a question of reality testing, it's a question of the limits of memory and of defensive distortions or wish-fulfilling distortions of memory. There is a relationship between memory and reality testing in an overlap that has to be taken into account. The way we usually talk about reality testing in the differentiation of transference and reality refers to the difference between internal and external perception and the capacity to not misconstrue or misconceive internal stimulation for immediate external perception. The difference between that and reality testing concerning distant memory or even more current memory is related, but it is a somewhat different function.

One of the points is that Hartmann also brought up the role of social reality and the influence of the parent in terms of giving permission to remember or prohibiting memory, so memory becomes a superego function as well. What is acceptable as memory, or what is specially valued as memory, is determined by social reality, not just the parents but the culture as a whole. That even leads to considerations today in our culture of the implanting of false memories, when you have therapists who tell the patient that they were abused, even in the absence of evidence. It becomes a kind of cultural popular approach that then interferes with memory functions because of the impact of the social reality.

Solnit: It could also be called malpractice.

Blum: Hartmann was at the very pinnacle of American psychoanalysis and has now faded into relative obscurity in the analytic literature, and among the many questions I asked was why. One of them had to do with idealization and inevitable disillusion; another one with the test of time, and I think we do have to consider importantly the whole question of the clinical relevance, the clinical utility of what Hartmann has contributed, its pros and its cons, and why so many analysts have apparently not found it useful in their clinical work, because we have to assume that, when Hartmann is not cited any longer and virtually disappeared from the literature, the ordinary analyst is not attending to his contributions.

Let me return now to the first point, idealization followed by devaluation and disillusionment. The theory, the conflict-free theory, in a way was bound to fall because psychoanalysis basically is looking at the psyche from the point of view of conflict. There is probably no area of psychic functioning that we can say is conflict-free. When Cliff brings up preconflictual period, I think that's a significant contribution, but one has to add, and I think Cliff would agree, that they often cause conflict. For example, a child born with a linguistic disorder will be more likely to have conflicts engendered about that and the parents will have conflicts about the handicapped child, whatever the handicap, which then influences the child's conflict. There is probably no area of psychic life that doesn't become imbued with conflict; even if its origins were preconflictual, it becomes amalgamated and condensed with conflict. To my mind, this was one of the major problems with Hartmann. He didn't want to be dogmatic. He really was more cautious than some of the statements we sometimes loosely attributed to him. For the most part, he spoke of relative autonomy. One can find in *The Ego and the Problem of Adaptation* statements to the effect that he's aware of the fact that all of the ego functions are in one way or another invested with conflict and regressively drawn into conflict, so the idea of a conflict-free sphere is a kind of purified ego, not purified plea sure ego but purified conflict ego. It's also for Hartmann, to some degree at least, an ideal fiction, and he can be quoted both ways. I think, in fairness to Hartmann, one has to say that he was not dogmatic and he wasn't trying to push this to the extreme form that some of his more zealous followers have taken it. Hartmann himself was circumspect and prudent about it and was aware of the problems even in his own constructs. The question also of autonomy is related to this because the autonomy again can be read in Hartmann both ways, both as completely autonomous and always as only relatively autonomous.

The idea of psychoanalysis in a general psychology is related to something else that appears in Hartmann, the way that he attempted by analogy to idealize the system to such a point of view that when he spoke of the energy transformations and changes, one would almost, at times, think that one was reading thermodynamics rather than psychoanalysis. He attempted to give a picture of psychoanalysis that was much closer to the natural sciences, much closer to chemistry and physics, and to an idealized view of chemistry and physics, which have their own set of problems.

This was another problem: there was the isolation of not just theory and technique, which we have alluded to here in the discussions, but also the isolation of theory and observation. There was a major gap between theory and observation, and the critics of Hartmann could say that Hartmann was engaging in armchair philosophy and armchair theorizing far removed from discourse that was related to clinical work and to people; that the discourse of energies and hypothetical energies and their extraordinary transformations, the exotic esoteric discussions of energies, the elitist and pretentious terminology of cathexis, anticathexis, decathexis, and so forth, gave it a kind of elegance that was only superficial. It was a kind of heuristic, pseudo-elegance and pseudo-scientific discourse that presented psychoanalysis in highly scientific terms and gave it an idealized view. Along with that was the fact that while attempting to look at the healthy part of the personality and what made possible growth, development, mastery, and adaptation, at the same time Hartmann attempted to present psychoanalysis as able to answer all those questions. He partly knew that it was impossible, that what he was attempting could not be accomplished. At the same time he presented it as not only a distant goal, but something that was almost within reach at the time.

This was the era in which there were other voices. It's difficult to talk about the Hartmann era in any way as if it's a unified era. Not only Brenner, not only Jack Arlow, but also at this time Phyllis Greenacre very interestingly raised the question of the idealization of psychoanalysis. There had been an idealization of Hartmann. This is one of our problems. This was not Hartmann's problem alone. Hartmann had been analyzed by Freud and possibly analyzed by Freud without fee. This was known to a few people, and there was always the tendency to idealize anyone who had had direct contact with Freud and was therefore a torch bearer. Those of Freud's analysands who had been directly in touch with the master remained loyal, had allegiance to the master, and continued the work and were given special prominence. They formed the elite group within analysis. This was the need of the analyst to maintain contact with the founder, and some of the same problems attached later to Anna Freud representing her father and representing the Freud legacy and continued even developing it. There was another example of wonderful collaboration between Hartmann and Anna Freud. I don't refer here to the theoretical—they differed in many ways—I'm referring to the professional and in some degree political alliance, and to the problem of excluding others who had different points of view, a tendency towards being elitist and exclusionary.

The metapsychology that was developed at first appeared to be an extraordinary advance and quantum leap. It was only with time that the terms and concepts fell into disuse, and it appeared as though the effort to formulate autonomous functions, to formulate a conflict-free sphere, and the larger effort to formulate a general psychology could be seen as idealizations that didn't hold up. They were isolated from observation, they were isolated from clinical data and from clinical utility. There were some dimensions that permeated important clinical work, but they were no longer directly identified with Hartmann or his followers.

Here the work of Kris and Loewenstein became important, because their papers were much more clinical. As Hartmann was almost totally theoretical, Kris and Loewenstein were very clinical and useful. Loewenstein's papers[56]

---

56. Loewenstein, R. (1951). The problem of interpretation. *Psychoanalytic Quarterly* 20:1–14; (1957). Some thoughts on interpretation in the theory and practice of psychoanalysis. *Psychoanalytic Study of the Child* 12:127–150. New York: International Universities Press.

on interpretation are underrated and to some degree semi-lost papers in the literature. They're really very fine papers and they attempt to use a number of the Hartmann concepts, although Loewenstein is an independent thinker. The way we talk to patients, the way we listen to patients, the way we formulate interpretations, and the way we render interpretations has changed under the influence of the Hartmann group, particularly under the influence of Kris and Loewenstein, though Hartmann's concepts were applied without attribution over a period of time. How did that change technically? The analyst became less of an id interpreter in the aftermath of ego psychology. In some ways, it's slowed down by attention to the surface, by the gradual appearance of material, by marshaling evidence, by presenting it to the patient in a form that the patient can assimilate, by showing the patient repeatedly how the different aspects of his conflict appear in his associations, the daydreams, the dreams, behavior, neurotic behavior, and symptoms. This was a different view. One can say that all this can be found in Freud, which is true, but the manner in which the patient was actually addressed had changed considerably and the patient became a much more active partner, not something just being interpreted to him and being told what his unconscious conflicts were, or what he was defending himself against or resisting, or this was his wish, he wanted to kill someone, or he wanted to have an incestuous relationship. A much more gradual unfolding process took place in the way the patient resisted insights, lost them, and regained them, going back to the vicissitudes of insight. Issues like that may be subtle, not very dramatic changes in technique, but they infiltrated and they gradually permeated psychoanalytic technique. I believe if you look at the few clinical reports before and after ego psychology, at least in the United States, there's a very different way of dealing with patients. The patients are listened to differently, and the analyst responds in a way that's quite different. The patient is a more active partner in the process, with an appreciation of the patient's talents, skills, ego resources, and capacity to both work in analysis and to not only lose insight, but to use it. The negative side of it is what Otto had referred to. I think this is certainly one of the criticisms that we all wonder about, which is: To what degree did they stay on the surface too long, to what degree would attention to the surface be used defensively to avoid interpretation of the depths? The idea that the ego psychologists defended against drive theory is questionable when you really look at the papers of the day.

With the idealization that occurred, the idealization of Hartmann, the idealization of ego psychology, the idealization of psychoanalysis as a general psychology, there was a further problem. Psychoanalysis itself was idealized as a panacea. We could treat all people; we could be all things; we could explain everything. Greenacre responded to this at the time with her paper[57] on the overidealization of psychoanalysis. It's a significant paper because it's a humbling paper. It introduces some humility where before there had been grandiosity. The grandiosity had a number of very interesting consequences. First of all, the analysts of the day loved it because it fed their narcissism, and the idea that analysis had this kind of reach not only as a theory, but as a way to reach so many different kinds of patients, was a quite different point of view than the one that we couldn't treat borderlines or very sick patients. The opposite point of view was simultaneously present, that we had the answers, that analysis was a panacea, that there are virtually no contraindications.

The disillusion was then not just with Hartmann, not just with the trio or the Hartmann era, but it was a general disillusionment with psychoanalysis. It had failed to be a general psychology; it had failed to be an all-embracing explanation; it didn't have the explanatory reach it claimed; and it certainly didn't cure everyone. The public became more and more aware of people in long analyses. Many analyses were in effect the same or worse, therapeutic impasses or therapeutic failures.

Another issue that I wanted to address is systematization. The effort to systematize psychoanalysis took a number of different forms. Hartmann wanted to pick this apart and describe the loose ends in theory. He wanted to address areas of theory that he felt had been given insufficient attention, including the development of ego function and the effect of the functions on each other, what he called *intrasystemic effects* as well as *intersystemic conflicts*. He helped to potentiate studies, even outside of psychoanalysis, within cognitive psychology, of what we consider to be ego functions and their somatic, let's say, foundations or the subsomatic substrates, studies of memory, studies of thinking, affect studies, seen in isolation unfortunately, but also important for us to consider. For example, some of the research on ethics[58] is important for analysts to think about and see the ways in which it might relate to our work.

The systematization leads to another extreme, though. It was thought that psychoanalysis could be so unified that we would have a systematic theory without all kinds of complexities and problems within it. One unfortunate consequence of the orthodoxy at that time was that when these papers were offered, there was little debate, little complaint, and little opposition. I heard, not officially but unofficially, that people would walk out, muttering under

---

57. Greenacre, P. (1968). Problems of over-idealization of the analyst and of analysis, in *Emotional Growth* 2:743–761. New York: International Universities Press, 1971.

58. Hartmann, H. (1960). *Psychoanalysis and Moral Values*. New York: International Universities Press.

their breath their dissent or their disagreement, but it was not said vocifer-ously. Tendencies towards dissent were muted, if not entirely absent. This held us back, but it also had some very positive consequences.

Where were the positive consequences? I'll mention one, and I refer here to what I know about, which is psychoanalysis in the United States. It may have been unique. I'm not really *au courant* of what was going on in Europe or in Latin America at this time. In the United States, one has to look at psy-choanalytic education before and after Hartmann. Psychoanalytic education was not at all systematized in the 1930s. In fact, the best thing one could do from the point of view of an American aspiring analyst was to go to Europe and hopefully get into analysis with Freud. The Rockefeller Foundation in those years actually offered fellowships for a number of Americans to go to Europe, to go to Austria to have an analysis with Freud or one of Freud's followers or someone that Freud recommended. Freud very interestingly would take people, knowing that it was a time-limited analysis. They would have funds, say, for 6 months of treatment and Freud would agree that would be their analysis—time-limited therapy. It may have been related to his idea of periods of analysis and coming back again after a time. Now, analysis was very informal in the United States. People went to Europe, they studied if they could with the master or one of his disciples. They took a few courses, usually very informally. They arranged for their own supervision. Sometimes the supervision in those days was done by the training analyst. The training analyst would act as both supervisor and analyst, and this particular prob-lem in that era was overlooked and it was thought that the training analyst would be in the best position to analyze the countertransference, which in those days was equated with resistance. The value of the countertransfer-ence for understanding the patient was not understood in the '30s. So psy-choanalysis in this country was really in a rather unsystematized state, and the arrival of the European immigrants in the United States actually trans-formed the landscape dramatically and radically, and psychoanalysis became extraordinarily systematized. One of the great advantages we had was that we developed a very elaborate system of psychoanalytic education with all kinds of controls and with really very lofty educational practices and goals. At the same time, one of the problems was the oversystematization, which led to its own form of distortions and also to a kind of a tendency towards consensus, orthodoxy, and homogeneity.

Bergmann: Thank you very much. I am particularly grateful that you touched on two questions, the systematization and the impact of the Hartmann era on technique.

Ostow: In regard to Harold's comment about cultural factors, I just want to elaborate on the analyst and the Jewish question. It's interesting the way different analysts managed and expressed their interest. Most European analysts who came here as refugees ignored the Jewish question. Some of them, however, felt that it was their obligation to speak out, and a few, like Loewenstein, wrote books about anti-Semitism.[59] Others wrote individual articles, but having made an initial statement they then dropped it, and it never again appeared in their bibliography. I read Loewenstein's book half a dozen times and I read it for the very simple reason that I can never understand it, even the last time. He comes out with some sort of statement like, "Christianity and Judaism are a cultural pair," and somehow or other this is supposed to account for anti-Semitism. I never understood why. His references to Jewish religious literature are very superficial and he doesn't identify the meaning of the various sources. He obviously did not write from knowledge.

On the other hand, Arlow is not a refugee. Arlow had no compulsion to write about Jewish cultural matters, but he did,[60] and he wrote because he felt that as a Jew he had something to introduce into analytic theory and applied analysis. He thought analysis helped to elucidate some of the aspects of Jewish literature, and so you have his interest in mythology growing out of his interest in Jewish mythology, and he wrote some splendid papers about that, even without the cultural compulsion. Then you have somebody like Martin, who addressed himself to both sides. Martin spent a long time dealing with the Holocaust. Martin also spent a good deal of time thinking about Freud's Jewish background and he contributed to that. Other than that, there is really not a lot until recent years. Again, within the context of greater pluralism within the American community and a greater freedom for analysts to state that they are Jewish and that they have an interest in the Jewish culture and Jewish religion. That's part of the history of the Jews in analysis.

Yorke: Could I comment briefly on a point made about the preconflictual phase? I was merely drawing attention to the fact that during that, during this phase, one couldn't properly speak of conflict except in the most limited way.

---

59. Loewenstein, R. (1951). *Christians and Jews: A Psychoanalytic Study.* New York: International Universities Press.

60. Arlow, J. (1951a). The consecration of the prophet. *Psychoanalytic Quarterly* 23:374–397; (1951b). A psychoanalytic study of a religious initiation rite: bar mitzvah. *Psychoanalytic Study of the Child* 6:353–374. Papers reprinted in M. Ostow, ed. (1982). *Judaism and Psychoanalysis.* New York: Ktav Publishing House, pp. 51–72 and 187–217.

This doesn't mean, as Harold rightly pointed out, that events occurring in that phase can't be drawn into conflict later, or contribute to it. He mentioned malformations and bodily defects and disturbances. In my paper I referred to a boy with congenitally short arms—the subject of a paper by Lussier.[61] This boy, whose arms were only about 8 inches long, learned to do a great many things he said he would do but which everyone thought at the time to be pure fantasies. He'd never swim! He'd never play the trumpet! He'd never ride a bicycle! But he learned to do all these things, and he learned to dive from a high board. He not only *played* the trumpet—he *taught* it. Years later I was asked to see him, and found none of these achievements had bolstered his self-esteem. The disability was deeply involved in conflict.

A further point relates to one brought up by Martin. Harold spoke of the elements of transformations during development. I think that's important, and has significance for infant observation. Some people take the view that behavior and attitudes that can be observed in infants can be seen and replicated, in later life, on the couch. They fail to acknowledge the fact the patient has undergone many transitions and *transformations* in the course of his development, and although what has happened in early life may have affected him, the analyst is dealing with a very different set of circumstances from those that obtained in early childhood. Even the memories and reconstructions of the early past will differ substantially from the reality at the time.

One last point, about the terms *cathexis* and *decathexis*. I was talking with Eissler last night and he raised the question of the revised *Standard Edition*. He thought *cathexis* would be better translated as "charge." Cathexis was pushed upon Freud, who finally agreed to it—much against his will, in Eissler's opinion. But I don't think we should critize Hartmann for using the term. He was simply using Strachey's translation, not his own.

Kernberg: The term *cathexis*, the translation is "investment." Freud used the term in a nontechnical way. This was a clear shift, and Hartmann spoke German very well. His using Strachey's efforts to scientificize Freud cannot be accepted at face value. It's not the same as a generation of American psychoanalysts who were led to confuse instincts and drives because of the *Standard Edition*. It was an entire generation of German-speaking immigrants that adopted that translation. In all fairness, Hartmann maintained the distinction of Freud regarding drive. I think that that terminology, cathexis, a mythological transformation, did a lot of harm to the scientific study of development.

---

61. Lussier, A. (1960). The analysis of a boy with a congenital defect. *Psychoanalytic Study of the Child* 15:430–453. New York: International Universities Press.

Is there really such a thing as preconflictual development? I would think that it's in the nature of the infant from birth on that the infant is extremely dependent on the caretaker's function and the caretaker cannot but frustrate the infant, who cannot diagnose the origin of the frustration. I'm thinking of work, for example, with children who have congenital defects of their digestive tract, children with chronic severe physical illness who develop intense aggression. Bill Grossman has written a paper[62] about this and he can talk about this much better than I can, but it seems to me that to think about a preconflictual stage is puzzling.

Yorke: It seems to me that Otto is speaking of frustration and satisfaction. That can lead to conflict with the mother or caregiver, and at that point one could speak of *external* conflict. I've already commented on congenital deformities, and on that point I wouldn't disagree with him. As for the term *cathexis*, I agree that it isn't a helpful word.

Neubauer: I also wanted to ask Harold, in his unusually rich presentation of the various factors that contributed to the topic, if we have a problem of definition of terms. When we speak about conflict historically, what is usually meant by the term is a neurotic constellation, based on interaction between superego, ego, and drive. This conflict one cannot see in the first few weeks of life. We can also use the term *conflict* as tension between the wish for gratification and the ego's attempt to achieve mastery. The term has different meanings depending on what period of life we are addressing. What is primary autonomy? Primary autonomy is any development that is not involved in conflict and, therefore, is conflict-free. The question arises whether Hartmann means by conflict-free, free from interference from the psychic apparatus, or free from forces that inhibit maturation? When Hartmann speaks of the secondary function of the ego, does he mean differentiation, integration, or reality assessment? These various forms of the ego are continuously at work. Each term would have to be defined in connection with what kind of ego functions, when we speak about conflict-free, when we speak about autonomy. This is really a historical question.

Grossman: This is all crucial. What Peter just said is why the goal of systematization in psychoanalysis has value. I associate an idea with Anna Freud, but I may be wrong because I know Freud talks this way too. She made a clear

62. Grossman, W. (1991). Pain, aggression, fantasy, and concepts of sadomasochism. *Psychoanalytic Quarterly* 60:22–52.

statement to the effect that there is no conflict before 18 months, or when it was presumed that there is a sufficient ego formation to have intrapsychic conflict.

Yorke: That point that Bill just made was also Glover's point.

Grossman: It's a crucial question. Here's an example of natural selection among ideas in the field. You end up with certain products that don't serve the function, or it would serve the function to correct the problem. That's why you need concepts like primary and secondary autonomy, and conflict-free, or relative, always relative because of the principle. The products of conflict are immediately involved in a new kind of dual orientation to the drives and the ego. You can't get away from it, but it's relative. It was one of the important things about the Kleinian position, theoretically, from Susan Isaacs's paper[63] onward at least, that you could think about conflict as having a broader significance, of which intrapsychic conflict between agencies is only a special case. To elaborate the point that Rapaport made, if you say the first self-imposed delay involves the first structure mentally, it is the moment the infant learns not to cry when it hears the mother's voice and is now waiting to be fed instead of just crying.

Neubauer: When does function become structure? Immediately?

Grossman: We have to assume that, because if there is the possibility to respond you have a structure or it will become structure. It will become an agency, if you want to think that way, but it's already a structure. I don't say this with the expectation that I will find immediate agreement. I'm only saying it's a point of view whose virtues are many and that it offers great possibilities for conceptualizing development. According to this view, conflict is a principle of mental functioning, with the terms and organization of conflicts becoming more complex in the course of development.

Green: I would like first to quote a passage from Martin's paper on the historical roots of psychoanalytic orthodoxy. It's a quotation from Freud's (1914) *History of the Psychoanalytic Movement.* "Psychoanalysis has never claimed to provide a complete theory of human mentality in general, but only expected that what it offers should be applied to supplement and correct the knowledge acquired by other means." Martin goes on to say, "It is one of the ironies

---

63. Isaacs, S. (1948). The nature and function of phantasy. *International Journal of Psycho-Analysis* 29:73–77.

of psychoanalytic history that under the title of psychoanalysis, a general psychology, Hartmann and his co-workers launched one of the most productive periods of psychoanalysis, the Hartmann era of psychoanalytic ego psychology. To convert psychoanalysis into a general psychology was the very thing that Freud condemned in others."

To come back to Harold's comments about idealization: to assume that cure is possible by interpretation only is not only an idealization of analysis, it's an idealization of the patient, which sometimes calls for very unusual ways of interpretation. This is an important issue because we have to discuss today not only the progress from surface to depth, but to compare different styles of interpretation that are practiced all over the world. Another point that was raised by Harold was the change instigated by Hartmann, not only looking backward (reconstruction), but also looking forward from the beginning of development. This raises the question of whether the approach of going from the beginning of life to more advanced, adult stages fulfills methodologically the requirements and aims of analysis. We have to come back again to the problem of infant observation and infant research. To me, the humility of the analyst does not rest on the limitations of his craft. I think it rests in the recognition of his own madness in front of the patient. It is the patient's "madness," or splitting about his "madness," that compels the analyst to think "madly" to reach the patient's unconscious in his interpretations.

Blum: I'd like to respond to the really fascinating comments that everyone has made. Morty's comments were very interesting about the role of Jewish identity in analysis. Historically, it's important. When one goes back to the Freud/Jung struggle, Freud's misjudgment concerning Frank, his search for a non-Jewish heir, as he called Jung, a crown prince who would take over analysis. His own struggles with his own Jewish identity were then mirrored and recapitulated in so many other ways with so many of his followers in the ensuing years. It's a fact that most of the analysts in Europe at the time, probably 98 percent, were Jewish. If you add those married to Jews or those who were part Jewish, we get probably close to 100 percent. Psychoanalysis was founded by Jews who were on the border of society. They were in the mainstream and were also outside the culture. That includes Freud himself. Many of them were highly educated, belonged to a special subgroup of the Jewish community, and saw themselves as professional mainstream and as citizens of the world, as humanitarians. This resulted in part in a positive form in the contributions they made to culture and in the way psychoanalysis began to transform culture and was immediately applied to culture. The cultural contributions applied to psychoanalysis as we see it today. When we look back on it, they were not only pioneering, they were extraordinary considering the limited knowledge available. Consider Freud, for example, in his 1909 paper on Leonardo, and Abraham's early work. With that came at the same time an effort to deny Jewish identity, and this led to certain problems as Nazism arose. Denial, as we know, tends sometimes to move to other areas and spheres by displacement or by condensation and by preferential use of the same defense. The denial of impending disaster and catastrophe as Nazism arose, and as the Holocaust was really beginning, on the part of so many who were involved, spread to other areas and might even be related in some way later on to the denial of the contributions of those who were excluded from participating in psychoanalysis, who were outside, with a very strong feeling that one had to protect the central core of psychoanalysis and that extraneous issues such as Jewish identity could not be acknowledged. This led in our country to such excesses as analysts who would insist that Jewish patients come to treatment on Yom Kippur and would charge them if they didn't come, but who themselves would take off Christmas and would even celebrate it. These issues were not analyzed. This was accepted. It was the way one practiced analysis. It was ego- and superego-syntonic, and this continued in many ways right up to the present day. There were further ramifications historically of this problem in terms of identity, and one could even relate it to the introduction by Erikson, who concealed his own Jewishness, of the term *identity* into a major position in psychoanalytic thought.

I'm very interested in the term conflict and how we define it. There are those who think of conflict in the first days of life, there are those who even think of it *in utero*. If conflict is conflict between the ego and a drive derivative, then conflict cannot occur in the first days of life unless one believes that the ego is already present from birth onwards. If you start with the idea of an undifferentiated phase and that the ego gradually evolves in complicated ways, not in a linear form, but hierarchically and from nuclei that coalesce but also differentiate, it's a very complicated mechanism. There are those like Balint[64] who postulate a primary object relationship. For them the conflict might well begin at birth. If you believe in the capacity for primary object relationship, then conflict is indeed present from birth. Our knowledge of early infancy is really very primitive. All we can do is attempt to infer and conjecture. We might conjecture that beginning with the capacities for delay, for anticipation, for certain other signs of a functioning ego, for a child attending specifically to the mother's voice with the capacity for imitative identification, first appearances, that with a number of issues that come up in early life, we begin

---

64. Balint, M. (1953). *Primary Love and Psycho-Analytic Technique.* New York: Liveright.

to infer the presence of ego as an educated guess. I myself lean towards a more gradual differentiation of ego functioning and I prefer the term *organismic stress* for the earliest phase of life. I think that may be part of the answer to your impossible question, Peter, because there's no way we can really resolve the issue.

Neubauer: Your definition does not take into account the presence of the apparatus in Hartmann's term because perception, sensory reactions, all of these things are already present at birth. Two assumptions are possible: an undifferentiated phase on the one hand, or ego nuclei that emerge, not out of an undifferentiated phase, but are present already and later become the ego.[65]

Kernberg: Just another alternative is to think of an early ego/id, not undifferentiated, but an ego/id in which there is an internal potential split between the elated and painful states, insofar as elated and painful states occur in relation to the same caregiver, so there may be intrapsychic conflict that is not intrasystemic.

Furst: And you don't want to call them differentiated?

Kernberg: I prefer to talk about the primary ego/id.

Grossman: It isn't intersystemic.

Kernberg: It is not intersystemic. I reserve the term *system* for ego. If you want to call the conflict between contradictory nuclei of ego/id as system, then you can call it intersystemic too, but then you have to say that we're using the term intersystemic for both those kind of systems and later on for the conflicts between ego, superego, and id. This is semantics.

Kris: There is another alternative, which is to revise one's idea of what is conflict. The model that has been mentioned has been the standard analytic model and is what I call *convergent conflict*, which occurs as an intersystemic conflict. Its prototype is the relationship between an unconscious element and the push component of repression. Divergent conflict doesn't require that. It's not all that hard to demonstrate in very young animals and people that they have approach-approach conflicts and that correlates with what I call *divergent conflict*. These conflicts appear in a variety of forms, generally known as *intra-*

---

65. The concept of the ego nuclei was introduced by E. Glover. See his (1968). *The Birth of the Ego: A Nuclear Hypothesis.* New York: International Universities Press.

systemic. Their prototype is the relationship between an unconscious element and the pull component of repression. Another early version of divergent conflict appears in the concept of bisexuality.

Blum: I think that we should not confuse the issue of what might be pre-conflictual. Whether conflict begins at birth can't be resolved because in this earliest phase all we can do is have our own conjectures and educated guesses or our own preferences or, conversely, biases. It's very different from the issue that Hartmann raised about the conflict-free sphere.

I want to turn to that in relation to technique. Hartmann survives in our present struggle in another form as a challenge today to the objectivity and neutrality of the analyst. The analyst's capacity to stand apart from the conflicts, not only to be aware of his own madness but also to retain rationality. The analyst has to be a beacon of rationality for the irrational patient and be able to formulate rational, not crazy interpretations. This capacity to expand outside the conflicts, to be able to look at his own conflicts and the patient's conflicts in a rational form, to, in effect, maintain enough secondary process not invaded by the primary process. The analyst remains reasonably neutral so as not to be drawn into taking sides in one way or another, and to be able to analyze his own conflicts so that they don't interfere excessively. We know there will always be some interference. There will always be some intrusion of the analyst's own conflicts, but not so excessively that the process cannot proceed. Otherwise, we have a completely irrational system. I speak of relatively rational, because no one is completely objective, no one is completely rational, no one is rational at all times. These formulations of technique that we take for granted were fortified by Hartmann. Unfortunately, when he talked about the conflict-free sphere, he took it to an absurd position. He acted as if the countertransference did not exist, which some of the analysts tried to deny at that time. We know now that we operate in a transference–countertransference field, a field of forces, and issues of rationality are always relative.

One final comment, a point in the paper that was not fleshed out: ego psychology is a misnomer. It was never just ego psychology. It was really a structural and systematizing psychology and in fact, Hartmann wrote a very interesting and important paper,[66] "Notes on the Superego," and he made important contributions to the theory of morality.[67]

---

66. Hartmann, H. and Loewenstein, R. (1962). Notes on the superego. *Psychoanalytic Study of the Child* 17:42–81. New York: International Universities Press.

67. Hartmann, H. (1960). *Psychoanalysis and Moral Values*. New York: International Universities Press.

Bergmann: If we are talking about the madness of the analyst, I don't see how André can remain silent. May I ask you to comment?

Green: Freud believed, even if others didn't, in Eros and the destructive drives. He assumed that there is a conflict from the beginning between these two groups of drives. He also put it otherwise on more common terms: binding and unbinding. The question is too complicated to be exposed in all its dimensions. There is also a basic conflict at the root of psychic activity, in Bion's opinion: whether to tolerate, in the case of frustration, inner tension for elaboration or to get rid of it in evasion through discharge. So the fact that we usually refer to conflict as a mental issue can also enable us to detect elementary forms of conflict that are not yet mentally structured in the way neurosis shows us.

About the question of madness, of course, Harold was right. We are caught up in the analysis of our own "private madness," as I have called it, made of passion and irrationality but, as far as interpretation goes, the issue becomes more difficult. The "crazy" interpretation can have an extraordinary impact in the session. This is not a theoretical statement. I am referring to Winnicott with his most famous interpretation, maybe the boldest in the contemporary history of psychoanalysis. A patient comes to Winnicott who has had many analyses before and Winnicott says to him, up to a point, "I listen to a girl. I know perfectly that you are a boy, but I am hearing a girl. And that girl speaks of penis envy." The patient is struck and says; "I could never talk about that because I was afraid of being considered psychotic if I did say that to the previous analyst." Winnicott says, "No, no, it's not you who are mad, it's me. It's me by thinking that I'm listening to a girl when I know you are a boy."[68] What Winnicott had in mind was that the mother of this patient wanted, unconsciously, to see him as a girl, she favored in him the creation of a false self and enhanced an acute splitting of this feminine part of him, which could not lead to normal bisexual integrated disposition. The patient had to split off this feminine part as something totally mad. Winnicott is talking of a patient who had several analyses. He has to say something sharper than what has been said to the patient until now to get closer to this split-off part of himself. So the analyst's mind functions in an identification with what he supposes to be the hidden "psychosis" of the patient and he knows that he has to reach it through an interpretation, in the transference, putting himself in the place of the "mad" mother. But doing this, he acknowledges it. In proceeding like this, he is differ-

---

68. This comes from Winnicott's paper on the splitting between masculine and feminine in *Playing and Reality*, Tavistock Publications, 1971, Chapter 5, Creativity and its origins, pp. 72–76.

ent from Anna Freud, and from Melanie Klein too. He beautifully invents the technique that is appropriate to his theory, on the role of the environment. One of the compliments that appeals to me the most is when a patient of mine replies to my interpretation, "You're mad. I have a mad analyst." Then, I know, I am right to the point, whenever I have the feeling of a splitting in the patient.

Bergmann: I have a small anecdote to add to this. When I was a very young analyst, a patient came in and I asked him about his previous analyst. He said, "He was a good analyst for healthy people, but not for me."

AFTERNOON SESSION, OCTOBER 19TH

Solnit: There is a special area called *infant observation*. Ernst Kris finally convinced Anna Freud that direct observation of children, including infants, could be very valuable in understanding, in elaborating, and in fact in reframing psychoanalytic theory. This is still a controversial subject, I'm going to ask Clifford if it's true; she delivered the eulogy after Ernst died, she acknowledged that she had been wrong and he had been right about the way direct observation can enrich.

That leads into my other area. One of the problems in talking about Hartmann's work and the Hartmann era is he didn't promise you a rose garden. He actually said it would be desirable to work toward psychoanalysis as a general psychology. The word *a* and *the* are quite different. He always referred to problems, he referred to comments, he referred to issues, but he did not have the data or a way of validating some of the ideas, and these were offered to see if they were useful. I found them enormously useful and continue to, especially because of my special interest in the area of applied psychoanalytic theory. If you look at Freud's work, he was always interested in things like humor, the functions of human personality that were not limited to the psychopathology or to conflict, and in that sense Hartmann's suggestions and additions are useful in a number of areas. When you look at Hartmann's work, you cannot really separate it from Kris's and Loewenstein's work, because they sparked each other and they each had a different area in which they developed their own curiosity and interests, and they created together with Anna Freud a journal because there was no other place at the time that would be a repository for that kind of dialogue, that kind of exploration, that kind of effort to build theory. Theory needed to be used in order to be revised. That's one of the reasons I really enjoyed Martin's paper, because you catch the dynamic of that, and even the title is clever because it captures a certain attitude trying to add to our theoretical and practical knowledge by a group of followers. When you read Hartmann, you cannot escape Kris, or Loewenstein, the importance of the drives, the importance of the id. You can't talk about all of them at the same time with the kind of intensity and the kind of sharp focus that they wanted to address. From its inception, *The Psychoanalytic Study of the Child* had a section on applications. Sometimes that's one of the parts that gets criticized the most, because we've had difficulty saying what the boundaries of application are, how far away you can get, for example, in literary criticism or in looking at aesthetic propositions or creativity, which Ernst Kris was so interested in. There was a trio. You can call it the Hartmann era. You could have called it the Kris era. You could have called it less accurately the Rudy Loewenstein era, because he was not nearly as focused on theory building as he was on its application to the clinical psychoanalytic situation, in which his work was terrific. His work on anti-Semitism was extraordinarily interesting and a useful way of understanding that terrible social problem. Hartmann himself was not Jewish, but he was married to a Jewish woman.

Blum: Dora was Jewish; Hartmann was one-quarter Jewish.

Solnit: But not raised as a Jew. I think that in our discussions here, there is a friendly dissonance about Hartmann that is worth understanding, and I don't pretend to fully understand it but it does show the amount of adrenaline that can be stimulated by Hartmann's ideas, and that I welcome. He strongly agreed with Freud that psychoanalysis was not a *Weltanschauung* or could lead to a philosophy, that he dissociated himself as did Freud from that, but it was his effort to do what many scientists do, which is to make predictions about what the data might reveal if you leap ahead. Whether it's in physics or sociology, and extrapolating from what they know as to what also will be the next theoretical building block, that could be useful. I think that Hartmann was very pragmatic, as was Kris, as was Loewenstein.

Bergmann: We will go to Tony's paper.

Kris: I come back to the point that is in the title: technique. For me, what's most important is what was wrong with the technique and how it got that way. I do believe it is the technique on which the era foundered. That may be because I can't follow all the philosophical issues, and all the nuances of theory are not as comfortable to me. I don't believe in them. So it may be that that's why I'm more interested in the technique, but there are real questions about the technique. It seems to me there is an interrelated group of components of the Hartmann era, all of which have been mentioned. None of this will be entirely new, but we do want to put them together in a new view. One of them is the countertransference rule, which says you must not have countertransference. If you have countertransference, you have a problem and it ought to be dealt with at a minimum in self-analysis, or by going back to analysis. This, as far as I can see, is Freud (1912) unchanged, a powerful position.[69]

A second interrelated component, though how they are interrelated one may disagree about: The Hartmann group did not understand the preoedipal world in the way the Kleinians did, in the way that apparently the French did, certainly not as Lacan did. They did not know how to include the preoedipal world, and sooner or later it was bound to get them into difficulty. The prohibition against countertransference and the antipathy to the preoedipal world combined to limit understanding. The equation of preoedipal pathology with psychosis was pejorative. From another perspective, the Oedipus complex took on overwhelming importance in their thinking. In the history of Freud's writings up to 1907, shame and guilt are approximately equal; after 1907, it's all guilt. Shame appears once, and it is to the credit of Heinz Kohut that he brought it back.

Neubauer: Nunberg emphasized shame.

Kris: The focus on the Oedipus is a third component. Everything had to be interpreted as oedipal, and everything therefore had to be a particular kind of conflict, what I refer to as *convergent* conflict. This rigidified their focus. Having done a fairly large number of second and third analyses, my impression is that my teachers did not know how to get to the Oedipus complex in difficult cases. Maybe they got to the Oedipus complex in cases that weren't so difficult, I mean narcissistic difficulties. I do not share the strategy of Kohut to say that narcissism is a phase and narcissistic pathology is a particular kind of pathology of a libidinal phase or of a narcissistic developmental phase or a self-developmental phase. I see narcissistic pathology as occurring at each of the potential developmental phases. I have spelled out what I think about narcissistic pathology.[70] Very briefly, I see a vicious cycle that starts with punitive

---

69. Freud, S. (1912), The dynamics of transference love. *Standard Edition* 12:97–106, and recommendations to physicians practicing psycho-analysis where Freud said, "I cannot advise my colleagues too urgently to model themselves during psycho-analytic treatment on the surgeon, who puts aside all his feelings, even his human sympathy, and concentrates his mental forces on the single aim of performing the operation as skillfully as possible." *Standard Edition* 12:115.

70. Kris, A. O. (1990). Helping patients by analyzing self-criticism. *Journal of the American Psychoanalytical Association* 38:605–636; (1994). Freud's treatment of a narcissistic patient. *International Journal of Psycho-Analysis* 75:649–664.

unconscious self-criticism, that leads to self-deprivation, that then correlates with entitlement or excessive demand, that leads to renewed self-criticism, round and round. This is the essence of narcissistic pathology, whether in borderline patients, those with character disorders, or neurotic patients. I'm impressed that my predecessors did not know how to deal with that, even in patients who were fundamentally neurotic. I believe that represents a very significant limitation in the armamentaria of the analyst, not to be able to help the patient who is under the influence of very great unconscious punitive self-criticism. If you can't help that patient because you tend to criticize the patient, implicitly or explicitly, if you can't evaluate your own countertransference that might lead you to see how you were critical, it's hard to function effectively with narcissistic patients. Here is the great influence of Merton Gill in the '80s saying that every interpretation is an action, analysts are doing things to their patients. Kohut and Gill between them corrected important mistakes of the Hartmann period. I'm trying to point out what I believe are the technical failures of that period. Kohut mentioned it very powerfully. It's one of the places I agree with him. As you know, I'm not very fond of his theory, but he said that you can't help these patients if your whole theory is one of lifting repression, if that is the only mechanism you have in mind. I do not like Kohut's solution to that problem. To solve that problem, he said, let us abandon the concept of conflict. I prefer to modify the concept of conflict, so that lifting of the push component of repression is not the sole model of conflict. Divergent conflict and convergent conflict, together, in interaction, provide a more serviceable formulation for me. To me, and here I am still totally allied with my father, psychoanalysis is essentially a conflict-centered field and what we do is to help patients resolve conflicts.

Bill Grossman and André Green emphasized the importance of metaphor. I quoted in my response to Martin's paper my father's statement that metaphor is an interference with clarity or systematization in theory, that Freud's use of metaphor was a conceptual error. That wasn't just a minor word error on his part. The Hartmann group thought, and I believe there is a lot of evidence for it, that they were following Freud's wish. They lost a great piece of Freud's intuitive appreciation of the preoedipal world and the world of uncertainty. They lost the potential for understanding how much metaphor is integral to the way people think. Arnold Modell[71] has written about that quite explicitly. That failure to allow sufficient place for metaphor was another com-

---

71. Modell, A. (1995). Metaphor and mind. Plenary address, American Psychoanalytical Association, December 15.

ponent in the interrelated factors that held them from a technique that could benefit narcissistic patients. Again, I mean narcissistic patients with developmental disorders at various levels. I don't believe that the consumers really would have demanded controlled studies, but I do believe the consumers felt injured. In this room, there are several people who have felt injured by the way the analytic teachers of that period behaved. One must add to that the considerable number of our failures.

Heinz Kohut very courageously changed his technique to respond to the problem of unconscious self-criticism, effecting a partial solution to the problem of technique. I think it was a very unfortunate consequence of his thinking that he then tried to revise theory totally and presented a totally new theory. (There have been many further steps toward leveling the field and some of them, I agree with André Green, can make you nervous. I think the field may have been leveled too much.) Other psychoanalytic groups had one or another advantage over the Hartmann group. The Kleinians who, as far as I can see, were every bit as authoritarian, had the preoedipal world and a tolerance of countertransference on their side. The interpersonalists had on their side that they were less critical of their patients. André Green tells us that the French, with the club of Lacan behind their heads, behaved themselves toward their patients insofar as they didn't criticize them or tell them that they were resisting. So those are my thoughts why the Hartmann era came to the bitter end it did. It might have for all the other reasons that have been discussed, but I am particularly interested in the question of technique, and this is the one thing I have been able to understand.

Bergmann: Thank you very much for a sobering and important contribution.

Furst: We've all talked about how psychoanalysis, in the hands of Freud particularly, developed as a technique, as a way of understanding and dealing with pathology based on conflict. Ultimately what you're addressing is that psychoanalysis began to experience difficulty when it dealt with pathology not based on conflict.

Kris: Can you amend that to intersystemic conflict, what I call convergent conflict? The interaction of self-critical conflicts and divergent conflicts gives a different picture.

Furst: I suspect that all of the difficulties have come up with regard to the question of treating narcissistic patients whose pathology is essentially based on developmental disorders. Mainstream psychoanalysis is really a technique for dealing with conflict, and when it attempts to deal with pathology that is not centered in conflict, it becomes far less effective. Some even said simply that narcissistic patients are not analyzable. When there was a plethora of patients, you could get away with it. I'm thinking of a project we ran on prolonged analysis. We arrived at the generalization that analyses that seemed to go and progress for a long time are invariably analyses with patients whose pathology is either narcissistic or developmental. Furthermore, we found that when these analyses, or long analyses, do benefit the patients, it's not because of the increased introspection and insight gained by the patient, but rather by relation to the analyst as new object. All the divergent schools in one way or another represent attempts to deal with this problem.

Kris: Balint and Winnicott had it solved to some extent when we didn't even know they existed.

Furst: I don't know that the other schools have had much more success than mainstream analysis. I don't know much about what kind of results the Kleinians get dealing with patients with pathology that's preoedipal, preconflict, narcissistic, nor do I know whether the Kohutians do, or the interpersonal school. We can speak admiringly or give credit to these other schools, as Tony does. I don't know that they harm patients any less than we do.

Kernberg: I can briefly summarize a few more things. I would like to make use of the opportunity to thank Martin for your wonderful essay, and for the invitation to talk in this group. I'm very acutely aware that some years back, there might have been a greater reluctance to invite me than nowadays. I'm deeply appreciative for the invitation. Because of my background, perhaps, I'm more critically inclined than others, but there may be a view of me as being more critically inclined than meets the facts, so let me go into a number of points.

One has to differentiate what Hartmann said concretely in his statements and the effect that his statements had. Bill has pointed out that we are doing it. Al stated that we are doing injustice to him by condensing the effects that he had and what he said. In many ways, he was flexible. I am really interested in the study of the effect of the approach, which is the Hartmann era, rather than Hartmann. If you look at my work, it is closely linked to Edith Jacobson. Hartmann redeveloped an edifice that permitted a number of people to develop the theory further. He gave them a theory that made the immensity of Freud's work more home-like. The advantage was an optimistic atmosphere. The disadvantage was that most people were not considered treatable when they were judged as primarily preoedipal in their pathology. Even those who were included in the treatment did not receive a full treatment because their preoedipal pathology was not included in the treatment. Now we are at the end of the era. That doesn't mean that it didn't have a positive effect for some time. That's on the positive side.

On the negative side is the active leaving out of alternative views. In any science, that is detrimental. It is true that it's a critique that one has to address Anna Freud, but with discretion. We have to acknowledge that Anna Freud, in the dialogue in London, was always involved with the Kleinians. She responded to them.

If a young analyst only quotes the senior people of his own institute, I don't mind, but somebody who has the freedom to do that shouldn't have done it. What did Hartmann leave out? Object relations theory or its development. That damaged the analysis of the Oedipus complex. He also left out the developmental study of the drives. To dismiss the concept of the death drive as an anachronism from a biological viewpoint is highly questionable. Psychoanalysis is the only science that has evidence of the intensity of aggression. We tend towards self-destruction. There's a tremendous temptation to do that. That's a major finding by Freud. If I had three hours, I could fill them with clinical evidence for that. Hartmann neglected to maintain the developments of the drives, both of sexuality and aggression (although the study of perversion and perversity went on slowly, particularly in France, in contrast to aggression, which was all over the place in Great Britain as well as in Europe), and here's the paradox, the centrality of the Oedipus complex. His neglect of the preoedipal pathology Tony already talked about. The focus on the preoedipal had curious consequence for the Kleinians. On the one hand, they pulled the superego into the first year of life, they pulled the Oedipus complex into the first year of life, because they wanted to combine Freud's statement about the relationship between superego and the Oedipus complex, but, on the other hand, the focus on the preoedipal dynamics was such that, for practical purposes in their clinical work, the Kleinians underemphasize sexuality to this day. If you look into the wonderful book by Roy Schafer[72] about the contemporary Kleinians in London and look at the clinical examples, you will note the relative neglect of sexuality. André has made this point often in conferences, that there is a neglect of sexuality is very true. The neglect of sexuality is also a consequence of the Hartmann era. It also has to do with the puritanical atmosphere of the American culture.

The whole concept of linear versus hierarchical development is a major problem of the Hartmann era. In all fairness, that was a radical contribution

---

72. Schafer, R., ed. (1997). *The Contemporary Kleinians of London*. Madison, CT: International Universities Press.

by Lacan, but Lacan did himself in by his crazy insistence on the brief hour. If Lacan had all his concepts but had continued with the standard analytic hour, he would not have been expelled and psychoanalysis would have been enriched.

The relationship to the two main boundaries, biology and sociology. In practice, Hartmann created an isolation between psychoanalysis and the other disciplines. This brings me to the crucial issue of the mind/body problem, because one could say that Hartmann protected a purely psychoanalytic perspective, but he really didn't because, on the one hand, in theory, he wanted to link the different disciplines and sacrifice depth if necessary. That was damaging to psychoanalytic development. We have to look at what's going on in biology. Affect theory is the traversible bridge between mind and body. Morty mentioned the direct influence of chemical substances for affects. There is clinical evidence that drugs affect sexual excitement and fantasy. Research evidence shows that what we call *empathy* can be described as affective communication by ways that can be observed and studied scientifically outside the psychoanalytic situation.

André's charge has a crucial point; it's the nodal point of theory formation. This is not the subject of today's meeting, but I would also want to comment. His presentation contains a wonderful summary of Freud's approach, plus André's contribution to it. If we think that the entrance of peak affect states into the mind are the representation of what's going on in the body, plus the motivational direction created by their object representation, as André has pointed out, then we can raise the question, do they create at the same time the rudimentary self-experience?

Green: Just let me add a comment. This can lead both ways, from the somatic to the object or from the object to the somatic.

Kernberg: This has implications. Think of theories of depression. There is no doubt that if somebody whom we love dies, we get depressed. I'm saying something banal, but what does it mean? That a human experience in reality triggers a catastrophe in the intrapsychic world and finally ends up in biology in the symptoms of depression. If we have the biochemical disposition to a disorganization of the system, this can be triggered from the inside, a catastrophe that transforms the external world. We have a two-way street there. That does not mean that we can easily and clinically go from the structural intrapsychic meaning to the structure of biology. We have to avoid this banal simplification. Drugs may not change psychic structure but by affecting intensity they can cause certain sexual fantasies to disappear even if they have no effect on sexual performance. Psychic structure cannot be reduced to biological structure. When I talk about psychic structure, I'm not talking only about the ego, superego, and id, but the structure of fantasy in self representative–object representative affect units: the object relations "building blocks" of psychic structure. When Freud spoke of the border between the body and the mind, he didn't imply that we would never get beyond his preliminary formulation.

Grossman: Does the affect or the drive change?

Kernberg: The change is in intensity of affect, but it affects the drive.

Grossman: Is it change in the drive that alters fantasy life?

Kernberg: From what we know, the affect is affected directly by chemicals. To say that the chemical effect directs the drive is an extrapolation for which we have no evidence. I believe that we are not born with the drives, the drives develop. I agree with Laplanche, not with André. This hypothesis is not an act of faith. I'm willing to change my view about it, but at this moment my view is that we are born with the capacity for highly differentiated intense affective states and that the affect states immediately create representations as well as discharge, and subjective experience, and facial expression. The affects are a package deal that contains what Freud attributed to the drives, except that the affects do not replace the synthesis that Freud achieved in his dual drive theory. If you try to analyze the patient's unconscious conflicts in terms of affect theory, you end in total chaos. If you analyze it further, you get conflicts and drives. This is clinically significant and permits conceptual clarity. Freud followed the right road by his tremendous intuition. I think that the integration of libidinally tinged pleasurable affects create the erotic drive and that the integration of the aversive painful affects create the aggressive drive. I am talking about both rage and hatred and the development of sexual excitement. I think that, clinically, the drives are the hierarchically supraordinate organization. They are expressed concretely in internalized object relations under the impact of peak affect states, always integrated in the relation between self and object representation.

Ostow: Affect and fantasy can be analyzed together.

Kernberg: They cannot be analyzed separately. Affect always has a cognitive implication, and primitive cognition always has an affect implication. I think that this conception also permits us to analyze the nature of primary process, condensation, and displacement. Language has a similar structure. For

Lacan, it was language. There is a similarity between the structure of affect and language, in addition to the fact that language gets infiltrated with conflicts. Style reflects unconscious conflict, which was contributed to mostly by David Lieberman, a Kleinian who nobody knows because he wrote in Spanish and he's a Kleinian ego psychologist.

Hartmann talked about neutralization, and I must confess that I cannot avoid thinking that he was in part responding to the Kleinians, who had a concept of neutralization and the integration of split or contradictory internalized objects. Hartmann was trying to pick up their conclusions, which clinically was incontrovertible, couldn't be argued with, but he took it out of context. This is what explains neutralization. I've tried hard to understand what he means by it. As far as I'm concerned, it's an empty statement and nothing else, unless you put behind it an object relations theory.

The next thing, the study of infant development and child development. There is one thing that I'm glad Al put in such a strong form, saying that "Hartmann and Anna Freud trusted that their observation of children would lead to significant changes in psychoanalytic theory." It is highly questionable, not because empirical research and observation cannot lead to influence our theories and change them, but because the road is infinitely more complicated. It's the same thing as saying that empirical research on sessions of patients will change psychoanalytic technique. I have been involved in psychotherapy research for 20 years. We are barely now at the point where we can start demonstrating a few key issues that psychoanalysts have known for 40 years.

Look at Lester Laborsky, who is probably the most distinguished empirical researcher. What has he done? He has demonstrated with complicated techniques that it is possible to objectify transference that seems to do justice to what's really going on between patient and therapist and, in turn, is related to the patient's improvement. Look at the depth of what I've just said. You may say that's trivial. Thirty years for that? How can it be true? It's just that we are beginning to develop methodology. It may take another 30 years, and to think that from the observation of children we're going to learn about the sexual excitement and the sexual fantasy of children in a culture that forbids research on child sexuality, in a country like the United States, where it's strictly forbidden. . . .

We know there are four factors about sexual development: core gender identity, gender role identity, object choice, and intensity of sexual excitement. Three of these issues are the kind of things we know about in development. The most important, however, whether we choose somebody from the other sex or somebody from our sex, is totally shrouded in ignorance because of the prohibitions against that aspect of research, and deep prohibitions in psychoanalysis itself are interfering. The interference with research at the point when it is most crucial will slow down the development of research.

In the long run, I trust that empirical research will have an important contribution, but the grandiosity of it has turned off those who are sitting on the "hermeneutic" side. I'm in disagreement with those who in principle reject empirical research. We will disappear if we object to our developing scientific research in a broader sense. Hartmann's attitude made us lose 20 years. You can say that we can't blame him. He couldn't know that. But the atmosphere that he created in psychoanalytic institutes, anybody who was doing research wasn't the right analyst. Anybody who wasn't doing anything in his daily life except doing analysis was not the right analyst. The rigidity, the death drive at work in our psychoanalytic institutions in this country, has been costly and now we are paying the price.

The nature of the Oedipus complex: that's perhaps less crucial, but there's so much to learn from that craziness of Oedipus at a primitive level. It was eliminated by eliminating primitive object relations theory. Again, I think we owe it to Lacan. There are very important things that have been learned there.

Just to go to the other boundary, to the social and cultural. It is true that during the Hartmann era the only thing we had was Bion's work on small groups. By 1959, Bion had written his book, *Experiences in Groups*,[73] and that was pre-Kleinian. Bion did it before he was brainwashed. Melanie Klein apparently forbade him to do that work, and he stopped doing anything on groups until she died and then he resumed.

Yorke: It largely stemmed from Bion's wartime experiences.

Kernberg: Pierre Turquet used Bion's concept to study the psychology of large groups. That happened in the late 1950s, and it is true, they couldn't have yet integrated it. Anzieu started working on this around the '60s.[74] There was an entire school in Switzerland and France to study mass psychology.

In the United States, Jacob Arlow's *Study of Myth* moved in the same direction. But he missed the connection with everything going on in Great Britain. In the United States the study of the connection between individual and group psychology, of the capacity for regression in groups, of our disposition to study mass psychology, was discouraged, as well as the study of the nature

73. Bion, W. (1959). *Experiences in Groups*. London: Tavistock.
74. Anzieu, V. D. (1966). Étude psychoanalytique de groupe reals (Psychoanalytic approach of natural groups). *Temps Moderne* 22:56–73.

of character and how it is molded by culture. For example, masochism in women takes the form of masochistic love relations. Masochism in men takes the form of masochistic submission to unreasonable work conditions. There is a world there to be explored: the integration of ideology into the superego. Talcott Parsons made a beginning of this, but we didn't pick it up psychoanalytically. The most important contribution to this was done by Edith Jacobson. Wilhelm Reich in *Character Analysis*, had already started to work on the relationship between character and social structure. He went bananas, but there were some real concrete issues that then were picked up in the study by the Palo Alto people on the authoritarian personality, outside the psychoanalytic realm. In expelling the culturalists, we lost interest in cultural research.

Regarding, technique, I would like to say that Ed Glover's textbook[75] on technique is really the first, and a magnificent textbook on technique. There are still today things in it that can be learned from it, although it's written in an old-fashioned terminology.

Bergmann: In 1927 Glover published an earlier version of that text in the International.

Kernberg: Ego psychological technique predates the Hartmann era and reached a culmination with Fenichel. Although Greenson expanded it, basically the main concept came from Fenichel. That led to the analysis of character and, if that had been matched with the Kleinian analysis of primitive object relations, it could have enriched enormously the technical approach. Ego psychology couldn't do it because of the elimination of object relations theory. Helen Tartakoff picked up the old descriptions from Riviere and from Abraham and from Freud. The material was there. We didn't use it technically because Hartmann's influence eliminated the other technical instruments that could have enriched an ego psychological approach, an important shortcoming. It is true that, within ego psychology, we had some important contributions, Tony's work, Paul Gray's work. In fact, you can go into the unconscious from various levels. The important aspects of technique were taken on by the Kleinians. By contrast, the technique of the Hartmann group suffered from superficialization: you have to be very cautious, you have to go slowly, the transference doesn't develop. We knew that the transference is there from session one, but in Loewenstein it's first the gathering of the transference, then comes the transference neurosis. The rigidity of the general schema interfered, and then led

---

75. Glover, E. (1955). *The Technique of Psychoanalysis*. New York: International Universities Press.

to Merton Gill's revolution, and then we went overboard into the other direction. I think that was a basic mistake in Merton Gill's approach that led to the
extreme position.

Kris: You mentioned Helen Tartakoff's paper.[76] So far as I know, the main
patient killed himself and, I think, at that time Helen Tartakoff and the group
of senior analysts didn't have a clue how to treat such a patient.

Kernberg: But that was the first step. If there hadn't been the censorship,
they would have been more successful. Joan Riviere wrote about technique in
the 1930s.[77] They would have been aware, but when Melanie Klein wrote about
envy and gratitude[78] she opened the entire field to technique, but that was
the book that, of course, was not taught in this country until the last 15 years.

Regarding Hartmann's differentiation between the ego and self, Hartmann
really made an important contribution in defining the concept of the self as
opposed to the concept of the ego, although that again opened a can of worms.
Edith Jacobson explored it in part. There are all kinds of adaptations. Our
capacity to interact at a conscious level with environment, to perceive, to have
memory, perception, action, many of these functions are really automatized
in the sense that the basic neurological structures that permit its functioning
are independent from conflict. It is true that we perceive colors, not because
we have solved oedipal issues. Even schizophrenic patients can pay a taxi. There
are a number of neurobiological functions that are gathered at the service of
the personality, but here we come to the self as a central ego structure and its
compositional self-representations, its relation to internal objects, and its translation into character, because when we talk about character and character
pattern we have to deal with the unconscious world of object relations and its
relation to the outside world. Freud himself used the term *Ich* to refer both to
that self-structure and to the impersonal functions. The whole emphasis on
the general neurobiological functions of the ego detracts from the fact that what
is essential in the personality is identity, and by identity I'm saying self-

---

76. (1966). "The normal personality in our culture and the Nobel Prize complex."
In *Psychoanalysis: A General Psychology, Essays in Honor of Heinz Hartmann*, ed. R.
Loewenstein et al. New York: International Universities Press.

77. Joan Riviere wrote the following important works: (1929). Womanliness as
a masquerade. *International Journal of Psycho-Analysis* 19:303–313; (1932). Jealousy
as a mechanism of defense. *International Journal of Psycho-Analysis* 13:414–424; (1936).
A contribution to the analysis of the negative therapeutic reaction. *International Journal
of Psycho-Analysis* 17:304–320.

78. Klein, M. (1957). *Envy and Gratitude*. New York: Basic Books.

concept, identity as the subjective part of character, or the behavioral part of identity. That's what we are interested in. I'm not saying that that doesn't include a number of neurobiological functions, but the whole discussion of autonomous ego dilutes what is essentially psychoanalytic. We go through life in many ways functioning objectively, doing work, cooking, and unconsciously trying to gratify aggressive and sexual needs that determine the nature of our relationships, happiness or unhappiness, self-destructiveness or effectiveness. That's what psychoanalysis is all about. George Bataille, a French philosopher who wrote a book[79] on eroticism that is probably the best book on eroticism that exists in the literature, says that our life oscillates between the ordinary time—space of daily life and the intensity of ecstasies, ecstasies of religion, of aggression and sexuality, and their interconnection. You can see the influence of psychoanalytic thinking behind that. Psychoanalysis has to deal with that dimension of ecstasy, the romantic dimension if you want. That's what we're all about and how this relates to ordinary life. What the Hartmann atmosphere did was to try to make it all uniform.

We have to work on the boundary with biology, concretely. We have to work on the boundary with sociology, but to work on the boundary of sociology by studying how the unconscious influenced the creation of the Nazi and Communist regimes and puritanical cultures. Psychoanalysis has to be concerned as much with external reality in this regard as with individuals. One day, when I expressed my interest in the psychoanalytic study of groups, I was told, "You have abandoned psychoanalysis. You have no business dealing with groups." We have to learn from our French colleagues. The Kleinians did the same for many years. In a strange way, Lacan freed the French psychoanalytic community from a rigidity.

Regarding psychoanalysis and psychotherapy, André spoke about doing psychoanalysis sitting up. What I've done is to try to treat patients who most people would not put on the couch, very sick individuals. I continue doing that with patients with antisocial behavior, severe self-mutilation, and chronic suicidal tendencies. Although I've had failures, I've also had very significant successes, which have been attributed to me as a therapist but I think that that's a way of denying the fact that I've been trying to contribute to a technique, and we have now proved that very different people can do exactly the same thing. This is an application of psychoanalytic theory to modification of technique for these sick patients. It is a technique that is not supportive; I'm sharply critical of the mixture of support and expressive psychotherapy. I am apply-

79. Bataille, G. (1957). *Death and Sensuality: A Study of Eroticism and the Taboo.* English translation, 1962. New York: Walker & Company.

ing a strictly psychoanalytic technique; it's not standard psychoanalysis. In this country, if I had said, this is psychoanalysis, I would now be dead. I called it *psychoanalytic psychotherapy* to survive, and it made no difference how it's called so long as it's clear what the technique is. The Kleinians say this is not analysis, and they are perfectly right. When I talk to the British independents, they say, "We've done this all the time, this is psychoanalysis." When I talk to the French analysts in a symposium on psychotherapy, they also told me that they do this all the time. One of the most intelligent leading analysts of the French-Canadian group told me, "You're not telling us anything new." So it could be called psychoanalysis there. The boundaries between psychotherapy and psychoanalysis are affected by ideology and our insecurity. It is also a consequence of the Hartmann era that we are so afraid, so insecure that we have to create very strict boundaries.

Kris: You just said it doesn't depend on the personality, other people can do it. I suppose you meant that it doesn't depend on your specific personality. It is hard to picture that you could work with such patients without using your personality.

Kernberg: Everybody has to use their personality. I have not talked about the use of medication because that has theoretical implications and practical ones. I have no problem with the practical ones.

Bergmann: It seems to me that we are succeeding to move rather well at the cost of some discussion to be sure, but if we can give Peter a chance, then we can give André Green a chance to speak about infant observation. Finally, we will have a chance to ask any questions.

Neubauer: I feel overwhelmed by all the things I've heard. For me, it is more important to determine why are there shifts from the Hartmann era to object relations theory, to intersubjectivity? What are the causes of the shift from one era to another? It reminds me naturally of Kuhn's work[80] on the paradigm. Does the lack of success in our practice demand new explorations beyond those that already have been undertaken? Or is the process of theory formation by itself in need of reformulation in order to accommodate new thoughts in order to assess the Hartmann era?

---

80. Kuhn, T. S. (1962). *The Structure of Scientific Revolutions*. Chicago: University of Chicago Press.

When I speak about the ego and its various aspects, I may be able to make connections outside the usual psychoanalytic area of investigation that are likely to lead outside of analysis proper. Some blame Hartmann for having led us astray, and we blame him for promising a theory of general psychology that he could not fulfill. Some blame him for somehow diminishing the psychoanalytic perspective. It is interesting for me to raise the question historically: Why was this period succeeded by the object relation schools? How did they come about? I can understand the transition from the first theory of anxiety to the second theory of anxiety, and from the topographical to the structural. Why then to object relations?

About infant observation, including observations during therapy, patients expressed themselves primarily nonverbally. We do not check what we observe. André's statement, "Theory depends on how it's going to be used." It's a question of finding further information. When we think about the infant at 6 or 8 weeks able to differentiate the social smile from the usual smile of physical pleasure, when we see at 7 or 8 months the stranger reaction, we speak of the developmental sequences and differentiation. We observe such milestones. What happens when analysts use this information and put it into the psychoanalytic frame of reference? What does one learn about the development of the ego that a social smile can occur, that the affective state of tuning has advanced so much at 6 weeks that there is already an orchestration on the affective level within the object and the self to produce such a smile? Can the stranger anxiety teach us something about primacy of drive representation or affect regulation and their differentiation? Take Margaret Mahler; her data came from observation in a nursery school. It did not come from the treatment of children.

Bergmann: It came from a theory that was imposed on the observation, and the theory came from Mahler being a psychoanalyst.

Neubauer: This is true when the analyst is an infant observer, but for some people these observations are outside the psychoanalytic province. There were six steps that Mahler had in sequences that she considered at that time to be ego areas, but obviously they are steps in the object relations function between the object outside and inside. What did we do with it? We employed it in our psychoanalytic work when we listened to patients. That means we use observation and data and check these theoretically and clinically.

All of this gives us information on how a certain level of knowledge has to be translated to fit into the psychoanalytic domain, for instance genetic reconstruction. The information that we get from infant observation and from observation of children is extraordinarily rich. It can be misused and can lead away from the psychoanalytic momentum or it can enrich us. However, when understood and used correctly, it contributes greatly to our understanding of our patients. A very good other example is the observation of play in children, by Winnicott.[81] Winnicott understood that play taking place in a space is more than children exposing their internal world. Expression in play was an important new source of information. He had the theoretical frame of reference to understand and explain the area of psychic life where play takes place.

Hartmann noted that early infancy is the period of the child's dependence on touch, perception, and object relations. What is primary autonomy? I think this term has to be separated from conflict-free sphere. The accent in the concept of conflict-free is on sphere, not on conflict-free. There are areas in the mind that are less engaged in conflict than others. What conflict is one free from? What is the nature of conflicts? Are there conflicts between the drives, between ego and aggression? Are there structural conflicts?

There are processes at work that follow certain patterns, which cannot just be explained by the conflictual model alone. Therefore, if autonomy refers to primary autonomy, in connection with object interaction, we then could follow it today. He speaks about primary autonomy as withstanding environmental influences. This is a point worthwhile to pursue.

Hartmann stayed with the observation of the ego and its structure. He was interested in developmental studies, but he did not pursue the developmental progression and the changes that occur over a period of time. The contributions of Anna Freud recognize the developmental dimension in a new sense. It was not genetics with extension, it was the forward reorganization and not only the reconstruction of the past. It was a study of the laws that govern the developmental processes.

Freud outlined the psychoanalytic theory of development. His three contributions made that incredible, original observation. He discovered phases of development that are discontinuous, where the earlier and more immature is left behind in order for new hierarchy to emerge, the phallic predominance to take over, the oedipal phase to supersede over it. Piaget then also proposes discontinuity in development. Freud did it by adding a new clinical development. His propositions permit us to state, with an adult or a child, in and to which phase of development there may be a regression or fixation. Freud showed us a linkage between normal developmental conflicts and pathology, but he did some-

---

81. Winnicott, D. W. (1971). *Playing and Reality*. London: Tavistock. See also Solnit, A., Cohen, D., and Neubauer, P. eds. (1993). *The Many Meanings of Play*. New Haven: Yale University Press.

thing much more. Thus the extension of psychoanalysis to include a study of development permitted Freud to propose new clinical vistas.

Mahler gives us the six stages. They are object related, very clear, precise and useful. She never could make a linkage between the separation individuation states and the libidinal phases of development. Even though John McDevitt[82] for the last 20 years has asked to study aggression from a Mahlerian point of view, he has not succeeded in linking the drive component with the object relations. I asked Mahler once why her separation individuation phases do not correlate with Freud's psychosexual phases. Mahler said that she could not do more than she has already contributed.

Infant observation and child observation can obviously be influenced by psychoanalytic theory, which informs the observer, and the other way around. It seems that we have a particular advantage in observing the infant in its early period. That advantage helps us to clarify speculations about the first year of life. Melanie Klein thought in terms of the first year of life.

Where psychoanalytic investigation by the method of psychoanalytic theory cannot explore early stages of development or ego functions such as the ego apparatus, data from observation and other fields will be of help to us. I have mentioned a number of attempts, in addition to Hartmann, that seek to determine new directions, at least give us additional data, to enlarge our knowledge. After the school of object relations, what will be the next focus that the history of psychoanalysis will take?

Bergmann: Wonderful. I think we should hear from André.

Green: I followed Peter's vibrant discussion on infant observation. The general position of the French admits the centrality of the Oedipus complex. We avoid using the expression preoedipal—though Freud used it himself—because we consider that the Oedipus complex starts from the beginning of life, because the parents' Oedipal structure has an influence on the infant at birth and even before. We speak of pregenital rather than preoedipal. All this is borrowed from Lacan.

Neubauer: Does pregenital mean prephallic?

Green: To some extent, yes, because the Oedipus complex is dominated by castration anxiety, therefore by the reference to the phallic stage. The reason

---

82. McDevitt, J. B. (1997). The continuity of conflict and compromise formation from infancy to adulthood: a twenty-five year follow-up study. *Journal of the American Psychoanalytic Association* 45:105–126.

for such terminology is that, under Lacan's influence, the Oedipus complex was not seen as a phase but as a structure. We use the word *structure* in a very different meaning from the one borrowed from Hartmann's terminology. This also should deserve a discussion. The structure as related to structuralism and the structure as related to Hartmann's theory are two different things.

The second point I would like to make is that it is a real pity that a small book on the death instinct, recently issued, has not been translated into English. This book collects the proceedings of a research conference of the European Federation of Psychoanalysis in Marseilles in 1984.[83] There were four main papers presented by Hanna Seagull, Reichert, Laplanche, and myself, with a discussion by Clifford Yorke. Not all of them agreed with Freud's theory of the death instinct. There were various points of view expressed, but it is interesting that the book, which is not very thick, has never been translated into English. Obviously the concerns of the Europeans are not shared on the other side of the Atlantic, as if the question was considered there as settled once and for all. Mr. President,[84] do something about it.

To come to infant observation: the sentence I selected from Freud was, "The possibility of an energic influence rests on quite definite preconditions which can be summed up under the term 'analytic situation'; it requires the development of certain psychical structures and a particular attitude to the analyst. Where these are lacking, as in the case of children, something other than analysis must be used."[85] For Freud, psychoanalytic theory could not be constructed genetically because *it was the end that provided the key to the beginning*. Freud anticipated T. S. Eliot. You have to wait until the structures arrive at maturity in order to see retrospectively how they had been constructed, in view of reaching what aims, but the goal is there from the beginning, though not quite detectable through observation. What is here implied is probably that the state of affairs that appears openly in the end is present *in germ* (i.e., sometimes not in any testifiable form) in the beginning. The opposite point of view (to start from the beginning) will never be able to detect these "germinal" features and, is likely to catch our attention and derive it on others, which may exist but are considered irrelevant or insignificant in view of a building of a psychoanalytic theory. A psychoanalytic theory implies the

---

83. Green, A. et al. *La pulsion de mort*. Paris: Presses Universitaires de France, 1986.

84. The reference is to Otto Kernberg, currently the president of the International Psychoanalytic Association.

85. Freud, S. (1925). Preface to Aichorn's *Wayward Youth, Standard Edition* 19:274.

postulate of the prevalence of the unconscious determinants of psychic activity. You will never reach the end goal by starting from the beginning, and trying to follow step by step where it goes because your assumptions of what is in the beginning will determine the end product, this is why, Peter, you very honestly recognized that Mahler's work could not coincide with Freud's work. We are dealing with two different theoretical attitudes.

I would like now to come to research. If I had only to listen to what you say, I would heartily approve. Unfortunately, this is not the current situation. Mahler's work was discussed and her conclusions rejected by modern infant researchers. Much if not all of Stern's work goes against Mahler and now we, as the analytic community, have the responsibility to evaluate Daniel Stern's ideas. If you look at Daniel Stern's work, there is nothing psychoanalytical in it anymore. Robert Emde, who is a psychoanalyst, turns away also from psychoanalytical theory and prefers the ideas of so-called scientific psychologists.

Kris: Spell that out a little bit more. Take time. Why is it not psychoanalytic?

Green: My paper[86] contains ten points against Daniel Stern's[87] concept of protonarrative envelopes, which is a total construct of science fiction. It uses a mixture of concepts borrowed here and there: some belong to psychoanalysis, some others to psychology, some others to phenomenology—a patchwork theory. Robert Emde's neglect of psychoanalytic concepts is remarkable. He published a paper[88] on imaginative reality that ignored the concept of psychic reality. His point of view is derived also from psychological concepts. Psychoanalytical concepts have little room in his work. Other contributions, as Emmanuel Peterfreund's,[89] show that this trend is not a recent fashion. He too is ignorant of psychoanalytic epistemology. He brings up empirical research to reformulate psychoanalytic theory. Instead of methodology we find analogy. To show such an oversimplification about the epistemological problem of what is methodology in psychoanalysis is deplorable. The latest example in

---

86. Green, A. Science and science fiction in infant research. Unpublished paper read before the London conference in October, 1997 (in press).

87. Stern, D. N. (1992). Enveloppe prenarrative du bébé. *Journal de la psychoanalyse de l'enfant* 4.

88. Emde, R. N., Kubicek, L., and Oppenheimer, D. (1997). "Imaginative reality observed during early language development." *International Journal of Psycho-Analysis* 78:115–134.

89. Peterfreund, E. (1978). Some clinical comments on psychoanalytic conceptualization of infancy. *International Journal of Psycho-Analysis* 59:427–441.

favor of this objectivistic approach is Peter Fonagy. He wrote a paper in 1982 that is thoughtful. But since he radicalized his opinion moving away from his cautiousness in the beginning.[90] What is the difference between Fonagy's work and some of the pioneers like Spitz and Mahler? Their work belongs to our discipline, their investigations try to fit with the requirements of science, but not at the expense of the originality of the facts seen with psychoanalytic eyes, that is, with their specificity and complexity as witnessed in the supposedly "nonscientific" conceptions born from the clinical setting. In contrast, in Fonagy's systematic approach, evidence would come from so-called scientific procedures that are alien to our discipline, and the conclusions are those in accordance to procedures that deny analytic specificity.

What are the grounds for infant observation? The ground is to observe as soon as possible the exchange between the baby and the mother. Most of the time, the results of observations are meant to confirm or to confirm the ideas of psychoanalytic theory. Infant observation means relating what one sees in a relationship between the infant or the child with an object, or what one sees and concludes from what can be deciphered by sight of the relationship between the child and his mother. This is an oversimplification of what is going on, because it does not take into account that the father is in the mother's mind since the beginning. Bion tells us that the mother has a capacity for reverie.[91] The reverie may be about the child or related to the father. Denise Braunschweig and Michel Fain emphasized this double relationship.[92] What is specific to the role of the mother?

In all these studies, mothers have no sexuality. They feed infants, but they do not feel anything in their breasts. They hold him tight, but this contact seems to be without feelings of pleasure. *In my own conception of the oedipal triangulation the mother is occupying a unique position, characterized by the fact that she is the only member of the triangular situation who has a bodily relationship to both the two others.* Neither the child nor the father has this privilege, and this totally changes the situation. It makes feminine sexuality a very conflictual issue for the woman, split between the spouse and the mother. What are the consequences of this state of things in the child–mother relationships, considering the role of mutual repressions? This can disappear in what is observable but does not suppress the effects of the repressed and in the unconscious, which will only be

---

90. Fonagy, P. (1982). The integration of psychoanalysis and experimental science, *International Review of Psycho-Analysis* 9:125–145.

91. Bion, W. R. (1962). *Learning from Experience*. London: William Heinemann Medical Books, pp. 35–36.

92. Braunschweig, D., and Fain, M. (1971). *Éros et Antéros*. Paris: Editions Payot.

testable through the return of the repressed. If the return of the repressed is not linked with the hypothesis of a sexual bond between mother and child, the findings are inconsistent. It makes things easier to "forget" the role of the mother's sexual feelings in the relationship. Who can deny that we have fallen back on pre-Freudian psychology? This does not mean that we are alluding to a full sexual relationship in these exchanges. We have the aim-inhibited drives to characterize them. An aim-inhibited drive is still a drive activity.

How can we guess anything about the intrapsychic within such a setting? In the past, I had a personal exchange with Margaret Mahler, whom I saw first at the symposium on personality disorders in Topeka in 1976. I was interviewed by her, asking what I thought about her work. I said that I believed that her work was very interesting for psychology, but not for psychoanalysis. She was, of course, not very happy. We continued our discussion the whole evening, and separated. Yet when we met socially two years after, in New York, she came, sat next to me, and told me, "So you still don't believe in my work." I said, "Yes, I'm afraid I have to say that." She replied to me, and I hope you'll trust my quotation, "You're right about the intrapsychic world. We cannot say anything with our methodology." She admitted that. How can we think as psychoanalysts that we will be observing a situation involving two partners, either the observer and the child, or the child and some other person, without thinking that what we observe is the result, at bottom, of the connection of two intrapsychic worlds? While you gain from seeing things from outside, you seem to forget that the intrapsychic world of each of the persons is completely out of reach. Or you adopt an interbehavioristic point of view, throwing away *two* black boxes. This is exactly contrary to the clinical situation, in which the analyst has always in mind what is supposed to happen in the patient's mind and what is supposed to happen in his own mind too, and tries to analyze the transference. This goes hand in hand with Tony's remarks about countertransference. Would you say you are able to guess the content of a book by observing someone reading it? Even if he talks about it to some other participant of the scene, are you not hearing what he is saying?

Now we shift to the concepts drawn from infant observation. The present trend in intersubjectivity says that you have to observe what happens in your body, in relationship to the patient. That refers to "enactment." This is a shift of models; the model is no longer representation, with all the varieties we have described, it is action. The concept of action comes to the fore in the form of interaction. "Inter" is less important than action. Action is meant to fill the gap created by our ignorance of what happens inside both poles united in action: subject and object. Throwing away the model of the drives was not a very productive intellectual approach. A highly qualified psychoanalyst like Owen Renick will say that first we have to notice the action and then construct the representation afterwards and that it is impossible to think before something happens in the field of action. I will not expand on that, but I believe that the change of model is the consequence of the progressive rejection, step by step, of drive theory. One should observe that drive theory also includes a reference to action (as a result of drive discharge) but with reference to an internal source that has to be worked through. A consequence of all approaches that focus on the interrelationship in a situation observed from outside, and not indirectly (and hypothetically) related to the inside world of the object you are investigating, which involves the necessity of the concept of representation, is to bring theory back to a causality that only considers the effect of an external relationship. Representation itself is a consequence of the pressure of drives.

Kris: In Owen Renik's mind, action is trial thought.[93]

Green: This is already in Freud's paper on "Two principles" (1911). This resurrection of the hypothesis of probe with small expenditures of energy is with the intersubjectivists in the context of a pragmatic model from which many theories of language have derived. Yet one is able to analyze this on an epistemological basis. It is the substitution of the mother as an active partner for her representation, which is at the basis of Freudian theory. The model of pragmatism is now predominant in all fields. You can witness the change in the conception of language from Chomsky's syntactic structures, to the model of the pragmatists (Austin, Searle), with the emphasis on the performative. In psychoanalysis it started with Schafer's action language and now is developing as a model; for Merton Gill, every interpretation is an action. This is less a discovery than an hypothesis, an epistemological strategy, a change of paradigm that calls for criticism. The differences remain in fact, otherwise you may advocate to act with the patient instead of talking to him. Here we are back to Ferenczi. What claims to be new has already occurred in the history of psychoanalysis in other circumstances in different forms. To blur the difference between thinking as action and action as acting is just a tactic to avoid building a specific theory of thinking in psychoanalysis based on the drive model and its working through representation. Of course, the drive model involves action, except that it is *internalized action*, less an action than a wish which wants to become a realization because of the impossibility to reach the object

---

93. Renick said speech is a form of action (p. 554) in his 1993 paper, Analytic interaction: conceptualizing technique in the light of the analyst irreducible subjectivity. *Psychoanalytic Quarterly* 62:553–571.

or to touch it, or, in other words, to act with it. To touch, to act are related to drive gratifications. The model of action is, in fact, reversed with the drive, because it is the journey from the source to the aim which makes the difference with the model of action which is stimulated by an external source and gives way to motor action. It is not right to neglect the difference because the drive model stresses the importance of the subject's structure to determine the meaning of his deeds. The subject is less "acting" than is "acted on" (by his drives). The action model which was created to define voluntary action is based on the illusion of consciousness as linked with will for the sake of reassuring the subject on his power having overcome his helplessness. The action inside draws you to act out, but you have to refrain, you have to repress or you have to transform.

Anna Freud's differentiated the real child from the reconstructed child. My assumption is that the real child is lost forever. It can never be recovered, reconstructed hypothetically. What is definitely lost is less what the child was but what *he* thought. We are dealing with the child *in the adult*. I do not believe that analysis is a work of reconstruction. I think it is rather the work of *construction*. What is the aim of construction? Arriving at a conception of the patient's mind that the patient can share with the analyst as being an approximation (Bion) to truth in a successful analysis. If patient and analyst agree that the picture built in an analysis is an approximation to the historical truth, it has necessarily some relationship with the past. Of course, it is not a photograph of the past. The picture is lost forever, if it has ever existed. You have to be consistent with what you have analyzed, and it is the consistency of the construction that is important *according to psychoanalytic thinking*. The consistency of the construction is based on the patient's mental functioning. Do I mean that there is nothing to say about infant observation? Not at all. Freud showed us with the "fort-da" example[94] how much he could draw from a very banal situation that everybody can observe, just as Winnicott[95] has also shown us that his very sophisticated thinking started from the awareness of the importance of transitional objects. Mothers have always known that children are very attached to a piece of woolen tissue, or to a blanket, or to a teddy bear, but Winnicott was the first to coin the function of what he called *transitional object* and to theorize its significance without using "scientific procedures." I disagree with the idea that the scientific method can, only by itself, promote

---

94. The fort-da example is borrowed from *Beyond the Pleasure Principle*, where Freud describes the game of his grandson with the cotton reel.
95. Winnicott, D. W. (1971). *Transitional Objects and Transitional Phenomena: Playing and Reality*. New York: International Universities Press.

these observations and I am pretty sure it does meet intrinsic limitations. There are two papers of Winnicott,[96] one on the string, the other on the spatula, that I consider major contributions to psychoanalytic theory; both lean on child observation, but both exist only through a psychoanalytic eye. Winnicott did not systematically film his children. He waited until something dawned upon him, just as Freud did.

We have here an epistemological choice. The most important paradigm of psychoanalysis is not the child, it is the dream. Whether you think of the dream as the central model or the child, you arrive at different conclusions. With the child, you have the idea of the prospective process from birth on to maturity. In analyzing a dream you analyze *in retrospect*. The patient mentions a dream that is *what has already happened to him*. He tells the dream, he associates, he evokes the day residues, and finally you become aware of the latent thoughts, which orients you to the dream work and to what has been important before the dream, the unnoticed, unconscious fantasy that led to this transformation that resulted in the dream. This is the basis of the *Nachträglichkeit* of which the French think so very highly. "Deferred action" is a bad translation.

If you look through all the works of the child researchers or infant researchers, you will see that they use the prefix *pre*—prerepresentation, prestructural, pregenital. This is a trick because what has to be explained and is supposed to come after the *pre* is explained already with the addition of the prefix *pre*. What follows the prefix in the word *pre-x* will include what is going to come, *x*, and waits for clarification. The important prefix in Freud is the *re*, the returning of, like in *re*presentation. What occurs in an event has little meaning because we have to wait till the mind has transformed it. Through the transformation we are able to know what is the work of the mind and what is the subject. The difference between the prospective and the retrospective approaches is that the latter went through the mind and cannot be reached by observing anything except what appears afterwards about it. At that time you can assume what the work of the mind has accomplished; that you cannot know before. This, for me, totally invalidates the model of the analytic interaction.

To come now to the question of the conflict-free sphere, the most important point for me, which has not been debated, is probably the impact of Piaget's work on Hartmann. Piaget never understood what psychoanalysis was about, though he claimed to have been analyzed. All of you remember Peter

---

96. Winnicott, D. W. (1960). String: a technique of communication. In *Maturation Processes and the Facilitating Environment*. New York: International Universities Press, 1965.

Wolf's paper[97] and the long debate that followed, questioning the present relevance of infant and child research to psychoanalytic theory. But the power of fashion is as strong as the power of illusion. The tendency to solve real psychoanalytic problems with tools that deny the specificity of psychoanalysis, and offer us answers that spare us the complexity of the facts our discipline tries to understand, has the effect of reassuring our intellect on its shortcomings and consoling ourselves on our ignorance.

Blum: I want to get to the issue of metaphor and multiple models, which has come up in a variety of ways. One of our problems is the reification of metaphor. Freud never meant the structural hypothesis to be anything more than metaphor. He never meant it to be taken concretely. One of our problems comes from Freud's own mixed metaphors. For example, the borderline, and transition between somatic and the psychic, can be looked on in terms of his metaphor of the body ego. Freud stated that the first ego is a body ego. You link the ego to the body, yet the ego is not the body. The body can be looked upon as the somatic substrate for the ego, but the ego is not really a body ego. The statement is a metapsychological construction. Take Hartmann's concept of the apparatuses: he tended to confuse the apparatus with the ego itself. What he was really talking about was the somatic substrate for certain ego functions. We have multiple models in Freud. We have the model of the child; we have topographic hypothesis optical models, we have fixation and regression military models, with so many troops being left behind and retreating and so forth. A study of models is of interest. For example, technically, he used archeological models, the lifting of what was buried and bringing it to the surface. We have to keep in mind at all times the advantages and disadvantages of metaphor and our own tendencies to concretize metaphors. Metaphors are indispensable, but we have to know how to use the metaphors, why we prefer specific metaphors, and the way in which metaphors may be reified.

I tend to agree with André's point about the dangers of child observations. One could discuss their use and abuse. I think he was somewhat pejorative about some of the people he mentioned. They may not know about psychoanalysis, but they do offer interesting research for us to think about and to evaluate its usefulness in relation to building psychoanalytic theory and

---

97. Wolf, P. (1996). The irrelevance of infant observations for psychoanalysis. *Journal of the American Psychoanalytic Association* 44:369–392. Followed by discussions by P. Tyson, B. Barrat, P. Fonagy, J. Osofsky, S. Seligman, T. Shapiro, and A. Wilson, pp. 392–474. See also Wolf, P. (1960). *The Developmental Psychologies of Jean Piaget and Psychoanalysis, Psychological Issues,* Monograph 5 (New York: International Universities Press).

understanding the psychoanalytic situation, for example, Otto's reference to affect research and to direct observation research. About the twin studies, they begin really *in utero* because the twins have a very different environment. They are usually of lower birth weight.

Neubauer: The second one is half a pound less at birth than the first one.

Blum: Sometimes more extreme. There's a greater probability of congenital defects with twins and a greater probability of low birth weight. So that the developmental line is impacted. On Hartmann's contributions and its limitations, he did introduce the term *genetic fallacy*, the tendency to misconstruct later aspects of development in terms of their earliest *anlage* because of developmental discontinuity. Some of the infant researchers fall into this error. The further one goes back, the more speculative our theories become; they become more a matter of conjecture and preference since there is no way of knowing what the intrapsychic world of the infant is.

As to the Hartmann era, the orthodoxy, the censorship, and the denial of what was going on in other areas of the analytic world and other areas of science was important. But it was not the only reason that the Hartmann era had such problems with dealing with borderline and narcissistic patients and the very ill. In 25 years, we've learned a lot more. It isn't just that they overlooked or refused to see, but that it took many years to really understand the developmental deficits, the developmental lags and disharmonies, the developmental inhibitions and arrests and the fact that some of the patients who failed had to come back. They couldn't separate and individuate. I am not prepared to completely discard Mahler. They couldn't separate and they had to come back because they needed the analyst as an organizing object; in Anna Freud's term it was an *auxiliary ego*. They also needed the analyst as a buddy to help them with the ordinary problems of life. It didn't become analysis for some of these people. It really became for some of them a supportive system or a safety net. Some of them came back again and again. Some of them ended up with psychotherapists. Looking back on it, with advances in theory and beginning integration of additional theory, we can understand these patients better, and begin to reformulate the way we thought about psychopathology. It was not only a matter of exclusion and rejection, but it was also a matter of the incremental learning that occurred over a 25-year period in analysis.

Bergmann: Clifford, I'm going to let you end the conference.

Yorke: I'm not capable at this stage of giving anything like the sustained and comprehensive addresses that we've heard this afternoon. I feel rather overwhelmed! I will simply comment on one or two points. Some of the observations made by my colleagues are so impressive that they call for a good deal of reflection. I would rather say, at the end of a conference of this kind, what an honor it is to be invited to take part in it.

On the matter of infant observation, I find it interesting to go back to the records kept by Anna Freud and Dorothy Burlingham[98] of the work at the wartime nurseries, to see how much that we take for granted today about development was discovered at that time. Some of the observations were very telling. For example, many parents then (as now) had the idea that, if children were sexually enlightened at an early age, it would be a great help to them and foster their sexual development in an appropriate way. It was found, in the wartime nurseries, that you could tell the children all the facts about sexuality, but subsequent observations showed that, even when they appeared to have understood, they hadn't changed their own theories one bit. Some educationalists could learn a lot from that. Incidentally, I am in accord with André in regarding the theories built up by Stern and Emde as no longer psychoanalytic.

Morty raised a question earlier that none of us addressed. It concerned the effect of drugs on psychic states. We know very well that drugs are capable of altering moods and affects. Some drug-induced psychoses show striking features. Amphetamine psychoses, for example, take the same form irrespective of the personality of the sufferer. There are always the persecutory delusions of a remarkably similar kind, and considerable fear surrounds them.

Peter referred to Anna Freud's work. Diagnosis—psychoanalytic diagnosis—was, for her, an essential prerequisite before *any* kind of treatment was considered. I always regarded the profile, as she had repeatedly said, as cross-section of the personality at the time the child (or adult) was assessed. But it needs to be supplemented by a consideration of the developmental lines. She herself regarded the developmental lines, collectively, as a different way of looking at diagnosis. I have always thought it helpful to put the two approaches together. At the Anna Freud Centre all children under 5 who were assessed diagnostically were also considered in terms of development lines (including the points along the line to which they had regressed, had been arrested at, or prematurely advanced towards), as well as by profile. I could never understand why one should stop at 5. I've never discovered an adult who'd reached the highest point on *every* developmental line. We all have defects somewhere. The profile and the developmental lines give a more complete picture of any

98. Freud, A., and Burlingham, D. (1943). *Infants Without Families.* London: Allen & Unwin. Reprinted in *Collected Writings, III*. New York: International Universities Press, 1973.

individual: they give both a vertical and cross-sectional view—a three-dimensional picture—of the individual.

Lastly, the question of the failure of psychoanalysis to help particular cases was a problem that Anna Freud was always keen to address. She thought we should look very closely at our failures. I recall a meeting in New York—at which Peter was present—when I presented a case that had failed to respond to analysis after some four years or so of analytic work. That presentation arose because some time before, Hannah Segal (who was president of our Society at the time) called me and said, "We've no Wednesday evening meeting this week because the person we signed up is ill and has canceled. Have you a case you could talk about?" I said the only case I had in my head that I could discuss at such short notice was a failure, and she said, "That's fine." Hannah Segal was in a chair and my fantasy was that many people would say the case was a failure because I hadn't handled it the right way; the Kleinians and perhaps many others would have handled it differently. Not a bit of it. Limentani opened the discussion and said, "I think that would have been a failure whatever had been done." And others, including Kleinians, followed suit. The case was one of developmental arrest. In New York, I remember that, at the end of the discussion, Peter said, "Thank God! I thought you were going to tell us that the case turned out all right!" People don't seem to mind presentations of failed cases; perhaps they feel they don't hear enough of them.

There are conditions that analysts can't help clinically, and we mustn't always relate our theory to conditions that respond to treament (this point was touched on earlier). A case of monsymptomatic hypochondriasis, for example, is virtually impossible to treat by *any* form of psychotherapy because the patient is totally unable to be interested, for more than a second or two at a time, in anything else except the part of his body in which he's so heavily invested. There are many other conditions, such as the depersonalization syndrome, that are refractory to psychoanalysis, but *that* shouldn't stop analysts from trying to understand the psychology of these states and conceptualize them. As long as we continue to try to do that, we may still be doing a useful job.

Bergmann: At the beginning I hoped that the sum total of what will emerge from the conference would be more than what is already in your presentation. My hope was more than fulfilled. We lived up to the model of Plato's Symposium, which the Oxford classical dictionary defined as "the setting for a series of contrasting speeches on a single philosophical topic, diversified by exchanges of dialogue." The original symposium was also a drinking party, and I hope that many readers of this work will find nourishment in it and stimulation for further work. This was a wonderful conference and I want to thank you all.

Neubauer: Martin, may we thank you for the preparation, for the platform you gave us for our discussion, for bringing us together, and your selection was excellent, particularly since you included me, and for the wonderful way in which you conducted it. I did not know that you had so much energy to cut us short sometimes, but I think we all owe you a debt and applause for what you did.

Furst: I want to thank you all on the part of the Fund. This has been truly one of our more memorable meetings. I must say that the level and openness of discussion here was truly exemplary. I'm now encouraged by the fact that we're going to go ahead and publish the results of our meeting as quickly as possible. What has been said here, and the papers that have been presented here, will be a landmark to be studied by interested people for a long while to come, and for that I'd like to thank you all.

EDITOR'S POST-CONFERENCE STATEMENT

Although the task of editing the minutes of this conference was not an easy one, my rewards were great. What the distinguished participants said spontaneously, even if not always expressed as clearly as they would had they written for publication, contains an unusual wealth of ideas, hunches, and premonitions, amounting to a real feast. The participants have been very generous in praise of my original monograph, but the reader will find that they deepened our understanding of the Hartmann era far beyond what I myself could have imagined.

Index